Federal Aid to Education

Lexington Books Politics of Education Series
Frederick M. Wirt, Editor

Michael W. Kirst, Ed., *State, School, and Politics: Research Directions*
Joel S. Berke and Michael W. Kirst, *Federal Aid to Education: Who Benefits? Who Governs?*

*Supported by Ford Foundation Research Grant 690-0506
to the SURC Policy Institute*

Federal Aid to Education

Who Benefits? Who Governs?

Joel S. Berke and Michael W. Kirst

with contributions by:

Stephen K. Bailey
Alan K. Campbell
Laurence Iannaccone
Edith K. Mosher
Seymour Sacks
Jay D. Scribner
Frederick M. Wirt

with the editorial assistance of:

Jenne K. Britell

Lexington Books
D.C. Heath and Company
Lexington, Massachusetts
Toronto   London

Project Personnel

Advisory Committee
Stephen K. Bailey
Alan K. Campbell

Project Director
Joel S. Berke

Coordinator of State Studies
Michael W. Kirst

Principal Finance Consultant
Seymour Sacks

Research Associates
William Wilken
Paul Irwin
Gerald Calderone

Editors
Jenne K. Britell
Dorothy Sickles

Consultants

Jesse Burkhead   Edith K. Mosher
John Callahan   Jerry Miner
Anthony M. Cresswell   Harold Pellish
Laurence Iannaccone   Jay D. Scribner
Laura Irwin   Donna Shalala
Paul M. Irwin   Robert Stewart
Eugene McLoone   Frederick M. Wirt

Research Assistants

Morris Bailey   Joseph Panaro
Janet Fendrick   Thomas Perloff
Robert Firestine   Richard Strauss
Lawrence Goldman   Susan Van Wiggeren
Richard Kuzmack   Dwayne Ward

Berke, Joel S.
    Federal aid to education.

    Result of a joint project conducted by the Policy Institute of the Syracuse University Research Corporation and the Maxwell Graduate School of Syracuse University.
    1. Federal aid to education—United States. I. Kirst, Michael W., joint author. II. Syracuse University Research Corporation. Policy Institute. III. Syracuse University. Maxwell Graduate School of Citizenship and Public Affairs. IV. Title.
LB2825.B44   379'.12'0973   76-167981
ISBN 0-669-75812-4

Published simultaneously in Canada.

Printed in the United States of America.

International Standard Book Number: 0-669-75812-4

Library of Congress Catalog Card Number: 76-167981

Contents

List of Tables

Foreword

This study had its origins in the winter of 1968-69 when John W. Gardner, then chairman of the National Urban Coalition, began to speculate on the degree to which federal education programs were assisting the urban school systems of the nation. As he sought an answer to this question, he rapidly became aware that information was simply unavailable on the types and the proportions of federal aid that particular school districts were receiving, as well as on the decision making processes that shaped those patterns of aid allocation. At his urging, his then deputy, James A. Kelly, began discussions of this problem with us. Together, we outlined a joint project to be conducted by the Policy Institute of the Syracuse University Research Corporation and the Maxwell Graduate School of Syracuse University. Joel S. Berke, then special assistant to the chairman of the Policy Institute and an adjunct professor of political science at the Maxwell School, was selected as project director.

This book is the result of that study. Its purposes are three: first, to chart the patterns of allocation of federal aid to education (i.e., who benefits?), second, to study the decision making that determined those patterns of distribution (i.e., who governs?), and third, to recommend needed changes in both distribution formulas and in administrative practices.

In the summer of 1969 the project got under way with the support of a generous grant from the Ford Foundation. Seymour Sacks, of the Economics Department of the Maxwell School, served from the beginning as the principal consultant on the financial aspects of the work. A few months later, Michael W. Kirst, Professor of Education and Business Administration at Stanford University, became involved in our work and served as coordinator for the state case studies of administrative and political behavior.

The role of the authors of this foreword was to be an advisory committee, and we followed the development, progress, and findings of the research with fascination. While we both had conducted previous studies of our own on intergovernmental aid, educational politics, and the administration of federal aid programs, we became increasingly convinced that this project was breaking new ground. The massive tracing of all major federal programs in 575 school districts over a four year time period, and the relating of those federal aid flows to the state and local funding systems and to the social and financial characteristics of the school systems under study, presented a series of challenging methodological problems. The analysis through parallel state studies of the politics of federal aid allocation, the investigation by Professors Porter and Warner of selected school system practices, and the analysis of the federal role in administering aid by the principal authors of this volume contained important new information and insights.

The fiscal aspects of the study covers the four fiscal years between 1965 and

1968, a period in which federal aid to education doubled after the first year and then stabilized at the end of the period. While the most recent financial data discussed in this volume, therefore, are now several years old, the interesting fact is that our continuing research, and that of others, has shown no significant alterations in the patterns that we found. The questions that we raised in the beginning of the study are, once again, in the national limelight. For the inequities in school finance that characterize state and local school funding have recently been declared unconstitutional by courts in five states. In response, policy makers in Washington and state capitals across the country are seeking ways in which federal aid can assist in resolving the problems that the courts have brought to public attention.

This is, therefore, a time of unparalleled interest in school finance reform, and one of the major questions under debate is what should be the new federal role. The research in this volume will be of major assistance to scholars, public spirited citizens, and policy makers who can gain from it a better understanding of current patterns and processes related to federal aid allocation and administration that will help them as they design new programs.

When we first discussed the possibility of launching this project, we meant it to provide information and guidance to policy makers at the same time that it satisfied the demands of scholars for methodological and theoretical rigor. Those were ambitious goals. It is our judgment that Professors Berke and Kirst and their colleagues have more than fulfilled our hopes. They have, we believe, provided a useful model of the way in which interdisciplinary social science can provide significant assistance in the formulation of more effective public policy. We hope the work is given a wide and careful reading.

Stephen K. Bailey
Chairman, Policy Institute of the
Syracuse University Research
Corporation

Alan K. Campbell
Dean, Maxwell Graduate School of
Citizenship and Public Affairs
Syracuse University

Preface

This book has been three years in the making. It has involved the cooperative efforts of scholars from eight universities and research organizations representing at least four scholarly disciplines and varied backgrounds in public affairs at the local, state, and federal levels. The work of the participants named on the title page, and the much larger number of advisors and assistants whose names appear on the list of project personnel, was conducted as part of a two year research project supported by the Ford Foundation. The background of that project was described in the Foreword to this book by Stephen K. Bailey and Alan K. Campbell, whose advice and experience played a key role in the development and conduct of this research.

The field research involved in securing the financial and demographic data for the four year sample of 575 school districts was undertaken in the summer of 1969. The direction of that effort and of the analysis during the following year was very much a joint effort of Joel S. Berke, of the Syracuse University Research Corporation, and Seymour Sacks, of the Economics Department of Syracuse University. The number of other individuals who were helpful at various times and in various ways is beyond our ability to express here, but three acknowledgments cannot be omitted: Eugene McLoone of the National Education Association and the University of Maryland; Carol Hobson Smith, who was bureau chief of the Elementary and Secondary Education Division in the National Center for Educational Statistics of USOE; and John Polley, Assistant Commissioner of the New York State Education Department. As is often the case in academic research, the men in the trenches were a group of able and dedicated doctoral candidates whose names appear on the list of project personnel. Clearly, without them this effort would still be no more than an interesting research design.

The plan for the conduct of research on who governs the allocation of federal aid to education, with emphasis upon the role of state governments in the process, was developed in a series of discussions between the fall of 1969 and the spring of 1970 by the two principal authors of this volume. Our initial research plan was refined and developed in meetings we held with our advisory committee and the consultants whose names appear as authors of the individual state studies. The field work for their chapters was conducted under Professor Kirst's direction in the summer of 1970, and their draft reports were completed relatively quickly thereafter. Without the cooperation of the many public officials in the United States Office of Education, state and local education agencies, governors' offices, state legislatures, and teachers associations, that research could not have been conducted. In the time that has intervened, we have gone through a prolonged period of analyzing and editing in which we have sought to identify the elements of commonality and those of diversity in the rich harvest of information and thorough analysis we received from the state researchers. While each of the authors proceeded with a uniform set of research assertions to validate or negate, and while coordination of approach was basically maintained, much of the parallelism of treatment and uniformity of format in the final product is owed to the superb editorial assistance we received from Jenne K. Britell.

Studies of the practices of local education agencies in mobilizing their budgetary resources were conducted by David Porter of the University of California at Riverside and David Warner of the City University of New York. While space limitations prevent our inclusion of their reports in this volume, the insights we gained from their investigations and theoretical constructs have influenced our conclusions and recommendations.

There have already been a number of interim products of this study. They include articles and book chapters, congressional committee prints and testimony, reports for executive agencies of the federal government, state study committees and expert testimony in the *San Antonio* v. *Rodriguez* landmark school finance case presently under review before the U.S. Supreme Court. This volume, however, is the first attempt at integration of the many and varied aspects of the project.

The book consists of nine chapters. The first discusses the financial factors that affect public education and analyzes the impact of federal school aid in California, Massachusetts, Michigan, New York, and Texas. The second discusses the politics and administration of federal programs and describes the research approach that is employed in Chapters 3 through 8. Each of those chapters analyzes the politics of federal aid in one of the five states above plus Virginia, the last added to provide a study of southeastern school politics. At the beginning of each case study chapter are research assertions which governed the study and the conclusions that were reached about these hypotheses. Comparisons among the states can, therefore, readily be made by reading these introductory sections. Chapter 9 discusses the intergovernmental relations that exist in the implementation of federal aid programs and summarizes the major conclusions and recommendations that we reached as a result of our research. A relatively brief overview of the book may be had by reading Chapters 1 and 2, the research assertions sections of the case study chapters, and Chapter 9.

As we have finally brought all the elements together, we have been awed by the unsatisfied debts of gratitude that we have accumulated during the three years since we began our study. Clearly, they are beyond the scope of this preface to acknowledge, but there are a few people whose roles cannot go unmentioned. William Wilken's work was essential to the success of the project. He collated and programmed data, developed working tables, and conducted statistical analyses from September 1969 to May of 1970. Donna Shalala, Robert Goettel, and Gerald Calderone helped with the preparation of Chapter 1.

To Kathleen Kennedy, secretary to the project director, all who have had any contact with the project are grateful. Her handling of the many administrative details involved in work of this kind as well as the typing of succeeding drafts and communications was done with skill, good humor, and common sense. To the many other secretaries who have had a part in this project, and particularly to Pat Iacoune, who patiently and accurately typed hundreds of pages of intricate tables that went into the statistical workbooks, and Dorothy Sickles, who assisted in the editing of Chapter 1, we acknowledge our very deep appreciation.

At the Ford Foundation, which supported this research, Edward J. Meade and James A. Kelly have been continuing sources of encouragement. Lastly, to the colleagues whose names appear on the title page of this work, we must acknowledge openly and frankly that this work is as much theirs as it is ours. While as director and coordinator of this research we accept full responsibility for the studies conducted under our leadership, the burden of that responsibility is a light one to carry because of the brilliance and the care that our colleagues brought to this study. We look forward to continuing associations with them in our research on the finance, politics, and policies of American public education.

Joel S. Berke
Washington, D.C.

Michael W. Kirst
Stanford, California

Federal Aid to Education

1 Federal Aid to Public Education: Who Benefits?

Joel S. Berke, Seymour Sacks,
Stephen K. Bailey and Alan K. Campbell

Introduction

Federal aid to education has probably stimulated more controversy per dollar than has any other domestic aid program. Over its long history, debates over federal support for education have pinched the most sensitive nerves of the American body politic, the nerves of religion, race, and states rights. Frequently, those debates center on questions of educational finance.

At present, for example, the hopes of parochial school proponents for added financial support from the federal government have been buoyed by the report of a recent Presidential Commission and have been dimmed by decisions of federal courts. Supporters and opponents of integration, busing, separatism, and segregation continuously raise questions about the purposes and uses of federal aid to education. Those who prefer block grants and revenue sharing contend with others who want increased emphasis on categorical programs, and their discussions frequently raise the traditional dilemmas inherent in American fiscal federalism.

But there is a special quality to this debate about the federal role in American educational finance these days, a sense that we are in a period of change and reform, where new approaches are under active consideration. While a number of familiar factors have interacted to bring this moment in history—the "financial crisis," the "taxpayer revolt," the "crisis in confidence" in American public education—the most immediate cause has been the series of legal cases declaring that state school finance systems characterized by wealth-based disparities in spending among school districts violate the Fourteenth Amendment's equal protection clause. Since the first of these decisions, *Serrano v. Priest*, was handed down on August 30, 1971, Washington has been abuzz with efforts to develop a federal response to the newly emerging court doctrines.[1] Plans to provide federal money for relief from property taxes, plans to provide incentives for states to decrease the range of wealth-based disparities in educational spending, and programs designed to achieve greater equality of educational opportunity through compensatory spending on the disadvantaged have all held the attention of influential officials in the legislative and executive branches.

As these programs are developed and debated, the discussions are handi-

1

capped by critical gaps in knowledge. There is a deplorable paucity of useful information available to anyone—public official, researcher, educator, or interested citizen—who seeks to understand the fiscal impact of the federal contribution to American educational finance.

The frustration of a recent panel of academic experts and top education officials, the 1969 Urban Education Task Force of the Department of Health, Education, and Welfare, is symptomatic:

> The difficulties encountered by the committee and others in focusing attention on the aggregate impact of federal aid on a particular type of local district, say urban districts, underscores the presently fragmented patterns of thinking about federal aid to education. Federal policy toward a particular district is primarily a function of the relative distribution of federal dollars; today, we discuss future policy without really knowing what present policy is.[2]

This chapter attempts a systematic evaluation of the role that federal funds play in the total local-state-federal complex of educational finance. The basic issue for investigation is this: what is the impact of federal aid to education on the finances of elementary and secondary public school systems? More specifically, we sought answers to these questions:

1. Are the problems of educational finance in urban areas distinctive?[3]
2. Does federal aid favor central city, suburban, or rural areas most?
3. Is there a difference among the various federal programs in the degree to which they aid central city, suburban, and rural areas?
4. Are school districts with low capacities to finance education being aided more or less than richer districts?
5. Are districts with greater and more expensive educational needs receiving more federal aid than those whose needs are less severe?
6. What has been the trend over the last few years in the distribution of federal aid?
7. What outstanding administrative problems dilute the impact of federal programs?
8. And, most important of all, is federal assistance commensurate with the problems facing public education?

The answers to all these questions differed somewhat from state to state. Indeed one of our clearest conclusions was that the pattern and mix of federal aid allocations varied markedly among states, but some generalizations did emerge.

First, in the most urbanized areas of the nation we found a unique crisis in educational finance caused by a general deterioration in their fiscal situation combined with higher demands and costs—for education and for other public services—than existed in neighboring communities.

Second, we concluded that central cities received more federal education aid than their suburbs, but that the amounts were too small to compensate for the suburban advantage in local wealth and state aid. The districts that received the most federal aid, both absolutely and as a proportion of their total revenues, were those in non-metropolitan, largely rural areas.

Third, there were significant differences in the patterns of individual programs. Title I of ESEA was most responsible for the overall tendencies noted above. It locked in on urban and rural poverty in a manner unmatched by any other aspect of the entire local-state-federal fiscal system.

Yet the patterns of other programs varied immensely and defied the development of consistent pattern or explanation. In a number of important cases, as in ESEA II and III, Vocational Education, and NDEA III, major cities have received even less aid than should have been allotted to them in view of just their proportion of the state's pupil population. When considerations of comparative costs or student need are taken into account, the pattern appears far more discriminatory.

Fourth, if fiscal capacity to support education is seen only in terms of property value per pupil, there is little compensating effect through federal aid. But if capacity is seen in terms of income levels, then the pattern described above does show a compensating or equalizing pattern, again due largely to Title I of ESEA.

Fifth, if one takes the proportion of poor and minority pupils in a district as one proxy for educational need—and the authors of this chapter do—federal aid tends to be significantly related to educational need. Districts with lower income and higher proportions of non-white pupils received more aid than those with lower proportions of such pupils. Title I showed this phenomenon more than the other programs, and by and large even the other federal aid programs in which the state has discretion as to their distribution seemed to be more responsive to educational need than was state aid.

Sixth, over the four-year period of our study, amounts of federal aid reported by individual school districts varied erratically because of the bizarre timing of federal fund appropriation and administration. Furthermore, during the last year studied, almost half of the districts in metropolitan areas reported an actual decrease in per pupil amounts of aid.

Seventh, although questions of program administration and design are discussed later in this work, we did think it useful to comment on some outstanding problems which we noted in the course of our research. ESEA money, for example, has often gone for a variety of special and ancillary programs and has not been utilized to improve the central portion of the curriculum presented to disadvantaged children. The failure to concentrate funds on the students most in need of compensatory education has frequently resulted in a superficial veneer of fragmented programs and new equipment, rather than in an integrated, high impact intervention to achieve major educational change.

Dilution of the educational impact of federal aid has also come about through the improper but widespread use of Title I as general aid for system-wide purposes.

Eighth, and last, federal aid is intended to provide strategically useful funds for educational purposes not otherwise receiving adequate support. Our study suggests, however, that the amounts of aid are simply too small in view of the problems that confront public education. At present, for the nation as a whole, federal aid constitutes less than 7 percent of public elementary and secondary school revenues. For the five industrialized states of our study (California, New York, Michigan, Massachusetts, and Texas), the proportions ranged from little over three percent in New York to ten percent in Texas. In per pupil terms, statewide averages of federal aid ranged between $22 and $50 per pupil. Given our findings on the threatening fiscal crisis facing urban education, these amounts are patently insufficient to overcome the financial problems of the urban public schools.

The data, analyses, and conclusions of this chapter are contained in three sections. This section gives an overview of the chapter. The second describes the urban fiscal context in which federal aid is currently operative. The third section sets forth the findings and conclusions we have drawn as to the impact of federal aid. Appendices to this chapter describe: (a) the shortcomings in present information systems relating to federal aid and educational finance and (b) a more detailed description of the methodology utilized in this chapter.

Scope of the Study

Two related but separate research techniques have been utilized in preparing this chapter. First, to analyze the fiscal context of urban education, we have sought to relate the financing of education to general trends in population movement, business conditions, and governmental finances in thirty-seven large metropolitan areas. Second, in order to assess the impact of federal aid to education, we have conducted an intensive investigation of the distribution of federal aid to a large sample of school districts in five industrialized states.

A. The Fiscal Context of Urban Education.[4] Emphasis in the first portion of the analysis is placed on the social, economic, and fiscal disparities found in the nation's thirty-seven largest Standard Metropolitan Statistical Areas (SMSAs) between the central cities on the one hand and their surrounding suburban areas on the other. While we recognize the marked variation among the kinds of districts located within the suburban rings of metropolitan areas, the magnitude of the overall disparities we found indicates that cities and their suburban rings face very different fiscal problems and have very different capacities to deal with those problems.

Furthermore, technical problems dictate analysis based on comparisons between central cities and the aggregates of all school districts in the remainder of their SMSA. Comparisons among individual school systems are complicated by the fact that the boundaries of school districts seldom correspond to those of other governmental jurisdictions. Since most social, economic, and fiscal data are collected for general purpose governments and only partially for school districts, comparisons between central city districts and individual suburban districts for .all but a minimum of characteristics are difficult. Where social and economic data are concerned, the problem can be handled by allocating population characteristics among jurisdictions by the proportions of population contained in each jurisdiction. The problem is far more difficult, however, when we place educational finance in the larger context of non-educational revenues and expenditures for general governmental purposes. Unlike population characteristics where the basic unit is persons, which can be allocated by the number or proportion of persons, revenue and expenditure characteristics are available only by jurisdictions and are allocable only in total or with much arbitrariness to any partially overlapping school districts.[5]

Some allocation, of course, was necessary to separate the central city from the outside central city areas. Since there are usually a number of governments overlying the central cities in the thirty-seven largest SMSAs, finances had to be allocated between the cities and their suburbs by relative population or tax collections, as appropriate. In the case of allocating overlying governmental revenues, central city finance reports from the cities in question were examined to determine the amounts of taxes collected within the city by these overlying governments.

B. The Pattern of Distribution of Federal Aid to Education. Research on the pattern of distribution of aid to education was conducted by examining 575 school districts located in the five urbanized states. The sample was designed to insure that all larger school systems were included in its coverage. It contains better than half the pupils in the five states. Our data and conclusions, therefore, are primarily applicable to the cities and suburbs of these industrialized, largely metropolitan, states where more than two-thirds of the nation resides. Although our primary interest is in those metropolitan areas, sufficient coverage exists in our sample of school districts to draw some conclusions about the impact of federal aid in non-metropolitan, largely rural, areas as well.

Special emphasis in our report is placed upon states as units of analysis. Most similar studies of national policy base their analyses on samples constructed as microcosms of the nation, giving attention to regional representativeness, but seldom seeking to include sub-samples that are even roughly representative of constituent states.[6] Our concern, however, is with studying the units that make decisions on the allocation of federal aid to school districts. Since the federal statutes, regulations, and administrative practices place major responsibility on state education departments for making those allocations, states are obvious units for such a study. Furthermore, since we are interested in the interrelationship of local, state, and federal finance, our analysis must contain units representative of different state-local systems of educational support. Since states take distinctive approaches to raising and distributing revenues for their public schools, it is appropriate to select states as analytical units for that reasons as well. While our sample selection was intended to emphasize the metropolitan regions within states, our samples were large enough so that our data permits reasonably accurate conclusions to be drawn about the fiscal behavior of the individual states in our study.

The study reports on a four-year period, beginning with the 1965 fiscal year and continuing through the 1968 fiscal year. The starting point provides a baseline just prior to the large increase in federal education spending that came with the implementation of the Elementary and Secondary Education Act of 1965. The use of the three succeeding years permits us largely to overcome interpretive difficulties caused by the unevenness and bunching of federal fiscal flow in any one year, and allows us to see trends over time. It is worth noting, too, that changes in the levels and purposes of federal appropriations for elementary and secondary education have been minor in the fiscal years that have followed those studied, so that our data and conclusions remain characteristic of the present system of federal aid to education at this writing.

All federal aid for elementary and secondary education reported by the school districts in our sample was included in the analysis. Eight major programs of aid were examined individually. They represent more than 80 percent of total federal revenues for elementary and secondary education, and more than 95 percent of such revenues actually going to school districts. (Headstart and other OEO programs, which account for an additional 15 percent of federal revenue for elementary and secondary education, are often channeled through poverty agencies.) The remaining 4 percent consists of minor federal programs usually reported in a residual or miscellaneous category by local districts.

The eight major programs are:

1. Title I of the Elementary and Secondary Education Act of 1965 (ESEA), financial assistance to local educational agencies for the education of children of low-income families;
2. Title II of ESEA, school library resources, textbooks, and other instructional materials;
3. Title III of ESEA, supplementary educational centers and services;
4. Title III of the National Defense Education Act of 1958 (NDEA), financial assistance for strengthening instruction in science, mathematics, modern foreign languages, and other critical subjects;
5. Title V-A of NDEA, guidance, counseling, and testing;
6. Vocational Education (aid for vocational education from all federal programs);

7. School Lunch and Milk Program; and
8. School Assistance in Federally Affected Areas, including Public Law 874 (general aid to offset increased school costs related to federal employees) and Public Law 815 (school construction money for similar purposes).

Our original intention had been to trace payments to school districts from each federal program providing assistance for elementary and secondary education. Initial conferences with state and federal officials and surveys of fund reporting, however, quickly demonstrated that information was unavailable on many of the smaller programs—at least by any research techniques that could be undertaken within reasonable time and expense limits. Allotments to states could be found, but the receipts reported by individual school districts were lumped together—and therefore lost individually—in such categories as "all other" or "miscellaneous outside revenues."

Some important programs proved impossible to trace to the district level within acceptable ranges of accuracy and effort. Headstart expenditures, for example, were often allotted to prime contractors by the Office of Economic Opportunity, and then subcontracted. The final point of expenditure often went unreported, so that actual time periods and expenditures could not be ascertained with sufficient precision for our purposes. In addition, Headstart amounts expended by public school authorities were frequently but a small proportion of Headstart monies being expended within the school districts. It seemed necessary, therefore, to omit expenditures for Headstart from our study.

One final word of caution should be stated for those who have not had experience with educational finance data. Despite rigorous efforts and substantial resources, we experienced enormous difficulty collecting and comparing data, even for jurisdictions as large as school districts. In our survey, differences in reporting among districts within states and among states themselves posed constant problems. There are at the present time, neither uniform definitions nor common sources for many important items of educational information. For example, methods of counting attendance vary significantly from state to state. In addition, some desirable data is simply unavailable. In a number of districts the category of "all other federal aid" is larger than the combined aid from specific titles. Furthermore, even though our sources of information were the official figures reported to state educational agencies by local school districts, project researchers uncovered a number of inaccuracies and discrepancies in the "official" figures. Lastly, we want to acknowledge that collecting data on more than forty categories of revenues and expenditures for 575 school districts for each of four years leaves room for error on our part; however, during the twelve months of analysis and data refinement that followed the collection of the raw information, the material was subjected to as rigorous an attempt to assure accuracy as we could devise.

The Fiscal Context of Urban Education

Raising adequate revenues for the support of education is a threatening problem in a large proportion of the nation's school systems. There are, of course, exceptions to this statement: enclaves with high nonresidential taxable resources relative to the number of school children; wealthy suburban communities with high levels of residential property, income, and educational expectations; and rural districts with stable or declining populations and relatively minimal educational demands. But in most cities, suburbs, and rural areas, heightened demand for educational services and salaries are running head-on into local taxpayer resistance, state economy drives, and a pause in increased federal spending. In many areas of the country, school boards faced with fiscal crises have resorted to school shutdowns, the elimination of special projects, and increasing average class size.

Hardest hit of all are the larger cities of the nation where three interacting phenomena strike most directly. First, because of problems common to highly urbanized areas—a declining fiscal situation combined with steeply rising demands and costs for education and other public services—large cities find it more difficult than most other areas to support educational services from their own tax resources. Second, education in central cities imposes higher costs than are found in less densely populated places. This is true because of the composition of the city student population, because of inherently higher urban cost factors, and because of aggressive and effective teacher unions. Third, cities frequently function under a legal framework that is far more restrictive and state aid laws which are far less generous than is true of suburban and rural school districts. Together, these factors have caused a crisis in urban educational finance. This section will discuss that crisis.[7]

Metropolitan Developments

The roots of the crisis in large city educational finance are found in the redistribution of population and economic activities that has taken place in the last two decades. The shifts have not been random. A sorting-out process has occurred—leaving the poor, undereducated, aged, and non-white in the central cities and taking heavy manufacturing, many retail establishments, and other kinds of business activities to the suburbs along with middle and upper income families. The result is that the tax base of cities has become insufficient to meet the resource needs of the high cost city population.

City poverty, in other words, often exists only a few miles from substantial suburban wealth. This adjacent ring of relative affluence complicates the plight of large city school districts because cities and suburbs compete for tax dollars, for instructional personnel, and for the quality of their schools. In this competition, cities are at a marked disadvantage. This is not to suggest that many suburbs, particularly the older ones, do not share central city problems. In fact, there are suburbs in this country which are increasingly taking on central city characteristics and consequently have similar resource needs.[8] For reasons already given, however, our data on SMSAs were dichotomized into central city and outside central city, and the statistical analyses were performed accordingly. Yet because the data on suburbs are diluted and distorted by the urbanized areas they contain, all comparisons between city and suburbs understate the real plight of urban areas. The following statistics, therefore, express only in part the stark fiscal situation in urban America.

A. Social, Economic, and Fiscal Trends. Population growth in large cities has nearly ceased in recent years, while their suburbs are enjoying a dynamic rate of increase: between 1960 and 1970, core cities in the nation's thirty-seven largest SMSAs grew by only 6.4 percent, while their suburbs increased by 26.7 percent.[9] Despite this slower city growth—and in some cases the total absence of growth—population densities in the cities continued to exceed those in the suburbs fifteen to twenty times over.

Within these differential growth rates lie marked differences in the characteristics of the metropolitan population. Central city black population, for example, has risen from 20 to 26 percent over the last decade while surrounding areas have remained fairly stable at 5 percent.[10] Income differences also are extreme, with central city family incomes averaging nearly $1500 less than suburban incomes.[11] Significantly higher proportions of poor families and significantly lower proportions of families in more comfortable circumstances live within rather than outside core cities.

Economic activity shows a similar picture of central city disadvantage. Between 1958 and 1967 in the thirty-seven largest SMSAs suburban retail sales increased at a real rate of 106 percent, central city sales by only 13 percent. These differing rates of growth resulted in a decline in the central city share of metropolitan retail sales from 63 percent in 1958 to 54 percent in 1963 to 49 percent in 1967 (Table 1-1). Other indicators tell a similar tale. Employment in manufacturing and wholesaling is declining in central cities while increasing in the outlying areas.

B. Tax Base Deterioration. One major consequence of these trends for educational finance is seen in the decreased capacity of urban communities to raise and to devote resources to the support of their schools. The population and economic shifts noted above have combined to depress the income base of central cities relative to their suburbs and to cause a much slower growth in the urban property tax base. Since the income of its residents is a major source of public resources, the relatively new position of cities as comparatively low-income areas is a basic problem for educational support.

Table 1-1
Retail Sales, Deflated by General Price Increase, for 37 Largest Metropolitan Areas, 1958-1967

Metropolitan Areas	Percent of Retail Sales in CC Portion of SMSA			Percent Increase in Retail Sales 1958-1967	
	1958	1963	1967	CC	OCC
Northeast	(50.7)	(42.6)	(37.7)	(−.3)	(75.2)
Washington, D.C.	52.1	42.1	32.9	10.5	134.8
Baltimore	71.4	58.1	53.4	4.9	128.2
Boston	38.9	31.2	26.0	−1.4	79.2
Newark	30.0	25.8	21.2	−14.1	37.1
Paterson-Clifton	36.0	23.9	24.6	.9	74.5
Buffalo	52.2	40.1	38.9	−9.9	54.7
New York	72.9	67.1	64.8	9.7	60.2
Rochester	60.4	52.9	48.5	18.1	91.3
Philadelphia	51.5	43.4	40.2	6.2	65.4
Pittsburgh	37.5	34.1	33.5	7.8	28.7
Providence	55.7	50.4	31.2	−36.3	73.1
Midwest	(66.0)	(56.2)	(48.8)	(9.5)	(127.1)
Chicago	65.3	56.9	51.5	5.3	86.6
Indianapolis	76.8	65.5	60.4	20.0	160.8
Detroit	51.1	42.7	36.1	.7	86.4
Minneapolis-St. Paul	73.4	61.5	54.4	7.9	149.7
Kansas City	59.9	63.3	50.1	55.2	64.3
St. Louis	48.1	37.5	32.7	−7.6	76.2
Cincinnati	64.2	57.0	45.0	4.6	129.4
Cleveland	74.0	54.8	39.6	−15.2	269.1
Columbus	80.2	69.0	67.2	22.8	141.9
Dayton	60.5	47.4	41.3	3.6	125.5
Milwaukee	73.1	63.1	58.4	7.4	108.3
South	(74.4)	(68.6)	(64.5)	(28.7)	(108.3)
Miami	54.9	40.4	37.5	−2.5	98.2
Tampa-St. Petersburg	75.4	66.6	65.8	30.9	108.9
Atlanta	71.4	62.8	57.6	37.7	153.9
Louisville	70.5	64.0	57.5	14.0	101.8
New Orleans	79.0	71.3	65.3	21.0	141.9
Dallas	77.7	71.2	68.4	36.6	119.2
Houston	75.7	82.4	74.8	55.9	63.3
San Antonio	91.2	90.0	89.6	36.4	79.9
West	(74.4)	(68.6)	(64.5)	(28.7)	(108.3)
Los Angeles-Long Beach	48.8	41.3	39.9	22.2	75.4
San Bernardino	44.9	42.1	NA	NA	NA
San Diego	64.0	56.4	53.9	25.6	91.8

Table 1-1 (cont.)

Metropolitan Areas	Percent of Retail Sales in CC Portion of SMSA			Percent of Increase (Real) in Retail Sales 1958-1967	
	1958	1963	1967	CC	OCC
San Francisco	54.5	48.0	43.4	16.3	81.6
Denver	70.5	55.9	53.3	11.1	132.4
Portland	76.3	58.8	59.6	28.1	180.3
Seattle	71.7	63.5	54.3	18.0	152.5
37 SMSAs	63.0	54.1	49.3	12.6	105.8

Source: Advisory Commission on Intergovernmental Relations. *Metropolitan Disparities—A Second Reading.* Bulletin No. 70-1, Washington, D.C.: the Commission, January, 1970. A Joint Project of the ACIR and the SURC Policy Institute.

More directly, however, it is the property tax base that is tapped for virtually all locally raised revenue for education. The traditionally higher city property tax base has been threatened in recent decades by a very slow rate of growth. In the northeast, the most recent studies show that suburban property values climbed an average of three times as much as did those of the central cities; in the midwest, suburban property appreciation was more than six times that in the core cities. For all sections of the nation, suburban property growth rate was more than two and one-half times that of the central cities (Table 1-2).

Growth in educational expenditures has far outstripped this slow rate of growth in the urban property tax base. Professors James, Kelly, and Garms documented this phenomenon in fourteen large cities between 1930 and 1960.[12] They found that per pupil educational expenditures rose three times as fast as property values.

C. The Problem of Municipal Overburden. Taxable resources are becoming increasingly more scarce in the core cities than in the rest of metropolitan America. But what makes the picture even bleaker is that cities are unable to devote as large a share of their resources to education as can suburban districts. Cities possess a high-cost population and an older physical plant which produce greater demands for general government services than in the suburbs—demands for greater health, public safety, sanitation, public works, transportation, public welfare, public housing, and recreation services. Central cities devote nearly 65 percent of their budgets to non-educational services, while their outlying communities devote less than 45 percent (Table 1-3). Put another way, core cities assign only a third of their funds to education, while neighboring communities consistently spend over half of their public monies for schools.

Cities raise about 30 percent less per capita for education from local taxes. On the other hand, central city residents tax themselves considerably more

Table 1-2
Growth of Property Values in Central Cities and Suburbs, 37 Largest Standard Metropolitan Statistical Areas

Area	Total SMSA Property Value (Millions)[a]		Percent of Value in Central City		Percent of Growth in Value, 1961-66	
	1961	1966	1961	1966	Central City	Suburbs
NORTHEAST			43.1%	37.8%	18.2%	53.2%
Washington, D.C.	$ 5,406	$ 8,686	43.0	34.9	30.2	83.6
Baltimore, Md.	4,124	5,074	47.9	40.6	4.3	40.3
Boston, Mass.	5,799	4,462	23.1	16.7	2.3	52.8
Newark, N.J.	2,864	7,095	20.8	17.6	109.0[b]	157.9[b]
Paterson-Clifton-Passaic, N.J.	1,774	8,289	NA	NA	NA	NA
Buffalo, N.Y.	2,405	2,555	44.6	42.1	0.3	11.0
New York, N.Y.	32,703	40,738	79.8	78.3	22.1	48.5
Rochester, N.Y.	1,349	1,644	49.4	41.6	2.5	40.8
Philadelphia, Pa.	6,901	9,055	58.4	48.4	8.8	62.6
Pittsburgh, Pa.	3,978	4,407	30.2	27.9	2.2	14.5
Providence, R.I.	1,766	2,001	33.7	29.7	−0.2	20.2
MIDWEST			48.8	41.3	6.9	38.9
Chicago, Ill.	16,339	18,915	49.4	44.5	4.5	26.8
Indianapolis, Ind.	1,110	1,462	50.1	43.4	14.0	49.5
Detroit, Mich.	6,830	8,570	48.9	37.2	−4.6	54.3
Minneapolis-St. Paul, Minn.	840	1,039	59.6	49.1	1.8	56.0
Kansas City, Mo.	1,150	1,362	55.0	52.8	13.8[c]	24.1[c]
St. Louis, Mo.	3,744	4,348	32.8	29.8	5.7	21.2
Cincinnati, Ohio	2,548	3,548	42.3	30.6	7.4	67.5
Cleveland, Ohio	4,389	4,915	40.4	34.3	−5.1	23.5
Columbus, Ohio	1,487	1,810	57.9	56.0	21.9[c]	31.6[c]
Dayton, Ohio	1,392	1,665	NA	30.3	NA	NA
Milwaukee, Wis.	3,213	3,916	51.6	46.5	9.7	34.9
SOUTH			62.4	48.4	87.4	129.9
Miami, Fla.	2,540	5,556	NA	29.2	NA	NA
Tampa-St. Petersburg, Fla.	1,849	2,763	NA	NA	NA	NA
Atlanta, Ga.	1,157	1,859	43.5	33.7	24.7	88.4
Louisville, Ky.	959	3,524	50.9	49.1	227.3[b]	251.8[b]
New Orleans, La.	769	899	83.0	78.2	10.2	49.6
Dallas, Texas	1,028	1,461	NA	NA	NA[c]	NA[c]
Houston, Texas	1,710	2,237	NA	51.7	NA[c]	NA[c]
San Antonio, Texas	494	577	72.3	NA	NA	NA

Table 1-2 (cont.)

Area	Total SMSA Property Value (Millions)[a]		Percent of Value in Central City		Percent of Growth in Value, 1961-66	
	1961	1966	1961	1966	Central City	Suburbs
WEST			49.7	44.3	16.5	44.4
Los Angeles-Long Beach, Calif.	10,552	14,928	40.1	41.6	44.4	39.4
San Bernardino-Riverside-Ontario, Calif.	1,199	1,811	NA	NA	NA	NA
San Diego, Calif.	1,303	1,651	54.5	54.3	26.2	27.3
San Francisco-Oakland, Calif.	3,731	5,316	39.6	33.3	19.6	57.4
Denver, Colo.	1,444	1,795	55.7	49.9	11.2	40.8
Portland, Oreg.	1,177	1,190	53.0	40.2	−23.4[b]	28.8[b]
Seattle, Wash.	1,064	1,532	55.5	46.7	21.2	72.4
TOTAL			48.9%	41.9%	21.1%	54.4%

Sources: U.S. Department of Commerce, Bureau of the Census, Census of Governments, 1962 and 1967. Volume II, Taxable Property Values. Washington, D.C.: Government Printing Office, 1963 and 1968.

[a]Refers to gross locally assessed real property before exemptions.
[b]Assessment.
[c]Annexation.
From *Metropolitan Disparities—A Second Reading*, op. cit.

heavily than is the case with their suburban counterparts; city per capita tax effort (taxes as a percent of income) is over 40 percent higher (Table 1-4) than in surrounding areas. In short, core cities spend less per pupil than do other parts of metropolitan areas while taxing themselves more heavily.[13]

Higher Urban Educational Costs

One additional consideration lends particular poignancy to the plight of urban finance: dollar for dollar, central cities get less education for their expenditures than do other parts of metropolitan areas. In other words, city education generally costs more per unit than does education elsewhere. There are two reasons for this phenomenon. First, the social and economic character of the urban school population requires an exceedingly high-cost educational program; second, many expense items in the school budget simply cost more in the cities.

A. Higher Costs Imposed by the Character of Urban Enrollment. The major factor accounting for the inherently more costly nature of schooling in the large

Table 1-3

Per Capita Total, Education, and Noneducation Expenditures, 37 Largest SMSAs, Central City and Outside Central City Areas, 1966-1967

		Total Exp.		Ed. Exp.		Non-ed. Exp.	
		CC	OCC	CC	OCC	CC	OCC
Northeast							
Washington, D.C.	D.C.	$564	$316	$148	$179	$416	$137
Baltimore	Md.	375	286	124	168	251	118
Boston	Mass.	482	321	92	137	390	184
Newark	N.J.	540	390	169	144	371	165
Paterson-C.P.	N.J.	270	273	97	151	173	122
Buffalo	N.Y.	392	372	128	207	264	165
New York	N.Y.	518	520	146	260	372	260
Rochester	N.Y.	499	403	158	265	341	138
Philadelphia	Pa.	293	255	126	139	167	116
Pittsburgh	Pa.	319	232	104	137	215	95
Providence	R.I.	241	201	94	109	147	92
		(408)	(317)	(126)	(160)	(282)	(145)
Midwest							
Chicago	Ill.	339	234	103	155	236	79
Indianapolis	Ind.	312	268	139	173	173	95
Detroit	Mich.	362	352	130	209	232	143
Minn.-St. Paul	Minn.	369	424	113	231	256	193
Kansas City	Mo.	303	238	137	127	166	111
St. Louis	Mo.	295	266	133	146	162	120
Cincinnati	Ohio	460	200	201	107	259	93
Cleveland	Ohio	328	282	132	144	196	138
Columbus	Ohio	299	267	111	162	188	105
Dayton	Ohio	353	228	161	132	192	96
Milwaukee	Wis.	416	383	151	165	265	218
		(349)	(286)	(137)	(159)	(211)	(126)
South							
Miami	Fla.	346	281	136	136	210	145
Tampa-St. Pete.	Fla.	305	216	113	113	192	103
Atlanta	Ga.	316	279	134	154	182	125
Louisville	Ky.	284	250	126	161	158	89
New Orleans	La.	233	318	93	143	140	175
Dallas	Tex.	219	290	91	177	128	113
Houston	Tex.	260	326	113	209	147	117
San Antonio	Tex.	204	208	101	145	103	63
		(271)	(271)	(113)	(155)	(158)	(116)

Table 1-3 (cont.)

		Total Exp.		Ed. Exp.		Non-ed. Exp.	
		CC	OCC	CC	OCC	CC	OCC
West							
Los Angeles-L.B.	Calif.	454	376	164	184	290	192
San Bernardino R & O	Calif.	471	435	202	219	269	216
San Diego	Calif.	383	391	135	209	248	182
San Francisco-Oak.	Calif.	486	463	131	216	355	247
Denver	Col.	342	278	131	164	211	114
Portland	Ore.	378	256	150	172	228	84
Seattle	Wash.	326	376	127	226	199	150
		(406)	(368)	(149)	(199)	(257)	(169)
Unweighted average 37 SMSAs		363	308	136	170	230	138

Source: Advisory Commission on Intergovernmental Relations. *Metropolitan Disparities—A Second Reading.* Bulletin No. 70-1. Washington, D.C.: the Commission, January, 1970. A Joint Project of the ACIR and the SURC Policy Institute.

cities is the composition of the urban school population. Higher proportions of the educationally disadvantaged, of the poor, of the handicapped, of the non-white, and of immigrants are located in central cities. The special educational needs of these groups require far greater educational resources to enable them to achieve normal grade level performance. Examples of such expensive programs are: education for the culturally disadvantaged, programs for non-English-speaking adults and children, programs for children to whom standard English is virtually a foreign language, adult education in general, summer school, programs for the physically and emotionally handicapped, and vocational schools.[14]

The percentage of non-white student population (primarily black, Puerto Rican, and Chicano) is another rough but useful index of the need for more educational resources. Non-white students tend to come from homes where parents have lower average years of schooling, schooling frequently acquired in inferior segregated schools. A host of recent studies have demonstrated the importance of parental educational background to the quality of a student's achievement in school. Those studies indicate that what the home does not provide, the schools must help to make up if educationally disadvantaged children are to approach their more fortunate classmates in achievement. The implications for the cost of the school program are clear.[15]

What should be kept in mind is that the non-white child is represented in even larger proportion in the schools than in the total population of the largest cities. For example, in 1970 the non-white percentage of the general population of Chicago was 40 percent, yet the non-white percentage of enrollment in public schools was 64 percent. Similar patterns may be found in all parts of the nation.

Table 1-4
**Taxes as a Percentage of Personal Income for 37 Largest Metropolitan Areas,
1966-1967**

Metropolitan Areas	Local Taxes as a Percentage of Personal Income	
	Central City	Outside Central City
Northeast	7.2	4.8
Washington, D.C.	9.1	4.4
Baltimore	7.2	3.5
Boston	8.4	4.0
Newark	8.8	5.5
Paterson-Clifton	6.4	6.2
Buffalo	7.7	5.2
New York	8.0	5.6
Rochester	6.4	4.8
Philadelphia	6.2	4.0
Pittsburgh	5.8	3.9
Providence	5.4	5.6
Midwest	5.9	3.9
Chicago	5.2	3.9
Indianapolis	5.3	3.9
Detroit	4.9	4.2
Minneapolis-St. Paul	5.1	4.8
Kansas City	6.3	3.4
St. Louis	7.0	3.8
Cincinnati	6.3	3.5
Cleveland	6.4	4.2
Columbus	4.8	3.9
Dayton	6.8	3.2
Milwaukee	6.4	3.9
South	4.7	3.3
Miami	6.7	4.6
Tampa-St. Petersburg	5.3	4.2
Atlanta	5.1	2.9
Louisville	4.6	3.2
New Orleans	3.7	2.1
Dallas	4.5	3.3
Houston	4.0	5.3
San Antonio	3.3	1.0
West	6.1	5.5
Los Angeles-Long Beach	6.3	6.3
San Bernardino	8.2	8.0
San Diego	5.2	6.1

Table 1-4 (cont.)

| Metropolitan Areas | Local Taxes as a Percentage of Personal Income | |
	Central City	Outside Central City
San Francisco	7.1	5.7
Denver	6.5	5.0
Portland	5.9	4.2
Seattle	3.7	3.5
Total	6.1	4.3

Source: Advisory Commission on Intergovernmental Relations. *Metropolitan Disparities—A Second Reading.* Bulletin No. 70-1. Washington, D.C.: the Commission, January, 1970. A joint Project of the ACIR and the SURC Policy Institute.

Table 1-5 compares, for 1960 and 1970 the proportion of non-white public school enrollment. This difference in population and enrollment proportions is a result of age distribution, family composition, and the greater tendency of white parents to send their children to private and parochial schools.

Table 1-5
Non-White Population and Non-White School Enrollment for Fifteen Largest Cities: 1960-1970

| City | Percentage Non-White of Total Population | | Percentage Non-White of School Population | |
	1960	1970	1960	1970
New York	15	31	22	54
Chicago	24	40	40	64
Los Angeles	17	36	21	46
Philadelphia	27	.35	47	61
Detroit	29	45	43	64
Baltimore	35	47	50	66
Houston	23	38	30	45
Cleveland	29	40	46	58
Washington	55	77	78	98
St. Louis	29	42	49	64
Milwaukee	9	17	16	28
San Francisco	18	28	31	46
Boston	10	19	16	34
Dallas	19	33	26	43
New Orleans	37	49	55	70

Source: Computed from Census data compiled in *General Social and Economic Characteristics*, Series PC(1)-C (Washington: Government Printing Office, 1972).

B. Urban Cost Differentials. In addition to the inherently costlier nature of the urban school population, city schools must pay more for many items in their budgets than do school systems in other areas. Take, for example, instructional salaries, the largest item in any school budget. In a study for the U.S. Civil Rights Commission, Professor Charles Benson pointed out, "City costs are characterized by a general expenditure raising phenomenon, namely, the age of their teachers. Also, for institutional reasons, cities tend to make promotions internally. On both counts, central cities tend to have school systems that are staffed primarily by teachers of substantial seniority. Again for institutional reasons, teachers are paid largely on the basis of seniority. It follows that central cities must pay higher salaries for teachers." In the last few years, of course, another factor has operated to increase instructional expenditures in large cities: militant teacher unions. Through tight organization and aggressive tactics, unions in the nation's metropolises have won substantial salary increases and other cost-raising benefits.

In addition to instructional salaries, personnel expenses for maintenance, secretarial, and security services are also higher in central cities as shown by Bureau of Labor Statistics reports. Higher incidences of vandalism also plays a role in pushing costs upward.

Land for school buildings is also more expensive in cities. While comparisons are complicated by the more sprawling campus-style architecture of non-urban schools, the extraordinarily high costs associated with assembling even small plots for city schools appears to outweigh those in the suburbs. For example, an intensive study of education in Michigan found that in 1967 Detroit paid an average price per acre of $100,000 in contrast with approximately $6,000 per acre in surrounding school districts.[16]

State Regulations and State Aid

Urban education systems, of course, are conducted within a legal framework and a financing system that involve a large measure of state participation. Both state regulations and state aid leave cities at a disadvantage relative to suburban and rural areas.

The costs of retirement systems, for example, are often assumed by state governments, but in many states the large school districts are omitted from the state program and must bear retirement costs primarily from local revenues. Even where smaller districts are responsible for retirement contributions, a heavier assignment is usually charged to the large city school district or its overlying government.[17]

When we examine the impact of state aid for education, we find that aid systems continue to bear the marks of their origins. Educational aid formulas were designed in the first decades of the century to compensate for disparities between the rich cities and the poorer outlying areas. Relative fiscal positions are now reversed, but the formulas continue to give lesser proportions of aid to cities than to suburbs, and to give more aid to rural than to metropolitan areas. Those conclusions have been drawn in many previous studies. One of the most recent was conducted by the United States Office of Education to compare eighty-four large city school systems with statewide revenue averages. It found that in the 1968 school year, seventy of the cities received less than the average state aid per pupil. Even when total local and state funds were considered, fifty-one of the cities received less revenues per pupil than the statewide average.[18]

Data collected for our own study is consistent with this pattern. In our five state analysis we found that in New York, Texas, and Michigan, metropolitan areas get anywhere from $17.00 to $58.00 less per pupil in state aid than do non-metropolitan areas. Only in California is the reverse true. Within the metropolitan areas we found that the central cities in all states except Massachusetts get less aid than their surrounding suburbs. As Table 1-6 shows, the difference can be considerable. Looking at individual metropolitan areas, the gap is often larger. For instance Syracuse, New York, in 1968 received $170.00 less per pupil than its surrounding area in state aid. Los Angeles for the same year received $95.00 less. Of the five major metropolitan areas in our five state study, only in Boston did the central city receive more state aid than its metropolitan area. Data on the thirty-seven largest metropolitan areas showed the disparities to be even greater: suburban areas received one-third more educational aid per capita in 1967 than did the core cities.[19]

Why do these discriminatory state aid patterns exist? Politically their roots lie in the rural dominance of state legislatures made possible by malapportioned representational systems. Since the 1960s and widespread reapportionment under one man—one vote judicial strictures, a coalition of rural and suburban interests have come to control most legislatures and these groups have continued to protect the old formulas which work to their advantage.

Why formulas work to their advantage? The most important and common

Table 1-6
State Aid Per Pupil by Metropolitan Areas, 1967

State	Total	CC	OCC	Diff. in Favor OCC
New York	$475.20	$392.90	$485.88	$ 92.98
California	271.65	250.73	274.06	23.33
Texas	206.21	183.01	210.48	27.47
Michigan	263.06	227.88	268.41	40.53
Massachusetts	118.41	223.07*	114.93	−108.14

Source: Computed from official state records by the SURC Policy Institute.
*Boston figure overstates amount of state aid because of payment scheduling associated with the implementation of a new aid program.

factor is the reliance on real property value to measure the capacity of school districts to support education. The higher the property value per pupil, the lower the state aid payment under equalizing aid formulas. Since cities tend to rate higher than other areas in property value because of the greater concentration of commercial and industrial property and the lower proportion of pupils in big cities, they qualify for less state aid than do suburban and rural school districts. Were almost any other recognized measure of fiscal capacity to be used (median family income, percentage of families in poverty, property value per capita rather than per pupil), cities would not look so rich and they would qualify for more realistic amounts of aid. Their position would be even more improved were aid formulas redesigned to take into account factors discussed above, i.e., higher urban cost levels, higher demands for non-educational public services, and more costly pupil populations. While the recent state and federal court cases if upheld by the U.S. Supreme Court, will require revision of state school finance systems, such revision may or may not result in formulas more favorable to urban interests.[20] Thus the aid patterns described above may be characteristic of school finance for some time to come.

Summary

Though raising adequate revenues for education is a serious problem in all areas of the nation, we have found that the fiscal crisis is most threatening in the larger cities of the nation. The trend in metropolitan development has left them with a less affluent population and a resource base that is failing to grow at a rate sufficient to meet increasing needs. Because large urban areas have higher public service needs, a much lower proportion of their expenditures can be devoted to education than is true in suburban areas. The result is, of course, proportionately lower educational expenditures in cities than in their environs despite higher tax efforts in the cities. Unfortunately these problems are compounded by the inherently more costly nature of urban education; expenses are higher in big cities and pupil populations there include more children in need of expensive supplementary educational techniques. State regulations and state aid rather than compensating for these urban disadvantages often act to exacerbate them. Whether the school finance reforms eventuating from court decisions will recognize the special problems of urban areas remains to be seen. This, then, is the fiscal context for our examination of the allocation of federal aid to education.

The Pattern of Allocation of Federal Aid to Education

Federal aid to education has a history that dates from the Northwest Ordinance of 1785. Even the modern form of assistance, categorical programs of grants-in-aid, has a continuous tradition stretching back more than fifty years to the Smith-Hughes Vocational Educational Assistance Program of 1917. A brief overview of the major developments in federal educational programs may be useful at this point.

During the depression of the 1930s, federal programs to furnish inexpensive milk and school lunches were begun. The Second World War brought impacted areas aid to school districts called upon to educate influxes of children whose parents were attached to military bases and other federal facilities. In the 1950s, spurred by the national trauma inflicted by the Soviet launching of Sputnik, federal assistance grew significantly through the National Defense Education Act aimed at upgrading programs in science, mathematics, foreign languages, and other critical areas.

Then in 1965 Congress passed the Elementary and Secondary Education Act (ESEA) to serve two ambitious and challenging educational goals: (1) achieving equality of educational opportunity by targeting funds for the education of children from low income families and (2) raising the quality of all education by supporting experimentation and innovation. In programatic content and in level of funding, ESEA represented a quantum jump in the federal role.[21]

Throughout this history, federal aid has served both to meet educational objectives and to assist school districts in bearing the costs of the most expensive domestic governmental service: elementary and secondary education. This section concentrates on the second of those purposes. It analyzes the impact federal programs have on the financing of public elementary and secondary education in the United States.

The Concept of Equity and Federal Aid

In selecting the areas of inquiry and the kind of analysis we would perform, the philosophy of the authors has played an important part. We feel it necessary, therefore, to make explicit our belief that one of the central questions to be asked about any governmental service is whether it is equitably distributed. In the case of state and local resources for education, we believe the distribution of services is basically inequitable.

The chief reason for this inequity is that the level of expenditures for education is determined primarily by the wealth of more than 17,000 individual public school districts in the nation. Local taxable resources, which provide more than half the revenue for running the public schools, vary immensely from district to district. For the children who live in those districts the quality of education varies accordingly. State aid laws, which supply an additional 42 percent of school revenues, fail to overcome the disparities among districts and in many states actually reinforce them.

That the level of support devoted to one's schooling should vary markedly depending upon where one happens to live is, we believe, both rationally and ethically questionable. But when the variations in school spending are in inverse relationship to the incidence of the need for educational services, the inequity is compounded. As discussed in the previous section, the greatest need for educational resources exists where the handicaps to learning are greatest, namely among the poor, the handicapped, and the victims of prejudice and neglect. These groups tend to be concentrated where taxable resources are least available for education, notably, in impoverished rural and in highly urbanized areas, particularly the large cities of the nation.

In analyzing the pattern of federal aid to education, therefore, we accordingly consider aid to be equitably distributed when it tends to offset disparities among school districts in regard to wealth (income and property valuation), when it provides assistance to urbanized areas in proportion to their fiscal disadvantages, and when it supplies proportionately more money to districts with higher numbers of educationally disadvantaged pupils.

Within that framework our findings indicate that:

1. federal aid to education in the aggregate has only a slight equalizing tendency at best, and that within a number of metropolitan areas it displays distinctly disequalizing characteristics;
2. the degree of equalization, where it does exist, is usually too small to offset pre-existing disparities among school districts, and
3. although Title I of ESEA does flow in greater proportion to poorer and higher need school districts, a number of other federal programs operate to help the rich districts get richer.

To be more specific, we found that:

1. Non-metropolitan areas, largely rural and small town in character, tend to receive more federal aid per pupil than do metropolitan areas.
2. While central cities get more total federal aid than their suburbs, the amount of federal aid is too small to offset the suburban advantage in local and state revenues. Suburbs averaged $100 more per pupil in total revenues than their core cities in four of the five states in the study.
3. With the exception of ESEA Title I, federal programs frequently provide more funds to suburban districts than to central city districts. Large cities appear to receive less money from programs such as ESEA II, ESEA III, NDEA III, and Vocational Education than their proportion of statewide enrollment would suggest.
4. Districts with lower income tend as a general rule to get somewhat more federal aid than districts with higher income, but there are numerous glaring exceptions. With regard to property valuation, federal aid shows no overall equalizing effect.

5. Somewhat more federal aid goes to districts with higher proportions of non-white students. However, the amounts are not in proportion to the magnitude of the added costs in educating the educationally disadvantaged.
6. During the four-year time period under study, the amounts of aid received by local districts varied erratically. Almost half the metropolitan areas in the sample reported an actual decrease in revenues during the last year of the study.
7. ESEA I has focussed needed funds in districts with the greatest educational and fiscal problems. However, its use is frequently in afterhours or summer programs rather than the core curriculum presented to the educationally disadvantaged. The failure to concentrate it on pupils most in need of compensatory education and its improper use as general aid for system-wide purposes have diluted its educational impact.
8. The amounts of federal aid are simply too small to be of anything but marginal help to financially imperiled educational systems. In comparison with total revenues from all sources which ran from $475 to $1,000 per pupil in the five states, we found total federal revenues averaging only $22 to $50 per pupil, or from 3.3 percent to 10 percent of statewide average district revenues. These amounts are inadequate in face of the massive financial problems facing education.

Federal Funding for Education—The National Picture

Before we begin our discussion of the findings in detail, let us briefly trace the levels of federal educational funding and their relationship to educational expenditures for the nation as a whole. The growth of federal aid to education over the past decade had been both significant and erratic (Table 1-7). Over that entire period, aid grew nearly five-fold, from just under $600 million to nearly three billion dollars. Between 1957 and 1964 federal funds almost doubled. They doubled again in one year, 1965-66, as a result of the passage of ESEA. However, during the last five years this overall growth pattern slowed and, if allowance is made for inflation, has actually declined in real terms. Furthermore, as a proportion of total educational revenues, federal aid rose consistently over a decade to a high of 8 percent in 1967-68, but has since slipped steadily to 6.9 percent in 1970-71 (Table 1-8).

In any case, while the proportion of federal educational support has not been impressive, federal aid has exerted programmatic or financial leverage in certain areas of national policy. In the areas of vocational and agricultural education, and more recently, science and language instruction and education of the disadvantaged, federal funds have had an important impact. In some program areas such as language laboratories, federal funding constitutes the preponderant proportion of support. In short, federal aid to education provides a small but important proportion of total educational expenditures.

Table 1-7
Revenues for Public Elementary and Secondary Schools (in thousands)

School Year 1	Total 2	Federal 3	State 4	Local 5
1960-61*	$15,320,340	$ 582,301	$ 6,096,983	$ 8,641,056
1961-62	17,527,707	760,975	6,789,190	9,977,542
1962-63*	18,769,388	681,964	7,379,522	10,707,902
1963-64	20,544,182	896,956	8,078,014	11,569,213
1964-65*	21,962,262	834,202	8,722,937	12,405,123
1965-66	25,356,858	1,996,954	9,920,219	13,439,686
1966-67*	27,256,043	2,162,892	10,661,582	14,431,569
1967-68*	31,092,400	2,472,464	12,231,954	16,387,982
1968-69*	34,756,006	2,570,704	13,866,782	18,318,520
1969-70*	38,192,011	2,767,045	15,627,751	19,797,215
1970-71*	41,936,556	2,892,957	17,226,776	21,816,823

Source: National Education Association, Research Division, *Estimates of School Statistics*, 1971, Table 29, p. 36.

Table 1-8
Percent of Revenue Received from Federal, State, and Local Sources for Public Elementary and Secondary Schools

School Year 1	Federal Sources 2	State Sources 3	Local Sources 4
1960-61	3.8%	39.8%	56.4%*
1961-62	4.3	38.7	56.9
1962-63	3.6*	39.3*	57.1*
1963-64	4.4	39.3	56.4
1964-65	3.8*	39.7*	56.5*
1965-66	7.9	39.1	53.0
1966-67	7.9*	39.1*	53.0*
1967-68	8.0*	39.3*	52.7
1968-69	7.4*	40.0*	52.6*
1969-70	7.2*	40.9*	51.8*
1970-71	6.9*	41.1*	52.0*

Source: National Education Association, *Estimates of School Statistics*, 1971, Table 30, p. 37.

Federal Aid Distribution

An understanding of the levels of federal educational funding provides an orientation to an analysis of the impact of federal aid to education. Our concern, however, is with federal funds as they actually reach school districts. It is only there that the real impact of aid programs can be felt. Ideally, we would have liked to have reported finances by individual schools, but such data are currently unavailable. The statistics that follow, therefore, have been assembled from official reports of local districts to their state education departments.[22]

A. Rural and Metropolitan. One of the most consistent patterns of impact that emerges from our data is that school districts in non-metropolitan areas, largely rural and small town in character, get more federal aid per pupil than do metropolitan areas (Table 1-9). In California, Texas, and Michigan, non-metro-politan areas receive an average 50 percent more aid per pupil than do the metropolitan areas. The greater importance of federal aid in the rural areas is underscored by the fact that such aid provides a consistently larger proportion

Table 1-9
Revenue Sources by Metropolitan and Non-Metropolitan Areas, 1967

State	Federal Aid	% of Total Revenue	State Aid	% of Total Revenue	Local Aid	% of Total Revenue	Total Revenue
California							
Metro	$37	5.1%	$272	37.3%	$420	57.5%	$730
Non-Metro	54	8.4	237	37.0	350	54.6	641
New York							
Metro	35	3.4	484	47.3	504	49.3	1023
Non-Metro	31	3.4	542	58.7	350	37.9	923
Texas							
Metro	42	8.8	207	43.4	228	47.8	477
Non-Metro	63	11.8	250	46.7	222	41.5	535
Michigan							
Metro	18	2.7	264	39.6	385	57.7	667
Non-Metro	30	4.8	305	48.5	294	46.7	629
Massachusetts							
Metro	39	5.9	126	19.0	498	75.1	663
Non-Metro	n.a.	n.a.	n.a.	n.a.	n.a.	n.a.	n.a.

Source: Computed from official state documents by the SURC Policy Institute.

of educational revenues there than it does in metropolitan school districts. New York State comes as an exception to these findings because of the immense impact of New York City with its high concentrations of families receiving welfare payments (AFDC) and thus qualifying for large amounts of ESEA Title I funds.[23]

B. Central City and Suburban. Examination of aid distribution within metropolitan areas—between central cities on the one hand and their suburbs on the other—reveals that while core cities receive more aid than their suburbs, the amounts of federal aid are insufficient to overcome the suburban advantages in locally raised revenues and state aid. With the exception of Michigan, where there is a small ($17.00) revenue edge favoring central cities, suburbs have an average of $100 more to spend per pupil than do the central cities (Table 1-10).

In Massachusetts, for example, central cities receive almost twice the dollar

Table 1-10
Federal Aid and Total Revenue By Central City, Outside Central City, and Non-Metropolitan Areas, 1967

State	Fed. Aid	Total Revenue	% Fed. Aid
California			
Central City	$39	$ 684	5.8%
Outside Central City	40	817	4.8
Non-Metropolitan	54	641	8.4
New York			
Central City	68	876	7.7
Outside Central City	31	1037	3.0
Non-Metropolitan	31	923	3.4
Texas			
Central City	38	479	7.9
Outside Central City	36	485	7.4
Non-Metropolitan	63	535	11.8
Michigan			
Central City	29	683	4.2
Outside Central City	17	666	2.5
Non-Metropolitan	30	629	4.8
Massachusetts			
Central City	69	675	10.2
Outside Central City	38	779	4.8
Non-Metropolitan	n.a.	n.a.	n.a.

Source: Computed from official state documents by the SURC Policy Institute.

amount of federal aid per pupil as the suburbs ($69 and $38), and federal aid represents 10.2 percent of all central city revenues compared to 4.8 percent in suburbs. Despite this important difference, suburban school districts in that state still receive 15 percent ($104) more per pupil from all sources than do central city districts. This pattern is repeated in New York and Michigan. Thus, while central cities in three of the five states receive more federal aid both absolutely and proportionately than do their suburbs—and essentially the same amounts in the remaining two states—federal aid has failed to close the wide gap in revenues available to education between cities and their suburbs. But these data reflect only one dimension of the problem of raising sufficient revenues for education in cities. As we noted above, the higher costs of providing comparable educational services in cities compound existing disparities.

C. Central City and Rural. In comparison with the non-metropolitan or rural portions of the five states, central cities fare less well. Only in New York is there a clear central city advantage. In both California and Texas rural areas receive considerably more federal aid, and in Michigan the two areas receive virtually the same amounts. In regard to total revenues for education, there is no clear pattern, with non-metropolitan areas and central cities each leading the other in two states (Table 1-10).

D. Title I of ESEA. As the largest federal aid to education program, ESEA Title I deserves special mention. Although its educational impact and administration have frequently received criticism, as a fiscal device we find it an immense success. Decidedly higher levels of Title I funds go to school districts with 1) central city or rural location (Table 1-11), 2) higher proportions of minority pupils (Table 1-12), 3) lower income levels (Table 1-13), 4) greater educational need as measured by average achievement scores.[24]

Title I amounted to $17.26 per pupil in the states in our sample in 1967.[25] This amount was almost half (46 percent) of the total federal aid received. Even more than total federal aid, ESEA I has had a greater impact in rural areas than in metropolitan regions. In 1967, non-metropolitan areas received 85 percent more Title I funds per pupil than did metropolitan areas ($25.50 to $13.85). This difference more than accounts for the overall disparity between federal funds to metropolitan and non-metropolitan areas.

In statewide averages, Texas and New York are relatively high in the amounts of ESEA Title I received ($18.25 and $16.27) while the other three states received between $10 and $12.

When the distribution of ESEA I within metropolitan areas is examined, the central cities uniformly do well in relation to their surrounding communities. The only major exceptions are Houston, Dallas, and Anaheim, which receive slightly less money per student from ESEA I than do the outside city areas.

Table 1-11

Comparison of Federal Aid Programs and State Aid for School Districts in Metropolitan Areas, 1967

All Areas Larger than 500,000 Population	ESEA I (Per Pupil)	State Discretionary Federal Funds (Per Pupil)	State Aid (Per Pupil)
California:			
Central city (N=7)	$19.64	$11.44	$234.29
Outside central city (N=119)	11.09	8.92	275.78
New York:			
Central city (N=5)	53.90	13.70	372.51
Outside central city (N=73)	12.35	11.44	494.06
Texas:			
Central city (N=4)	19.67	5.73	174.26
Outside central city (N=33)	12.25	10.38	209.35
Michigan:			
Central city (N=1)	37.15	7.27	238.13
Outside central city (N=31)	7.86	5.75	271.26
Massachusetts:			
Central city (N=1)	32.33	7.18	236.08*
Outside central city (N=26)	7.95	11.58	110.26

Source: Computed from official state records by SURC Policy Institute.

*Boston figure overstates amount of state aid because of payment scheduling associated with the implementation of a new aid program.

Table 1-12

Comparison of Federal Aid Programs and State Aid for School Districts in 5 Large Metropolitan Areas Based on Percentage of Nonwhite Enrollment (1967)

Districts in 5 Largest SMSAs Ranked by Racial Makeup (Number of Districts)	ESEA I (Per Pupil)	State Discretionary Federal Funds[1] (Per Pupil)	State Aid (Per Pupil)
New York SMSA:			
(8) 15 percent nonwhite or more	$30.89	$13.01	$413.17
(36) less than 15 percent nonwhite	10.62	10.48	523.62
Houston SMSA:			
(6) 15 percent nonwhite or more	10.21	11.38	193.25
(8) less than 15 percent nonwhite	19.31	8.35	188.49
Detroit SMSA:			
(5) 15 percent nonwhite or more	25.85	8.07	285.06
(22) less than 15 percent nonwhite	5.13	5.87	272.69
Boston SMSA:			
(1) 15 percent nonwhite or more	32.33	7.18	236.08
(26) less than 15 percent nonwhite	7.99	11.58	112.19
Los Angeles SMSA:			
(25) 15 percent nonwhite or more	15.30	8.63	296.26
(19) less than 15 percent nonwhite	6.28	7.21	236.72

[1]ESEA II, NDEA III, NDEA VA, Vocational Ed., Lunch and Milk.

Source: Computed from official state records by SURC Policy Institute.

E. Other Major Federal Programs. While the formula for the allocation of Title I funds works toward equity for central cities within SMSAs, the pattern of distribution of other federal education programs does not. The point is illustrated by the following example and by a survey of the fifty largest cities in the nation.

How a very wealthy suburb can garner substantially more federal aid than a neighboring deteriorating central city may be seen in the case of Schenectady and Niskayuna, New York (Tables 1-14 and 1-15). Schenectady, a central city whose depressed financial situation can be seen most readily in the fact that it qualifies for three times more Title I aid per pupil than Niskayuna, received only $60 per pupil from all federal programs. Niskayuna, probably the wealthiest

Table 1-13

Comparison of Federal Aid Programs and State Aid for School Districts in 5 Largest Metropolitan Areas Ranked by Median Family Income (1967)

School Districts in 5 SMSAs (Suburbs Ranked by Income Categories) (Number of Districts and Median Family Income Level)	ESEA I (Per Pupil)	State Discretionary Federal Funds[1] (Per Pupil)	State Aid (Per Pupil)
Los Angeles SMSA:			
(2) High ($12,000 to $8,600)	$0	$3.60	$230.25
(17) Moderately high ($8,600 to $7,400)	6.00	7.71	242.04
(12) Moderately low ($7,400 to $6,400)	14.39	7.86	272.63
(4) Low ($6,400 to $6,100)	24.19	12.72	380.70
(1) Central city ($6,896)	23.05	4.92	191.53
New York SMSA:			
(5) High ($17,000 to $10,500)	7.17	7.74	338.98
(13) Moderately high ($10,500 to $8,000)	11.86	12.18	494.20
(18) Moderately low ($8,000 to $6,500)	12.88	10.68	505.20
(7) Low ($6,500 to $5,500)	17.12	10.83	584.55
(1) Central city ($6,091)	68.72	8.89	329.74
Houston SMSA:			
(1) High ($8,900 to $7,200)	2.61	9.69	201.50
(5) Moderately high ($7,200 to $6,300)	4.03	10.34	179.03
(4) Moderately low ($6,300 to $5,000)	7.40	9.89	167.03
(3) Low ($5,000 to $3,700)	49.69	9.06	243.56
(1) Central city ($5,902)	14.32	6.92	172.60
Detroit SMSA:			
(3) High ($14,700 to $8,700)	1.70	3.07	206.68
(10) Moderately high ($8,700 to $7,400)	6.56	6.24	261.07

Table 1-13 (cont.)

Comparison of Federal Aid Programs and State Aid for School Districts in 5 Largest Metropolitan Areas Ranked by Median Family Income (1967)

School Districts in 5 SMSAs (Suburbs Ranked by Income Categories) (Number of Districts and Median Family Income Level)	ESEA I (Per Pupil)	State Discretionary Federal Funds[1] (Per Pupil)	State Aid (Per Pupil)
(12) Moderately low ($7,400 to $6,600)	7.52	5.45	297.90
(5) Low ($6,600 to $5,600)	12.28	7.03	268.46
(1) Central city ($6,069)	37.15	7.27	238.13
Boston:			
(3) High ($9,400 to $9,000)	$4.31	$7.81	$125.20
(6) Moderately high ($9,000 to $7,300)	5.16	12.57	121.78
(11) Moderately low ($7,300 to $6,300)	6.65	12.13	99.73
(6) Low ($6,300 to $5,900)	14.93	9.07	118.68
(1) Central city ($5,757)	32.33	7.18	236.08

[1]ESEA II, NDEA III, NDEA VA, Vocational Ed., Lunch and Milk.

Source: Computed from official state records by SURC Policy Institute.

suburb in the area, is able to take advantage of a sufficient range of federal programs to receive $84 per pupil, or 140 percent the amount of its proportionately poorer neighbor. State aid acts to reinforce the disparity. With a deteriorating fiscal situation and a school population with proportionately three times the number of disadvantaged pupils as its neighbor, the central city receives $100 less per pupil for education.

Table 1-14

Summary of Revenues Per Pupil, Schenectady and Niskayuna, New York, 1967

	Enrollment	ESEA I	Other Fed. Aid	Total Fed. Aid From All Sources	State Aid	Total Revenue
Schenectady	12,480	$28	$32	$60	$454	$1069
Niskayuna	4,708	6	78	84	471	1173

32

Table 1-15

Federal Revenue by Programs for Schenectady and Niskayuna, New York, 1967

	Schenectady		Niskayuna	
Federal Program	Amount	Per Pupil	Amount	Per Pupil
ESEA I	$348,800	$27.94	$ 26,300	$ 5.58
ESEA II	24,400	1.95	35,100	7.48
ESEA III			134,500	28.57
(Total ESEA	373,200	29.90	195,900	41.61)
NDEA III	19,600	1.57	21.700	4.60
NDEA V-A	5,500	0.44	5,200	1.10
Vocational Ed.	50,800	4.07	26,900	5.71
Public Law 874	143,300	11.48	103,100	21.89
School Milk & Lunch	27,500	2.20	28,100	5.96
Other Federal	129,100	10.34	16,005	3.40
Total Federal	749,000	60.01	396,905	84.30

Source: The University of the State of New York. The State Education Department Bureau of Educational Research. Albany, New York.

A study by the USOE examined entitlements under five federal programs to compare the share of state allocations going to large cities with the share of the state's student population in those cities. Except for Title I of ESEA, the study found that large cities were receiving less aid than their proportionate share of the state's population would imply. In other words, not only were federal aid programs not compensating for the special fiscal problems of cities discussed above; federal aid programs were not even giving cities their proportionate share (Table 1-16). In the fifty largest cities in the nation, with 21.3 percent of the pupil enrollment in their combined twenty-eight states and 26.4 percent of the disadvantaged by Title I count, their receipts by program were 15.9 percent of Vocational Education funds, 16.2 percent of NDEA Title III (instructional equipment), 18.1 percent of ESEA II (textbooks and library resources), and 20.5 percent of ESEA Title III (supplemental services and centers). Only under ESEA I did the fifty cities receive funds equal to their percentage of state's student population.

The twenty-five largest cities of the nation received $280 million for the six major education programs. With 12 percent of the enrollments in their states, this represented 14.7 percent of the state's federal aid, but only 10.4 percent of aid other than Title I. Similar conclusions were reached in a report by USOE in 1971 entitled *Finances of Large-City School Systems: A Comparative Analysis*. It, too, found that only in the case of Title I of ESEA were central cities receiving amounts of aid proportional to their pupil populations.

Federal Aid and the Capacity to Support Education

This section will examine the relationship of federal aid to some indicators of district capacity to support education: median family income, state equalized property valuation, state aid, and total revenues for education.

A. Federal Aid and Median Family Income. Let us look first at the relationship of federal aid to average income among school districts within each of the five states. When simple correlation coefficients are computed, we find an inverse relationship (signified by the negative values in the table) in every state in the sample, indicating that where income is lower, federal aid is higher. A perfectly inverse relationship would have a -1.00 coefficient, so it is clear that only in Texas ($-.67$) is the relationship a particularly strong one.

Correlations of Revenue from Major Federal
Programs with Median Family Income
in Districts of Metropolitan Areas

California	New York	Texas	Michigan	Massachusetts
$-.27$	$-.31$	$-.67$	$-.17$	$-.30$

We have looked more intensively into the income-aid relationship in the largest metropolitan area of each of the five states. As Table 1-17 shows, in all states except Massachusetts the wealthiest suburban districts received the least federal aid per pupil and the poorest districts got the most when central cities were not considered. However, if we look for a consistently equalizing effect the results are disappointing. In Houston and Detroit, for example, districts with moderately high family incomes get more federal aid than districts with moderately low income.

Even where the pattern is an equalizing one, it is frequently very mild in its effects. In the Boston metropolitan area, for instance, the wealthiest districts receive $29.00 in federal aid per pupil while the poorest receive $34.00, a difference of only $5.00 despite a nearly 50 percent differential in their average income levels.

Glaring examples of disequalization are found in each of the large metropolitan areas. Beverly Hills, the richest district in the Los Angeles area with a 1960 median family income of just under $12,000, received $17.00 per pupil in federal aid. The Hudson district, with about $6,700 in median family income, received only $14.00. In Massachusetts, Quincy (average income $6,800), which qualifies for large amounts of Impacted Areas (PL 874) aid, received $123.00 per pupil in federal money whereas Salem, with average income of under $6,000, received only $9.00 and Malden, with average income of $6,200, received only $18.00 in federal aid. In each of the cases mentioned above, the richer districts spend twice as much money from all sources per pupil as do the poorer districts.

Table 1-16
Central City Proportions of State's Federal Aid and Enrollment for 25 Largest Cities, 1967*

Cities	Enrollment	ESEA I Eligibles	ESEA I Funds	City Proportion of State's Federal Aid (less Title I)	City Proportion of State's Federal Aid (6 major programs)**	Federal Aid (in thousands)
California						
Los Angeles	14.6%	20.6%	20.0%	6.7%	11.7%	$22,909
San Francisco	2.5	4.5	4.4	1.0	2.3	4,474
San Diego	2.8	3.1	3.0	0.8	1.7	3,235
Colorado						
Denver	19.4	29.1	26.0	15.1	18.5	5,079
Georgia						
Atlanta	10.5	6.9	5.7	8.7	7.0	4,375
Illinois						
Chicago	26.5	50.9	53.9	24.1	40.2	34,763
Louisiana						
New Orleans	13.0	11.7	15.0	15.2	15.1	6,775
Maryland						
Baltimore	24.3	50.8	49.7	21.6	38.3	9,357
Massachusetts						
Boston	8.7	26.1	24.6	4.5	14.6	4,928
Michigan						
Detroit	14.8	33.3	35.0	17.3	26.5	16,271
Minnesota						
Minneapolis	8.5	12.6	11.2	11.0	11.1	4,175

Missouri					
St. Louis	13.9	18.9	19.4	12.1	16.1	7,098
New York						
New York	33.3	63.8	61.4	23.2	48.7	82,932
Buffalo	2.3	4.5	4.3	2.8	3.8	6,543
Ohio						
Cleveland	8.2	14.3	14.7	6.6	10.3	7,818
Cincinnati	3.8	8.5	8.6	4.6	6.4	4,870
Pennsylvania						
Philadelphia	12.7	25.4	24.6	17.8	21.5	19,151
Pittsburgh	7.6	6.9	6.6	12.1	9.1	8,134
Tennessee						
Memphis	14.7	9.3	9.3	5.2	7.6	3,813
Texas						
Houston	10.9	5.2	5.1	4.2	4.7	6,168
Dallas	5.9	3.8	3.7	2.4	3.1	4,035
San Antonio	5.3	4.4	4.3	5.6	4.9	6,463
Washington						
Seattle	13.5	15.7	14.8	13.5	13.9	4,486
Wisconsin						
Milwaukee	13.3	18.4	17.8	13.2	15.4	4,725
Average (unweighted)	12.0	18.7	18.4	10.4	14.7	

*Excluding District of Columbia.
**ESEA I, II, III, NDEA III, Vocational Education, PL 874.

Table 1-17
Comparison of Federal Aid Per Pupil Received by School Districts by Income Categories for Major Metropolitan Areas, 1967

School Districts	Los Angeles Range Median Family Income	Los Angeles Federal Aid	New York Range Median Family Income	New York Federal Aid	Houston Range Median Family Income	Houston Federal Aid	Detroit Range Median Family Income	Detroit Federal Aid	Boston Range Median Family Income	Boston Federal Aid
High	$12,000 to 8,600	$16	$17,500 to 10,500	$19	$8,900 to 7,200	$16	$14,700 to 8,700	$ 3	$9,400 to 9,000	$29
Moderately High	8,600 to 7,400	18	10,500 to 8,000	31	7,200 to 6,300	21	8,700 to 7,400	18	9,000 to 7,300	31
Moderately Low	7,400 to 6,400	26	8,000 to 6,500	32	6,300 to 5,000	19	7,400 to 6,600	12	7,300 to 6,300	39
Low	6,400 to 6,100	54	6,500 to 5,500	46	5,000 to 3,700	53	6,600 to 5,600	55	6,300 to 5,900	34
Central* City	6,896	37	6,091	78	5,902	21	6,069	80	5,747	69

Source: Computed from official state records by SURC Policy Institute.
*Central cities unranked because of different fiscal characteristics.

Core cities received more federal aid than any other districts in three of the states, more than their low income positions alone would suggest. This phenomenon is probably the result of the high proportion of welfare (AFDC) families residing in central cities. Yet even in those states where a relatively high amount of federal aid goes to the cities, the amount those cities spend per pupil from all revenue sources is consistently among the very lowest of the districts within the metropolitan area.

When individual federal aid programs are examined, even the mild overall equalization effect disappears except for Title I of ESEA. Taking one random district from each of the categories of median family income in the New York metropolitan area, we find that the pattern of distribution of individual programs defies simple explanation (Table 1-18).

Without ESEA I, totals of federal aid display an essentially disequalizing tendency. With the exception of Bellport, richer districts get more money than do poorer ones. Individually, ESEA II and Lunch and Milk money are fairly evenly distributed among districts. Other programs have no ascertainable relationship to median family income.

B. Federal Aid and the Property Tax Base. The concept of equalization has traditionally been linked to the size of the real property tax base of school districts. The uneven location of real property has long been seen as a major cause of inequality in the educational opportunities provided in different communities. To overcome these disparities, equalization formulas for the distribution of state educational aid typically allocate funds, to some greater or lesser degree, in inverse proportion to the level of property value per pupil. Aid ceilings, floors, and sharing ratios, however, often serve to defeat the nominal purposes of such programs. In addition, while property value may serve as a realistic yardstick of comparative fiscal ability among the relatively comparable school districts of the suburban and rural areas, its usefulness is limited in measuring the entirely different fiscal position of large cities and highly urbanized areas. There, as we showed above, the greater service needs of an urban population place a far higher demand upon the property tax base than is the case in less densely populated areas. Proportionately less locally raised revenue can, therefore, be devoted to education in the large cities than in the suburban and rural areas on an equal amount of taxable property.

Correlations of Revenue from Major Federal
Programs with State Equalized Property
Valuation in Districts of Metropolitan Areas

California	New York	Texas	Michigan	Massachusetts
−.18	−.03	−.21	.22	−.14

Table 1-18

Federal Aid by Program for Five School Districts in New York Metropolitan Area, 1967 (Average Per Pupil)

Districts	Median Family Income	ESEA I	ESEA II	ESEA III	NDEA III	NDEA V-A	PL 874	Voc Ed	Lunch-Milk	Total Without ESEA I	Total
High											
Great Neck	($14,451)	$4.66	$1.26	$11.31	.32	.00	.00	.62	3.86	17.57	22.23
Moderately High											
Huntington	(8,988)	22.60	2.40	2.22	1.45	.00	2.22	2.04	5.86	16.19	38.79
Moderately Low											
Hicksville	(7,908)	1.62	2.33	.00	1.64	.36	3.41	.75	4.07	12.56	14.18
Low											
Bellport	(6,237)	26.44	1.80	1.35	6.36	.70	29.23	.10	5.71	45.25	71.69
New York City	(6,091)	67.78	1.78	1.59	1.05	.34	.00	.57	4.99	10.32	78.10

Source: Computed from official state records by SURC Policy Institute.

Given the shortcoming of valuation as a universal measure of capacity, it is still interesting to note whether federal aid offsets district property tax base disparities. The simple answer is that it does not. Correlation coefficients display no significant relationships. While four out of the five states do show an inverse relationship (federal aid is higher where valuation is lower), the values are so low as to be meaningless. In one state the relationship is even reversed: in Michigan, as we saw, more federal aid goes to districts that are richer.

In the five major metropolitan areas, federal aid has at best a neutral and at worst a disequalizing impact. Leaving central cities aside, in many instances the wealthier districts do better than other categories of suburban districts in garnering federal aid. In the New York, Houston, Detroit, and Boston areas more aid goes to the wealthiest category than to the poorest, and in the metropolitan areas of New York and Detroit, the richest group of districts outside the core cities receives more aid than any other category (Table 1-19).

C. Federal Aid and State and Local Revenues. The relationship between federal and state aid is of great interest. Some observers have viewed federal aid as complementary to state aid, others as a measure to offset and redirect state priorities and patterns. Our results provide little support for either view; correlation coefficients showed virtually a random relationship, except in Texas where there was a slight (.29) correlation with state aid patterns.

Correlations of Federal Revenue with State Aid to School Districts in Metropolitan Areas				
California	New York	Texas	Michigan	Massachusetts
.07	−.18	.29	−.08	.06

The effect of federal aid when compared to local revenue is somewhat similar. Although the correlations are all negative, the degree of correlation is of an inconsequential order in all states except Texas, thus indicating that federal aid assists districts with less revenue for education as much as districts with greater funds for their schools.

Federal Aid and Non-White Enrollment

One measure of a district's educational resources is, as discussed above, the proportion of educationally disadvantaged students in the schools of the system. As a proxy for such data, we have taken the district's proportion of non-white students. We find that the flow of federal aid is significantly related to the proportion of non-white (primarily black, Puerto Rican, and Oriental) students

Table 1-19

Comparison of Federal Aid Per Pupil Received by School Districts Ranked by Valuation Categories for Major Metropolitan Areas

School Districts	Los Angeles		New York		Houston		Detroit		Boston	
	Range A.V.*	Federal Aid	Range A.V.	Federal Aid	Range A.V.	Federal Aid	Range A.V.	Federal Aid	Range A.V.	Federal Aid
High	$84,700 to 38,300	$19	$77,800 to 52,000	$38	$140,700 to 79,000	$23	$34,700 to 23,000	$40	$56,400 to 36,000	$33
Moderately High	38,300 to 10,000	23	52,000 to 23,000	33	79,000 to 53,500	26	23,000 to 10,000	14	36,000 to 22,500	41
Moderately Low	10,000 to 5,500	23	23,000 to 14,000	30	53,500 to 16,500	26	10,000 to 8,000	22	22,500 to 18,000	30
Low	5,500 to 4,600	27	14,000 to 10,500	29	16,500 to 12,000	21	8,000 to 5,200	16	18,000 to 13,500	30
Central City	16,908	37	41,141	78	37,533	21	16,665	80	14,021	69

*Range of State Equalized Valuation

Source: Computed from official state records by SURC Policy Institute.

in a school district. This relationship emerges from the correlation coefficients, which show a consistent positive relationship. The higher the proportion of non-white students, the more federal aid a district tends to receive. While the strength of the correlation is only of moderate power, collectively they are the strongest relationships that emerged from the variables tested.

Correlation of Revenue from Major Federal
Programs with Proportion of Non-White
Students in Metropolitan School Districts

California	New York	Texas	Michigan	Massachusetts
.33	.31	.21	.54	.43

To illustrate the phenomenon in more detail, we have compared the districts in the New York metropolitan area that have more than 15 percent non-white school populations with the average of their income quartiles. With the exception of one rather high income district in which rapid black immigration has been a very recent characteristic, districts with large black pupil proportions receive far more federal aid than do other districts of comparable income. Title I of ESEA is the primary source of these higher revenues (Table 1-20).

Offsetting the higher costs of education for the disadvantaged is an important

Table 1-20
Districts with over 15% Non-White Pupils by Income Quartiles, New York SMSA

Districts by Income Category	% Non-White	Total Federal Aid of District	Average Federal Aid of Quartile
Moderately High			
Greenburgh ($9,700)	35%	$13	$31
New Rochelle ($8131)	16	51	31
Moderately Low			
Freeport ($7,915)	17	49	32
Hempstead ($7,455)	65	80	32
Mt. Vernon ($6,873)	39	68	32
Copiague ($6,479)	27	33	32
Low			
Bellport ($6,237)	16	73	46
Central City			
New York City ($6,091)	40	78	n.a.

Source: Computed from official state records by SURC Policy Institute.

form of equalization. Since non-white populations tend to have a significantly higher proportion of educationally disadvantaged pupils, this pattern of greater amounts of federal aid, notably Title I aid, to districts with larger non-white populations constitutes a distinct equalizing effect.

The Trend in Federal Aid

One important factor in understanding the impact of revenue is the pattern of aid over time and its effects on educational policy. When school districts are confident of steadily rising amounts of aid, those aid programs are likely to become an integral part of the total educational planning of administrators and school board members. However, where aid varies from year to year, educational planners are handicapped by uncertainty as they develop next year's academic program, contract for facilities and equipment, and hire additional staff.

During the years covered by our study, federal aid reaching school districts has differed from year to year and has followed no discernible pattern. While all the states and metropolitan areas in the sample show increased per pupil aid for the four-year period, in the last year of the period almost half the districts in metropolitan areas reported an actual decrease in per pupil amounts of aid. An additional fourth of the areas maintained the same level of aid, and only the remaining 30 percent showed an increase. Yearly revenues reported by the major cities in New York State illustrate the phenomenon (Table 1-21).

Problems of Program Administration

To this point we have confined our discussion to an analysis of the patterns of allocation of federal aid to education. Subsequent reports, some already in preparation, will examine the decision-making processes on federal aid to

Table 1-21
Revenues From Major Educational Aid Programs for New York State Central Cities, 1965-68 (average per pupil)

	New York	Buffalo	Rochester	Albany Schenectady Troy	Syracuse	Utica-Rome	Binghamton
1965	$ 7	$ 4	$ 5	$16	$ 5	$48	$ 5
1966	31	39	28	49	30	68	12
1967	79	79	110	44	64	89	32
1968	40	52	99	73	75	71	24

Source: Computed from official state records by SURC Policy Institute.

education in school districts, in state education departments, and in federal educational agencies. In this report, however, we think it may be useful to make at least cursory mention of some of the outstanding problems of program administration that weaken the impact of programs of federal aid to education.

The operation of Title I is of particular interest because its funds are allocated on the basis of a poverty formula, thus providing substantial assistance to central cities and other communities with greater than average need for educational resources. The effect of the leveling of the rate of growth of federal educational aid is seen in its effect on Title I. In the 1968-69 school year, "cutbacks of $68 million combined with the growing costs of education resulted in $400 million less for disadvantaged pupils in the local schools this year than was available in the first year of the program," according to the Fourth Annual Report of the National Advisory Commission on the Education of Disadvantaged Children. In addition, the growth in the number of eligible pupils has made for a sharp decline in funds available for each Title I participant—both because of changes in the federal eligibility formulas and because many cities have experienced a marked increase in the number of pupils from families receiving AFDC payments (which increases the number of Title I eligibles). Testimony presented before the House Education and Labor Committee showed that in New York State, Title I funds per poverty eligible pupil had declined to little more than half, from $365.64 to $200.10 in the first four years of Title I operation (Table 1-22).

Dilution of the tendency of aid to overcome educational disadvantage has occurred not only because of total funding levels but also because of administrative procedures of many state and local education agencies. Since the poverty factors which are employed to allocate funds to the county and district levels are not used in determining the particular children who will benefit from Title I programs (poor educational performance is the criterion), school officials have considerable leeway in determining the particular beneficiaries of federal funds.

Table 1-22

Comparative Data on the Allocation of ESEA Title I Funds in New York State, 1966-69

Fiscal Year	Maximum Basic Grant	State Allocation	Proration Factor	Average Net Current Expense	Prorated Per Pupil	Total Number of Poverty Eligibles
1966	$109,667,000	$109,667,000	1.00	$366	$366	299,962
1967	159,451,000	111,091,000	.70	393	274	405,584
1968	195,228,000	115,776,000	.59	417	247	468,629
1969	265,611,000	113,601,000	.43	468	200	567,706

Source: Statement presented by Irving Ratchick, Coordinator of Title I, ESEA, New York State Education Department to the House Education and Labor Committee, Washington, D.C. on H.R. 514 on March 6, 1969.

By failing to concentrate funds to provide total educational effort directed toward students most in need of compensatory education, many school systems have spread Title I allocation thinly in order to include as many students as possible. The result is a superficial veneer of fragmented programs of new equipment rather than an integrated, high impact intervention to achieve major educational change. In statistical terms this may be seen in the average national expenditure for each pupil participating in a Title I program in 1970: $95.00. With average per pupil expenditure from all sources running at just under $700 per pupil nationally at the same time, this level of Title I spending is highly unlikely to achieve marked change in the quality of education afforded the educationally disadvantaged.

There are other reasons why Title I of ESEA has failed to bring the degree of aid for urban education problems that was originally expected. Because of the uncertainty and late availability of funds, a circumstance which has prevented educators from being able to plan for Title I as they develop their program months in advance of the start of the school year,[26] ESEA money has largely gone for a variety of special ancillary programs and has not been utilized to upgrade the central portion of the educational curriculum presented to disadvantaged children. Thus while Title I funds have been of importance to central city school districts and have helped to offset the imbalance of financing described in earlier sections of this chapter, the effect has not been even as helpful as the gross figures might suggest.

In December of 1969 a report by the Washington Research Project titled *Title I of ESEA Is It Helping Poor Children?* stirred wide interest. The report documented a series of instances in which Title I funds were being used for purposes other than assisting disadvantaged children. The report included the following conclusions:

We found that although Title I is not general aid to education but categorical aid for children from poor families who have educational handicaps, funds appropriated under the Act are being used for general school purposes; to initiate system-wide programs; to buy books and supplies for all school children in the system; to pay general overhead and operating expenses; to meet new teacher contracts which call for higher salaries; to purchase all-purpose school facilities; and to equip superintendents' offices with paneling, wall-to-wall carpeting and color televisions.

Though Title I funds are supplemental to regular money, there are numerous cases where regular classroom teachers, teacher aides, librarians, and janitors are paid solely from Title I funds . . .

Title I funds are not to supplant other Federal program funds. But the extent to which Title I funds have been used to feed educationally deprived children, to purchase library facilities and books, to provide vocational education for disadvantaged students, raises serious questions as to whether Title I funds are being used to supplant National School Lunch, Child Nutrition Act, Title II ESEA and Vocational Education Act funds.

Title I funds are not for the benefit of non-poverty children, yet teaching personnel, equipment, supplies, and materials purchased with this money are found in some of the most affluent schools where not a single educationally disadvantaged child is enrolled.

And Title I funds are not to equalize racially segregated schools. Yet many Southern school systems which have steadfastly refused to comply with the Constitutional mandate to desegregate use Title I funds to make black schools equal to their white counterparts. These funds are sometimes used to actually frustrate desegregation by providing black children benefits such as free food, medical care, shoes and clothes that are available to them only so long as they remain in an all-black school.[27]

Shortly after the publication of the report, Commissioner James E. Allen appointed an intragovernmental task force to improve the functioning of Title I. Among the early products of the task force was the "comparability requirement." Issued in the summer of 1970, it requires school districts to demonstrate that Title I schools are the equal of non-Title I schools in teacher pupil ratios and instructional expenditures *without and before* the expenditure of Title I funds. While the effects of such a requirement would be immense, problems of implementing it are also great. At present it is far too early to judge its effectiveness.

Conclusion

This section has examined the pattern of allocation of federal aid to education. The story in general is grossly disappointing. Rural areas receive proportionately more aid than central cities, far more than metropolitan cities as a whole. Many individual aid programs give more help to rich districts than they do to poorer ones. Fund flows over time are so uneven, both within fiscal years and from year to year, that harried school planners often end up shunting federal aid funds to the least pressing, least important of their academic priorities. And problems of program administration further dilute the effect of federal dollars. Most notable of all, the magnitudes of aid are so small—averaging from $22 to $50 per pupil in the five states of the sample and from 3.3 percent to 10 percent of total revenues per pupil (Table 1-23)—that they must be found wanting when compared with the enormous tasks faced by, and inadequate money available for, public education. That central cities—with their social, economic, and fiscal problems—should be averaging significantly and consistently less in total per pupil revenues than their less threatened suburbs is no less than a national disgrace (Table 1-23).

There are some glimmers of light. Overall federal aid provides proportionately more aid to the fiscally threatened core cities than to their more favored environs. Federal aid tends to go in greater proportions to districts with lower than average incomes and higher than average proportions of non-white students.

Table 1-23
Revenue Sources by States, 1967

State	Total Fed. Aid	% of Total Revenue	State Aid	% of Total Revenue	Local Aid	% of Total Revenue	Total Revenue
California	$40	5.6	$264	37.0	$410	57.4	$714
New York	34	3.4	501	50.4	459	46.2	994
Texas	50	10.0	224	44.8	226	45.2	500
Michigan	22	3.4	277	42.4	354	54.2	654
Massachusetts	39	5.9	123	18.6	501	75.6	663

These tendencies toward equity, however, are far too little to overcome the basic maldistribution of educational finances in this nation.

It may be well, in conclusion, to remind ourselves of what that maldistribution implies, for statistical correlations and dollar amounts have a way of hiding as much as they convey. The real impact of inadequate and discriminatory funding levels is evidenced in high dropout rates, student performance below grade level, difficulties in attracting and holding qualified teachers, and over-crowded classes held in aged and dilapidated school buildings. The costs of these conditions are varied and immense. They are reflected in higher welfare, law enforcement, and job training expenses of the cities, in the flight of the middle class to the suburbs, and in the human tragedy and property destruction of urban unrest.

Remedying the problems on the educational agenda will not be easy. It will require the development and implementation of new approaches and special programs. Retrained and better trained teachers will be needed. New class configurations and clinical techniques may also be called for. A variety of strategies will be employed but one factor will be common to all: they will be costly. Until the federal government assumes the responsibility for providing an adequate and equitable pattern of aid to education, the crisis in American education will continue.

Appendix A—A Note on the Information Gap in Educational Finance

The introduction section of Chapter 1 noted critical gaps in information necessary for the formulation of educational finance policy. On some of the vital questions underlying federal educational policy, e.g., the level of expenditures of individual schools, comparative data of even minimal reliability simply do not exist. But, in regard to most of what we need to know, the reason for the "unavailability" of important information may be traced to two problems. First, data remain scattered among and within major federal agencies like United

States Office of Education (USOE), the Office of Economic Opportunity (OEO), the Advisory Commission on Intergovernmental Relations (ACIR), and the Census Bureau, as well as among state and local education agencies and the National Education Association. With current staffing patterns, USOE cannot assemble and integrate materials from these varied sources.

To illustrate: OEO has detailed information on Headstart expenditures; USOE does not. Census and ACIR have valuable information on aspects of state and local finances relevant to the need and capacity for educational support; USOE does not utilize it. Aggregate data on federal expenditures for the nation and for states as a whole are available. But they are not available, either by separate titles or in total, on a district-by-district basis, to say nothing of separate schools within districts or of individual students. Yet to study the impact of federal aid to education, the researcher or policy maker must have figures more detailed than state-wide information. At present, he must deeply involve himself in the uneven and inconsistent record-keeping systems of the states themselves to obtain these data, or satisfy himself with the small sample of districts (1600 for the entire nation) contained in the Annual Elementary-Secondary General Information Survey annual publications of the Office of Education.

A second major reason for the absence of useful information is the lack of appropriate conceptual frameworks for examining questions of educational finance. The concept "federal aid to education" is generally interpreted by the National Center for Educational Statistics (USOE's major educational statistical bureau) to mean essentially "programs administered by USOE." Educational policy makers, therefore, often receive only the most gross of financial information related to programs like the Neighborhood Youth Corps, Operation Headstart, the Job Corps, and Manpower Development and Training.

Another problem of conceptualization relates to the penchant of schoolmen for isolating educational matters from all other areas of governance. In the world of the policy maker, however, education is but one of an infinite number of claimants for public support, and but one of a variety of services aimed at improving the quality of American life. Education, therefore, must be seen in relation to other factors for effective policy making. For example, financial need for state and federal aid in school districts is related to the total package of services receiving support from local taxes; yet collectors of educational data regularly ignore questions of municipal overburden.

The metropolitan context of the market for educational services is widely recognized by social scientists and administrators. Within metropolitan areas competitive salary levels are set and students compete for jobs after graduation. Yet educational statisticians neglect the importance of the concept of the SMSA as an interrelated regional area, and continue instead to generate county, state, and national data.[28] Another factor important in establishing national policy is the social and economic nature of communities, but again income, ethnic, and economic data are seldom integrated with educational material.

These varied symptoms of statistical myopia are reflected in some very tangible ways. As independent local governments in most places in the nation, school districts frequently have boundaries that are not coterminous with other governmental jurisdictions. Since most data on taxes, expenditures, income, population, and ethnic composition are collected by general governments (municipalities and and counties), they are not applicable directly to school districts. This lack of coterminality has proved a real inconvenience to those seeking to examine education in relation to other governmental activities and to the larger society. Even so, such inconvenience has been overcome by many careful researchers working with census tracts and school district maps. With a less restricted view of educational relevance, however, such anachronisms long ago could have been eliminated by the nation's education agency. It is commendable that USOE has recently completed some initial mapping of school district boundaries in relation to general boundaries to overcome the noncoterminality problem.

A start has now been made to break out of the inadequate procedures of data collection. Three years ago the National Center for Educational Statistics (NCES) began its Elementary and Secondary General Information Survey (ELSEGIS). A stratified sample of 1,400 school systems, later enlarged to 1,600, was directly surveyed to provide national totals on revenues, expenditures, and attendance.[29]

Belmont survey begun by the Bureau of Elementary and Secondary Education, and specifically the Consolidated Program Information Report (CPIR), will provide additional information by districts for program evaluation purposes, and will focus on many variables related to federal programs. That these efforts in their current stage of development can serve only imperfectly as a tool for analyzing major educational policy problems, especially urban problems, is not the point. What is important is that these new approaches are underway, and that they be supported, improved, and expanded.

The immensely valuable report of the USOE Advisory Committee for Educational Finance Statistics (the Kelly Committee), submitted to the U.S. Commissioner in March of 1970, catalogues USOE's information shortcomings. More important, it provides a series of proposals aimed at dramatically upgrading USOE's capability to provide useful material for national educational policy making. A summary of those proposals follows:

1. Organize USOE publications of school finance data around analytical common denominators relevant to significant public policy issues in American education.
2. Combine USOE data with local governmental data from the Census of Governments.
3. Solicit proposals for studies comparing ELSEGIS data with the 1970 census of population and housing when those data are available.

4. Expand ELSEGIS and other USOE survey data to include federal programs not administered by USOE.
5. Expand ELSEGIS sample to include samples within all SMSAs in which the largest 100 central cities are located.
6. Expand ELSEGIS (and Belmont Survey) sample to include all districts with more than, say, 5,000 pupils plus a random sample of school districts under that figure.
7. Collect data at the individual school and administrative unit level on educational programs, student population, personnel, revenues, expenditures, and outputs for a random sample of schools in big cities.
8. Collect and publish state data on (a) an annual basis and (b) by federal title as well as by federal act.
9. Develop mechanisms to coordinate USOE data collection activities with those of other agencies of the federal government that are in a position to provide USOE with useful data.

However, many of the recommendations of the Kelly Committee are as yet largely proposals, a blueprint for the future.

The National Center for Educational Statistics has requested funds to implement most of the proposals, but its requests have not in the main been granted. Educational statistics remains the most underfunded of all federal statistical activities.

For the present, the need of policy makers and the interested public for information on the financial impact of federal aid to education remains unmet.[30]

Appendix B—A Note on Chapter 1 Methodology

This study of the patterns of federal aid allocation has been conducted using a five-state sample (California, New York, Michigan, Massachusetts, and Texas) containing 575 school districts. This note will explain how and why we chose that sample.

In constructing the sample for this study, the basic choice that had to be made was between a nationally representative, cross-sectional selection of school districts or a sample which was representative of individual states. We decided upon the latter because it was more consistent with the major purposes of our research. Foremost among those were (1) a concern with governmental units that decide aid allocations going to school districts, i.e., states, and (2) an intent to see federal aid in relation to distinctive state-local systems of educational finance. In addition, serious methodological problems plague attempts to create a single national sample of school districts: for example, property valuations are not equalized to take into account the differences in assessment practices among states, and methods for counting enrollments vary from state to state. As a result, we have undertaken our analysis with a sample composed of separate sub-samples of school districts in five states.

Selection of States

In selecting the five states to be studied, we sought a group of states that would be broadly representative of the dominant trends in educational finance, particularly of the trends which affect metropolitan areas where more than two-thirds of the nation currently reside. The states from which our school system sample was drawn contain 31 percent of the nation's total population and of its public school enrollment through grade 12, and 39 percent of the country's metropolitan population and of its metropolitan public school enrollments through grade 12. In short, with a sample selected from only five states we encompass a substantial proportion of the nation's school population. Our selection was based on more than their sizable population. Specifically our criteria were: (1) region, (2) degree of urbanism, (3) social and economic characteristics, (4) arrangements for financing elementary and secondary education, and (5) patterns of school district organization.

Region. The choice of states provides substantial regional representativeness that includes the northeastern, north central, southern, and western states. All the examined states are within a different census regional division: California within the Pacific; New York, the Middle Atlantic; Texas, the West South Central; Michigan, in the East North Central; and Massachusetts, New England.

Degree of Urbanism. Each of the states whose school systems we studied exceeds the other members of their respective census regional divisions in the proportion of their population classified as metropolitan. This skewing of the sample was adopted in order to provide a vehicle for understanding the relationship between federal aid and the nation's metropolitan trends. In selecting our samples within those states, however, we did include sufficient districts in all states except Massachusetts to permit us to make statements about the rural areas as well.

Social and Economic Characteristics. In regard to social and economic characteristics, the five states of our study differ considerably with respect to one another, but are representative of their respective regions.

Comparing the 1968 household incomes, we find that Texas, with $8,618, falls below the national average of $9,592, while all the others rank above. Michigan, with $10,899, is the most affluent; followed by New York, $10,662; Massachusetts, $10,545; and California, $10,180. These average household incomes are significantly closer than those of any other state to the average income within their regional divisions.

The five states, though different in terms of household income, vary markedly in terms of the proportion of their black population. Massachusetts has 2.2 percent, California 5.6 percent, New York 8.4 percent, Michigan 9.2 percent, Texas 10.5 percent. These proportions deviate little from the appropriate regional division averages, except in the case of Texas which has a considerably lower proportion of black population than do other states in its region. However, the inclusion of Texas permits us to include urban school systems that contain large populations of Chicano children. Concentrated in the southwest, these school systems are among the poorest in the nation and therefore must not be ignored.

The sample states also differ widely in population density. With 657 persons per square mile, Massachusetts ranks as one of the three most densely settled states in the nation. Conversely, Texas with only 36 persons per square mile rates as one of the most sparsely inhabited. Population densities of the other three states are New York, 351; Michigan, 138; and California, 100. As with other characteristics, the densities figures for the sample states are similar to those of their respective regional divisions.

Arrangements for Financing Education. One of the key elements in understanding systems of educational finance, is the relative distribution of revenue responsibilities between the school district and the state government. Nationally, local governments raise approximately 52 percent of all revenues, the states 41 percent, and the federal government approximately 7 percent. Behind those national averages, however, is a wide range of diverse revenue responsibility. The states in our study reflect that diversity. In regard to the percent of revenues raised by local jurisdictions, Table 1-23 shows that the states in our sample accurately reflect national diversity, ranging from Massachusetts where 76 percent of revenues was raised locally to Texas where 45 percent was locally raised. State aid ranged from a low of 19 percent of total revenues in Massachusetts to a high of 50 percent in New York. In regard to federal aid, the states in the sample ranged from 3.4 percent to 10 percent. These states except Texas fell below the national average of better than 7 percent. In dollar amounts, our states varied from being among the highest in the nation to being somewhat below the average. Again our states appeared highly representative of the other states in their regional division.

Variety in state support programs was also evident. Massachusetts, Michigan, and New York, possess aid programs in which at least 80 percent of all grants is apportioned on an equalizing basis, i.e., in inverse relation to the relative fiscal ability of local school systems. In Texas slightly less than 60 percent of total aid is estimated to be equalizing, and in California, a flat grant state, it is only 33 percent. These figures, of course, do not begin to describe all the features and nuances of the various state aid systems, but they do give some idea of the strong differences which exist.

Table 1-24
Phase I Fiscal Data Collection Instrument

The following data has been collected on each of the school districts in the project sample for the 1965, 1966, 1967 and 1968 fiscal years.

Card No. (Cols. 8-9) 01

		Balances on Hand Beginning of Year			Revenue from Local Sources			
Identification	District Name	For Current Operations	Bldg RSRV & Serial Bond Interest & Redemption	Total Beginning of Year Balances	Taxation & Appropriations	Tuition & Transp Fees from Patrons	Other Local Revenue	Total Revenue from Local Sources

Card No. (Cols. 8-9) 02

				Revenue from Federal Sources, by Program				
Identification	District Name	Revenue from Intermediat Sources	Revenue from State Sources	ESEA Title 1	ESEA Title 2	ESEA Title 3	NDEA Title 3	NDEA Title 5-A	Public Law 815

Card No. (Cols. 8-9) 03

		Revenue from Federal Sources, by Program (cont.)							
Identification	District Name	Public Law 874	Head Start	Follow Through	Vocational Education	Nat'l Schol Lunch & Spc Mil Progs (Cash Only)	All Other Revenue from Federal Sources	Total Revnu from Federal Sources	Total Non-Revenue Receipts

Card No. (Cols. 8-9) 04

		Current Expenditures, School Year 1964-1965							
Identification	District Name	Tot of All Balances Revenues & Transfers	Incoming Transfers	Salaries of Professional Staff	Administration	Salaries of Non-Prof Staff	Total Salaries for Instruction	Other Instructional Expenditures	Total Expenditure for Instrcn

Card No. (Cols. 8-9) 05

Current Expenditures, School Year 1964-1965 (cont.)

Identification	District Name	Attendance Services	Health Services	Pupil Transptatn Services	Operation of Plant	Maintenance of Plant	Fixed Charges	Tot Allowable to Pupil Expenditures	Food Services

Card No. (Cols. 8-9) 06

Cur Expends, Sch-Yr, 1965-6, (cont.)

Capital Outlay

Identification	District Name	Student Body Activities	Comm Srvcs, Sum Schols, Adult Educ, & Jr Cols	Total Current Expenditure &	Sites, New Bldgs, Additions, Improvmnts	New Equipment	Total Capital Outlay	Debt Srv from Cur Funds

Card No. (Cols. 8-9) 07

Debt Service from Current Funds (cont.)

Identification	District Name	Amount Paid into Sinking Fund	Principl of Expends to Sch Housing Authority	Interest on Expends to Sch Housing Authority	Other Debt Services	Tot Expends for Debt Srvcs from Cur Funds	Outgoing Transfers	Principal of Debt	Interest on Debt

Card No. (Cols. 8-9) 08

Atnd & Mem, Sch-Yr 65-6

Identification	District Name	Average Daily Attendance	Average Daily Membership	Total Expenditurs

School District Organization. There is considerable variety in our sample with regard to the patterns of school district organization. All our states except Michigan possess some dependent school systems, and in Massachusetts, as in the other New England states, virtually every school system is a subdivision of a town-wide general purpose government.

California introduces a distinctive pattern. Entire school systems can be comprised of elementary grades or secondary grades or both. This arrangement complicates problems of studying educational finance, since there are considerable cost differentials in education of elementary and secondary school pupils, comparisons between districts with different grade levels of educational responsibilities must obviously be avoided.

In New York, Michigan, and Texas, a more typical pattern of school district organization exists. Common to them, as well as to the other states in the sample, a geographic pattern of district organization insures that there will be extensive social, economic, and fiscal disparities among districts in metropolitan areas. Effectively gerrymandered boundaries in all states permit privileged communities like Great Neck, Bloomfield Hills, and Alamo Heights to spend large sums on children with few educational problems while neighboring districts are able to spend relatively small amounts on students with fundamental impediments to learning.

Selection of School Districts

The process for selecting the districts within our sample was based upon the techniques of sample selection used in the USOE Elementary and Secondary General Information Survey. (Like the ELSEGIS sample, ours was chosen on a stratified, variable proportion random selection basis from the *1965-1967 Education Directory* of the U.S. Department of Health, Education and Welfare.) The first step in constructing the sample was to establish for each of the five states the number of school systems falling within the following size cohorts: (1) 25,000 and over; (2) 10,000-24,999; (3) 5,000-9,999; (4) 2,500-4,999 and (5) 300-2,499. School systems with less than 300 enrolled students were excluded entirely because they are located predominantly in two or three rural midwestern states.

The second step in establishing the representative cross-section was to decide upon the proportion of school systems to be selected randomly from each enrollment cohort. The ratio settled upon was as follows: 1 to 1 for all school systems with 25,000 and over; 1 to 1 for all school systems with 10,000 to 24,999; 1 to 2.5 for all school systems 5,000 to 9,999; 1 to 4.5 for all school systems with 2,500 to 4,999 and 1 to 17.5 for all school systems with 300-2,500 pupil population. These proportions were increased considerably from those used in the ELSEGIS project in order to give emphasis to the large school systems generally found in major metropolitan communities.

To select the districts for each cohort, a table of random digits was employed and the appropriate number of sample systems was selected. The result of this process was to give us a high proportion of school districts within metropolitan areas: 85 percent in California, 72 percent in Massachusetts, 71 percent in New York, 65 percent in Michigan, 58 percent in Texas. In terms of the number of school systems, the sample contains 15 percent of the total in California, 14 percent in Massachusetts, 13 percent in New York, 10 percent in Michigan, and 9 percent in Texas. Because of its metropolitan school system orientation, however, this sample represents 71 percent of the fall 1966 enrollment in California, 62 percent in Texas, 60 percent in New York, 52 percent in Michigan, and 45 percent in Massachusetts.

Collection of Data

Fiscal data was collected for each of the sample districts. Research assistants spent from three to six weeks in state capitals examining a variety of official sources that reported school district revenues and expenditures. In several cases we obtained copies of the state's own computer tape. In others data were copied from official publications. More than fifty categories of financial data were obtained for the 1965-1968 fiscal years (see Table 1-24).

Social and economic data were later assembled for each district. Since such data are collected on the basis of general government jurisdiction and census tracts, developing accurate data for school districts required that researchers overcome problems of non-coterminality by comparing school district maps with census tracts where possible and by assigning social and fiscal data to school districts on the basis of standardized assignment formulas where tracted maps were not available. A list of the social, economic, and fiscal variables is given in Table 1-25.

Table 1-25
Social and Economic Data Available for All School Districts in the Study

1960 nonworker-worker ratio*
1960 percentage of median family income under $3000*
1960 percentage of median family income over $10,000*
1960 percentage of population non-white*
1960 median family income*
1965 pupils per square mile of school district**
1965 state equalized full valuation per pupil**
State equalized tax rate expressed in mills**
1967 percentage non-white high school enrollments***

*Source: Bureau of the Census
**Source: Computed from appropriate state sources
***Source: National Center for Educational Statistics, *Directory*

Notes

1. For a description of the general inequities behind these recent court challenges, see John E. Coons, William H. Clune III and Stephen D. Sugarman, *Private Wealth and Public Education* (Cambridge: The Belknap Press of Harvard University, 1970). For a description of the inequities as they appear in the case currently before the U.S. Supreme Court, see "The Texas School Finance Case: A Wrong in Search of a Remedy," *Journal of Law and Education*, I, No. 4, (1972). (Joel S. Berke, Anthony Carnevale, Dan C. Morgan and Ron D. White.)

2. Wilson C. Riles, The Urban Education Task Force Report (New York: Praeger Publishers, 1970), p. 75. For fuller discussion see Appendix A of this chapter and Robert J. Goettel and Joel S. Berke, *Improving Information Systems for Educational Policy Making*, (Washington, D.C.. The President's Commission on School Finance, 1972).

3. A note on terminology: "urban" refers to cities and older, densely populated suburbs with many characteristics in common with central cities. "Metropolitan" refers to a Standard Metropolitan Statistical Area (SMSA) as defined by the Census Bureau. "Central City" (CC) denotes the core city of an SMSA. "Outside Central City" (OCC), "outlying areas," and "suburbs" refer to the remainder of the SMSA. All areas outside SMSAs are "non-metropolitan" or largely "rural."

4. The research on this aspect of the study was conducted in cooperation with the Advisory Commission on Intergovernmental Relations. See *Metropoliten Disparities—a Second Reading*, a study conducted by John J. Callahan, Bulletin No. 70-1 (Washington, D.C.: Advisory Commission on Intergovernmental Relations, 1970). Data drawn upon for this analysis were taken from published and unpublished materials of the 1967 Census of Governments. Population estimates were based on interim Census and Rand McNally estimates. Personal income data were allocated to cities and suburbs on information from *Sales Management* and *Survey of Current Business* (for the relevant years).

5. The census mapping project and other related projects sponsored by the U.S. Office of Education will combine first through fourth count census data with educational data for a sample of roughly 5,000 school districts. This immensely useful work, to be completed in 1973, will develop a broader selection of variables available by school district. It will not, however, provide a general public finance context for education finance data since it will not allocate fiscal data by school districts or resolve the problems involved in such allocations.

6. See, for example, the first two in the new series of reports summarizing the U.S. Office of Education's (hereafter referred to as USOE) Elementary-Secondary General Information Survey, *Statistics of Local Public School Systems* (Washington, D.C.: Government Printing Office (GPO), 1970-1971).

7. For a fuller description of these phenomena see Chapter I in Alan K. Campbell and Seymour Sacks, *Metropolitan America—Fiscal Patterns and Governmental Systems* (New York: Free Press, 1967).

8. See G. Alan Hickrod and C.M. Sabulao, *Increasing Social and Economic Inequality among Suburban Schools* (Danville, Illinois: Interstate Publishers, 1969).

9. Computed from *Statistical Abstract of the United States*, section I, Table No. 14: *Population of Residence and Race: 1950-1970* (Washington, D.C.: G.P.O., 1971), p. 16.

10. Ibid., Table No. 15: *Population Urban and Rural: 1950 and 1960, and by Race: 1950-1970*, p. 16.

11. Ibid., Section xi, Table No. 506: *Money Income of Families-Race and Residence by Income Level: 1969*, p. 318.

12. H. Thomas James, James A. Kelley, Walter I. Garms, *Determinants of Educational Expenditures in Large Cities of the United States* (Stanford: School of Education, Stanford University, 1966).

13. For a comprehensive treatment of the relative fiscal position of school systems in core cities and in their suburban rings, see Seymour Sacks, *City Schools/Suburban Schools: A History of Fiscal Conflict* (Syracuse: Syracuse University Press, 1972). For a more general treatment of fiscal pressures on central cities resulting from central city interaction with the remaining metropolitan community, see Hirsch, Vincent, Terrell, Shoup and Rosett, *Fiscal Pressures on the Central City: The Impact of Commuters, Nonwhites, and Overlapping Governments* (New York: Praeger Publishers, 1971). For comprehensive treatment of the relative fiscal position of different types of school systems in metropolitan and non-metropolitan areas, see Betsy Levin, Thomas Muller, William J. Scanlon, Michael A. Cohen, *Public School Finance: Present Disparities and Fiscal Alternatives* (Washington, D.C.: The Urban Institute, 1972).

14. One measure of the added costs of some of these programs was developed by the National Educational Finance Project. On the basis of current expenditure practices of selected school districts, they found the following cost differentials: compensatory education for the educationally disadvantaged, 2.0 times normal program cost; education for the mentally handicapped, 1.9 times normal program cost; education for the physically handicapped, 3.25 times normal program cost; vocational/technical education, 1.8 times normal program cost. See Roe L. Johns, project director, *Future Directions for School Financing* (Gainesville, Florida: National Education Finance Project, 1971), p. 28. For a more provocative approach to establishing the added costs necessary to provide equality of educational treatment for the disadvantaged that attempts to assess in dollar terms the extra funding necessary to compensate disadvantaged pupils for the additional educational capital embodied in middle class pupils by virtue of the value of their parental instruction, see Dennis J. Dugan, "The Impact of Parental and Educational Investments Upon Student Achievements," Social Statistics Section, *Proceedings of the American Statistical Association*, 1969.

15. For a useful discussion of a number of these studies, see James W. Guthrie et al., *Schools and Inequality*, Chapter III (Cambridge: MIT Press, 1971). For the debate as to whether a linkage exists between the quality of school services and pupil achievement see also James Coleman et al., *Equality of Educational Opportunity* (Washington, D.C.: G.P.O., 1968); Samuel S. Bowles and Henry M. Levin, "The Determinants of Scholastic Achievement: An Appraisal of Some Recent Findings," *Journal of Human Resources*, Summer 1968; Moynihan and Mosteller (eds.), *On Equality of Educational Opportunity* (New York: Vintage-Random House, 1972); Harvey A. Averich et al., *How Effective Is Schooling?* (Washington, D.C.: President's Commission on School Finance, 1971).

16. James W. Guthrie et al., ibid., p. 131.

17. Seymour Sacks, *City Schools/Suburban Schools: A History of Fiscal Conflict* (Syracuse: Syracuse University Press, 1972), p. 84.

18. Lynn H. Fox and Gordan E. Hurd, *Finances of Large City School Systems: A Comparative Analysis*, prepared for the Department of Health, Education and Welfare, U.S. Office of Education, National Center for Educational Statistics (Washington, D.C.: G.P.O., 1971), pp. 42-43.

19. Advisory Commission on Intergovernmental Relations, op. cit., Table X.

20. Joel S. Berke and John J. Callahan, "Serrano v. Priest: Milestone or Millstone for School Finance?" *Journal of Public Law*, XXI, No. 1, (1972)

21. For a thorough compilation of federal education legislation to 1968, see U.S. Congress, House, *Federal Educational Policies, Programs and Proposals: A Survey and Handbook*, I-III, House Document 398, 90th Congress, 2nd Session (Washington, D.C.: G.P.O., 1968). For an overview of the historic forces shaping modern federal education programs, see Stephen K. Bailey and Edith K. Mosher, *ISEA: The Office of Education Administers a Law*, chapter i (Syracuse: Syracuse University Press, 1968).

22. Figures for the states of our samples (for example, the proportion of federal aid to total revenues) may differ somewhat from the amounts of federal aid reported for states as a whole by state education departments as a result. For one thing, certain direct state expenditures will elude us. For another, small federal programs or those administered by multi-district authorities may go unreported by individual school districts while state officials are able to report the state's total allotment. Yet on balance, the most important consideration was to report finances as close as possible to the point where they are transformed into real educational resources (services, equipment, and facilities), a procedure that we have adapted from the recent innovation in data collection, the Elementary and Secondary General Information Survey of the United States Office of Education (USOE).

23. In determining the amount of Title I aid a district is eligible to receive, the major criterion used is the number of children whose parents receive Aid to Families with Dependent Children (AFDC).

24. Donald S. Van Fleet and Gerald Boardman, "The Relationship Between

Revenue Allocations and Educational Need as Reflected by Achievement Test Scores," *Status and Impact of Educational Finance Programs* (Gainesville, Florida: National Education Finance Program, 1971).

25. These amounts are not Title I funds per Title I eligible. Rather, they are presented as Title I money per pupil in the entire district, in order to more clearly indicate the overall fiscal impact of Title I funds.

26. Bailey and Mosher, op. cit., Chapters IV and V.

27. The report by the Washington Research Project of the Southern Center for Studies in Public Policy and the NAACP Legal Defense and Educational Fund, Inc., *Title I of ESEA Is It Helping Poor Children?*, December, 1969, p. 57, 58. Several recent projects conducted since that report were completed and have found that many of these problems continue.

28. The Elementary and Secondary Education General Information Survey does break out overall "metropolitan central," "metropolitan other," and "non-metropolitan" but it does not deal with the school districts in particular metropolitan areas in relation to each other. For an example of the latter, see Advisory Commission on Intergovernmental Relations, *Metropolitan Fiscal Disparities*, (Washington, D.C.: Government Printing Office, 1967).

29. For a study of the 1969-70 school year, a larger sample consisting of 5,000 districts has been used, but the smaller sized sample, inadequate for developing state-by-state samples, has been utilized for subsequent years.

30. Robert J. Goettel and Joel S. Berke, op. cit., Chapter 3.

2 Federal Aid to Public Education: Who Governs?

Michael W. Kirst

Research Considerations

In a recent review of the literature, Segal and Fritchler characterized the subfield of intergovernmental relations politics as "largely untouched—a kind of methodological Cinderella after midnight."[1] Consequently, research designs in this area are pioneering and must be based in large part on concepts from other subfields of political science. For instance, intergovernmental politics focuses on a "relationship," and the concept of sovereignty was borrowed from the study of nation states. The concept of dual sovereignty and the "states rights" ideology followed.[2] Stressing that nearly every function is shared by almost every level of government, Morton Grodzins subsequently demolished the myth of dual sovereignty. His analysis of the relationship was highlighted by the rubric "cooperation,"[3] and he contended conflict occurs not between governments but among branches of the same level of government.

From 1958-1970, federal grants to states and localities grew more than five-fold, from less than $5 billion to an estimated $25 billion in the 1970 fiscal year. Federal grants-in-aid as a percentage of total federal expenditures has risen from 6.1 percent to 12.8 percent.[4] As this growth has occurred, the Grodzins' cooperation-conflict dichotomy has become too general to be very useful. Between 1960 and 1970 the basic character of the typical federal assistance program changed from helping state or local governments accomplish *their objectives* with perfunctory general federal review, to using state governments as an *administrative convenience* under some explicit controls for accomplishing *specified federal objectives.*[5] Surely, such a change would lead to tension between federal authorities and would require a new theory of intergovernmental relations.[6] Indeed, Sundquist warns that the conflict has grown to such an extent that the federal system is threatened by "the power struggles and treaty negotiations among mutually jealous federal-state-local agencies." In his view, intergovernmental struggles often change the basic substance of the federal program. A 1970 survey, however, revealed 75 percent of the local federal aid coordinators (usually in a mayor's office) still elected the first alternative for describing their relationships with the federal government.[7]

Cordial and friendly, noncompetitive	102
Friendly competition	25

61

Cautious and guarded negotiation   11
Hostile

A similar state response would indicate that intergovernmental conflict is rarely overt and usually kept on a subtle professional basis. Indeed, state professional educators probably are more at ease with federal educators, who share the same general values, than with general government executives or parents and community groups. These issues are analyzed in depth in Chapter 9 but this chapter also highlights the preeminence of traditions and state political culture in allocation decisions.

The state studies were conducted in part through elite and specialized interviewing. The techniques followed those outlined in *Elite and Specialized Interviewing*, by Lewis Dexter. The interviews frequently led to the discovery of relevant published and unpublished hard data. Documentation for these studies included state plans prepared for the U.S. Office of Education, state guidelines and reports, internal SEA memoranda, and other pertinent articles and books.

To insure that the five researchers were primarily investigating the same issues, we standardized key components of the case studies. All of the researchers considered the following topics in their intra-state analyses:

I. Historical
    —State political culture—particularly the impact of "localism" on the influence of state officials
    —Traditional political pattern of urban-rural conflict and/or cooperation
    —Role and effectiveness of state political coalitions among education interest groups
    —History of professionalism, performance and politicization of the SEA.

II. Role of Governor, Legislature, Parties, and Interest Groups
    —Interest in federal funds
    —Staff for oversight.

III. Coordination and Overall Priorities for Federal Education Aid
    —Use of state comprehensive planning including relationship of federal categories to state funds
    —Impact of federal categories on balkanized organizational structures
    —Central management capacity.

IV. Title-by-Title Analysis
    —Distribution formulas within the state; changes over time
    —Importance of federal regulations and guidelines
    —Interest group constellations for each Title
    —Influence in setting program priorities
    —Monitoring, enforcement, dissemination by the State Education Agency.

Research Assertions

Before the study commenced, we formulated six major assertions to be tested in each state study. If these six assertions were confirmed in the states, they would together provide a theoretical framework to explain and predict the distribution of federal aid in additional states. In effect, future research could move from our "hypothesis-generating" stage to "theory confirming" cases and deviant cases. Consequently, it is desirable to analyze these six broad assertions before moving to a more detailed examination of each federal title.

The six assertions are listed below:

1. There will be less involvement and political influence by the governor and legislature on federal aid in comparison with state aid. General government executives will leave allocation decisions and negotiations to state education professionals.
2. The influence and impact of the urban school lobby on the state allocation of federal aid will not be significant. Cities will not form state coalitions or use existing coalitions to direct more federal aid to their needs.
3. As federal aid increases and states have more discretion in allocation, pressures will increase on state government from organized interests. Consequently, a longitudinal analysis would show a gradual change in interest group intensity.
4. The state education agency will attempt to minimize political conflict and pressure by using existing state aid formulas for allocation of federal funds. Most of these state aid formulas are not adjusted very well for core-city needs.
5. Federal aid, except in a manner restricted by federal guidelines or requirements, will flow within a state as it has in the past. Once the pattern of state distribution is established based on Assertion #4., then the flow will only be altered by explicit and vigorously enforced federal regulations.
6. SEA personnel are socialized so that they view their proper role as providing technical assistance to the LEAs, not enforcing or policing federal requirements or setting program priorities. This rather passive, technical assistance role vis á vis the LEAs would preclude such things as setting reading priorities or restricting Title I aid to elementary schools.

If it had been validated, this set of assumptions would have resulted in the following scenario for state allocation. The federal money flows to the SEA where the governor and legislature are largely unaware and uninterested in the decisions. The impact of lobbies on state allocation decisions is minimal but growing incrementally. The SEAs use the distribution criteria in the state aid formulas and change these only when federal regulations are enforced by threat of fund termination. SEA personnel maintain cordial relations with LEAs and stress their technical assistance role.

These assertions highlight the potential usefulness of organizational choice theory for predicting state allocations of federal aid. In effect, the SEA operates in an environment that permits bureaucratic standard operating procedures and routine administrative programs to predominate over governors, legislatures and pressure groups (which are unaware or ineffective). State education departments frequently end their search for possible allocation alternatives with familiar state aid concepts which represent satisfactory, rather than optimal, solutions embedded in politically viable state aid formulas. These standard operating procedures of state governments are disturbed only by federal regulations that signal a mandatory change. The relations of state departments with local districts proceed according to historical patterns of behavior. The routines and customarily appropriate procedures in the existing SEA organizational repertoire, however, vary widely among states. Variations are caused by such factors as different state political traditions and the SEA environment. Organizational theories would lead us to predict that the menu of alternatives considered by state education departments in their allocation decisions would be very limited in both number and character. In short, allocation decisions on federal aid are constrained greatly by existing organizational goals and procedures, as well as overall state political factors.

While our assertions proved to be relatively accurate descriptions of major tendencies found in our six studies, there were striking exceptions. In California, for instance, the legislature has extensively earmarked the federal aid allocations. In Michigan, the SEA has employed a needs assessment and has targeted funds to urban areas to counter the state aid flow—thus contradicting our fourth assertion. (From the standpoint of organizational choice theories the Michigan SEA is an interesting case of an organization changing its goals and standard operating procedures.) Coalitions of urban districts have not concentrated their efforts on federal aid as yet, but Detroit and New York have hardly been as unaware or passive with respect to state allocation of federal aid as our second assertion would suggest.

Large-scale changes in the flow of federal dollars in Michigan and California were *not* related to changes in federal regulations or enforcement policies—clearly exceptions to our fifth hypothesis. Many of the titles across the states, however, show a strong similarity to state aid formulas, primarily with respect to uniform per pupil allocations and the merger with state formulas on teacher units or teacher salaries. The service and technical assistance role attributed to SEA personnel in our sixth assertion is not generally followed in certain titles (particularly Title III of ESEA).

To assist the reader in making interstate comparisons, we have summarized the outcome of the research assertions before the detailed analysis of each state in Chapters 3-8. A number of crucial overall observations are discussed below. Chapter nine also summarizes both general findings and important exceptions and desparities.

State Political Culture and Federal Aid

The political culture and traditions of state education politics—different in every state—principally determine state distribution and administration of federal aid. Federal aid is channeled into an existing state political system and pattern of policy; a mixture distilled of federal priorities and concerns and frequently different state priorities and concerns emerges. The federal-state (and local) delivery mechanism also insures that the implementation and policies are *not* uniform among the states. State policy with respect to federal aid is very different in Michigan than it is in Texas or Virginia. The sanctions and incentives available to the federal government are insufficient to alter drastically the traditional pattern of state education policy. Federal money can be considered a stream that must pass through a state capital; at the state level, the federal government is rarely able—through its guidelines and regulations—to divert radically the stream or reverse the current. Consequently, the specific political context in each of the six states needs to be carefully examined by the reader. Yet, over a long period of time, federal administrators and guidelines have a perceptible impact on state policy, providing the federal objectives are not changed.

Each of the state studies examines the political culture and historic attitudes in which state education politics is embedded. The "religion of localism" in Massachusetts or the "audit mentality" and unassertive state government in Virginia are the key contextual elements within which federal and state aid operate. These contextual elements help to establish and to sustain the organizational routines of the SEA. As Edith Mosher stresses for Virginia:

... the changes (from increased federal education aid) were brought about in accordance with the state's characteristic mode of orderly and consensual decision-making. Its elements are: a strong and astute governor, a relatively compliant legislature, low profile interest group activity, and an unassertive bureaucracy, including the State Department of Education. It is apparent that even Governor Holton does not consider his election as a mandate for dramatic policy upheavals, since during his first year in office he has displayed the conciliatory tone, deliberate pace, and regard for continuity to which Virginians are accustomed in the conduct of public business.[8]

With regard to urban-suburban-rural priorities, the state allocation decisions are also embedded in a tradition of political relationships. The New York case highlights the traditional political interactions between Albany and New York City. The lack of priority in state funds for Boston is the reflection of years of Massachusetts political history. While several states (Virginia, Texas, and California) display an emerging urban alliance, concerted multi-city action has not yet had a decisive impact on federal aid decisions. The traditional rural concern in Texas education politics is most graphically reflected in the distribution formulas for vocational education and NDEA. In all of the states, the core cities are currently attempting to create alliances and are gradually becoming more aware of the potential impact of federal aid. State interest group activity with respect to federal aid appears to be on the increase.

Each of the studies analyzes historically a number of SEA characteristics. Although the major portion of recent SEA growth has been underwritten by federal funds, federal money is funneled through an SEA administrative structure and pattern of policy; again, state factors influence its eventual distribution. In Michigan, a statewide assessment program, comprehensive planning, and priority setting have ordained a consistent urban priority even in federal programs without such mandates. In Massachusetts, the religion of localism has led to an absence of state priorities—urban or otherwise—and a passive service orientation. Department personnel in Massachusetts apply gentle persuasion with respect to federal regulations, but retreat when an LEA protests vigorously. In short, state departments and units within state departments display administrative styles along a continuum from aggressive leadership to passive technical assistance. In some state contexts, particular administrators— Riles in California and Porter in Michigan—can move a state from one administrative style to another. But in Massachusetts and Texas, the overall state political culture imposes such great constraints that a more activist program priority orientation for the SEA is not feasible.

The states also vary enormously with respect to the partisan political image of the SEAs. The apolitical image, paramount in Texas and Virginia, deterred gubernatorial and legislative concern and intervention. On the other hand, California Superintendent Rafferty was viewed as immersed in politics; because he was not considered an "objective educational expert," the legislature interceded in federal aid administration.

Discordant educational interest groups fragment educational politics in California, Michigan, and New York; administrators feud openly with teacher and citizens' groups. By contrast, the Texas State Teachers Association remains unified, including administrators and urban school districts under one roof. We see a pattern in which divided educational interest groups encourage intervention in federal aid policy by governors and legislatures. If the educators can not agree and appear to be out only for their own parochial interests, governors and legislators are more likely to intercede in the administrative and allocation decisions of the state bureaucracy. Only in California, however, did we find sufficient staff to enable governors and legislators to oversee the implementation of federal aid. Other governors and legislators lack the information and analysis needed to intervene in federal aid administration.

A detailed summary of the political culture and style of each of the six states would only detract from the richness and in-depth treatment by each of the authors. Some striking elements are (1) the importance and diversity of state political culture and standard operating procedures for determining federal allocation policies; (2) the consequent variation in state political and financial outcomes—e.g., no standard federal aid policy exists; (3) the substantial discretion and leadership of administrations in some states, and the overwhelming constraints on state leadership in others; (4) the traditional estrangement of city lobbies from SEA decisions, and the very recent urban-district awareness of the potential for changing state policies to enlarge the flows of federal money to cities.

Coordination, Comprehensive Planning, and Monitoring

The degree and character of state planning for the use of federal resources; the coordination among federal programs and between them and state priorities; and the way in which the administration of the federal programs was monitored were also important questions for investigation. By and large, we found little evidence of systematic attempts to shape the various federal programs to serve integrated and carefully articulated educational priorities. We looked for such evidence as consolidated application forms; emphasis on comprehensive management information systems, and a coordinated approach of the monitoring of LEA programs. Only in Michigan did we find a basis for planning of this kind. We must hasten to add, of course, that the federal government has not itself maintained any sustained commitment to this concept of comprehensive planning. The Texas study, for example, examined the abortive attempt of the Texas Education Agency to implement a program of this kind in the face of a wavering federal-state commitment and a lack of statutory encouragement.

In view of this weak federal attachment to more systematic use of federal resources, the Michigan comprehensive planning needs assessment program is especially noteworthy.

The assessment provides data on achievement, school services, and the social-economic background of the pupils; it has been the basis for targeting federal funds to disadvantaged children, regardless of the lack of explicit priorities in particular federal statutes—e.g., Title III of ESEA. The immediate intellectual force behind the current Michigan assessment effort was provided by staff members in the Michigan State Department's Bureau of Research.[9] Enthusiastically supported by State Superintendent John Porter, the programs were successfully negotiated through the governor and legislature.

The assessment is complemented by *Common Goals of Michigan Education,*[10] prepared by a task force of educators, students, and lay citizens. The assessment's documentation of the extremely low social-economic background of many Detroit pupils was instrumental in the targeting of federal aid to Detroit and the initiation of a special state aid formula for disadvantaged children. Because assessment fostered accountability within the MDE bureaucracy, top level priorities were able to influence the federal aid decisions made by the various divisions responsible for day-by-day federal aid policy. The comprehensive planning and priority setting establishes a standard for lower level administrators. Recent information indicates that Michigan has moved even further in its concentration of federal aid on the disadvantaged than the case study in this volume indicates.

In Michigan, the state superintendent and state board were able to seize the initiative and set priorities in part because of the factionalism among educational interest groups; discord reigns among teachers, administrators, and school board members, among others, and no group has been able to establish inordinate influence.[11] Beholden to no interest group, the MDE could play each one off against the other in order to chart its own course. The superintendent's needs assessment and priority setting program enabled him to fend off the importuning of specific lobbies, such as vocational educators, when they conflicted with his priorities. The low visibility (only 7 percent of Michigan's total expenditure) and complex categorical nature of federal aid have deterred the governor, legislature, or political parties from interceding in MDE allocation decisions. As Scribner points out, legislators and gubernatorial staff only vaguely understand federal aid; thus these general government officials do not consider the issues very relevant or exciting. Scribner concludes:

—The proportion of federal aid is too small to arouse serious, lasting public attention.

—Public awareness over federal aid issues in Michigan is negligible and to an extent blurred by the more immediate and intense issues of state and local concern.

—Though the governor has budgetary powers, he lacks any direct influence on the functions of the state department of education.

—The legislature possesses some fiscal control and passes legislation affecting the state department, but has very little influence over actual execution of state programs.[12]

State Boards of Education and Federal Aid

On paper, state boards of education have enormous formal prerogatives to determine state education policy making. Although we have almost no studies of the policy role of state boards, the predominant suspicion is that the boards rarely exercise these impressive formal powers.[13] The state board appoints the superintendent in twenty-five states and in the others must approve the major policy proposals of the chief state school officers (CSSO); nonetheless, the state board reputedly is dominated by the SEA or immobilized by other political forces. In view of the contradictory evidence, this study paid particular attention to the impact of the state board on federal aid.

We found state boards of education to be severely hampered by the same constraints that local boards face. Indeed, because state board members do not live in the state capital and meet only once or twice a month, these constraints are greater than those faced by local boards.[14] State boards lack expert, independent staff. Laymen with other demanding positions, members are usually not presented with performance criteria or objective output data upon which to question the judgment of the CSSO or his *large* staff. The complex categorical nature of federal aid—in contrast with state goals and priorities—is difficult for lay boards, untutored in phraseology or rationales, to understand.

The method of board selection contributes to the state board's lack of impact. Sroufe described the election as a "non-event" in which most candidates put out only one press release. The public remains unaware of the issues or candidates. Consequently, rarely does a board member have a policy mandate from his campaign or a constituency to represent. All of these constraints result in the state board being, at best, a forum for and most likely a captive of the education professionals. Only in California did the board have a significant impact on the state administration of federal aid. In the other states, the board may have routinely approved federal aid issues, but the lack of interest group activity on these issues made approval routine.

The California case is noteworthy because of the ideological split between the CSSO (Rafferty) and a state board composed of holdover members appointed by Governor Edmund Brown, a liberal Democrat. The California State Board reviewed federal aid proposals carefully with little regard for Rafferty's opinions. Indeed, the California legislature specified that Titles I and III of ESEA should be administered by lay advisory commissions responsible directly to the state board—thus completely bypassing Superintendent Rafferty. Wilson Riles, the present state superintendent, thrived under this political arrangement when he was the head of the Division of Compensatory Education. Possessed of the state board's confidence, Riles was influential in the appointment of many members of the Title I Advisory Commission. When he became state superintendent, Riles moved swiftly to trim the power of the legislatively-established independent Advisory Commissions and to reconcentrate power in the Office of State Superintendent. The state legislature approved most of his requests for reorganization. The state board's review of federal aid decisions is also less intense under Riles.

Specific Allocation Decisions

The lack of general policies and comprehensive statewide planning for federal aid necessitates a title-by-title analysis. No state policy for federal aid exists; there are only policies and guidelines for each federal title. Moreover, the federal categories display no consistent priority or coherent policy. Some are directed at a target group—the disadvantaged; others, at equipment and books; still others, at such concepts as innovation. If the states do not put them together in some fashion, it is unlikely the locals will. Each of the state studies devotes considerable effort to the individual titles. Again the most striking fact to emerge from a comparative analysis is the diversity of state policies and underlying political structures and traditions. The search for conclusions without exceptions is frustrated frequently. At one end of the continuum, California and Michigan promulgate and monitor specific policies to concentrate funds on disadvantaged children. In his study of Michigan, Scribner discusses the state monitoring team that reviewed Detroit's Title I program in detail and the changes that ensued. At the other end, Massachusetts' administrators restrict their Title I enforcement to friendly persuasion. Iannaccone summarizes the Massachusetts situation:

The Massachusetts SEA has generally not seen its role as one of using its discretionary power to maximize aims through the establishment of high quality standards for programs in the local education agency, neither demanding sophisticated methods for program development, careful operating procedures, tough criteria for program proposal review, nor careful evaluation requirements. In short, the Massachusetts Department of Education in allocating federal funds and administering federal programs has, in effect, generally transmitted to the local educational agencies the discretionary powers which the federal government and federal legislation give it.

Briefly, where federal mandate requires the Massachusetts Department of Education to exercise control over (local) programs and specify in detail the nature and/or form of such control, the . . . Department has complied with federal regulations. Otherwise, it has not availed itself of the discretion available to it.[15]

In essence, title-by-title policies in any state are established and executed according to a general state department administrative style. A specific program or bureaucratic unit, however, may deviate markedly from the normal pattern of state policy; in Massachusetts, the Title III ESEA Office is staffed by more activist and research oriented personnel than are the other federal program offices.

The vocational education section in each state study deserves special mention. Vocational education appropriations have grown rapidly in recent years ($487 million), and the USOE is instituting a new program in "career education." Vocational education programs have always involved substantial state participation and discretion in allocation. As Chapter Nine emphasizes, the federal sanctions and incentives have been insufficient to reorient substantially the content the state allocation of vocational education programs—despite frequent congressional attempts to legislate significant program changes through detailed amendments.

Each of the studies examines the specific distribution formulas used in each of the state discretionary titles. The determinants and criteria of each distribution formula should be noted by the reader; federal regulations, lay advisory councils, local pressure groups, and top state administrators influence the formula's ultimate composition. Especially interesting are the changes over time in these specific distribution formulas as well as the reasons for the changes. The aggregate impact of these title-by-title decisions is displayed in Table 2-1 which shows the differential flow of Title I ESEA, state discretionary federal funds, and state aid as each affects central city and suburban school systems.

Values Underlying the Research

As with all research, the values of the researchers had considerable influence on both the design and conclusions of the study. For example, fiscal and political

Table 2-1
Comparison of Federal Aid Programs and State Aid for School Districts in Metropolitan Areas (1967)

SMSAs over 500,000 Population	ESEA I (per pupil)	State Discretionary Federal Funds* (per pupil)	State Aid (per pupil)
California			
CC** (N=7)	$19.64	$11.44	$234.29
OCC*** (N=119)	11.09	3.92	275.78
New York			
CC (N=5)	53.90	13.70	372.51
OCC (N=73)	12.35	11.44	494.06
Texas			
CC (N=4)	19.67	5.73	174.26
OCC (N=33)	12.25	10.38	209.35
Michigan			
CC (N=1)	37.15	7.27	238.13
OCC (N=31)	7.86	5.75	271.26
Massachusetts			
CC (N=1)	32.33	7.18	236.00
OCC (N=26)	7.95	11.58	110.26

*ESEA II, NDEA III, VA, Vocational Ed., Lunch & Milk.
**CC = Central City
***OCC = Outside Central City
Source: Computed from official state records by the SURC Policy Institute.

relationships between state government and core city schools were examined extensively in the six case studies. Our concern with these relationships drew substance in large part from the distressing, deteriorating fiscal plight of urban schools analyzed in Chapter 1. As a consequence of these statistics, the case studies focussed to a greater extent on the factors that determine the cities' share of intrastate federal funds than on those that determine the suburban and rural allocations. However, to ascertain the variables responsible for the urban share required the analysis of the suburban and rural capabilities for attracting federal aid as well.

The researchers espouse an aggressive and effective SEA for several reasons, and this viewpoint influenced the emphasis of our investigations. State aid formulas presently favor districts outside of core cities, particularly the suburbs. In our six state study, Massachusetts is the only exception to this trend, and Massachusetts provides a relatively small share of state aid compared to the other five states. A strong, independent SEA could use federal funds to correct the inequitable situation created by state aid. By invoking its discretionary power, the state department of education could redistribute federal funds to core cities—thus recognizing their special fiscal problems. Adoption of such a policy demands an intrepid SEA—unfettered by political alliances and unwilling merely to plug federal money into state aid distribution formulas.

Many of the federal statutes, particularly Title I and vocational education, delegate to the state the responsibility for insuring that federal funds reach the target population of disadvantaged youths within school districts. For instance, Title I aid must be channeled to schools with *high concentrations* of low income children, while nearby schools with many disadvantaged students cannot be assisted with the limited funds. Adequate and aggressive SEA application review, monitoring, and information dissemination staff are required to effectively administer the federal provisions.

Finally, the researchers favor the use of SEA discretion to insure that limited federal money is expended on a coherent, comprehensive program; though the federal statutes usually leave the mix of program and curriculum choices to local-state negotiations, they do permit the state to determine substantive thrusts. In California, for example, the Title I program demonstrates a clear preference for elementary programs; the programs must contain a number of components designed for comprehensive impact, e.g., teacher training, nutrition, and others in addition to an academic focus like reading. In our view, these program priorities will be related to the particular educational problems of each state and, consequently, there will be great variation among the states.

Research Methods for Determining Who Governs

This study was designed to integrate the case study and comparative methods. Because science aspires to generalize, the case study approach has always had ambiguous status. While a single case provides intensive data, it cannot be the basis for valid generalization. We did not, however, have the resources to research enough states to claim representative sample data. Our study falls under Lyphart's classification of hypothesis-generating cases:

Hypothesis-generating cases start out with a more or less vague notion of possible hypotheses, and attempt to formulate definite hypotheses to be tested subsequently among a larger number of cases. The objective is to design theoretical generalizations in areas where no theory exists yet.[17]

Hypothesis-generating case studies are distinguished from "theory-confirming" (or "theory-infirming") case studies because the latter are analyses of single cases within the framework of established generalizations. In essence, the case study or studies test and subsequently confirm (or infirm) a proposition. In the absence of any prior research on the specific topic, we attempted in this study to construct some tentative propositions. Although the comparative case approach limited our research to six states and precluded national generalizations, it was selected for several related reasons. First, the fiscal data presented in Chapter One demonstrated a significant variation in distribution patterns among those states. Although we have traced some aggregate patterns, the analysis of each federal title revealed a scatteration indicative of particular state factors—factors which could best be explored on an individual case basis rather than by a survey.

Second, other research indicated that surveys of structural factors of state government or of individuals with formal decision-making power could not explain federal aid distribution.[18] Survey data on the chief state school officer's fiscal independence or the governor's veto power would only mask the important political factors. Indeed, we suspected federal aid allocations were primarily bureaucratic decisions made by the SEA, with limited involvement by the legislature or office of the governor.

Third, we believed that division directors or bureau chiefs within the SEA were significant decision makers on intrastate allocations. Bureaucratic negotiations between division heads and local school staffs, as well as the complex federal negotiations between USOE officials, with their general guidelines, and state officials, with project approval power, required a case study approach.

Finally, the great diversity of state political culture, educational decision makers, and patterns of educational policy formulation, apparent in our initial findings, demanded a comparative case method of analysis. The methods and concepts of comparative government research seemed most appropriate. The range in the education policy-making process between Massachusetts, Texas, California, and Virginia, for instance, turned out to be enormous and would likely be obscured by aggregate statistical indicators of either an economic environmental or political structure nature.[19] In short, for this study we did not concur with Thomas Dye who states that his evidence suggests "that the linkage between socio-economic inputs and policy outcomes is an unbroken one, and that characteristics of political systems do not independently influence policy outcomes."[20] Such a viewpoint implies that case studies are not needed to probe the kinds of interest constellations that exist or the policy preferences of the key decision-makers. We concluded, however, that research on federal aid allocation *cannot* be done through statistical analyses and correlations among quantifiable state variables;[21] political variables must be considered if the patterns of federal aid allocation are to be understood.

Additional considerations influenced our choice of the case study as a method and the decision-making process as the major independent variable. As indicated in the Foreword, this study of public policy was designed to (1) chart the allocation of federal aid to education in selected states, (2) to describe the decision process by which that aid was distributed by state governments, and (3) to search for mechanisms to improve the flow and fiscal impact of those aid programs. A systematic analysis of demographic or economic variables, while of value for some purposes, does not suit our need to identify leverage points for change in public policy. Intensive case studies that clarify the intra-state decision processes and criteria that lead to the distribution outcomes, however, do. Such studies provide a policy-relevant base of knowledge that yields important clues for designing new policies and implementation mechanisms that can alter those patterns of allocation. Indeed educational policy makers cannot change the population and economic patterns that are illuminated by macroanalytic studies.

While this approach is not likely to lead to generalizations without some exceptions, it should work to identify the critical differences among states that must be understood if effective policy and implementation techniques are to be developed. Too often, as noted below, federal policies are framed with a monolithic model of state behavior implicitly in mind. An approach like ours will serve as an antidote to such thinking. Hopefully, it will also help to develop legislation provisions that meet the differential administrative and political patterns that shape the intra-state distribution of federal money.

A six-state study of politics and administration of federal aid is plagued by both a small number of cases and a large number of variables. To reduce the problem of many variables, Lyphart suggests that the comparative analysis be focused on "comparable cases."[22] By "comparable" he means "similar in a large number of important characteristics and variables which one treats as constants, but dissimilar as far as those variables are concerned which one wants to relate to each other."

In the context of our study we could accomplish this objective by limiting the geographic spread of the states examined to one region—perhaps the Southeast. We chose to include a range of states with widely varying characteristics because our audience of public policy makers needs to understand the diverse complexities of educational politics in the various states. Architects of public policy tend to devise general policies with only a few states in mind. As James Sundquist observed:

75

In drafting of federal aid legislation, a drafter's view of the role the states should play is likely to depend upon his estimate of state competence—and that is apt to depend upon which state he is thinking about. If his picture is of New York or California, he is likely to write his bill in terms of what the state can contribute. If his picture is of a small and backward state, he is liable to leave the states out of the administration channel in order to prevent them from impeding progress. In the drafting of the Economic Opportunity Act, an "Alabama syndrome" developed. Any suggestion within the poverty task force that the states be given a role in the administration of the act was met with the question, "Do you want to give that kind of power to George Wallace?"[23]

While the numerous variables impede comparative analysis, a far-ranging study is likely to result in more informed, intelligent public policy. Indeed, we found that generalizations on the variables investigated rarely hold for all six states. With an N or 6, the exceptions are important. A conclusion of substantial state variation argues for the federal government to adopt a differential approach, working through some states and bypassing others in the same education program.[24]

Notes

1. Morley Segal and A. Lee Fritchler, "Policy-Making in the Intergovernmental System: Emerging Patterns and a Typology of Relationships," paper presented at APSA meeting, Los Angeles, September 1970. For an interesting case see Martha Derthick, *The Influence of Federal Grants* (Cambridge: Harvard, 1970).

2. For a summary of leading American theories of federalism, see Daniel J. Elazar, *The American Partnership* (Chicago: University of Chicago Press, 1962).

3. Morton Grodzins (Daniel J. Elazar, ed.), *The American System* (Chicago: Rand McNally, 1966). A number of studies by Grodzins students have been brought together in Daniel J. Elazar et al. eds. *Cooperation and Conflict: Readings in American Federalism* (Itasca: F.E. Peacock, 1959).

4. See *Special Analyses*, Budget of the United States, Fiscal Year 1970, p. 209.

5. See James Sundquist, *Making Federalism Work* (Washington: D.C., Brookings, 1970).

6. Segal and Fritchler have made a start on such a theory in the APSA paper.

7. Segal and Fritchler, op. cit., p. 15. Response rate was 44 percent. They proposed a four-fold typology for federal-state relations: (a) joint policymaking, (b) mutual accommodation, (c) innovative conflict, and (d) disintegrative conflict.

8. Edith K. Mosher "State Decision Making for Federal Aid: An Intensive Analysis of the Commonwealth of Virginia," paper presented at Annual Meeting of AERA, New York, Feb. 6, 1971.

9. See C. Phillip Kearney, "The Politics of Educational Assessment in Michigan," *Planning and Changing*.

10. Michigan Department of Education, *The Common Goals of Michigan Education* (Lansing: MDE, 1971).

11. See Thomas H. Eliot, Nicholas A. Masters, and Robert H. Salisbury, *State Politics and Public Schools* (New York: Alfred A. Knopf, 1964), pp. 179-227.

12. Chapter 4 in this volume.

13. See for example Gerald E. Sroufe, "Recruitment Processes and Composition of State Boards of Education," paper presented at the annual meeting of the American Educational Research Association, Los Angeles, California, Feb. 8, 1969.

14. For a summary of evidence on local board impact, see Michael W. Kirst, *The Politics of Education at the Federal, State, and Local Levels* (Berkeley: McCutchen, 1970), pp. 3-133.

15. Laurence Iannaccone, "A First Step in Making Sense Out of Massachusetts," unpublished paper presented to the group working on the federal aid project reported in this volume.

16. See James March and Herbert Simon. *Organizations* (New York: John Wiley, 1958) and Richard Cyert and James March, A Behavioral Theory of the Firm (Englewood Cliffs, N.J.: Prentice Hall, 1963).

17. Arend Lyphart, "Comparative Politics and the Comparative Method," *American Political Science Review*, 65, September, 1971, p. 692.

18. See, for example, Herbert Jacob and Kenneth Vines, *Politics in the American States* (Boston: Little Brown, 1965), particularly those sections relating to the governor. For a reader on comparative state politics, see Frank Munger, editor, *American State Politics* (New York: Crowell, 1966).

19. For an example of macroanalysis stressing correlation rather than case data, see Richard Hofferbert, "The Relation Between Public Policy and Some Structural and Environmental Variables in American States," *American Political Science Review*, 60, 1966, pp. 73-82.

20. Thomas Dye, "The Independent Effect of Party Competition on Policy Outcomes in the American States," a paper presented to the American Political Science Association Meeting, 1965. He has subsequently published *Politics, Economics, and the Public* (Chicago: Rand McNally, 1966) that further documents the quoted statement.

21. The problems of multicollinearity in such studies are now being widely discussed. See Hubert M. Blalock, Jr., "Correlated and Independent Variables: The Problem of Multicollinearity," in *The Qualitative Analysis of Social Problems*, Edward Tufts, ed. (Menlo Park: Addison-Wesley, 1970), p. 424.

22. Lyphart, op. cit., p. 687.

23. See Sundquist, *Making Federalism Work*, p. 271.

24. For an elaboration of this differential concept see Ibid., pp. 270-272.

3

The Politics of Federal Aid to Education in California

Michael W. Kirst

Disparate political forces vie for control of federal aid to education in California. During the past ten years, the constant tilting of state legislature and state superintendent has effected an administrative environment in which some of the research assertions were confirmed and others disproved. The popularly elected state superintendent of public instruction from 1962-1970, a period of extensive federal legislation, was Dr. Maxwell Rafferty. In disagreement with his policies and actions, the legislature moved successfully to influence and shape the administration of federal aid to education in California.

While weakening the superintendent, the legislative activity promoted the emergence of another educational figure, Dr. Wilson Riles. As director of compensatory education and administrator of Title I in California, he achieved state and national recognition for the effectiveness of the California Title I program. Riles defeated Rafferty in the 1970 election and is the current State Superintendent of Public Instruction. This study concludes at the end of Rafferty's second term in office—1970. The transition from Rafferty to Riles might have a profound impact on the relationship between the State Department of Education and the Legislature that is highlighted in this study. It is probable, however, that an enduring pattern of policy and legislative orientation was established during Rafferty's era. Terms referred to by their initials here are explained on p. 130. For a brief explanation of the various federal titles discussed in this book, see pp. 6-7.

Research Assertions and Federal Aid in California

Assertion No. 1. There will be less involvement and political influence by the governor and legislature on federal aid in comparison with state aid.

In California this hypothesis was verified only for the governor. At present, the interest of the governor's office in federal aid is restricted to the identification of the types that California receives. The governor has not prized the stakes in federal aid highly enough to warrant active involvement. He has been reluctant to intercede in CSDE decision making unless important state issues are involved because of his relationship with State Superintendent Max Rafferty. He did not consider Rafferty a part of his cabinet or a close advisor; consequently, the superintendent did not consult the governor on federal aid. Governor Reagan has concentrated his efforts on higher education, with a minimal program at the

77

elementary and secondary level; thus, understandably, he would not consider federal aid an issue appropriate for the exercise of his influence with the legislature.

Governor Brown was indirectly more active in federal aid because his appointees to the state board of education more closely supervised the CSDE; however, Brown remained neutral in disputes between the board and Rafferty. Both governors, of course, took a great interest in state aid issues which consitute a large part of their budget.

The hypothesis did *not* hold for the legislature. This case study is replete with examples of legislative initiative and superintendence of federal aid. The legislative analyst subjects federal funds to the same scrutiny as state dollars, and the legislature has voted appropriations for a special field investigation of categorical federal funds. As state aid decreased because of stringent state finances, the legislature addressed itself increasingly to setting priorities and goals for federal funds. Even when state revenues were in better shape, the legislature established administrative mechanisms to insulate federal programs from Rafferty's control. Dissatisfied with the CSDE, the legislature has intervened across the board in administrative matters that other states leave to "professional experts."

Assertion No. 2. The influence and impact of the urban school lobby on the state allocation of federal aid will not be significant.

California has not developed a cohesive, active, or effective lobby among the large urban school districts for either federal or state issues. California's cities vary enormously with regard to demographic and social-economic indicators, except in one factor—a large number of pupils. As a group, the lobbyists have been more active in state issues.

The urban lobbyists and program people from the largest cities are aware of the details of federal aid allocation formulas; they try to intercede as individuals when it is appropriate and likely to be worth the antagonism from CSDE administrators and smaller school districts.

Assertion No. 3. As federal aid increases and states have more discretion in allocation, pressures will increase on state government from organized interests.

There is not a great deal of pressure group activity in federal aid at any stage. Individual districts were active, but CASA and CTA, the two main professional organizations, have chosen not to lobby on allocation formulas. They favor maximum local control in state administration of federal aid, but as one lobbyist put it, "we probably could not have changed much even if we tried." This reflects, in part, the sorry state of professional education organizations in California politics. The parent advisory councils that have developed around federal titles represent an emerging interest group; they will probably break away from the professional administrators who currently shepherd them on lobby trips to the state capital. There is no evidence of extensive lobbying by Model Cities, Community Action Program people, NAACP, or other traditional urban lobbies. Perhaps federal aid funds (roughly 5 percent of total school expenditures) must increase before interest groups exert greater pressure.

Assertion No. 4. The state education agency will attempt to minimize political conflict and pressure by using existing state aid formulas for allocation of federal funds.

California's state aid formulas are based roughly on ADA and assessed valuation; CSDE used these two determinants of state aid in federal -titles permitting the application of statewide formulas. Title II of ESEA was based simply on ADA and assessed valuation. Vocational education was theoretically a project competition system, but was actually, in large part, based on ADA, until the federal act required changes. ESEA-Title I is a federally established formula. ESEA-Title III, like the state *categorical programs*, emphasizes the legislative mandate of 50 percent priority for language arts and math in grades K-8. It has not been allocated on an ADA or assessed value basis, but relies on a project proposal system with outside reviewers. NDEA-Title III has always been a project grant. A study of NDEA from 1962-1965 found a positive relationship between district size and participation in NDEA. In addition, more than 50 percent of the elementary and unified school districts which received special state equalization aid (based primarily on low assessed valuation) participated in NDEA-Title III, while only 27 percent of the districts which received basic state aid (ADA only) because of their high property tax wealth participated.[1] We see a *participation* pattern along the lines of state aid formulas, but no explicit formula was employed. We cannot compare cash distribution against the published pupil participation factors.

Assertion No. 5. Federal aid, except in a manner restricted by federal guidelines or requirements, will flow within a state as it has in the past.

This is the so-called "cold turkey principle": Funds cannot be withdrawn from local districts all at once; withdrawal or large increases must be stimulated by federal changes and proceed gradually, if at all. California exhibited this pattern in every program. Even Title I administrators allowed large inequities to exist in the sub-county allocations for four years after the initial allocations were made on a simple ADA basis. The vocational education formula is the classic example. The federal minimum of 15 percent for the disadvantaged is included, and the rest of the formula is carefully constructed to preserve historic shares, particularly the 45 percent for community colleges. Backed by a lobby of county superintendents, the Title III supplementary centers have been supported for twice the period of any other Title III project; these supplementary centers still consume about one-third of the funds. Stability, however, may assist local planning in all of these federal titles.

Assertion No. 6. SEA personnel are socialized so that they view their proper role as providing technical assistance to LEAs, not enforcing or policing federal requirements or setting program priorities.

Federal program administrators in California exhibit styles and philosophies along the lines of Iannaccone's check-writers, political activists, and researchers.[2] The variety of styles and philosophies makes difficult generalizations concerning this research assertion. The Title I staff would qualify roughly as Iannaccone's "political activists." More recent CSDE employees, they saw the poor as their clients. Impatient with established patterns and modes of operation, they were much more concerned with federal intent than the LEAs desired. They would fight the professional establishment and were strongly supported by Washington. They had a strong urban focus; their chief reference groups were outside CSDE in other activist organizations or in the legislature. The ESEA III staff was more concerned with research design than the other offices and identified with university researchers. It valued open competition and granted awards to the "best" proposal. The group that come closest to meeting the implications of the assertion were the vocational education staff. For them, the "professional leadership" role is to gently encourage LEAs toward better proposals and to assist them in their pursuit of federal funds, not to police the federal requirements through detailed inspections or data. The vocational education staff value a relationship of long standing trust and avoid high conflict situations.

Political Factors Shaping Fiscal and Administrative Patterns

The Political Context

State government in California has always executed masterful strokes on the canvas of educational policy. In both policy formulation and implementation, its strong influence is manifest.

The California Education Code—the compiled laws on education passed by the legislature—exceeds 2,300 pages. The state adopts textbooks for statewide use and constantly revises its guidelines on courses from mathematics to morality. State financial aid has been decreasing recently as a percent of total expenditures, but still comprises 35 percent. The California State Department of Education has undergone substantial growth, and its salaries are among the highest in the nation.

Despite these impressive indicators of state control, however, the political tradition of localism strongly affects the implementation of the detailed state statutes and official policies. The tension between the centralized policymaking ideology of the legislature and the norm of local control of California schools is an important factor in the politics of federal aid. More important, however, is the conflict between lay groups and legislators on the one hand, and the faction-ridden professional educators on the other. Their disagreements on educational priorities and administrative policies spill over into federal aid issues. These opposing groups pull and push the state department of education in different directions. The department's elected chief administrator has his own views on these issues; buttressed by a statewide constituency, his opinions and actions add yet another dimension.

Such a complex political mosaic would not have confronted a researcher in the 1940s. The state superintendent of public instruction drew the bulk of his support from a clique of influential superintendents and professors of education administration who were also probably responsible for his appointment.[3] The superintendent was a "unity" candidate among educators, a supporter rather than initiator of educational policy, with a passion for anonymity. In 1945 this clique came up with a compromise candidate, who subsequently recounted his experience:

. . . The telephone rang. It was the Governor of California. I was totally surprised and astonished. I went to Sacramento and spent four hours with the Governor. . . . He offered me the position of State Superintendent of Public Instruction. I didn't even know I was being considered. I still don't know how I got it. I suppose it was because of my being past President of the Superintendent's Association. . . .[4]

During this earlier period, differences and conflict among the education interest groups were accommodated *within* a monolithic professional influence structure, the California Teachers Association; it was the spokesman before state government for all the groups, including administrators. As a leading local superintendent observed,

The leaders and council of CTA were administrators. There wasn't a need at that time for a militant administrator organization. They were all in CTA.

CTA! There was no problem! We were CTA. CTA was controlled by superintendents of schools, local schools.[5]

From this unified profession emerged a single policy initiative in state politics—and it was usually the *only* initiative in the larger political system. Governors, legislators, non-educational interest groups generally agreed to "leave it to the educational experts." "Friends of education" from the legislature and CSDE participated in the strategy sessions of the CTA before specific state policies were proposed; then they carried the ball during the legislative and administrative process.

Lack of party cohesion increased the influence of this earlier monolithic professional interest group. Strong political parties in a community are the result of an effective precinct organization, the ability to determine who shall be the party's nominees, and control of government patronage. In California, none of these three sources of strength exists. There is no way even to make endorsements at the state level, and political parties are excluded from city and county affairs.[6] The merit system is extremely effective; only a few desirable jobs, most of them in the judiciary, are available for patronage. Given the rapid growth and high mobility of California's population, it is unlikely that a strong party system could have been built even under ideal conditions.

Factional politics, the result of weak parties, had attained their apogee at the time the monolithic education structure operated. Organized around personalities, the state legislature developed in-house leadership cliques which spanned both parties. Formulation of public policy was delegated (or relegated) to the special interest groups—alcoholic beverage control to the liquor lobbies, highway policy to the highway contractors, and education policy to the professional interest groups. There was little motivation to develop systematic or comprehensive programs of educational policy. Those legislators inclined to initiate policy in the complex area of educational finance could rely on little independent staff.

If federal aid had been channeled through the political system described above, the allocation pattern would have been quite different. In the 1940s the state board of education and the legislature reacted to initiatives from the "experts" in the CTA and its ally, the state superintendent. Indeed, as we shall see, the influence structure for allocating 1958 NDEA funds was very different from that for ESEA-Title I funds in 1965. Before discussing specific titles, however, we need to look at the variations that distinguish the present political landscape from the earlier one.

The New Education Politics

The structural characteristics of state educational policymaking in California have always enhanced the possibility of conflict and deadlock. The detailed and restrictive Education Code requires the legislature to pass on large numbers of routine education bills. The California state board is appointed by the governor, with the approval of two-thirds of the Senate, for staggered terms of four years. The board has extensive authority, but does not appoint the state superintendent, a constitutional officer elected on a statewide nonpartisan ballot.

It is not the objective of this study to evaluate the relative importance of the factors which transformed state politics of education in California from that of the 1940s and 1950s. Apparently, the first major change was the fragmentation of the professional education interest groups. Leading superintendents and professors subsequently lost their influence. CTA was divorced by CASA, which represented the administrators; after the separation, CASA split into several more subgroups. Moreover, the cacophony produced by warring professionals shattered the image of educators as "objective experts," above politics, and revealed, instead, an ordinary pressure group looking out for its own good. After this debacle, the legislature increasingly seized the initiative in education policy (including federal aid), an initiative supported by a large new legislative staff.

The conflict era ended the ability of the professional to influence or control the election of the state superintendent. A non-establishment candidate, Max

Rafferty, was elected in 1962; viewed as a "dissident" among administrators, he did not espouse the principles of the leadership clique of the forties. The "superintendent's superintendent" did not even make it to the run-off. Rafferty's opponent was a professor, who, it was rumored, had close ties to the militant teachers of the CTA. A widely circulated anecdote among administrators at election time was: "If you had to vote for President of AMA, and you had a choice between a chiropractor and a Christian Scientist, who would you vote for?"[7]

The election of 1962 gave State Superintendent Rafferty a great deal of public support. Thereafter, the state superintendent's public wrath could cost aspiring politicians the support of Rafferty-oriented voters. The power Rafferty derived from this popular support, "public regarding power" in Edward Banfield's term,[8] affected the behavior of statewide officers such as the governor much more strongly than it did individual assemblymen and senators.[9] Consequently, the governor adopted a hands-off strategy with regard to public disputes except where major state issues emerged. Federal aid issues did not seem important enough for the governor "to take Max on."

After his election, Rafferty strived to maintain and enhance this public regarding power, rather than to bargain with individual legislators in terms of specific pieces of legislation or administrative policies. While Rafferty's appeals to the public were successful in preserving his popularity with the voters, he never succeeded in maneuvering the legislature or restricting their initiatives in many areas of educational policy. The legislative initiative in federal aid has been extensive and almost always in a direction opposed by the CSDE. Indeed, much of the legislation was designed to erode the state superintendent's influence over the administration of federal aid. Moreover, Rafferty's authority to appoint CSDE officials was limited, and any attempt to increase it until 1969 was opposed by the state board.

Rafferty's ability to endorse the educational policies of a potential candidate for governor was useful in preventing the governor's direct intervention in federal aid issues. The governor, however, appoints the state board of education; its influence has been substantial. In effect, Rafferty's public regarding power lacked a "connector" in the state board of education and in the Assembly and Senate Education Committees. Within the CSDE he has refrained from disciplinary actions (leaving those to his Deputy Calvert) and preserved a "friendly leader" image. If one considers that the Democratic party and its governor, the state board, the professional education interest groups, and key legislators were originally arrayed against him, Rafferty's partial success at the federal policy level is a tribute to his statewide constituency. When his own Republican party was in control of the state government and a number of his strongest opponents in the CSDE were replaced, the major opposition regardless of party affiliation came from the legislature.

After Rafferty's 1962 election, the relationships among the superintendent, the state board, and the legislature were summarized this way:

The Superintendent would make a proposal; the Board, usually the President (Braden), would strongly (in some cases angrily) criticize the Superintendent; the major newspapers would give broad, front page coverage to the controversies; some local parent or political groups would issue statements for or against positions taken by the participants . . . The reaction of the Board publicly was one of unity, but privately, a minority was extremely disturbed.

The Speaker of the Assembly (Unruh) saw the Superintendent as a threat to Democratic party hegemony in the state and vigorously attacked him for a long period of time during the year. The Speaker's attack was for the purpose of getting the Superintendent out in the open from behind his shield of non-partisanship when he was obviously running for governor (according to the Speaker's aide) . . . The Governor (Brown) was in the painful position of seeing his political friends on the Board of Education in a furious fight with a Superintendent who represented his political rivals and was, in fact, a potential candidate against him, yet he had to maintain a cautious neutrality.[10]

Interest Groups

For the major education interest groups, the years up to 1960 were devoted to building a strong alliance with the dominant Republicans.[11] As we have seen, the various interest groups had split apart; the seven administrative organizations, the CTA, and the State School Boards Association were rarely able to agree. After the switch to Democratic control of the legislature in 1958, the educational organizational leaders could not make the adjustment to the Democrats' orientation or their determination to make education a major state issue. CTA became preoccupied with teacher welfare legislation; after its defeat over credentialing in 1962, it became even more impotent in the areas of general education improvement and federal aid. Tables 3-1 and 3-2 present the CTA sponsored legislation in 1963 and 1965. This orientation toward teacher welfare does not enhance CTA's image as objective education experts, nor would it lead to a concern and involvement in the significant allocative issues of federal aid.

CTA has restricted its interests in federal aid (as well as in state aid) to the narrow confines of teacher welfare. It has been embroiled in a dispute with CASA concerning the certification and tenure of teachers who are paid entirely from federal aid. CASA believes that issues in state aid are more urgent for its one-man Sacramento staff: "Federal aid has not been high on our priority list. I doubt we could do much about it even if we tried."

CASA opposes the legislature's establishment of priorities in federal funds and supports local discretion. It advocates a straight line of authority within the CSDE and opposes separate divisions such as compensatory education. CASA reacts to legislative proposals for federal aid by occasionally adopting a position; but it does not forcefully communicate the position to legislators.

Table 3-1
CTA Sponsored Legislation, 1963

Bill	Fail Pass	Nature of Content	Policy Area
SB 57	P	Retirement Allowances	Teacher Welfare
SB 79	P	Licensing of School Personnel	Teacher Welfare
SB 109	P	Substitute Teacher Earnings	Teacher Welfare
SB 152	P	Certificated School District Employees	Teacher Welfare
SB 171	P	Tenure	Teacher Welfare
SB 467	P	Fines for Abuse of Teachers	Teacher Welfare
AB 198	P	Teacher Salary Schedules	Teacher Welfare
AB 484	P	Teacher Retirement	Teacher Welfare
AB 2759	P	Teacher Retirement	Teacher Welfare
AB 235	P	Re-employment of Certificated Staff	Teacher Welfare
AB 3003	P	Leave of Absence, Accident or Illness	Teacher Welfare
AB 579	P	Higher Ed. Tuition Fees, Cert. Staff	Teacher Welfare
AB 107	F	Death Benefits	Teacher Welfare
AB 181	F	Minimum Salary	Teacher Welfare
AB 271	F	Teacher Retirement	Teacher Welfare
AB 310	F	Medical and Health Benefits	Teacher Welfare
AB 312	F	School Support Levels	School Finance
AB 620	F	Probationary Certificated Employees	Teacher Welfare
AB 2190	F	Payment of Attorney Fees	Teacher Welfare
ACA 5	F	School District Indebtedness	School Finance

Source: *1963 Legislative Digest* California Teachers Association, Sacramento, California, 1963).

CASA represents all administrators in the state and consequently steers clear of CSDE allocations or project awards. Any stance on a bigger share for urban areas, for example, would splinter the organization. The CASA staff does not consider it appropriate to intercede before the CSDE on a project award that might favor one member over another.

The two major interest groups, CTA and CASA, evidence little inclination to expend any of their already meager stock of influence on federal aid. Neither the CTA or CASA newsletters and communications to their members have ever mentioned federal aid in the two years the author reviewed them. While politics abound in California's federal aid allocation decisions, it has not been injected by interest groups.

The Legislature

The major control over CSDE is exerted by the legislature. Interviews with legislators of both parties reveal an overwhelming displeasure with the compe-

Table 3-2
CTA Sponsored Legislation, 1965

Bill	Fail Pass	Nature of Content	Policy Area
SB 156	F	Appointed State Supt. of Public Instr.	Judicial
SB 1	F	Attorney General's Opinion	Judicial
SB 936	F	Single Salary Schedule	Teacher Welfare
SCA 6	F	Appointed State Supt. of Public Instr.	Judicial
AB 230	P	Probationary Dismissal	Teacher Welfare
AB 257	P	Transfer of Sick Leave	Teacher Welfare
AB 362	P	Accident and Illness Leave	Teacher Welfare
AB 1474	P	Mandated Negotiations Procedure	Teacher Welfare
AB 1999	P	Concealed Electronic Snooping Devices	Teacher Welfare
AB 2003	F	Death Benefits	Teacher Welfare
AB 3193	F	Contractual Agreements	Teacher Welfare
AB 191	F	Health-Welfare Tax Authorization	Teacher Welfare
AB 203	F	Health Benefits	Teacher Welfare
AB 204	F	Retirement Benefits	Teacher Welfare
AB 314	F	Appointed State Supt. of Public Instr.	Judicial
AB 1806	F	Legal Fees	Teacher Welfare
AB 2103	F	Escalator Adjustment of Salaries	Teacher Welfare
AB 427	F	Death Benefit Increase	Teacher Welfare
ACA 11	F	Appointed State Supt. of Public Instr.	Judicial

Source: *Final Status of CTA Sponsored Bills, 1965*, California Teachers Association, Burlingame, California, September, 1965 (Mimeographed).

tence and performance of the CSDE in administering federal funds. Surprisingly, this viewpoint is held by leaders of both parties; Republican control of the legislature did not lead to any change in attitude toward the CSDE and the Republican state superintendent. Indeed, the legislature's output indicates its dissatisfaction with the leadership of the entire California educational system since the early 1960s.

Dissatisfied with the state superintendent, state board, and professional interest groups, the California legislature created in 1961 a special, full-time staff for the education committees. This staff provides a high quality of analysis and advice—thus decreasing the legislators' dependence on the education lobbies and state agencies that they had grown to distrust. The specialized education staff is augmented greatly by the staff of the legislative analyst. Table 3-3 shows the staff available to all legislative bodies in California state government.

California's legislature has not conformed in the last decade to the pattern Ferguson found in 1960 in a survey of four states.[12] Ferguson concluded that 94 percent of the state legislators in California thought the solutions to the problems of education were financial as contrasted with 4 percent who ranked

Table 3-3
Legislative Staffing

1. Legislative analyst's office	37 professional
a. Works for Joint Legislative Budget Com.	12 clerical
b. Prepares analyses of the budget and all bills requiring expenditures	
2. Legislative Counsel	48 professional
a. Assists members in drafting legislation	40 clerical
b. Prepares a digest of each proposed bill	
c. Provides advice to legislators, agencies, courts on legislation and constitutionality	
3. Auditor General	
a. Works for Joint Legislative Audit Com.	35 professional
b. Provides an independent audity for legislative and executive use	& clerical
4. Legislative Reference Service—Library*	
5. Printing Plant*	
Total	172
Senate Staff	
Approximately 245 professional and clerical positions are reported†	
Total	245
Assembly Staff	
Committee Staff Consultants (full-time)	40
Office of Research	15
Republican Staff (Speaker's Office, majority floor leader and caucus chairman)	15
Democratic Staff	17+
Legislative Interns	10
Operational Staff	
Desk—Rules Committee	17
Sergeants	41
Secretaries, clerical, printing staff	220
District Staffs (in member's district office)	
Administrative Assistants (one per member)	80
Secretaries (one for each member)	80
Clerical help (part time)	60
Total	595

*Included in executive budget.
+California Legislative Handbook, pp. 94-105.
+Includes two staff members assigned to the minority party on the Ways and Means Committee.
Source: "Professionalism, Public Policy and the California Legislature" a paper by Gerald Calderone of Syracuse University Research Corporation, unpublished.

curriculum change highly. Since then the legislative record in both state and federal aid shows a concern by both parties that more money is not sufficient. Bill after bill has demanded administrative and curriculum reform, thereby extending state control of local educational policies.

The lack of program priorities for federal aid within CSDE has led to legislative mandates for emphasis on language arts and math. The lack of confidence in local educators has resulted in requirements for statewide PPBS and numerous cost-effectiveness studies. A Joint Legislative Committee on Goals, Standards, and Evaluation has been formed. The legislature was continually changing the administrative structure in CSDE in order to divest control from Rafferty. Again, these trends continue regardless of which party is in power.

The legislative analyst and committee staffs often provide the expertise that drives this legislative initiative forward. The office of the legislative analyst compiles each year a 400-page analysis of the education budget and any proposed education legislation with a budgetary impact. The legislative analyst is required by law to make specific recommendations on each item of appropriation in any appropriation bill. Alan Post, the legislative analyst since 1948, is pushing for PPBS through his fifty-man staff. His top education analyst received an MBA from Stanford and then worked as an efficiency expert at Lockheed. Approximately four professionals work full-time on education; in the writer's opinion, the staff is as highly qualified as the one in the U.S. Bureau of the Budget. Mr. Post hires people trained generally in economics and public administration and stresses that they should be "management oriented."

The finance department under the governor has had its staff cut back and is not as active in field visits as is the analyst. It devotes too much time to budget control (voucher checking, audits, etc.) to be very active in assessing the effectiveness of education programs. In 1970 the governor's finance director termed the CSDE a "fiscal nightmare," but has not been active in federal funds.

Post's philosophy on federal funds is: "Our office is program oriented. We don't give a damn if it's federal or state money—it's still money." The analyst now publishes a comprehensive inventory annually of federal funds that have a bearing on state funds. Current federal legislation is analyzed and reported as to its impact on California.

The Republican chairman of the Assembly Education Committee, Victor Veysey, has been particularly concerned about the allocation and effectiveness of federal aid. In May, 1970, he commented:

What a tragedy that over half a billion dollars of scarce education money has been poured out by Washington in California with minimal results. There is need for straight-thinking at the federal level . . . for insistence on results rather than more 'business as usual' by the education establishment.[13]

In 1969 Veysey had sponsored a bill directing the legislative analyst to conduct "an independent fiscal review and analysis" of major federal and state categorical aid programs in California. The legislature voted six positions and $180,000 to explore the following issues:

1. What measurable evidence is there that the expenditures have produced results?
2. Is there evidence which indicates programs have failed to achieve their stated objectives?
3. What measurable factors account for either success or failure in supplementary education programs?
4. What legislative action can be taken to insure a greater proportion of successful programs?

The analyst used a review team approach; the team underwent an intensive period of training and observation concerning the background of federal programs. Fifty-three districts, representing 59 percent of the total Title I apportionment in California, were selected for priority review. The analyst's preliminary findings will be discussed under each title in subsequent sections. In general, his findings were critical of CSDE. Although the analyst has been in office since 1948, he serves both parties, and enjoys a reputation of objectivity and nonpartisanship. Nevertheless, Rafferty claimed the criticism was politically motivated. The analyst's report was released about a month before the 1970 primary for the state superintendency. Rafferty charged:

To bring this upon the eve of a political campaign seems rather questionable to say the least. All I'm saying is the time is most peculiar. I've been around here for several years. The budget has changed very little in that time. If he (Post) had any criticism, he should have stated them long before now.[14]

Post retorted that his annual reports for the past six years had been critical of CSDE handling of federal money. He suggested lawmakers prescribe more guidelines for spending federal funds intended for educational improvement. CSDE handling of federal money contributed to the "weakness" of many federally financed programs. "This has resulted in a large number of projects of questionable value."[15] Post also charged there is "ample evidence to indicate" that reorganization of the department is lagging behind what the legislature intended. Wilson Riles, Rafferty's opponent, attempted to make a major campaign issue out of the legislative analyst's report on federal funds.

The Governor and Federal Aid

The California governor is classified in most studies as at the upper range of power or strength compared to his colleagues in other states.[16] The governor has extensive appointive powers and a line-item veto over the budget. But the California governor does not appoint the state superintendent of public instruction. Moreover, as in other states, the governor spends little time on departmental administration and the oversight of administrative details compared with the time spent on maintaining his political standing. A review of the literature in this area indicates that the governor's small personal staff fights fires and rarely coordinates administration.

His [the Governor's] duties as 'representative of the people,' as the political leader of the state, and the hard facts of a huge and sprawling bureaucracy simply make it unlikely that any governor can act as a day to day administrative overseer . . . The practical realities of the governor's office are not those of the reorganizer's theory: the governor does not know what is going on until there is some reason to pay attention to a trouble spot in the administrative system.[17]

In some states, the governor can compensate for weak formal controls if he has an undated letter of resignation from the chief agency administrator in his files. Governors in California, however, must deal with a major statewide political figure elected on a nonpartisan ballot. Both governors have been cautious in their "interference" in the policies of the CSDE and have avoided overt conflict. Indeed, as a statewide officer, the governor is more responsive to Rafferty's constituency than individual legislators, appointive officers, or civil servants. Governor Brown, through 1966, never openly attacked the superintendent.[18] After that period, attacks were rare. In issues that offended his Democratic appointees to the state board, Governor Brown remained neutral. He contended that the prestige of the superintendent's office entitled Rafferty to special respect.[19] Any governor regards public battles with Rafferty as politically costly. Consequently, the issues must be major and the stakes high. Interviews with the governor's staff reveal that federal aid does not fit in these categories:

The Governor might be able to get a change through the State Board, but we have bigger issues than federal aid we have not pushed. The superintendent would fight hard to preserve his prerogatives. He is not considered a member of the Governor's Cabinet and does not attend Cabinet meetings.[20]

The governor's staff indicated a high degree of frustration over their inability "to get a handle" on federal aid to education. In their view, the programs, during Rafferty's tenure, were running "wild and loose," and the state board was a rubber stamp for CSDE recommendations. The governor's finance office has divisions for budget, planning, and program policy which exert quite a bit of control over state aid, but just attempt to keep track of federal aid. The governor's office also has a new Office of Intergovernmental Management with about thirty-five professionals. This office is a clearing-house for federal grants covered under U.S. Budget Bureau circular A95, but education is not included in A95. The office deals with 9,000 grants a year; it spends all its time just trying to find out what federal funds come into California from federal agencies covered by A95. As yet it has little time to make the critical comments on state plans that A95 envisioned. The office heads believe the federal government should legislate more involvement of governors in education grants. CSDE employees never go through the Washington branch office of the governor's finance director. They negotiate directly with their USOE counterparts.

The author could not find any significant involvement of the governor's office in federal allocation questions. The political barriers are reinforced by Governor Reagan's preoccupation with higher education. His public statements stress that elementary/secondary education is a local problem, and additional state funds are not likely to be spent effectively until local schools are managed better.

The State Board of Education

There is a dearth of empirical studies of state boards of education. We know something about the backgrounds of state board members and how they are selected.[21] Bailey's New England study in 1961 discusses the role and influence of the state board in some state finance issues. This federal aid study of the allocation of federal aid can be useful, however, in providing a comparative state analysis of state board activities in a number of recent issues.

The ten members of the California State Board of Education are by statute the policymaking and monitoring body for the educational system, including the junior colleges. The board, which meets monthly, must approve each project and meet guidelines under almost all federal titles (NDEA is the major exception). A major constraint on the board's influence is a lack of independent staff similar to the legislature's. Board members view the CSDE as their staff. The state superintendent nominates a CSDE staff man to serve as a "liaison officer" who also handles public correspondence. The men on the board all have full-time outside jobs.

Until the late 1950s the board and superintendent had few public disagreements; neither led a very vigorous life. The Governor, Pat Brown, a Democrat, appointed several people who were not content with the historical mold of board behavior in California. They desired a more active policymaking role and were inclined to question the recommendations of professional educators. Rafferty's relations with the board appointed by Governor Brown deteriorated to such a state that Rafferty in 1963 addressed a series of questions to Attorney General Mosk to this effect:

1. Does the State Board have the right to order the State Superintendent to do something he does not want to do?
2. What happens if the Superintendent does not do the action?
3. Whose legal right is it to give orders to the employees of the State Department of Education?
4. What would happen in the case of conflicting orders on the part of the Superintendent and the Board?[22]

Although the legal opinion asserted the primacy of the state board, the execution of the board's policies became highly uncertain. The board can order the superintendent to support a particular bill before the legislature, but he either can decline to do so or render only token support. The superintendent is not obliged to honor board requests for information that is essential to policy formulation. The board's response is to go around the superintendent directly to subordinates in the CSDE and to rely on outsiders for information and help.

In Federal aid the state board has not always been a rubber stamp for CSDE recommendations. In the mid-sixties it revised the ESEA II distribution formula. It was influential in establishing the administrative insulation for Wilson Riles, the director of compensatory education. The legislature's establishment of advisory commissions for ESEA Titles I and III has tended to inject more lay influence over educational policy; but the state board is a second court of appeals on federal projects for the LEAs after they have appealed to the advisory commissions. The advisory commissions have probably complemented the state board's influence since the board's subcommittee on federal aid can meet only one evening a month.

A review of the minutes and the pre-meeting documents mailed to California State Board members during 1969-1970 indicated no significant changes in CSDE recommendations on federal aid. Projects were routinely approved, and major policy questions on guidelines were briefly examined. The state board's normal disposition is to respect the department's expertise in federal program matters since the dialogue is carried on categorical title by categorical title. A comprehensive state plan which interrelated several titles might elicit considerably more debate and investigation.

Federal Funds: A Big City Viewpoint

The big five cities, Los Angeles, Oakland, San Diego, San Francisco, and San José, have full-time representatives in Sacramento. The writer had several interviews with the representatives of one city, some of whom are based in this district's central office. While federal issues are usually handled by program or categorical title coordinators, the Sacramento legislative lobbyist attempts to keep track of major issues.

It is clear that the five big cities have never formed a united front on a federal aid issue; they have just begun to hammer out common stands on major state aid changes. As yet the big five do not feel that they have federal aid problems in common. They say their minority groups have very different patterns. The superintendents in all five cities have changed recently; Oakland, San Francisco, and San José appointed new superintendents in 1970; in Los Angeles and San Diego, the superintendents have been in office only one to two years. The five Sacramento-based legislative offices operate in isolation that is surprising since they all share adjoining suites in the same office building. Reconciling view-points among Title I coordinators is also difficult because the coordinators come from different bureaucratic echelons, and many cannot speak for the superintendent.

CSDE includes several of the big cities (and usually Los Angeles) on its advisory commissions to help formulate guidelines or the project rating panels. As the representative of one city put it:

You are one voice in a committee of fifteen. Very few of the things we recommended went into the guidelines and formula. We could go back to Washington and complain, but where does that leave you in the state? We need those smaller districts in some crucial intra-state issues. When we go to D.C., we get the image of a big city pushing its weight around. When we seek something special from the legislature, we are viewed with suspicion. We have won sometimes, but you can't put on a political power play over everything. We are always in the position of saying we are a little bit different than the other 1,134 districts. You hear it said around the legislature, "here they come again." On the four bills we introduced today, I got another district to front for us in order not to give them the kiss of death.[2 3]

The big cities hold their fire until major issues in federal aid hang in the balance, and the antagonism of other districts is outweighed by the large gains. The central office and lobbyist representative of this big city were very knowledgeable about the details of federal allocation decisions and frequently chose not to intervene. Two cases from Title I will illustrate their strategy.

In 1965, the Division of Compensatory Education used a simple ADA count to make allocations within the counties for Title I. The federal formula earmarked amounts at the county level, but left it to the states to divide the money to school districts *within* the county. CSDE preferred to use AFDC data, but none were available, so the department had to use ADA data. The next year, CSDE was able to compute the intra-county allocations on the basis of AFDC data. The central city was to gain an enormous amount; at the same time, an outlying area would have lost $1.1 million, (the decrease from $1.8 million to $700,000). CSDE proposed a four year phase-out. Even though it would forfeit large amounts, the central city decided not to press the issue:

What we would have gained in dollars would not have been worth it. We needed those other districts in the county on some major bills in the state legislature. We stepped aside on this one. The interesting thing was that this was an in-house issue, but it involved large amounts of money. No one in the legislature or public knew it, but $13 million was at stake.[2 4]

A contrasting case concerned updated AFDC data for Title I. Title I allocations in California are based on the latest available AFDC data. The central city made an arrangement to get the pay tapes from the local welfare department. The state was using older sample data which showed a much lower allocation. The city appealed to John Hughes, head of Title I in USOE. Hughes put a hold on all California Title I projects for three months while USOE studied the issue. The three-month hold evoked resentment from the other districts for the central city. USOE decided in favor of the central city figures. In this case, the increase for the central city was not at the expense of other California districts. California qualified for a larger part of the *national* total.

Given its acute financial problems, this particular central city has been gratified by CSDE's attitude under the related ESEA II and NDEA III. The ESEA II formula does not have any factor designed for urban areas, but "was the quickest and easiest way to get a distribution in 1965, in view of the money arriving after the school year began." CSDE, however, helped this city to obtain a waiver on maintenance of effort, or else no money could have been committed. In view of its inability to maintain past effort, this city does not feel it has any cause to complain about the changing of the Title II formula. The big problem with NDEA III is the requirement of 50 percent matching money, and CSDE has been helpful when the city can match.

The central city people agree with CSDE administrators that their failure to get an ESEA III grant in the years of state operation stems from their large requests and the small amount of uncommitted money. Most of the Title III projects are around $50,000; two or three city projects would use up all available funds.

These big city representatives provided good supportive evidence that CSDE Title I administrators enforced the guideline program priorities. CSDE has contended that some types of educational approaches are more effective than others and has disputed the city's applications on this ground. The Title I state people also made the city cost out Title I on a school by school basis.

This city's representatives reported no attempts to use organized groups like the NAACP to lobby their cause. They did stress, however, the importance of the parent advisory councils required under ESEA Titles I and III:

We bring these parent advisory groups to CSDE when we negotiate projects, and they participate and protest cuts. Our parents were against CSDE's guideline to eliminate high schools from Title I. Riles arranged for the parents to go to Washington and see Jack Hughes. While we were there, we also visited 15 Congressmen. You know those Congressmen seemed to pay more attention to the views of those parents, in many cases, than they did the school district spokesmen.[25]

Impact of Federal Legislation on State
Categorical Programs

The California legislature passed several compensatory education and preschool programs shortly before or after the advent of the Elementary and Secondary

Education Act of 1965. These include the MacAteer Compensatory Education Act (very similar to Title I): the Miller-Unruh Basic Reading Act (to employ reading specialists); State Preschool Education; the Special Teacher Employment Program (to reduce class size in poverty areas); and the Educational Improvement Act (to provide compensatory projects in reading and math). Appropriations for the MacAteer program stopped growing after the advent of Title I; the program now involves only fourteen research projects to develop innovative teaching techniques. Miller-Unruh has grown to $22.3 million and is by far the largest of the other categorical programs.

The impact of federal funds has been to decelerate or abort state programs that had the same general focus as federal categories. If state funds have explicit program priorities for language arts and math that are narrower than federal programs, they have not been hindered by potential overlap. Miller-Unruh and the Educational Improvement Act are viewed as specialized efforts which complement but do not overlap federal programs. General fiscal constraints and Governor Reagan's lack of support have now curtailed their expansion, but together they account for about $30 million annually.

The California State Department of Education

CSDE and the Political System

As Robert Salisbury has noted, any state department of education is an arena of potential political conflict; departments tend to suppress this conflict and to preserve the illusion of a non-political administration guided by professional education standards.[26] This is simply not possible in California where events and people have forged a highly political image for the CSDE. A political image hampers a department's activities in its various bailiwicks. Goldhammer found that local administrators discounted the leadership performance and influence of state departments which were embroiled in politics:

It is also felt (by local superintendents) that the political concerns of the department personnel interfere with their assuming adequate professional roles and responsibilities. Where the state superintendents are concerned about their political relations, there is a feeling that the state departments of education avoid effective involvement in important issues and side-step strong leadership, either in the development of adequate legislative programs or the formulation of major approaches to the solution of educational problems, or both.[27]

In California the visible political free-for-all has definitely eroded the CSDE's influence and authority with the LEAs. The significant growth of the department within the past decade results solely from the infusion of federal funds. About 40 percent of the department's personnel is funded from federal sources.[28] In 1962 there were only 93 federally funded positions. By 1968 there were 454—a 388 percent increase! In contrast, during the same period, positions supported by state dollars increased from 575 to 669—only a 19 percent increase. Moreover, the 1970 legislature cut the CSDE budget more than any other state agency's, removed major educational programs from Rafferty's control, and required an extraordinary number of progress reports to the legislature. As Frank Lanteman, the chairman of the Conference Committee on the Budget, remarked, "He (Rafferty) is knee-deep in bureaucratic fat and has been for years."[29] Rafferty told the state board he would attempt with federal funds to cover officials whose salaries the legislature eliminated.[30]

The department's critics want more leadership and tighter controls over local spending in order to insure conformity with federal and state laws. Superintendent Rafferty responded in this manner:

The supposed need for more "expenditure controls" is mentioned when the fact of the matter is that California State Government is, if anything, over-controlled now.... The State Board of Education and the Department of Education, under a constitutional officer or superintendent elected by the people, plus controls by the Department of Finance, present statutes, and State and Federal auditors afford enough controls; in spite of the analyst wanting to freeze more controls into the statutes.[31]

Dr. Rafferty's criticism of federal aid reaffirms his strong support of local control:

Once the Federal Government begins direct financing of schools, you're going to see the end of local control. I don't think it's necessary. If the Federal Government would return to the states the tax sources it has been taking away from them, every state would easily meet its school costs.[32]

His philosophy would more accurately indicate the CSDE's political behavior if he had controlled the CSDE internally; the separate bureaucratic baronies, state board intransigence, and legislative restrictions limited his influence. Despite these constraints, the department's administrative performance has often been much more assertive of state control than Rafferty's public statements would lead one to believe.

Coordination, Priorities, and Comprehensive Planning for Federal Programs

The efficacy of our present array of federal categorical grants for education has been increasingly challenged. While the grants reflect distinct problem areas of national concern, they do not embody any explicit *overall* federal policy.[33] Each federal category has focused on a somewhat separate problem or objective; in many cases the categories overlap.

At the federal level, "hardening of the categories" set in quite early, whereby each title was administered in splendid isolation from the others. A federal executive for each categorical program was matched by an equally specialized state counterpart. Lines of communication ran up through the categories but rarely across them.

Seeking to create a pattern from the pieces, the U.S. Office of Education and the Federal Advisory Council for State Departments of Education have urged state departments to adopt statewide comprehensive planning—to integrate, coordinate, and direct diverse federal categorical programs within the state.[34] In effect, statewide comprehensive planning would provide priorities and criteria for allocating scarce federal funds to competing LEAs. It also would specify the types of programs to receive funding priority, a priority that would probably be applicable to several different federal categorical programs. Centralized administrative leadership at the apex of the state department of education as well as a sophisticated state planning and assessment staff to oversee all federal categorical programs are also implied.

Coordination and priority setting for federal programs in California would be a major undertaking. As Table 3-4 indicates, about $284 million will pour into California from federal aid to education in 1970-71. Both the CSDE leadership and its critics acknowledge that statewide planning, priority setting, and coordination for these federal funds have never developed. The legislature and the previous state board charge that the CSDE leadership does not desire or possess a sound strategy for coordination and statewide priorities. CSDE leadership contends that the legislature vetoes proposed reorganization plans, a first step toward central direction of the categorical programs.

Rafferty was never particularly concerned with the internal administration of the CSDE.[35] His policy within the department has been accurately described as "hands off."

His power here (within CSDE) consists of his refraining from disciplinary actions within his department and maintaining his friendly leader image. Actually the "hands off" policy is a bit more complex. He is respected for such a policy and is liked for it. But much of his popularity comes from the fact that his deputy Calvert does the disciplining, and he is the person who is disliked. Rafferty seldom interferes, and when he does, his modifications are minor.[36]

Our extensive interviews confirmed this earlier research. Even if he were so inclined, the state superintendent can only appoint four top jobs. Rafferty rarely interceded on promotions. A picture emerges of little stress or resources for internal program coordination and priority setting. Although Deputy Superintendent Eugene Calvert was the chief administrator, federal program issues almost always halted at the level of Eugene Gonzales, associate superintendent of public administration; in turn, Dr. Gonzales left negotiations with USOE to the categorical program operators. In our interview, he indicated that the department has never had the resources to coordinate much of anything,

Table 3-4
Budget Estimate of Federal Aid for Public Schools in California 1970-71

Program	California's Federal Aid (Estimate)
Elementary and Secondary Education Act	
Title I Compensatory Education	$ 78,954,564
Education of Migrant Children	6,000,000
Title II School Library Resources	4,166,500
Title III Supplemental Educ. Centers	8,544,780
Title IV Educational Laboratories	4,000,000
Title V Department of Education	2,000,000
Title VI Special Education	2,277,633
Title VIII Dropout Prevention	500,000
Follow Through Program	841,617
National Defense Education Act	
Title III Improvement of Instruction	5,335,635
Title V Guidance and Counseling	1,324,875
Education Professions Development Act	996,363
Vocational Education Act	17,000,000
Adult Basic Education Act	1,690,787
Manpower Development and Training Act	12,900,000
Unruh Preschool Program	9,721,000
Economic Opportunity Act	
Operation Head Start	25,000,000
Public Law 874	70,000,000
Public Law 815	10,000,000
Child Nutrition Program	22,736,435
Total Federal Assistance to California	$283,990,189

Source: Legislative Analyst

including federal programs. Admitting a pressing need for coordination, he stated that the proposed planning unit was never cleared by administrative offices external to CSDE.

Reorganization of CSDE

Reorganization of the department to enhance central direction has become a political football, tossed between CSDE, the legislative analyst, and various legislative committees. As long ago as 1964, Arthur D. Little Inc. made a study of CSDE and was generally critical of the lack of policy direction at the state level.[37] In 1967, Arthur D. Little presented another report to the state board indicating management, coordination, and planning problems remained unsolved.[38] The report criticized the excessive "divisionalitis" within the department and urged the use of multidisciplinary teams. It recommended first the initiation of long-range comprehensive planning with explicit priorities. It emphasized the necessity of reducing the confusion and inefficiency present in new program planning. This recommendation applied particularly to programs which (a) are funded from federal or multiple sources; (b) draw on the professional skills of more than one division; and (c) serve population segments which traditionally have been targets for other division programs and services.

The Little proposal advocated that two officers, a deputy superintendent for major programs and a deputy superintendent for administration, be responsible for the department's existing functions and programs. This arrangement would enhance the coordination of existing state and federal programs and reduce "divisionalitis." The two deputy superintendents would be empowered to require the divisions' pursuit of policies designed to foster cooperation and coordination.

When Rafferty left office virtually none of the reorganization had been executed; "divisionalitis" was still rampant; comprehensive planning and coordination did not exist. The CSDE and the state board proposed a different plan from the Little proposal. The legislature and Department of Finance in the governor's office have reacted by stalling all plans and cutting back proposed positions. The 1969-70 report of the legislative analyst sums up the situation in this way:

Although the proposed reorganization of the Department of Education has been studied, discussed, and "committed" for almost five years, and although the State Board of Education has finalized its own proposal, the 1969-70 budget does not include any proposed positions for the implementation of any reorganization proposal. We understand that the department has requested a total of 55 positions costing in excess of $900,000 for the implementation of the State Board plan but that the Department of Finance has not yet granted approval for the positions nor is it actively supporting the State Board's proposal.

We also understand that the department may establish some of the positions and finance them with Federal funds available under the provisions of Title V of the ESEA. In our opinion, no move of this sort should be made by the department until the fiscal and policy implications of each proposal be thoroughly reviewed by the legislature.[39]

The problems of coordination and comprehensive priorities are especially acute in California because of the overlap of state categorical programs with similar federal categorical programs. In the area of compensatory education, various political considerations have culminated in a separate Office of Compensatory Education that reports directly to the state board, not to the state superintendent. As the legislative analyst emphasized,

The department is presently responsible for the administering of the Adult Basic Education Program, the Vocational Education and Manpower Development Programs, the Basic Reading Act of 1965 (a state program), several preschool programs, in addition to Titles III and V National Defense Education Act which have compensatory education components.

Ideally, these interrelated programs should be coordinated, and there should be some type of a common review of district applications for state and federal assistance. Presently there is no coordination of these programs and a completely separate Office of Compensatory Education will not facilitate it.[40]

Federal categorical programs have not caused balkanization of CSDE; they merely reinforced existing baronies and "divisionalitis." The political conflict surrounding education program administration in California is the force that sunders the state education establishment. As the California legislature itself concluded in 1967:

Educational administration in this state, as it exists in Sacramento, consists of a chaotic, unplanned collection of boards, agencies, commissions and officers, connected sometimes by dotted lines of authority and sometimes by no lines at all. It resembles nothing so much as a blunderbuss approach to satisfying the pinpointed and crucial needs of public education in the nation's most populous state . . . As an elected state official, the superintendent has a right and, indeed, a duty to speak out on educational issues of the day. When he does so—and his views conflict sharply with those of the Board of Education—misunderstandings and eventual harm to education are bound to ensure.[41]

Attempts to Overcome Fragmentation

All arrangements devised to overcome fragmentation have been stymied by political crossfires. In 1969 the legislative analyst recommended a consolidated federal application form and the development of improved application and disbursement procedures for federal categorical aid. The present application process or "grantsmanship" was found to be complicated and time-consuming. The applications for each program must contain a description of the proposed project, a detailed budget, and various assurances that the proposal meets the requirements of the particular law. The suggested reforms were not adopted during the Rafferty era.

The relationship between Rafferty and the legislative analyst's office is summed up by this quote from Rafferty's response to the FY 1971 report:

This year Governor Ronald Reagan's economy move to cut his 1970-71 budget to approximately 20% below the 1969-70 level of expenditures really left little for the Legislative Analyst to do in the way of cutting. This frustrating situation for the analyst is the most generous justification that can be made for the analyst's report which criticizes many, many things in general with little, if any, justification and gets into many policy matters that should hardly be his zone of responsibility. In any event, a great many severe attacks on the Department of Education are either groundless or dead wrong.[42]

Title V Impact

The analyst saw Title V of ESEA, a program to upgrade SEA capabilities, as a particular target: "We believe that the addition of staff through this type of funding (Title V) has been one of the major contributors to the irrational organization that existed."[43] Tables 3-5 and 3-6 summarize state expenditures for Title V ESEA.

From these tables we conclude that (1) individual Title V projects are very small and involve a low portion of the state's total allocation; (2) once established, projects are seldom terminated; and (3) the projects lack strong central direction. Although some projects deal with coordination and leadership, their impact is negligible because of limited scope and lack of priorities. The analyst recommended the enactment of legislation to provide guidelines for the department's allocation of Title V funds. The proposed guidelines would include (1) state priorities for the allocation of funds; (2) a formalized system of project approval; and (3) annual reporting of results to the legislature. The analyst concluded:

Proposals are generally conceived at the bureau level and submitted to the department's cabinet by the operating head of the division involved. There is little in the way of project planning or budget development and no formal application procedure.

It is important to note that a proposal under Title V is an indication of weakness in an area of the department's operation. This could be a damaging admission for a divisional administrator to make to the policy body of the department. This has resulted in the large number of projects of questionable value.[44]

Federal Aid Administration: A Title-by-Title Analysis

ESEA—Title I

The changes in the California political landscape prior to 1965 affected the administration of Title I. Tempered by their earlier clashes with CSDE and the superintendent, the state board of education and the legislature determined to exert substantial influence on the federal legislation. California had passed its first state compensatory education program (the MacAteer Act) in 1963, two years prior to ESEA. At the time, the legislature expressed its desire to insure that compensatory education programs were not "absorbed and lost" in CSDE.

Table 3-5
Title V ESEA Funding Expenditures, Fiscal Years 1965-66 through 1968-69

Abbreviated Title of Project (Funded Since Program Inception)	1965-66 Expenditures	1966-67 Expenditures
A.D. Little Survey	$ 202,770	$ 5,749
Committee of Seven	4,571	–
Program Planning Unit	83,919	153,817
Advanced Placement	12,285	61,750
English Framework	4,030	34,207
Social Sciences Framework	31,772	79,947
Science Framework	9,704	27,147
Bill of Rights	48,481	64,614
State Comm. Pub. Education	44,763	188,190
School Bus. Admin. Workshops	2,639	24,407
Transportation Supervision	855	–
School Planning	15,430	36,245
Test Kitchen	7,000	17,005
J.C. Advisory Panel	19,403	63,756
Data Processing Educational Info. Systems	70,835	110,821
Innovation Exchange	1,651	4,645
Mexican American Children	15,061	74,986
Teacher Supply-Demand	53,040	473
Instructional TV	4,376	28,177
Arts and Humanities	3,458	26,047
Staff Inservice Training	1,074	30,084
Intergroup Relations	2,674	–
Study of Desegregation	1,162	5,481
Junior High Schools	12,607	29,781
Review Education Code	44,822	–
Economics Education	16,407	25,071
Editor Services Project Talent	10,472	–
Adult Spanish Surnames	9,399	20,828
Conservation Educator	3,117	1,593
Teacher Records	148,033	28,025
Strengthening Admin. Services	–	34,065
Health Instruction Guidelines	–	32,000
Reading Grades 1 & 2	–	27,000
1st Grade Reading Test Analysis	–	8,100
Textbook Evaluation Study	–	25,408
Progress, Physically Underdeveloped	–	18,000
Special Education Data Collection	–	40,000
State Board Clerical Assistance	–	–
NDEA III Strengthening Crit. Subjects	–	–

Table 3-5 (cont.)

Abbreviated Title of Project (Funded Since Program Inception)	1965-66 Expenditures	1966-67 Expenditures
NDEA X Imp. Stat. Services	–	–
Departmental Reorganization	–	–
Accreditation Workshop	–	–
Curriculum Mentally Gifted	–	–
Adult Education Adv. Committee	–	–
Continuation Education Workshops	–	–
Curriculum Abstracts	–	–
Education Prof. Development Act Admin.	–	–
P.E. Framework	–	–
Model Inservice Programs	–	–
Drug Abuse Education Program	–	–
Reading Workshops	–	–
Foreign Language Framework	–	–
Civic Education	–	–
Distribution to LEAs	–	–
Selection of Test Instruments	–	66,058
Bulletin Laws Except Child	–	5,000
Departmental Administration	–	–
Blind/Multihandicapped	–	20
Common Data Base	–	51,546
Think-In on Gifted	–	3,520
Role Ethnic Minorities	–	10,000
Student Councils	–	10
Tests for Certification	–	29,655
Test Bilingualism	–	24,000
Analysis State Test Results	–	14,000
Totals	$1,739,654	$1,699,999

Source: Table compiled from annual listings in the Legislative Analyst, *Analysis of Budget Bills*; 1970-71 (Sacramento: California Legislation) pp. 184-85.

Thus it divorced compensatory education from State Superintendent Rafferty's control and established an independent seventeen-member advisory commission to supervise state and, later, federal compensatory education programs. Of the seventeen members, eleven were appointed by the governor; two were from the Assembly; two, from the Senate; and two, from the community. The chief administrator, the director of compensatory education, was appointed by the commission and reported directly to it and the state board. At the outset of Title I, Wilson Riles, the director of compensatory education, indicated he would not shrink from a tough stance on priorities and program quality:

Table 3-6
ESEA Title V Estimated Expenditures 1969-70 Departmental Activities by Divisions

	Man-Years	Salaries	Contracts	Equipment	Other	Total
Departmental Administration						
State Board Clerical	3.0	$ 19,600	0	$ 100	$ 7,300	$ 27,000
Innovative Exchange	0	0	$ 1,500·	0	3,500	5,000
Management Information System	16.0	154,509	0	0	20,491	175,000
Departmental Reorganization	2.0	28,200	1,200	0	5,600	35,000
Strengthening Adm. Services	10.0	79,535	0	22,812	15,653	118,000
Staff Inservice Training	4.0	$ 40,428	$16,000	$ 1,930	$31,642	$ 90,000
Subtotal	35.0	$322,272	$18,700	$24,872	$84,186	$450,000
Public School Administration						
Improving Statistical Services	2.8	26,734	4,221	0	14,045	45,000
Textbook Utilization	1.5	20,375	0	1,017	6,608	28,000
Business Adm. Workshops	2.0	25,766	1,440	0	4,794	32,000
School Planning Services	4.7	64,810	11,055	260	31,875	108,000
Subtotal	11.0	$137,685	$16,716	$ 1,277	$57,322	$213,000
Compensatory Education						
State/Federal Preschool Coord.	5.0	$ 55,260	$ 2,000	$ 65	$17,675	$ 75,000
Intergroup Tensions	1.5	20,218	800	0	5,982	27,000
Subtotal	6.5	$ 75,478	$ 2,800	$ 65	$23,657	$102,000

Source: Legislative Analyst, *Analysis of the Budget Bill*, 1970-71 (Sacramento: California Legislature), pp. 185-86.

I've been around (the CSDE) for eight years. What usually happens is that the district sends its budget man up. He is concerned only with how to get the dollars, not with methods or programs. He doesn't bother with that. If this is to be a program operation, we must have mechanisms to ensure that when they come for money, we can nail them. We make them start with identifying the target area, the most pressing needs of youngsters, strategies and programs to meet those needs and how to evaluate results. *Then* we talk in terms of how much funding is needed to carry out their objectives. My viewpoint is that this is not just money to help districts build buildings or buy projectors, it is to meet the needs of deprived children.[45]

The advisory commission promptly criticized the state superintendent for not providing adequate staff and office space to handle the big new federal school aid program.[46] Wilson Riles, who owed a good part of his appointment to his relationship with Senator MacAteer, had a significant influence on who was appointed to this advisory commission. The commission membership was drawn from both parties; was very liberal; and believed that Riles would do a good job. They viewed their role as supporting him in any political battles and offering helpful advice. Confronted with the political obstacles of the state board and advisory commission, Rafferty abdicated and left Riles in charge.

Riles commenced to write Title I guidelines and to recruit staff. He selected people from across the state on the basis of their accomplishments. He explained,

I've found that if you've got the people who can operate a program, the program operates, I don't care what chart you draw. Flexibility allowing me to choose staff was critical. I only chose four out of many departmental applicants.

We are dealing in an area in which the school system has been insensitive. You don't just grab up someone and make him a consultant on the disadvantaged. I brought in those I wanted from within and without the department. I couldn't have done it without a separate division. It enabled me to avoid the established bureaucracy.[47]

A high-ranking CSDE official indicated the legislature's intervention was crucial in preserving the focus of the compensatory education program: "No doubt they (the CSDE planners) would have taken Title I and spread it through the department. There are arguments on both sides, but, operationally, look at the results obtained."[48]

The division's independence, however, isolated it from other federal and state categorical programs; but this isolation could not impede overall coordination since CSDE was not organized for comprehensive planning and priority setting.

At the earliest USOE regional meetings on Title I, the OE officials used a draft guideline which stated, "It is expected that the total number of children served by the program of a local agency will approximate the number of children on which that agency's formula grant is based."[49] Pressures from Congress and the chief state school officers forced a USOE retreat on this issue. The California Division of Compensatory Education, however, decided to enforce the guidelines to assure the funds were not spread so thinly as to negate the Act's "threshold effect" and "critical mass."

Riles' success in not compromising this stance is a good example of the political support a state agency needs to carry out a "hard line." While the original idea came from OE draft guidelines, CSDE used its required annual evaluation to compare effectiveness with expenditure level. CSDE used the suggested relationship of a minimum of $300 per pupil as a "partisan policy analysis" to support its viewpoint. This research and evaluation data enabled CSDE to parry LEA challenges and objections and to persuade the advisory commission on compensatory education and the state board. Compensatory education staff stress they never could have enforced concentration without the support of the advisory commission and state board. The members of both bodies were sympathetic to state leadership and especially to Riles. The local districts found solid resistance to their objections to tight guidelines on all state fronts:

The local agencies took their complaints to Riles. Once the State Board voted 10 to 0 against a large city district using a lot of Title I to build high schools, the word got out it was useless to appeal to the State Board. They were viewed as being 100 percent behind Riles and his staff. After all, they had strongly supported Riles for the appointment.[50]

The evidence is that the state legislature did not intercede on program or project decisions after establishing an administrative structure "independent of the establishment." The MacAteer Act embodied some priorities for in-service education and early childhood, but these were encompassed in CSDE's comprehensive program approach. Local agencies appealed to Riles and sometimes to John Hughes, the USOE Title I head. Hughes, however, saw the CSDE operation as a national model and would not undercut it.

This initial victory on concentration led to a series of program guidelines on such things as targeting, program priorities, integration, and parent advisory councils. These ideas were designed by Riles' bureau chiefs, cleared with Riles, and then brought to the advisory commission and state board. State board members were informed of the proposed policies for the first time when they reached Sacramento for their evening subcommittee meeting. Both the advisory council and the state board were apprehensive about becoming "too dictatorial." They were impressed, however, with the data in the evaluation reports, which supported CSDE recommendations, and trusted Riles.

Contending "the federal guidelines were too vague and confusing," CSDE staff sent out their own state Title I guidelines. Each LEA received guidelines, program suggestions, planning procedures, bibliographies, and evaluation reports. These state communications became increasingly detailed over the years. Desirous of ending single component programs providing only remedial reading, CSDE staff proposed and obtained the following requirements for each local program:

instructional
   —language development and mathematics
   —others, if appropriate

supportive
   —parent involvement and participation activities
   —auxiliary services, such as nutritional, health, counseling, and psychological services
   —inservice training of project personnel

—intergroup relations activities to alleviate racial, social, or linguistic isolation. This may include desegregation, planned human relations' activities, and ethnic studies.

This comprehensive program was reinforced by an explicit priority for elementary programs, advocated by staff members with a background in elementary education. Their views were supported by a review of the generally weak high school proposals and some evaluation data which showed greater gains at the elementary level. The guidelines state:

... priority in designating target area schools shall be given to elementary schools; and only after a comprehensive, longitudinal program from kindergarten through grade six is established at the eligible elementary schools, may a junior high or high school be selected.[51]

Authority for this priority setting was included in the state legislation setting up the advisory commission. The CSDE staff took this literally and, indeed, as we have seen, Riles had an important hand in designing the original legislation.

Although USOE in 1965 changed its guidelines to require that Title I money be targeted to areas of *high* concentration of low income families rather than to areas of *highest* concentration, CSDE guidelines continued to demand *highest*. Moreover, the USOE guidelines specify, "districts in which recent integration has been completed shall use the year prior to integration as the base year for determining attendance areas from which students may participate." California has relied on the most recent AFDC data as the basis for determining the extent of low income families in any district or attendance area.

California was the first state to mandate parent advisory councils. Again, the idea was advanced by a bureau chief in the division of compensatory education; discussed in a meeting with all bureau chiefs; approved by Riles; and then reviewed in detail with the advisory commission and the state board. These latter bodies were needed as political buffers, and the advisory commission members were regarded as "sympathetic experts." An "appendix plan" is required for each application.

Experience with "hidden segregation" led to a guideline prohibition on certain types of classroom grouping:

Title I projects will not be approved if they (1) create special tracks for the educationally disadvantaged; (2) establish adjustment, pre-grade or junior grade classes for the educationally disadvantaged; (3) isolate Title I children from the mainstream of school life for a period of time greater than one-half of the regular school day.[52]

The California State Guidelines are replete with examples of this sort. For instance, five components are specified for each staff development (inservice) project. One of the advisory commission members was instrumental in requiring in-service training in all Title I programs.

The involvement of the governor's office in these program and allocative restrictions imposed by CSDE was minimal. Governor Brown appointed liberal board of education members who supported Riles in numerous ways, but direct involvement was nonexistent. Governor Reagan has evidenced no interest in Title I, and his staff regard it as a "welfare program."

If strong state leadership and guidance are favored, the California Title I administration has been exemplary. Despite this generally strong performance, several major problems have appeared.

The legislative analyst's field investigators found that the use of AFDC data for allocating Title I funds within the state works against low-income cultural groups, such as Mexican-Americans and Chinese, in which "cultural constraints tend to inhibit the acceptance of welfare."

All districts visited have reported large low-income disadvantaged populations of either Oriental or Spanish surname individuals who do not apply for welfare. Spanish surname under representation on AFDC, for example, is estimated to be over 50 percent by school and community officials in those districts visited.[53]

The analyst believes California and the southwestern states are net losers of Title I funds because of AFDC criteria, while northeastern and southern states probably gain.

The analyst's investigation also revealed that the parent involvement guidelines were not being implemented. The analyst saw "little meaningful participation" and observed that more than 200 parents had attended CSDE's statewide meeting of program administrators and voiced similar complaints. The analyst made several interesting policy recommendations:

1. Parent Advisory Committees should have a sign-off function on all Title I applications similar to that presently accorded to local Community Action agencies.
2. Advisory Committees should periodically receive expenditure data throughout the life of the Title I project.
3. Parent Advisory Committees should receive copies of the CSDE monitor and review team reports now sent only to the district superintendent.
4. Methods of selecting parents should be revised so LEAs cannot "stack" the committees with teacher aides and spouses of school employees.

CSDE officials also admit that the present LEA budget categories and fiscal systems do not permit objective testing of maintenance of effort. The California guidelines carry maintenance of effort to attendance areas within the LEA. Until comparability is clarified, the federal regulations extend only to the LEA as a whole. CSDE has only three staff people to check expenditure data. The fiscal staff spends its time checking the arithmetic on applications and acting on complaints.

Perhaps the CSDE's unsystematic monitoring procedure from 1965-1969 merits the greatest criticism. Monitoring was termed "informal" and admittedly poor. In the past two years, however, a well-planned monitor and review team periodically reviews individual Title I projects in selected school districts. The form and check list used are comprehensive and probe all crucial allocation questions including targeting, concentration, and comparability. A crucial issue is that these reports do not reach the public. A leak of the Oakland Title I report led to press headlines and considerable pressure by the Black Caucus to reorient the programs. CSDE's philosophy has been to work the problems out with local public school officials. The evidence indicates the division of compensatory education has the political support and drive to bring about project changes based on these monitoring visits. Whether the changes would satisfy local citizens and activist parents is unknown.

In general, the division of compensatory education has been more stringent in its requirements than USOE. The staff and director aspired to national leadership and had sufficient political support in the state to achieve it. Although some of the ideas (like concentration at $300 per pupil) came from USOE, the California State Department of Education frequently outstripped USOE and needed after-the-fact OE interpretations to uphold California policy stands.

Vocational Education

In vocational education, unlike Title I of ESEA, primary influence on programs and allocations is exerted by CSDE; outside agencies play only a marginal role. CSDE, however, passes a great deal of its discretion under the federal law to LEAs. From the George Barden Act until 1968, USOE never displayed any interest or concern with the intrastate distribution of money in California. The department administrator said he made an interstate study in 1952, and no two states had the same distribution systems. Only after the Vocational Education Act of 1968 did USOE probe into the intrastate distribution of funds within California. The Office of Education was most concerned about the lack of state plans for specific allocation formulas.

Prior to the 1968 federal amendments, California operated the part of the Act pertaining to support of instructional programs under a modified project system. Although projects from local districts were theoretically judged by outside review panels of experts and funded on their merits, a split based on ADA was also used in conjunction with the prior funding levels. CSDE administrators said the allocation system was very subjective and operated with virtually no priorities or guidelines. One admitted, "Our staff spent a lot of time checking the typewriters and other objective paperwork, but the money decisions were based on subjective judgments we could not defend."[54]

An annual deluge of applications—about 1,500 proposing to spend four times the available money—was the result. Large city districts often submitted fifteen to twenty separate projects. A very amorphous state plan which was never altered between the federal acts of 1963 and 1968 governed CSDE operations.

The section on "allocation of federal funds" said simply "due consideration" shall be given to:

(a) the vocational education needs of all persons of all age groups in all communities in the state, and
(b) the results of periodic evaluation of state and local vocational education programs and services in light of:
   (1) current and projected manpower needs and job opportunities;
   (2) the need for maintaining, extending, and improving existing programs and developing new programs of vocational education.[55]

The state plan sent to USOE did not include the criteria to be considered by the project review teams of non-CSDE consultants. These were included in the instructions for applicants sent to LEAs:

— There is administrative support in terms of adequate supervision and coordination of the program;
— the occupation-centered curriculum is set up and maintained with the advice and cooperation of the employee-employer representatives concerned;
— the instructional program is directly related to existing employment opportunities and is based on the advice and counsel of representatives from the occupational community being served;
— vocational guidance . . . is a continuing part of the program;
— training for an occupation is carried to the point of developing marketable skills . . . sufficient to enable the trainee to get and hold a job;
— occupational training is offered as close to the actual time of job entry as possible;
— instruction provides effective learning situations and duplicates as nearly as possible conditions in the occupation itself;
— personnel possess adequate professional qualifications for teaching; and
— the cost and district effort are reasonable in terms of the objectives of the project.[56]

None of these criteria establish priorities among types of districts, target populations, or programs, such as agriculture or office occupations. The review teams were "composites of the users of the funds" and "sound vocational education people." Outside reviewers were chosen by the vocational education staff in CSDE and included vocational education teachers, superintendents, county office administrators, and community colleges representatives. The department did not hesitate to use "administrative adjustments" to make sure the projects (1) did not cut the past level of support, and (2) were not greatly at variance with the vocational education ADA of the district. As a lobbyist for a large urban district expressed it:

Under the project system we knew exactly how much we were going to get come hell or high water. Maybe we sold out for 30 pieces of silver but we could plan for it and thereby use money more effectively. Obviously, our allotment was too low because any type of entitlement system based on a need factor gave us more money.[57]

While the 1968 Vocational Education Act was the greatest stimulus to change in allocation patterns, two outside forces were partly responsible for the dissolution of the project system.

In 1967 Arthur D. Little Inc. had made a comprehensive study of vocational education in California and reached the following conclusions:

(1) The vast majority of the state's 943,665 vocational enrollment are in older and more traditional programs. Conversely, a relatively small percentage are in growth fields.
(2) High school occupational training programs are particularly weak. Girls outnumber boys by three to one in such programs and a large emphasis is being placed on low-level clerical training.
(3) Special programs for persons with special needs, persons who cannot benefit from regular vocational education programs (primarily disadvantaged pupils), are virtually nonexistent.
(4) The current federal definition of vocational education [before the Vocational Education Act of 1968] is a major obstacle to the development of state-level priorities regarding the content of occupational training programs and the development of an improved allocation formula. The definition of vocational education is so general that almost any curricula may be defined as vocational and thereby qualify for federal support if the training is keyed to an occupational field.[58]

The 1968-69 *Report of the Legislative Analyst* included several alleged weaknesses:

Some of these weaknesses include a lack of precise definitions regarding what courses of study ought to be or ought not to be included in the definition of vocational education, a lack of state level priorities for the allocation of funds, a lack of state and regional planning of comprehensive programs, a lack of articulation of vocational education programs with compensatory education programs and a noticeable lack of articulation of high school programs with junior college programs.[59]

The congressional amendments of 1968 required a focus on the disadvantaged and handicapped which heretofore CSDE had never enforced. The new amendments also required attention to maintenance of fiscal effort, variable matching based on ability to pay, and reasonable tax effort. CSDE had paid scant attention to maintenance of effort, saying supplanting could not take place "unless special conditions warrant and a full explanation is given." Until 1968, surveys of manpower needs did not seem to have an important part in CSDE project decisions.

Wesley Smith, the state director of vocational education, had been dissatisfied with the project system for several years. He invoked the federal mandates to assemble a panel of five finance experts who were instructed to develop an equitable automatic entitlement system similar to Title I of ESEA. This entitlement system would build in the constraints of the 1968 Act and provide the local district with a "bank account" expendable after CSDE approved the specific programs. Smith favored an entitlements system additionally because it would force LEAs who had not applied for large vocational education grants to refuse an earmarked amount.

The formula for the entitlement system became the key component of "who gets what" in California vocational education. The finance experts' recommendations were tested in advisory panels, but the real decision was made by the Joint Committee on Vocational Education, composed of three members of the state board of education and three from the governing board of the California Community Colleges. California, in the early 1950s, had broken the federal barrier against using federal funds for junior colleges. Unlike the high schools, California junior colleges had been enthusiastic about using federal vocational funds, and prior to 1968 their share built up to 45 percent of the total. As one who was in on the formula decision said: "We thought our number one consideration was how to come up with a figure that would satisfy the community colleges. We knew they had to get what they got before, but yet there were new earmarks in the federal act."[60]

The vocational education staff presented the joint committee with three alternative formulas based on weighted ADA. For instance, the disadvantaged could have been given one ADA, .5 ADA, or .2 ADA. Because it was necessary to preserve a large community college share, the formula with the lowest weight (.2 ADA) was selected. Morever, the joint committee stipulated that actual district apportionments should not vary by more than 10 percent from previous funding levels. Consequently, the entitlement system applied only to federal money in excess of the prior year's appropriation. Again, the community college spokesmen seemed to be able to win their case. As Wes Smith said, "Our blue ribbon advisory panel said we must pay attention to past history in application of an entitlement system. Unless you have good evidence of gross inequities in the past, you just can't cut people off. We had no evidence of gross inequities."[61]

The entitlement formula works in the following way, based on a local district's ADA. A regular secondary ADA has a weight of 1; an adult, 1.5; a handicapped is .2 ADA, and disadvantaged, .2 ADA. Junior or community college ADA is then counted with a weight of 2.6. Community colleges received the highest weight (2.6 ADA) in order to permit their total share of all funds to approximate the traditional 45 percent. In effect, disadvantaged are counted once as a regular ADA and again (.2 ADA) under the disadvantaged factor. Counts of the disadvantaged, which are based on AFDC, are not kept at the junior college level.

This formula provides the minimum for disadvantaged under the federal law but is heavily weighted in favor of total school population and junior colleges. A comparison of Oakland Unified with wealthy Palo Alto Unified and a rural junior college in Humboldt County demonstrates the formula's effects:

		Oakland	
ADA Type		Weight	Weighted ADA
Regular	17,406	1	17,406
Adult	747	1.50	1,121
Special Education	709	.20	141
Disadvantaged	5,072	.20	1,014
		Palo Alto	
ADA Type		Weight	Weighted ADA
Regular	5,542	1	5,542
Adult	586	1.50	879
Special Education	81	.20	16
Disadvantaged	58	.20	12
	Redwoods Junior College (Humboldt)		
ADA Type		Weight	Weighted ADA
Regular	2,060	2.6	5,356
Adult	408	1.5	6.2

Although USOE challenged the California formula on the basis of need, it did not recommend any changes because of its inability to define need. CSDE administrators believe all districts need vocational training. They do not see any objective way to rank school districts in order of priority as OE wanted. The formula did gratify USOE because it incorporated weights for assessed valuation and tax rates in computing the variable matching share. For instance, the poor Compton school district outside Los Angeles must put up only $0.25 for every vocational education dollar while wealthy Patterson must match $3 for every federal dollar.

The formula was determined without significant involvement of the governor's office and legislature. The legislature has been concerned about the program, but as a key staff person noted, "We can't find a legislative handle that makes sense to control the program." The 1970-71 *Report of the Legislative Analyst* states:

We believe that the entitlement approach is a more effective system of apportioning vocational education funds. Further, we believe the limitations placed on the approach (not reducing any LEA by more than 10 percent) were justified because it was the first year of the new system and there were no new federal funds. However, in the future the legislature should view such restrictions on the entitlement system with concern.[62]

The California State Plan for vocational education allocation cannot have been very informative to USOE. The entitlement formula is described in general and vague terms; the weights are never clearly elucidated. The disadvantaged is called a "general priority," but this priority does not emerge from an analysis of the formula. State program priorities are supposedly based on a relation to manpower needs, but this is also not reflected in the formula. CSDE communications clearly indicate that local programs are to be based on one- and five-year manpower projections. As everyone concedes, the problem is that the local manpower data are unreliable. The Office of Education questioned the "skimpy data" on manpower needs and job opportunities; the department administrators contend they are aware of the urgent need for better data—especially five-year projections—but add, "We do think, however, the Human Resources Administration data is too subjective. If there is a riot in Hunters Point, San Francisco, they make this a priority. We can't go along with this."[63]

The department is just beginning to make project grants under the other parts of the Vocational Education Act of 1968 (cooperative, homemaking, work-study). It will use outside reviewers but will not set geographic or target population priorities beyond those required by federal law preferring to "let the best proposals determine whether the money flows to cities or rural areas."

With seventy-five people in three regional offices, CSDE has a substantial field staff to monitor projects; however, a staff member commented, "The main thing we do is to get acquainted with the local staff and answer questions. We want to acquaint them with our services and downgrade the inspection phase unless we get complaints. We rely on the county and LEA vocational education directors as safeguards." Since the passage of the 1968 Act, CSDE has more substantive areas to monitor, particularly the five-year plan and the balance among occupational areas. Nevertheless, much of the staff still conceives its responsibility to be guidance and suggestion.

The vocational education program has been characterized politically by a low profile, with little pressure for projects and few complaints to legislators. The federally-mandated advisory council is just getting organized, and no one can predict its impact.

The legislature, an active participant in other allocation programs, has now turned to vocational education; a 1970 Assembly bill with broad and impressive bipartisan sponsorship represents its initial efforts. The bill requires CSDE to develop a plan to integrate vocational education with the regular high school curriculum. If this move gains momentum, some federal funds may be earmarked as they are in Title III of ESEA.

NDEA-Title III

The administration of NDEA-Title III, enacted in 1958, reflects influences and pressures different from those that shaped the administration of ESEA I. A state plan program with minimal federal guidelines, NDEA III embodied the concept that "the State provides a broader base for educational leadership and planning than is possible at the local level, yet one which is far closer to the local school, or to the local college than the Federal Government."[64]

The superintendent of public instruction chose Dr. J. Graham Sullivan as NDEA director and established the following administrative precepts:

1. Minimize state control and maximize state service and leadership.
2. Keep Department of Education administrative costs as low as possible.
3. Involve school district personnel continuously in all aspects of state level program planning and evaluation.[65]

A "think group" of nine prominent educators from school districts and higher education came to Sacramento to discuss guidelines, regulations, and the state plan. However, according to Millstein,

This group provided a sounding board for the department, but critical decisions were made during the first several months by an intradepartmental Task Force. The mainstays of the Task Force were the Chief of the Division of Instruction, the Chief of the Division of Public School Administration, the Bureau Chiefs for Elementary and Secondary Education, and the new director, Dr. Sullivan. Because he was responsible in the final analysis, more often than not, discussion and debate revolved around his conceptualizations. . . Out of this thinking and subsequent actions of the program director came the philosophical base of the first California State Plan and the administrative pattern of the NDEA Bureau.[66]

The California State Plan was submitted on February 9, 1959, and was immediately approved by the U.S. Commissioner of Education. Sullivan resisted the Office of Education's attempts to require great detail in the state plan. He drafted a general plan that enabled the bureau to "do anything the contract (state plan) would let it do."[67] This assumed actual decision-making power at the state level. The USOE did not issue a formal set of NDEA guidelines until September 1963—five years after the legislation was passed! The Act did not mention evaluation of the funds' impact. Consequently the federal regulations only hint at evaluation, and the California guidelines merely suggest some evaluative procedures. NDEA III has had a poor valuation record.

The state superintendent finally approves NDEA III projects; the state board is not even informed. The California NDEA guidelines do not mention priorities or criteria for intrastate distribution. Administrators contend that NDEA is "for all types of districts" and that neither the legislation nor the Office of Education discuss urban-rural priorities. They assert that decisions are based on the quality of the entire project, including project objectives. From 1958-1964 applications amounting to approximately $6 million were filed for the $5 million available in federal funds. After the eligible subject categories were expanded in 1964, requests exceeded available funds by more than three-to-one.

A CSDE internal planning paper illustrates the department's attitude on priorities or legislative mandates limiting the use of funds to types of students or classes of schools (such as urban disadvantaged). The CSDE had sampled LEA opinion on fund restrictions and reported three main problems:

— a feeling there would be a community reaction to further concentration of funds in the area of compensatory education;
— belief that it would result in significant losses of teacher enthusiasm and effort; and
— a feeling that such an action would be interpreted as a direct attack upon local control.

The department summarized the viewpoint with which it identified by quoting from a local administrator:

This community would not support any further concentration of funds in the area of compensatory education. Local initiative is fundamental. Each district must decide for itself where its problems are. To do otherwise is destructive of teacher morale and invites massive retaliation by the community.[68]

To decide among competing projects, CSDE employs a rating scale of the use, quality, and quantity of the equipment. This includes such categories as durability, appropriate quality for the grade level, relation to project objectives, mobility, etc. The rating is then considered in light of "priorities" such as:

— Degree to which the objectives relate to NDEA III basic purposes;
— Degree to which project will improve instruction;
— Competencies of staff;
— Degree to which new equipment and materials will contribute to the achievement of the objectives.

The ratings are done by CSDE staff and ad hoc panels of LEA people such as department chairmen, subject matter specialists, curriculum coordinators, and others who are able to come to Sacramento for a week. There is a review panel of five in foreign languages and three in mathematics. Expecting that some will be dropped, the local districts often submit four or five projects. The CSDE administrators aspire to give some money to each district that applies. If a small district submits a poor application, the state staff or consultants will help to rewrite it. Such a system minimizes pressure from local districts for favoritism, and no district has ever requested a hearing by the state board.

The NDEA staff all have school administrative backgrounds plus some curriculum depth. There has never been anybody on the staff from large cities. The top administrator told us that his staff was too small to conduct a sophisticated monitoring plan. The monitoring theory for NDEA is summed up this way by an NDEA official: "I don't think we want to be a policing agency in terms of following up to see if people did what they said they were going to do. The key to our success is that most of the decision making is done at the district level. They know their abilities, needs, and financial situation."[69]

In sum, NDEA III is very much under the control of department staff; it recommends outside consultants for the rating panels and makes final decisions. There is no review by the State Board. The state plan permits a maximum amount of flexibility, and a search of the department files shows almost no Office of Education concern with improper expenditures after the first year. The legislature has regarded NDEA III money as too categorical and too small to intervene. The legislative analyst has continually criticized the lack of evaluation data on the effectiveness of the program.

ESEA-Title II

In 1965 Title II was initially assigned to the Bureau of Audio-Visual and School Library Education. After the state board of education rejected several of the bureau's proposed state plans, the program was shifted to the NDEA bureau. Delayed approval of the state plans caused postponement of the program until March 1966, when entitlements were established.

The initial state plan allocated money under a formula which considered only the district's assessed valuation and the average daily attendance. This type of formula does not favor the cities which typically have higher assessed values than suburbs.

The specific formula was

$$X = \frac{S}{(d)} \ (W) \cdot (Y)$$

X = the district's entitlement for a given year;
S = state average assessed valuation per unit of ADA in the state;
d = district assessed valuation per unit of ADA of the district involved;
W = the average amount of money per child in the state available for acquisition of materials under Title II; and
Y = a district's average daily attendance.

Table 3-7, provided by CSDE, shows the formula applied to four school districts. During the first few years, no one in California paid much attention to Title II.

Table 3-7

Formula Applied to Four Unified School Districts Having an ADA of 1500 or More (1964-65)

Average assessed valuation (adjusted) per unit of ADA in the State: Elementary $12,725, Secondary $31,806*

Estimated average amount of money (Phase I) available per child to State, $1.36

District**	Adjusted Assessed Valuation	ADA (1964-65)	Entitlement
Beverly Hills (1)	$ 235,470,864	5,530	$ 1,828
San Francisco (0)	1,692,567,439	100,181	74,568
Temple City (52)	33,917,948	4,366	6,933
Travis AFB (105)	20,165,951	3,212	6,652

Note: Actual entitlements will be based on adjusted assessed valuations and on ADA figures which will include the elegible private school attendance in the district.

*Rank of district among 105 unified school districts having an ADA in public schools of 1500 or more; rank based on 1963-64 unadjusted assessed valuation per ADA.

**Public schools only; information on private schools not available at this time.

The legislative analyst did not discuss it, nor did the big cities challenge the formula under which approximately $8 million was distributed. Indeed, very few people knew about the formula; its components were not even mentioned in the guidelines and information sent to the local districts, and a table of statewide distribution was not publicly available. Local districts were asked to pledge that "Title II funds will supplement, and in no way supplant, local effort." The CSDE staff suggested assessed valuation as a basis for need and the State Board accepted it. The department also specified that no district would get less than $200 in total or more than $10 per child.

In 1968, however, the Office of Education began to enforce the "relative need" part of the Act and requested additional need factors in the formula. Negotiation of a new formula ensued. The department, following OE's general stance, presented the state board with five factors, including the number of books in a school district's possession. The board argued that five were too many; the department then returned with three factors, but the board wanted tax effort to have a higher priority. Upon resolution of these issues, the current formula, which determines the allocation of 75% of the Title II funds, was established. The entitlements determined by the formula for the city of Oakland and for a fast-growing, white, middle income suburban district outside of Sacramento are compared in Table 3-8. Table 3-9 illustrates the effects of the formula for two districts in Contra Costa County, a suburban area of San Francisco and Oakland. Note all suburban districts demonstrate more "need" than Oakland, with its large disadvantaged population.

Twenty-five percent of the Title II funds is reserved for projects judged

Table 3-8

Determination of Disbursements of ESEA II, Phase I Funds, 1969-70 Fiscal Year

	Oakland Unified		San Juan Unified	
	Elementary	Secondary	Elementary	Secondary
	Relative Need Factor		Relative Need Factor	
State Average Assessed Valuation per ADA ÷ District Assessed Valuation per ADA	$\frac{14,752}{19,182} = 0.77$	$\frac{36,993}{49,796} = 0.74$	$\frac{14,752}{9,209} = 1.60$	$\frac{36,993}{20,235} = 1.83$
District Tax Rate ÷ State Median Tax Rate	$\frac{4.1130}{3.5300} = 1.17$	$\frac{4.1130}{3.5300} = 1.17$	$\frac{4.4850}{3.5300} = 1.27$	$\frac{4.4850}{3.5300} = 1.27$
State Book Average per ADA ÷ District Book Average per ADA =	$\frac{6.00}{13.75} = 0.44$	$\frac{9.00}{13.93} = 0.65$	$\frac{6.00}{6.00} = 1.00*$	$\frac{9.00}{9.00} = 1.00$
Total Relative Need Factor	2.38	2.56	3.87	4.10
Public and Private ADA	x 51,480	x 20,264	x 40,335	x 17,829
District Allowance Factor	122,522.40	51,875.84	156,096.45	73,098.90
Disbursement per ADA per Allowance Factor	x .16030	x .16030	x .16030	x .16030
Total District Entitlement	$19,640.3407200	$8,315.6971520	$25,022.2609350	$11,717.7536700

*Those districts (including San Juan Unified) who contract for school library services are given a relative need factor of 1.00. The actual average books per ADA is: Elementary = 3.60; Secondary = 5.96.

Table 3-9
Determination of Disbursements of ESEA II, Phase I Funds, 1969-70 Fiscal Year

	Walnut Creek Elementary Relative Need Factor	Acalanes Union High Relative Need Factor
State Average Assessed Valuation per ADA / District Assessed Valuation per ADA	$\frac{14{,}752}{19{,}957} = 0.74$	$\frac{36{,}993}{31{,}527} = 1.17$
+		
District Tax Rate / State Median Tax Rate	$\frac{3.1810}{1.8900} = 1.68$	$\frac{1.8810}{1.7100} = 1.10$
+		
State Book Average per ADA / District Book Average per ADA	$\frac{6.00}{12.54} = 0.48$	$\frac{9.00}{7.16} = 1.26$
=		
Total Relative Need Factor	2.90	3.53
Public and Private ADA	x 4,721	x 7,406
District Allowance Factor	13,690.90	26,143.18
Disbursement per ADA per Allowance Factor	x .16030	x .16030
Total District Entitlement	$2,194.6512700	$4,190.7517540

exemplary by CSDE staff and library consultants. The stated objectives of these exemplary projects indicate the pattern of allocation:

To provide throughout California a wide geographic distribution of pilot project libraries that are easily accessible to members of governing boards of school districts, teachers, administrators, student teachers, and others who may wish to observe an effective instructional materials program in operation.[70]

In sum, the principal allocative decisions in the administration of Title II have been made by the CSDE staff and the state board. The legislature and lobbyists have been notably absent. Although the state board played a crucial role in changing the formula, the initiative came from the office of education.

The comparison of the Oakland and San Juan Unified districts demonstrates that the current formula does not favor the big cities. Thus its effectiveness in satisfying USOE's 1968 stipulation of "relative need" is open to question.

ESEA-Title III

The administration of Title III etched a new pattern of federal-state relations in California. During the initial years of NDEA, California administrators protested the "improper communications" that flowed directly from the Office of Education to the local districts.[71] This concern with Washington's modus operandi diminished after 1959 but was rekindled by ESEA-Title III. Under Title III, the department could only review and recommend on LEA-submitted proposals; the Office of Education granted final approval.

CSDE countered by establishing a Program Planning Unit headed by an experienced NDEA operative, Donald Johnson. Johnson contended CSDE had three alternatives with respect to Title III: (1) to ignore the requirement for commenting on local applications and thereby refuse to participate; (2) to recommend *all* proposals regardless of merit, leaving the entire onus of approval or disapproval on USOE; or (3) to accept the recommendation requirement at face value. Johnson said after many sessions, "We decided that USOE should never be allowed to make decisions without the guidance of CSDE. Therefore, we decided to do a thorough ranking of our recommendations. This was a major policy decision."[72]

Millstein concluded USOE and CSDE have agreed on 80 to 85 percent of the California Title III proposals without any discussion. He quotes Office of Education officials as asserting "the CSDE's review process for ESEA III has become as thorough and well done as ours." The distribution pattern that CSDE inherited when Title III reverted to state control was largely of its own making.

During 1965-66 a rough breakdown of approved projects in California showed:

Type of Project	No.	Amount
Supplementary Centers	21	$3,365,283
Data Processing Centers	10	441,540
Exemplary Programs	58	3,824,873

Supplementary Educational Centers. Twenty-one of these centers were spread throughout the state in locations determined by the neighboring county superintendents of schools. This spread the money in a geographically equal fashion throughout the state, with no particular concentration in any one area. The centers were to be multipurpose and to mobilize local educational, cultural, and community resources. Their cost remained at approximately $3 million during the entire OE stewardship.

Data Processing Centers. Regional data processing centers were designed to provide local school districts with data processing services which they otherwise could not afford. Additional centers have been created, increasing the amount committed to over $1.6 million.

Innovative programs. These programs were individual or cooperative district projects. Their funding increased to $10.6 million in 1967-68.

The 1967-68 *Report of the Legislative Analyst* charged Title III was not coordinated with other categorical programs and exhibited no clear priorities. It attributed these problems to the Washington-based decision-making structure. The analyst was also dismayed by the lack of evaluation data.

Title III of ESEA follows very much in the tradition of Title I; the legislature and advisory commissions became principal architects of the state administered program. At the time of the shift from USOE to state control, there were "State Board Policies for Implementation of Title III." The analyst's 1968-69 report contended these were "not very encouraging."

Vague priorities for innovative and exemplary programs drew the most criticism.

— First priority was to be given to projects of statewide significance, on the basis of the State Board's determination of priority of need for the state as a whole, and to continuing projects during the three years of federal funding on the basis of an annual evaluation of the effective functioning.
— Second priority was to be given to projects of regional significance approved by the boards of the supplementary educational centers, on the basis of the boards' determination of priority needs for the county or region.
— Third priority was to be given to proposals which seek solutions to problems not identified as being top priority of need.

The analyst's view, later shared by the legislature, was:

None of these priorities emphasize the importance of programs in critical areas such as elementary reading and mathematics, compensatory education and urban educational problems which have all been identified by the legislature as critical program areas which require comprehensive and coordinated local and state attention . . . We recommend that the legislature develop policy guidelines for the allocation of Title III funds, similar in concept to the guidelines established by the MacAteer Act for Title I and the legislature direct the State Board of Education to include such guidelines in the State plan for Title III.[73]

Distrustful of the quality of local proposals and concerned with the possibility of departmental passivity, the legislature moved once again to specify priorities and guidelines. It established the Educational Innovation Advisory Commission composed of legislators, the superintendent of public instruction, and eleven members appointed by the State Board of Education. Projects are initiated by the local educational agency, reviewed for form and content by CSDE's Bureau of Program Planning and Development, and presented for approval to the commission. Projects are then recommended to the state board for final approval.

The drive to wrest control of Title III administration from the Republican state superintendent had bipartisan support. The legislative establishment of the advisory commission was followed by the passage in a Republican-controlled legislature of five additional bills limiting CSDE's Title III discretion. Together these bills earmark more money for special purposes than exists in the total state allotment. In effect, there is so much legislation that none of it is very binding. Title III has become a happy hunting ground for legislators who want to initiate innovative schools or cost effectiveness studies.

In addition to over-zealous stipulation of available funds, Title III administration is impeded by the existence of three overlapping advisory commissions:

1. The Educational Innovation Advisory Commission was established to administer the State plan; it is required by federal law to advise the State Board on policy matters, to determine criteria for approval of applications, to review, and to evaluate innovative educational programs.
2. The Educational Research Commission was established to administer the Experimental Schools Program and to provide funding from Title III-ESEA monies; this commission can hire personnel; receive and expend funds; operate experimental schools; and determine the program of instruction.
3. The Advisory Committee on Program and Cost Effectiveness, a special committee, was established to evaluate and advise the State School Board on projects to be approved for Titles I and III of ESEA and the Miller-Unruh Basic Reading Act.

The CSDE reacted with dismay to this overlapping and earmarking of priorities. The department particularly objects to the diversion of Title III funds to pay administrative costs for EPDA and Title VIII dropout prevention and complains vehemently about OE's refusal to disallow this kind of expenditure. Moreover, the state plan submitted to USOE is not really a guide for action or even a plan, if one considers the legislative earmarks. The legislature contends that it can set priorities and make its decisions stand as the California state plan.

The large continuations of prior Title III projects and the legislative restrictions have made impossible CSDE consideration of programs other than language arts and mathematics for grades K-8. The Act requires that 50 percent of Title III must be spent for language development and mathematics in grades K-8, but 20 percent of the money is still locked into the supplementary centers. CSDE administrators have a low opinion of the quality of OE-funded central cities projects which also must be continued. They view Title III as an innovation program that should not be diverted to an urban focus if wealthy suburbs are willing to do something different. In their view, the central cities projects wasted large amounts on existing community action efforts and "more of the same."

In FY 1970 CSDE could fund only twelve new projects in language arts and mathematics. They do not solicit projects but rely on the regional supplementary centers to do it indirectly. One administrator alleged, "If we get too active the politicians will complain that their area did not have an even chance." CSDE relies for project rating on an elaborate system of outside panels. The panels work in four-man teams including specialists in evaluation, the program focus (e.g., mathematics), fiscal analysis, and management. The program specialist is selected by CSDE from a local public school; the fiscal analyst is usually a local school business manager; and the management representative is usually from a supplementary service center. There are twelve teams who read proposals for five days. If one team cannot arrive at a consensus, the proposal is referred to another one.

The results of this process in FY 1970 were to provide no money for central cities. CSDE did not use any "administrative discretion" to change the ratings, in large part, because a big city performance contract with a lot of political pressure behind it was denied. The big cities are hampered because the approved projects cost approximately $50,000-$80,000, and this amount would have little impact in a city. CSDE officials say the reviewers they select seem to prefer projects that cost approximately $80,000. Reviewers.are chosen from nominations by local or county offices and universities.

Local districts bring pressure to bear prior to the meeting of the review teams, usually in the form of endorsements by state legislators and local public officials. Some big cities have come up to see the reviewers, after decisions have been made, and complain the reviewers have never dealt with large projects. The cities can only speculate how they would fare if large amounts of money were available.

The state plan and guidelines enunciate some special considerations which have little influence on the ratings or decisions. The state guidelines read:

Taking into consideration the criteria listed in the preceding sections, if two or more proposals are judged to be of substantially the same high quality, proposals will be funded first from the area in the state which has persons with the greatest relative need, and second from the geographical area of the state which has not previously been awarded a project.[74]

CSDE administrators say that they have never been able to operationally define relative need although it is in the federal guidelines. In the past, "geographical distribution" has meant reference to the pin map of project locations and a search for a "reasonably good project for around $20,000" in an uncovered area. The reviews are then "administratively adjusted."

The guidelines also state, "Proposals submitted by districts making a special tax effort will receive special consideration." Again CSDE has no clear operational definition, but says it sometimes considers districts with several citizen-approved tax overrides. The state legislature wrote in a legal priority for districts in lowest reading quartile. CSDE has not enforced this priority because their test data is three years old. Indeed, Title III, to CSDE, implies "open competition," and these other factors are viewed as inhibiting and "political."

The supplementary centers have been a particular favorite of CSDE administrators and they have enjoyed twice the life span of other projects. The county superintendents played a crucial role in setting the boundaries and furnish good political support. Many of these centers are seen as developing capability in planning, evaluation, and needs assessment.

Monitoring has been greatly restricted by the poor example set by USOE when it controlled 100 percent of the money, and lack of staff. CSDE is still establishing monitoring plans, and four staff members visited two projects in 1970 for two days. The major sources of feedback are the continuation application and final reports. Department administrators concluded by saying, "If we get complaints, we go out and look."

In Title III as in Title I, the legislature has played a major role in the allocations. It has established program priorities and several advisory commissions who report directly to the legislature or state board. However, the Commission on Innovation has changed the review teams, and CSDE recommendations only twice in two cycles. The legislative mandate for experimental schools, on the other hand, has set up an independent commission that does not rely much on CSDE and does not even report to the State Board!

Conclusion

The distribution of federal aid in California has been influenced significantly by the overall state political climate. The elected State Superintendent of public instruction, Dr. Maxwell Rafferty, a Republican, clashed frequently and bitterly with the Democratic State Board of Education and the Democrat-controlled state legislature with its extensive legislative staff resources. Even when the legislature and state board became more conservative, the pattern continued of overturning or circumscribing the state superintedent's policies on federal aid.

Specifically, we found that Assertion No. 1 did not hold for the legislature. The California legislature is unequaled in the quantity and capacity of its staff. The legislature has urged this staff to investigate and make specific recommendations on federal aid. Legislative distrust of Rafferty's ideology and administrative style led to a series of CSDE reorganizations and independent commissions to insulate federal programs from Rafferty's control. Both Governors Brown and Reagan, however, have not regarded the stakes in federal aid to be high enough for their active intervention in the decisions of a state superintendent who possesses a potent statewide constituency and a formal status independent of the governor's cabinet.

California has not developed a cohesive and active lobby coalition among the large urban school districts for either federal or state distribution issues. Individual urban districts are aware of the details of federal aid allocation formulas and will exert pressure on the department when enough money is involved. Overall, there was not a great deal of pressure group activity in federal aid at any time. CTA and CASA, the two main professional organizations, concentrate on professional benefit and welfare issues.

All of these themes are woven into the score of federal aid allocation in California.

Title I subcounty allocations were originally based on ADA of the local districts but have been shifted to AFDC by the compensatory education director, Wilson Riles. Riles enjoyed legislatively mandated autonomy from Rafferty and operated through a sympathetic advisory commission.

Vocational education and ESEA II formulas reflect the traditional patterns of distribution in the state aid formulas—ADA and assessed valuation. The vocational education formulas devised after the Vocational Education Act of 1968 have been altered to insure that present distribution (particularly for community colleges) does not depart too widely from the previous project grant history of winners and losers.

NDEA III is a project grant with guidelines that give no hint of priorities or criteria for intra-state distribution. Administrators stress that decisions are based on the quality of the proposals, including use, quality, and quantity of the equipment.

ESEA III distribution has been determined largely by a 1966 emphasis on regional service centers (for a county or several rural counties) and subsequent legislative earmarks for innovative projects, particularly in basic skills in grades K-8.

From the standpoint of the cities, Title I is effective through the use of AFDC. The vocational education and ESEA II formulas are not well designed to properly respond to special urban needs. NDEA III and ESEA III judge the quality of proposals without any priorities for types of districts.

The quality and extent of CSDE leadership varied with the individual categorical title. There was no department-wide mechanism for comprehensive planning, coordination, or integration of either federal or state categorical programs. Rampant "divisionalitis" made the establishment of overall substantive priorities impossible. The legislature called for more coordination on the one hand, and on the other divided and conquered various divisions. The state superintendent was critical of the concept of federal aid and seemed content to leave whatever policy leadership was possible to his trusted staff. But much of the superintendent's discretion was legislated away, and the largest federal program was administered independently by Rafferty's chief political rival, Wilson Riles.

Consequently, California presented a variety of styles and philosophies in federal program administration. The Title I staff were political activists impatient with established patterns of operation and very cognizant of federal intent. They had close links with their Washington counterparts. The ESEA III staff were the most research oriented. Most of the others in the department perceived "professional leadership" as assisting LEAs to obtain federal money and avoiding conflict over federal intent.

Notes

1. David N. Evans and I.T. Johnson, *The Impact in California of NDEA* (Sacramento: California State Department of Education, 1967), pp. 22-23.

2. Laurence Iannaccone, "Federal Program Administration in Three Styles: Check Writers, Political Activists, and Researchers," unpublished paper prepared for a meeting of this research team, Chicago, Illinois, April 1970.

3. See Dean Bowles, "The Power Structure in State Education Politics," *Phi Delta Kappan*, February, 1968, pp. 337-340.

4. Bowles, op. cit., p. 337.

5. Ibid., p. 337.

6. See James Q. Wilson, *The Amateur Democrat* (Chicago: University of Chicago, 1962).

7. Bowles, op. cit., p. 338.

8. Edward Banfield, *Political Influence* (New York: Free Press, 1961), pp. 10 ff.

9. Francis Galbraith, "The California State Superintendent of Instruction: His Uses of Power, 1963-1965" Ph.D. dissertation, University of California, Berkeley, 1966.

10. Ibid., pp. 43-44. Galbraith feels the governor believed neutrality was the wisest political position.

11. Harold Irving Goodwin, "A Framework for Education Policy Formation in California" Ph.D. dissertation, University of California, Berkeley, 1964.

12. Leroy C. Ferguson, "How State Legislators View the Problem of School Needs" in Robert Crew, ed., *State Politics* (Belmont: Wadsworth, 1968), p. 481.

13. *San Francisco Sunday Examiner and Chronicle*, May 3, 1970.

14. *Palo Alto Times*, March 10, 1970.

15. Ibid.

16. Herbert Jacobs and Kenneth Vines, eds., *Politics In the American States*, (Boston: Little Brown, 1965), p. 229.

17. Duane Lockard, *The Politics of State and Local Government* (Princeton: Princeton University, 1969), p. 360.

18. Galbraith, op. cit., p. 83.

19. Ibid., p. 83.

20. Comment in Interview with the researcher, April, 1970.

21. See Gerald E. Sroufe, "Recruitment Processes and Composition of State Boards of Education," presented at the annual meeting of the American Educational Research Association, February 8, 1969, Los Angeles, California.

22. *San Francisco Examiner*, February 21, 1963.

23. Comment in an interview with the researcher, April, 1970.

24. Comment in an interview with the researcher, April, 1970.

25. Comment in an interview with the researcher, May, 1970.

26. Robert Salisbury, "State Politics and Education," in Jacob and Vines, op. cit., pp. 331-335.

27. Keith Goldhammer, *Issues and Problems in Contemporary Educational Administration* (Eugene: University of Oregon [Center for Advanced Study in Educational Administration], pp. 88-89).

28. *Analysis of the Budget Bill: 1969-1970, Report of the Legislative Analyst* (Sacramento: California Legislature, 1968), p. 234.

29. *San Francisco Chronicle*, July 20, 1970.

30. Ibid.

31. Max Rafferty, *Response to the Report of the Legislative Analyst*, unpublished memorandum.

32. *New York Times*, May 24, 1970.

33. See Michael W. Kirst, "Federalism and Urban Education," *Education and Urban Society*, February, 1970, pp. 219-231.

34. For an example of this policy urging, see U.S. Office of Education, *Focus on the Future Education in the States* (Washington, D.C.: GPO, 1968).

35. This is carefully documented by Galbraith, op. cit., passim and Myron Millstein, "Functions of the California State Department of Education as They Relate to Two Federally Funded Educational Programs," Ph.D. dissertation, University of California, Berkeley, 1967.

36. Galbraith, op. cit., p. 88.

37. Arthur D. Little, Inc., *The Emerging Requirements for Effective Leadership for California Education* (Sacramento: California State Department of Education, 1964).

38. Arthur D. Little, Inc., *A New Organizational System for State-Level Educational Administration* (Sacramento: California State Department of Education, 1967).

39. Legislative analyst, *Analysis of the Budget Bill, 1969-1970* (Sacramento: California Legislature, 1969), p. 221.

40. Legislative analyst, *Analysis of the Budget Bill, 1966-1967* (Sacramento: California Legislature, Feburary, 1966), p. 261.

41. *The Tangled Web: Final Report of the Assembly Interim Committee on Education* (Sacramento: California Legislature, January, 1967), pp. 10-13.

42. Maxwell Rafferty, *Response to the Report of the Legislative Analyst: 1970-71*, unpublished, p. 1.

43. Legislative Analyst, *Analysis of the Budget Bill: 1970-71*, op. cit., 236.

44. Ibid., p. 187.

45. As quoted by Millstein, op. cit., p. 113.

46. *San Francisco Chronicle*, October 26, 1965.

47. As quoted by Millstein, op. cit., p. 100.

48. Comment in interview with the researcher, May, 1970.

49. U.S. Department of Health, Education, and Welfare, Office of Education, *Guidelines: Special Programs for Educationally Deprived Children* (Washington, D.C.: USOE, 1968).

50. Comment in interview with the researcher, April, 1970.

51. California State Department of Education, *Guidelines: Compensatory Education* (Sacramento: California State Department of Education, 1969), p. 5.

52. Ibid.

53. Legislative Analyst, *Progress Report: Fiscal Review and Analysis of Selected Categorical Aid Education Programs* (Sacramento: California Legislature, April, 1970).

54. Comment in interview with the researcher.

55. California State Department of Education, *California State Plan for Vocational Education* (Sacramento: California State Department of Education, 1967), p. 3.

56. California State Department of Education, *Instructions for Applicants: Vocational Education Act* (Sacramento: California State Department of Education, 1966), p. 5.

57. Comment in interview with the researcher, June, 1970.

58. Arthur D. Little, Inc., *A New Organizational System for State-Level Educational Administration* (Sacramento: California State Department of Education, 1967).

59. Legislative Analyst, Analysis of the Budget Bill: 1968-69 (Sacramento: California Legislature, 1969), p. 156.

60. Comment in interview with the researcher, April, 1970.

61. Interview with Wesley Smith, State Director of Vocational Education, (Sacramento, May 1970).

62. Legislative Analyst, *Analysis of Budget Bill: 1970-1971*, p. 261.

63. Comment in an interview with the researcher, April, 1970.

64. Ewald B. Nyquist, *Emergent Functions and Operations of State Education Departments*, a paper prepared for the Conference on the Emerging Role of State Departments of Education, Columbus Ohio, February 27, 1967, p. 27.

65. Donald W. Johnson, "The Dynamics of Educational Change," *Bulletin of the California State Department of Education*, 32, 3 (September, 1963): p. 6.

66. Millstein, op. cit., p. 50.

67. Sullivan, as quoted by Millstein, p. 74.

68. California State Department of Education, *Impact of Title III NDEA Upon Selected California School Districts*, 1968 (unpublished).

69. Quoted by Millstein, op. cit., p. 152.

70. California State Department of Education, *ESEA–Title II: Manual of Information* (Sacramento: California State Department of Education, 1968), p. 14.

71. Millstein, op. cit., p. 160.

72. As quoted by Millstein, op. cit., p. 162.

73. Legislative Analyst, *Analysis of Budget Bill: 1968-1969*, (Sacramento: California Legislature, p. 215).

74. California State Department of Education, California State Plan: *Title III of the Elementary and Secondary Education Act* (Sacramento: California State Department of Education, 1970), p. 64.

Abbreviations not Explained in Text

CSDE California State Department of Education
CASA California Association of School Administrators
CTA   California Teachers' Association
ADA   Number of pupils in average daily attendance
SEA   State Education Agency
LEA   Local Education Agency
PPBS Program Planning Budgeting System
A95   Required that federal agencies notify governors when grants were made to their state
AFDC Aid to Families with Dependent Children, a federal public welfare program

4

The Politics of Federal Aid to Education in Michigan

Jay D. Scribner

The Michigan Department of Education (MDE) allocates federal aid undaunted by education interest groups, state government, or the public. Education interest groups wrangle unceasingly as to purpose and goals; fiercely partisan politics divide and conquer the legislature and the executive branches of state government; and federal aid issues do not impel Michigan citizens to action. The major architect of the patterns of allocation in Michigan is the state superintendent of public instruction.

In many instances, the federal legislation permits the state to decide how much discretion it will exercise in the allocation of federal funds. Under Ira Polley, state superintendent from 1966 to 1969, and John C. Porter, current state superintendent, the department has often used its discretion to channel funds to areas of the greatest need, even though the federal act may not require such distribution. The department's determination of these areas is facilitated by Michigan's comprehensive planning-needs assessment program, unique among the states studied.

Not a monolith, united in purpose and action, the department is divided internally between the traditionalists, who favor a service role for the department, and the reformers, mainly newer personnel, who envision the department as the champion of educational equality in Michigan. Although the reformers now hold the policy-level positions, the traditionalists are still largely responsible for the administration of federal programs.

But the lack of external participation is both an asset and a liability. While lack of external *influence* (and opposition) has enabled the department to allocate funds discriminately, lack of external *support* hinders the department's campaign for educational equality and progress in Michigan.

Research Assertions and Federal Aid in Michigan[1]

Assertion No. 1. There will be less involvement and political influence by the governor and legislature on federal aid in comparison with state aid.

The Michigan governor and legistature exerted limited influence on federal aid allocation. While state aid allocation policy proposals or decisions were not the central focus of this study, the research tends to support the assertion that political involvement falls along a continuum—from a lower level for federal aid allocation decisions to a higher level for state aid allocation decisions.

Assertion No. 2. The influence and impact of the urban school lobby on the state allocation of federal aid will not be significant.

This assertion was borne out in the study. No direct evidence indicated that urban lobbies influence state department officials in the allocation and distribution of federal funds. However, the needs of the cities appeared to have increasingly high priority among the funding patterns of the federal programs studied. Moreover, Detroit school officials responded immediately and comprehensively to rebut the negative findings set forth in state site-visitation team reports. The possibility of an active urban lobby in the future is suggested by Michigan's apparent political division into a rural-industrial and urban poor-labor alliances.

Assertion No. 3. As federal aid increases and states have more discretion in allocation, pressures will increase on state government from organized interests.

Although study findings did not corroborate this research assertion, external pressures on the state department of education appear to be on the rise. Attempts to reform the department through the abolition of the state board and the appointment of the state superintendent of public instruction by the governor have been unsuccessful; if such reforms should succeed in future years, the department will be brought squarely into the political arena—no longer protected from state and local interest groups. At present, federal aid represents a relatively minor share of the state education budget. The special purposes of categorical federal aid are undoubtedly only vaguely understood by the general citizenry. With little immediate impact on a large proportion of those concerned with local and state taxes, the programs lack the issue relevancy necessary to generate sharply focused public opinion.

Assertion No. 4. The state education agency will attempt to minimize political conflict and pressure by using existing state aid formulas for allocation of federal funds.

State aid formulas in Michigan provide grants-in-aid primarily on a general aid basis and secondarily on a categorical aid basis. Monies are first distributed on the basis of the state equalized valuation for each public school pupil; this distribution constitutes approximately 90 percent of all state support. The remaining 10 percent is distributed for certain special programs, such as transportation, special education, and aid for underprivileged children.

Although the distribution of ESEA-Title I funds essentially adheres to the federal guidelines, in some of the other federal programs, state aid formulas are used in the allocation of federal funds. For example 45 percent of ESEA-Title II funds are allocated on a student enrollment per capita basis; NDEA-Title III provides up to 55 percent of the funds on a variable ratio requirement which approximates the ratio of per pupil allowance established by the School Aid Act (Michigan's grants-in-aid provision). Clearly these programs indicate, if not an adherence, an approximation of existing state formulas. After the application of other criteria, ESEA-Title III provides that geographic distribution must be considered. Federally funded vocational programs also involve minimal criteria which make possible a base percentage of reimbursement for broad distribution of up to 10 percent; if districts comply with additional criteria, the rates can be increased. Thus, although Michigan has developed significant distribution strategies to meet critical educational problems and to reach the state's poverty pockets, our data appear to support this assertion. One can only speculate on the result if all districts did not receive some funds. The Thomas Report (*School Finance and Educational Opportunity in Michigan*)[2] scores Michigan state aid because all districts, even the richest, receive some aid—thus negating the possibility of equalization. This conclusion also has a measure of tenability with respect to federal aid to education in Michigan.

Assertion No. 5. Federal aid, except in the manner restricted by federal guidelines or requirements, will flow within a state as it has in the past.

Implicit in this assertion is the notion that the discretion allowed in allocation decisions on federal aid programs will be used sparingly in the newer programs. While there is no evidence to support the "cold turkey principle" (as illustrated in Michael Kirst's study of California), the ambiguous, vague distribution criteria permit various interpretations of local intent. Such flexibility leaves much to the expert judgments of state department officials. Nevertheless, upon close scrutiny of the federal programs included in this study, in several instances, department officials have strived, within federal guidelines, to target federal funds equitably among schools on the basis of need. Title I criteria have been adopted for selected federal programs to insure that disadvantaged youth receive a larger proportion of benefits. Furthermore, MDE officials have established administrative safeguards to insure that federal aid would not flow in the same manner within the state as it did prior to, or immediately subsequent to, passage of the 1965 Elementary and Secondary Education Act.

Assertion No. 6. SEA personnel are socialized so that they view their proper role as providing technical assistance to LEAs, not enforcing or policing federal requirements or setting program priorities.

This assertion was most accurate when applied to ESEA II and NDEA III; both of these programs were marked by more routine administrative practices and were less likely to involve serious monitoring or evaluative activities. Titles I and III of ESEA and Vocational Education were either designed initially as innovative programs or involved actual target groups of pupils. Although professional personnel at all levels of the department were found to perpetuate localism traditions and to take a "non-policing" service role, more of the reformers within the department were involved in the more innovative and socially relevant programs; these programs aspire to ameliorate the problems of the poor and to develop new methods, content, and organizational approaches. The atmosphere within the department seemed to be affected substantially by the leadership style of the state superintendent and by the balance of power, between those individuals oriented toward localism and the service ideal and those oriented toward educational reform and strong state leadership.

Patterns of Allocation of Federal Aid to School Districts

Great discretion rests with the states in the administration of many of the federal programs. In several instances, the Michigan Department of Education has invoked this discretionary power to distribute funds to areas of the greatest need, rather than to all the districts in the state. Former Superintendent Ira Polley, current Superintendent John C. Porter, and their supporters have successfully incorporated relative need criteria in the several programs. The federally mandated priorities of ESEA I have been adhered to; and in vocational education, the state has tried to meet the varied needs of its citizens. NDEA III and ESEA II State Plans both contain priorities which stress that funds should be allocated to "districts where economic, social, and other population characteristics create a substantial concentration of deprived students." To determine such a concentration, these two programs utilize the ESEA I allocation formula. In many instances, however, lack of staff makes it impossible to administer the programs as effectively as would be desired.

Federal guidelines are quite specific on the distribution of ESEA I funds. Michigan cities with the highest concentration of Title I eligibles are receiving a proportionate amount of funds; school districts located in highly populated areas have a higher concentration of Title I eligibles and thus receive more funds. Of the thirty school districts receiving the largest proportion of Title I funds, sixteen school districts are in the southeastern region (which includes Detroit); thirteen districts are in the southern region of the state (mostly independent, rather than metropolitan or urban fringe cities); and one school district is in the more rural area of the upper peninsula. In 1970-71, the department started to measure costs of Title I programs on an individual school basis rather than on a district-wide basis. The department has also tried to insure that non-public school pupils receive the funds to which they are entitled and has stressed the funding of long-range rather than summer programs.

Vocational education programs in Michigan also reflect the department's determination to put the funds to the best use. Michigan's rapidly developing industry, increasing urban population, and high unemployment rate in rural areas require a multi-purpose program. Michigan has attempted to develop and fund different kinds of programs to meet the different needs. In order to use the limited funds most effectively, area vocational centers have been proposed. Although a greater number of centers are proposed for urban areas which, in turn, have a larger number of ESEA I eligibles, the centers would be distributed throughout the state, including the rural areas of the upper peninsula.

Ninety-three percent of Michigan school districts participate in the NDEA III program. The first priority stipulates that 35 percent of all funds are to be allocated for educationally deprived children, but the state was unable to secure enough funds for the 50-50 matching basis of reimbursement. Fifty-five percent of the funds are allocated on a variable ratio basis of reimbursement, which approximates the ratio of per pupil allowances established by Michigan's grants-in-aid provision.

Under ESEA II, 45 percent of the funds are allocated on a student per capita basis. The second largest share of resources is distributed on the basis of relative need, determined by the special requirements of children of low income families

In ESEA III, the department has spent more than the national average on staff development and dissemination. When two or more programs are of the same quality, the school district that makes the greater tax effort in relationship to state equalized valuation and average personal income receives priority.

Although the researchers found instances where federal funds were being used in lieu of state and local funds and where guidelines were not being followed, Michigan has achieved some success in its efforts to target funds on the basis of need.

Political Factors Shaping Fiscal and Administrative Patterns

A Case of Limited Involvement

Major interest groups, political parties, and branches of state government do not weigh heavily in the decisions of the Michigan Department of Education on the allocation of federal aid. It is not at all clear why the political context of the MDE is, in fact, a case of limited involvement. Is it because federal aid constitutes only a small proportion of the state education budget? Is it because the majority of cities are either unaware or unaffected by the federal aid provided in the programs under study? Or is it the result of a high-pressure political context in which conflict over a variety of issues of concern to the state curbs the influence of any one of them. Undoubtedly, it is at least a combination of all these circumstances. Whatever the reason, respondents in this study consistently and unequivocally stated that interests external to the MDE had little effect on federal allocation decisions.

Michigan's political context is not static nor is public interest in education dormant. As in most states, education issues arouse the interest of Michigan citizens in varying intensities; but their demands and claims are usually projected at state or local issues, rather than at actual activities and programs resulting from federal involvement in Michigan's educational system. State finances, religion and the schools, school district reorganization, inequities in the educational status, and other issues typical of many states contribute to the level of interest and resultant conflicts over education in Michigan.[3]

Despite the presence of these concerns, the MDE is able to allocate federal funds unfettered by obligations to special interest groups, political parties, and state officials. This freedom is the consequence of a unique combination of events and circumstances. Education interests in Michigan are greatly fragmented; little structure exists for aggregating and articulating clearly distinct and unified proposals; and the role of various groups and their interests have only limited and occasional indirect effect on MDE operations. Distinct political ideologies demarcate the Michigan political landscape and the conflict between their supporters diminish the potential influence on the MDE. Finally, although they have evinced considerable interest in education, the executive and legislative branches possess little influence—beyond constitutional and statutory provisions—over the ongoing operations of the state department of education.

In their evaluation of the ability of the major education interests to achieve consensus, Masters, Salisbury, and Eliot observe: "In Michigan there is no continuous or regular pattern of decision-making, or at least none that is easily visible. The final outcome of recommendation cannot be safely predicted. . . . That is, there is no process in Michigan to eliminate or modify the factors that cause conflict over education issues."[4]

Statewide Educational Organization Interests

The influence on MDE allocation decisions exerted by the six major education groups in Michigan depends largely on three interrelated concepts: (1) the bargaining power of the group, (2) the strategies it invokes, and (3) its leverage in the larger political system. Masters et al.[5] have provided detailed descriptions of the political participation of the six groups—Michigan Association of School Administrators (MASA); Michigan Association of School Boards (MASB); Michigan Education Association (MEA); Michigan Federation of Teachers (MFT); Michigan Association of County School Administrators (MACSA); and the Michigan Consolidated Parent Teachers Association (MCPTA). It should be noted that the MACSA is no longer effective since, subsequent to the Masters, Salisbury, and Eliot study, a reorganization of intermediate agencies in Michigan took place.

The bargaining power of education groups varies both in degree and kind. Yet none of the groups has successfully amassed the elements of power necessary to force governmental decision makers to respond directly and affirmatively to their demands. Lack of consensus among the various organizations and different power bases further dissipate their bargaining powers.

Organized interest groups are generally considered less satisfactory than political parties to express broad public interest.[6] Of all the educational interest groups, superintendent and school board organizations come closest to approximating the broader interests of both the educators within the system and the public outside the system. The education group with the greatest potential influence in Michigan is MASA. Representing nearly every community, its members (school superintendents) are regarded as "authorities" on education matters at the local level. Because superintendents are generally perceived to promote the welfare of the entire district, MASA holds the strongest bargaining position. Similarly, local school board members, who feel they represent both the school and the taxpayers, are viewed as without the vested interests of teachers and administrators. Members of the MASB are more apt to have better rapport with state legislators, since, like legislators, most are elected by their own local constituency.

The MEA relies on a large membership and a perceived representativeness of all education interests. Because of competition for membership, and an attitudinal change among teachers, particularly those in urban and large suburban districts, the MEA has tended to move more actively toward a teacher welfare orientation. On the other hand, for the MFT bargaining power lies in the support of organized labor. While it has been described as primarily concerned with teacher welfare, the MFT is more directly involved in urban education issues and, consequently, finds some support from the Detroit and Wayne County Democratic legislators.

Finally, the bargaining power of the intermediate administrators is practically non-existent. Small in number, lacking in prestige among education groups in Michigan, limited in access to legislators and with almost no job patronage for legislators to use, intermediate administrators have never been able to exert much influence on the state legislative process. The MCPTA also has exerted limited influence. Although parents are numerous, reflect varying amounts of prestige, and can rely on face-to-face contact with state legislators, the MCPTA has never achieved a cohesive statewide organization or mounted a militant campaign—requisites for effective lobbying.

The diverse strategies used by the six major groups compound and further illustrate the lack of consensus on education issues. Most effective has been the strategy employed, but sparingly, by MASA, which has organized teams of superintendents throughout Michigan, who contact local administrators and who, in turn, contact their legislators about specific state legislation. MASB capitalizes on the legislative view of school board members as community representatives by playing the "watchdog role." They not only work to influence the opposition or support of legislation; they also sponsor their own legislation through key legislators. The MEA relies on a well-staffed research bureau and provides the "necessary" information to legislators. The MFT relies on its strong democratic support and its ability to borrow some influence from other education groups, especially when Michigan elects a Democratic governor. Since they lack the bargaining power of the other groups, rarely are the intermediate administrators (MACSA) or parents (MCPTA) able to exert much collective influence at the state level.

While the four most active groups seemingly possess much potential leverage, their actual leverage has been less than formidable in effecting responses to their demands. MASA, insisting on its political independence of other groups, has been reluctant to use its potential influence; MASB, reflecting a strong localism tradition, has actually weakened the collective leverage of education groups by occasionally lining up against them on education issues; MEA, perceived as partisan (Democratic),[7] offers an information service which is regarded with suspicion; and MFT, comprised of an urban, Democratic-dominated membership, alienates Republicans, frequently in control of the state legislature.

In summary, there appear to be several natural restraints on the power of any of the statewide educational organizations in Michigan. These restraints not only limit direct influence over the policy process within the MDE, but also indirect influence such as the initiation of state legislation which might affect state department activities. As one government official put it: "Pressure tactics by education groups are frequently futile. They even have a boomerang effect causing the legislator to not just vote negatively, but also to actively oppose a given bill."[8]

Consequently, these same restraints curtail the involvement of educational interest groups in federal aid allocations.

Political Party Interests

Before inferences can be drawn about the motivation, attitudes, and values that underly citizen demands and governmental response, a system's political culture must be understood. In Michigan, the best index of political culture is the diverse—if not polarized—party ideologies. On the surface, the apparent cohesion among Republicans, on the one hand, and Democrats, on the other, would seem to have potential significance for the decision-making behavior of the MDE. Even when parties participate in the selection and recruitment of state board members, this is clearly not the case.

It is important to note the pattern of party affiliations as reflected in the popular vote at presidential elections, the composition of the state legislature, and the occupancy of the governor's office. Until the 1970 election, with the exception of the sweeping Republican defeat in 1964 (with most of the losses occurring in states such as Michigan, where Barry Goldwater's candidacy hurt Republican chances at every level of office), Michigan's electoral decisions have followed a relatively consistent pattern. Table 4-1, shows Michigan's support of the Eisenhower Republican candidacy in popular votes by margins of 11.4 and 11.5 percent; excluding the 1964 election, it also shows an increasing trend in the popular vote for Democratic candidates—2.1 percent margin for Kennedy and 6.7 percent margin for the losing candidate, Hubert Humphrey, in 1968.[9]

Table 4-1

Political Party Affiliation in Popular Vote, State Legislature and the Governorship

Year	% Total Popular Vote Presidential Election			Number of Rep. and Dem. State Legislators				Governor's Party Affiliation	
	Rep.	Dem.	Margin	Rep.	Dem.	Rep.	Dem.	Governor	Party
1952	55.4 (Eisenhower)	44.0	11.4	25	7	66	34	G. Mennen Williams	Democrat (term began 1949)
1953	–	–		24	8	66	34	G. Mennen Williams	Democrat
1955	–	–		23	11	59	51	G. Mennen Williams	Democrat
1956	55.6 (Eisenhower)	44.1	11.5	–	–	–	–	G. Mennen Williams	Democrat
1957	–	–		23	11	61	49	G. Mennen Williams	Democrat
1959	–	–		22	12	55	55	G. Mennen Williams	Democrat
1960	48.8 (Kennedy)	50.9	2.1	–	–	–	–	G. Mennen Williams	Democrat
1961	–	–		22	12	56	54	John B. Swainson	Democrat
1963	–	–		23	11	58	52	George Romney	Republican
1964	33.1 (Johnson)	66.7	33.6	–	–	–	–	George Romney	Republican
1965	–	–		15	23	37	73	George Romney	Republican
1967	–	–		20	18	56	54	George Romney	Republican
1968	41.5 (Nixon)	48.2	–6.7	–	–	–	–	George Romney	Republican
1969	–	–		–	–	–	–	William G. Milliken	Republican
1970	–	–		20	18	53	57	William G. Milliken	Republican

The state legislature (excluding the aftermath of the Johnson-Goldwater election) shows a consistent Republican domination, but during recent years the Democrats have gradually increased their number. Finally, in the 1970 election, the Democrats attained a majority in the state legislature. Occupancy of the governor's office, on the other hand, traditionally has been out-of-step with Michigan political trends. Democratic Governor G. Mennen Williams held office from 1949 until he was replaced in 1961 by John B. Swainson, lieutenant governor. Both governors, seen as supporters of educational programs (Williams definitely the more vigorous leader), were weakened greatly by a lack of legislative support, a consequence of Republican domination (as shown in Table 4-1).

Governor George Romney and his successor, former Lieutenant Governor William G. Milliken, were both Republicans at a time when Democrats were gaining strength in the state legislature. Their relative success in support of state education legislation may be attributed to party affiliation and their ability to work effectively with majority leaders in the state legislature. Michigan's political culture is best characterized as fiercely partisan, where ideological doctrine is expressed and demonstrated through party membership; thus even Republican governors—when supported by a Republican legislature—find it difficult to gain support for public policy proposals which contradict the conventional doctrine of their own party.

Differences in Democratic and Republican value preferences on almost any issue consistently present each Michigan voter with options related directly to the party ideology of his choice. This distinct ideological cleavage between the two parties has enabled the local citizen, especially the party member, to reach personal conclusions on policy proposals, including state educational policies. Thus, through the party structure, the citizen and his state representative may channel their interests and private attitudes toward different policies.

Although this study produced no concrete evidence to suggest that the distinct party ideologies directly affect MDE decisions, Michigan's intense political culture has important implications and perhaps future consequences for educational policy. For example, a research team supported by the Urban Coalition found evidence in Michigan to suggest that high quality school services are provided for students from high socioeconomic backgrounds and low quality school services are provided to students of low socioeconomic backgrounds.[10] A disparity of this sort is extremely important when one considers the traditional rivalries among political parties which tend to divide on rural-industrial alliances versus urban poor-labor alliances. As will be noted in the discussions of state governmental interests, legislative actions historically have tended toward state aid programs that favor the higher valuation school districts.[11] Similarly, the mere suggestion of a partisan state school board in Michigan causes some concern over the equitable treatment of children in school districts relying primarily on revenues derived from a tax base that is distributed unevenly.

A likely association of party ideology with educational policy in Michigan may be found in the traditional rivalries of the political parties over urban-rural and management-labor interests. Positions taken by political parties on decisions related to such concerns most likely would follow the pattern implied in this statement:

... the public school interests have operated in a political context where the economic posture of two parties varied more perhaps than in any other state. Republicans accused the Democrats of being "fiscally irresponsible," "dominated by labor," "anti-free enterprise," and "socialistic." Democrats attacked Republicans with equal vigor and dispatch at the slightest provocation. Democrats viewed the Republicans as being "dominated by business interests," "friends of the rich and enemies of the poor," "anti-progress and pro-stagnation," "right wing and authoritarian," and "rural and backward in outlook."[12]

Within these limits, the patterns of influence emanating from Michigan's political culture seem readily calculable. Democrats, typically pro-labor and residents of the larger cities, look more favorably on the use of scarce fiscal resources to improve the welfare of low income groups; Republicans, on the other hand, would favor new services and programs which would not adversely affect big businesses, such as the automobile manufacturers, or the higher income groups and the rural farmers. Because of these irreconcilable differences, political party interests in Michigan are not likely to contribute substantially to the amelioration of educational problems peculiar to the poor, especially within the inner city, but also outside the central city.

The State Board of Education

Partisan interests also suffuse the recruitment and selection of members of the State Board of Education. The board, the policymaking arm of the MDE, consists of eight members, two elected in each biennial election, who serve eight year terms. The board appoints the state superintendent of public instruction, the chief officer of the department, who serves at the board's pleasure. The eight member board was created by constitutional amendment in 1963. Prior to this revision, the board consisted of four members, elected for six-year terms, and the superintendent was popularly elected for a two-year term. All candidates, including those aspirants for the top positions and those making bids for minor political offices, of which the state board is considered to be one, work as a political unit to bring the major election issues before the public. Such unity would imply subsequent access of party members to the decision making apparatus of the MDE; according to the current and past state superintendents of public instruction, however, board-member behavior does not conform to any predetermined pattern based on party membership. Indeed, its critics have argued that the state board inadequately meets the educational crises in Michigan, is essentially unaccountable to the governor, the legislature, and even the nominating parties, and should be abolished.

The *Report* of Governor Milliken's Commission on Educational Reform, discussed in more detail later, submits the following:

Once the conventions have nominated their choices, the public's role is limited to attempting to select among these. Such a board, members of whom are nominated almost as an afterthought by both political parties, brought into office on the tide of presidential or gubernatorial elections, forced to function in a political unit which is apt to be fiercely partisan, and given only limited power to fulfill the requirements of their office, is bound to fail, and has failed as an effective governing body.[13]

The divergent interests of each party and the structural feature of a partisan elected board are ample grounds for assuming the linkage of political interests to federal aid allocation decisions. Empowered with little authority and relegated to a constitutionally defined position, however, the board is primarily dependent on professionals within the MDE; this dependence effectively isolates the board from external partisan influences, influences present in the executive and legislative branches of Michigan government.

State Governmental Interests

A thorough analysis of gubernatorial and legislative effect on the department demands an in-depth investigation of the informal relationships of legislators, the chief executive and his staff, and other elected executives of state government, and their impact on the decisions and goals of the MDE. Logistically, this study did not allow for such in-depth analyses. Instead, the researchers examined the major attempts of state government to influence, if not restructure and redirect, the organizational development of the MDE. In addition, several leaders of the 1970-1971 legislature, including the Speaker of the House and the Minority Leader, were interviewed.

The researchers in this study relied substantially on two major sources of information: *School Finance and Educational Opportunity in Michigan,*[14] a comprehensive survey supported by the Michigan Legislature and submitted in April, 1967; and *A Chronology of Educational Reform in Michigan,*[15] a report commissioned by the executive branch which reviewed the survey proposals and recommended specific legislative actions. The Chronology was submitted to the governor in January, 1970. These two documents and the impetus and preparation involved in their emergence represent a more formal state governmental strategy to effect changes in the organization and administration of Michigan's educational system, particularly at the state level. At this writing, however, the state legislature had acted upon few of the resultant resolutions and legislative bills.

School Finance and Educational Opportunity in Michigan—"The Thomas Report"

This survey, frequently referred to as the "Thomas Report" after its director, Dean J. Alan Thomas of the University of Chicago, has been acclaimed as the most comprehensive study of elementary and secondary education in Michigan's history. In authorizing this survey, initiated in October, 1966, the Michigan legislature opened the way for a most carefully designed and conducted study on school finance, one that already has received much attention in professional circles throughout the nation. It was proposed by the state board and carried out under the leadership of Ira Polley, who became state superintendent of public instruction shortly before the study was initiated. The Thomas Report was conducted with the assistance of a forty-member Citizens Advisory Committee, numerous state consultants, a National Advisory Committee (comprised of professional leaders of national repute in school governance and school finance), the Midwest Administration Center at the University of Chicago, and several research assistants from universities in Michigan. In its conclusions, the Thomas Report summarized the conflicts and problems in Michigan education:

1. While enrollments in the elementary grades show signs of leveling off, and secondary enrollment continues to grow, both adult education and pre-kindergarten enrollments have been expanding.
2. There is great variation in the educational opportunities available to students in the State of Michigan.
3. There exist critical problems in the financing of urban education. These problems demand adequate financial support from the citizens of the state.
4. In comparison with many other states, vocational education in Michigan is inadequately supported from state funds. Full programs of special education services are not available in certain parts of Michigan. Even where they are available, they may not be provided at the level which is to be desired.
5. The present procedures for the financing of school construction are very costly.
6. The pre-constitution portion of the teachers' retirement funds is presently in serious financial difficulty.
7. Although there has been progress in the reorganization of districts, problems of inequality in educational opportunity and inefficient operation resulting from the persistence of very small districts are still in existence.
8. The procedures for distributing state aid to school districts are overly complex, and do not accomplish the purpose of equalizing educational opportunity.
9. A revenue crisis also faces Michigan's non-public schools. There is a proportional shift in the student body from nonpublic to public school enrollment.[16]

Clearly, the Thomas Report has enormous implications for the overall attainment of equal educational opportunity in Michigan. Not only did the survey detail the status of educational programs and services, it also enabled the state board, legislature and executive branch to knowledgeably deliberate and pursue alternative measures for the achievement of educational opportunity.

A Chronology of Educational Reform in Michigan

The Commission on Educational Reform, author of the *Chronology*, consisted of six distinguished Michigan citizens and Governor Milliken, the chairman. The commission's task was to assess statewide interest and expectations and to present specific policy proposals for state governmental action. It held public hearings in the upper peninsula (the more rural sector of the state), in Detroit (the central city of the state's largest metropolitan area), and in Lansing (the state capital). In addition, the commission established a forty-three member Citizens Advisory Committee which included representatives of the major educational and non-educational private organizations and interest groups. Governor Milliken's commission report begins with this fundamental statement: "....We asked ourselves, and many others, what in our present circumstances stands between the people of Michigan and an adequate and responsive educational system."[17] Its response to the question can be summarized in this assertion, taken from the report:

The organization of public education at the state level in Michigan is a classic case of arrested development. Evolving as it has from a 1908 constitutional provision which merely required the State "to continue a system of primary schools whereby every school district in the State shall provide for the education of its pupils," the State, despite the new Constitution of 1963, still plays a passive role, generally exercising only its custodial charge to "continue" local school districts and see that *each* provides for *its* pupils.[18]

While the commission's report went beyond the recommendations of the Thomas Report in a few of its resolutions, it incorporated many of Dean Thomas's specific alternatives. The commission advocated the abolition of the State Board of Education and its replacement with a state superintendent of public instruction appointed by the governor. More important, the commission recommended substantial changes in the financing of public education, institution of a statewide property tax and the elimination of local school taxes, increased state funding, an enrichment levy, increased excise tax on cigarettes, and the cancellation of property tax credits. An extensive assessment program, the establishment of neighborhood centers for school dropouts, and the development of teacher incentive programs were other areas of reform specified by the commission.[19]

The commission's findings suggest that the MDE is shielded from the governor and the legislature and, therefore, has no accountability. The report declares that the governor's responsibility is very limited; while he has budgetary powers over the operations of the state educational structure, he cannot directly influence the functions of the state board or the state superintendent of public instruction. Likewise, the legislature exercises some fiscal control and enacts legislation affecting the operations of the MDE; yet it has little control over the actual execution of state programs. An elected body, the State Board of Education, according to the commission report, has no direct obligations to the governor or the legislature other than, of course, those mandated by the constitution or legislative action. The governor's commission alleged that the state board has failed to effectively perform its duties.[20]

Finally, the governor's commission proposed far-reaching structural changes in the position of the state superintendent of public instruction. The commission deplored the current status of the state superintendent:

The Superintendent of Public Instruction, who should be the central and key figure in making the state structure function, is selected by a majority of the State Board and serves at its pleasure. While he serves as chairman of that Board, he has no vote, and his impact on the Department is largely a function of the Department's confidence that he will be able to continue to keep a majority of the Board voting to employ him.[21]

The commission proposal to abolish the State Board of Education and to provide for a state superintendent, appointed by the governor, was still another attempt both to strengthen the governor's hand in educational affairs at the state level and to make the department, including its executive officers, accountable to the state government.

The Legislature: Partisan Views on State Governmental Interests

In order to ascertain the Democratic and Republican views on (1) legislative involvement in the allocation of a federal aid; (2) the governor's reform proposal; and (3) the recruitment and selection of state board members, the researchers interviewed William A. Regan (Democrat), Speaker of the House, and Clifford H. Smart (Republican), Minority Leader.

Speaker Regan represents the 3rd Representative District, which includes Detroit and part of Wayne County. Initially elected to fill a vacancy in January, 1958, he has been re-elected to the House in each succeeding session. He corroborated the study findings of little legislative involvement in federal education programs. He suggested, "Federal aid programs are not a concern of legislators . . . primarily because no one [public interest] brings problems of federal aid program distributions throughout the state to the legislator."[22] He noted, however, that Michigan legislators have been very concerned and active in increasing *state* aid to the poorer districts. He felt this trend was the result of two concrete state policies—the 1965 reapportionment and Michigan's split distribution formula. In analyzing Michigan's distribution formula, the Thomas Report found contradictory results and suggested that Michigan's approach to the provision of an adequate financial base not only resulted in gross inequities between wealthy and poor districts, but also failed to stimulate local educational improvements.

Addressing himself to Governor Milliken's (Republican) reform proposals which had achieved little success in the legislature, Speaker Regan cited the "top dog approach implicit in the proposals and at the expense of local autonomy" as the main reason for legislative recalcitrance. He described legislators and their constituencies as less than enthusiastic about the proposed abolition of the state board and appointment of the state superintendent. Accountability and control appeared to be the central issues. Moreover, the governor's proposed budget process was regarded as too lengthy, requiring 12-15 months as it evolved from the state superintendent to the governor and, ultimately, to the legislature. Speaker Regan also claimed that such a process would call for beefing up the intermediate and MDE offices, a task of enormous proportion and one that should precede any change in the existing budget process.

Speaker Regan felt the method of state board selection was insignificant. He noted that the board had been dominated by Democratic nominees, which undoubtedly accounted for the governor's favoring abolition. In 1961, when the new Constitution was instituted during a Republican-controlled legislative session, Republicans called for elected boards. This Constitutional Resolution was implemented under a Republican governor. At the time of the present study, the circumstances were reversed.

Minority Leader Smart, a Republican, represents the 94th District, which includes two counties (Genesee and Oakland) north of Wayne County. Representative Smart had been elected to the legislature in 1964, 1966, and 1968. His interpretation of the legislature's interest in federal education programs in Michigan and the trend toward equalization of educational monies in the state was similar to Speaker Regan's. Representative Smart concluded that: "Federal funds are largely ignored by state legislators even in deliberations over state aid measures." Further, he suggested that the consequences of the thrust toward equalization have caused serious stresses on the citizens of the state: "Michigan has a financial crisis on its hands with respect to funding schools—the tax structure is causing a rebellion in the state."[23]

While Minority Leader Smart agreed that the governor's reform proposal met with little legislative success, he emphasized that the state's attempt at statewide assessment and the appropriations for neighborhood centers were discernible results. He claimed that the Thomas Report had very little new in it and was not innovative as far as "experienced people in these matters" were concerned. He did add, however, that the Thomas Report, by bolstering the governor's proposals for assessment and accountability, increased the visibility of such issues. He also attributed legislator recognition of the growing urban education problem to the Thomas Report.

Republican legislators, according to their minority leader, viewed the predominantly Democratic state board as partisan whenever possible. Of all those interviewed, within state government and the MDE, Representative Smart was the most explicit on the matter of partisanship vis à vis Michigan's State Board of Education. He argued that the state board: ". . . attempts to plan programs and make proposals with tongue-in-cheek to the legislature, requesting programs costing huge sums of money."[24] Moreover, rather than the governor's proposed abolition, he supported an executive appointed board because: (1) it would strengthen the quality of board membership; and (2) it would enhance the governor's opportunity to bring about educational reform, regardless of party.

Representative Smart also suggested that board members are generally "unknowns," do little statewide campaigning, and are elected on the coattails of other candidates. Thus, Republicans instituted the elective method earlier during a Democratic governorship so as to reduce the "political" behavior of state board of education members, and later have called for an executive appointed state board for precisely the same reasons.

In these interviews, both parties in the legislature acknowledged a lack of interest in the distribution and allocation of federal education monies in Michigan. Assuming that their comments represent genuine "partisan view-points," their disagreement on the selection of the state board and state superintendent are easily understood. Since Democrats are gaining greater support and state board members ride in on the crest of victory, not surprisingly, Republicans favor appointment by the governor (who favors abolition), and Democrats favor the present elective system. Changing the system would not necessarily rectify its shortcomings, since MDE officials, legislators, and the governor's representatives agree that partisan politics has little impact on state board decisions.

State governmental interests in Michigan thus have had little consequences for the department's implementation of state and federal programs. Cognizant of the possible influence of the legislature, most interviewees denied any political influence beyond the formal passage of a given bill. Legislative action as a result of the Commission's report is a case in point. At the time of our study, the majority of the proposals either had failed to pass the legislature, were still in committee, or had been altered from their original state. Moreover, the governor failed to find the necessary support even among Republican legislators. The current stalemate is but the newest chapter in Michigan's history of minimal legislative and executive involvement in educational decisions.

The Michigan Department of Education

Policy and administrative decisions at the Michigan Department of Education are molded by two forces: primarily by the prowess and style of the state superintendent of public instruction, the department's leader; and secondarily by the almost contradictory value orientations that divide department personnel into two groups, which the researchers have categorized as traditionalists and reformers. The traditionalists believe that the department's role is a service one—to assist local districts when the districts request assistance. In contrast, the reformers want the department to provide innovative educational leadership in Michigan; this leadership would include evaluation and planning to achieve equalized educational opportunity. A reflection of the state's political culture, the different conceptions of the department's role profoundly affect the administration of federal programs.

Background

At the turn of the century, the state department of education assumed responsibility for education in Michigan, formerly the charge of the legislature. The department's superintendent was limited to appointing non-professionals and a few assistants in preparation for the Smith-Hughes Act of 1917; subsequently, he was restricted to reinforcing the department's capacity both to administer its statistical and rural divisions and to regulate, supervise, and inspect its operations at the local level. The depression years weakened the developing department and halted what little progress had been made. During the years prior to and following World War II, the state superintendent's primary responsibility was to maintain the department—a department with few services to offer local educational agencies.[2 5]

Not until the mid-1950s and the arrival of the space age was this trend reversed. Sputnik and mounting concern for American educational superiority increased demands on the MDE, as on other state departments of education; these new demands and the responses they entailed enabled the MDE to expand its activities. During the last fifteen years, three men have held the office of Michigan State Superintendent of Public Instruction: Lynn M. Bartlett (1957-1965), Ira Polley (1966-1969), and John C. Porter (1969-   ). Their respective styles of leadership substantially molded MDE decisions during the years of increased federal involvement in education.

The Bartlett Years (1957-1965)

Like most of the popularly-elected officials in the upper ranks of Michigan state government during his tenure, Lynn Bartlett was a member of the Democratic party. Although an elected superintendent, he had an extensive background in education as a teacher and administrator in the public schools and as a college instructor. He was a member of many educational organizations, including MEA and MASA. His background and the elective nature of his office forged an educator-politico style of leadership.

Every two years, or four (1957, 1959, 1961, and 1963) of the eight he served as state superintendent of public instruction, Bartlett sought the approval of the voters. Owing his election to the votes, the campaign funds, party work, and the efforts of those who elected him, he had to be aware of the desires of his constituencies and to satisfy them. This, of course, brought the department and the formulation of state educational policy closer to the political arena. However, the department itself was shielded from outside political involvement. As one informant confided, "There just weren't any burning issues involving the MDE. Only two major issues really evolved during this era, and they involved a $200.000 increase in teacher retirement and the introduction of horology into the curriculum."[26] Both subjects clearly lacked the intensity and social impact of contemporary demands on public education.

Bartlett's identification with the Democratic party posed a serious handicap to his capacity for leadership. As indicated earlier, the legislature traditionally has had a Republican majority and consequently perceived Bartlett's legislative proposals as enshrouded in Democratic programs. Superintendent Bartlett's dilemma has been summarized as follows:

... having to maintain a partisan stance toward public school issues in order to retain the strong support of his party and thus remain in office, while at the same time he must support a bipartisan program in the legislature in the hope of legislative victory.

The nature of the office of superintendent of public instruction compounds the difficulty. To gain acceptance and respect within the public school system, he must be regarded as an educational statesman, not a politician. This informal requirement has given the superintendent very little political leverage for the promotion of his own programs even when they bear the Democratic label. Unlike the governor, for instance, who is in a stronger political position, it is difficult for the superintendent to transfer his ballot box popularity into voter support for his programs in the legislature.[27]

The department experienced its most rapid growth during Superintendent Bartlett's term; it shifted gradually from the stricter administrative and regulatory functions of earlier times toward a broader service orientation that included statistical services, school plant planning and curriculum services. This service orientation is still reflected in both the attitudes and behavior of personnel who joined the department during this term and continued to occupy positions during Superintendents Polley's and Porter's terms. Bartlett also used his official status to attempt to modify the state aid formula and to reform the state system for financing education. During his final term, Superintendent Bartlett placed the financial crisis in Michigan education squarely before the predominantly Republican legislature. Shortly before his final term expired, he said:

Two years ago when I spoke to you, I pointed out that if we consider the percentage of all funds (current, building debt) obtained from local and state tax sources, we would find that during the past several years there has been a definite trend to shift more and more of the financial burden to the local level. This trend has not stopped. In 1950-51 the state was contributing 52 percent. Now we find that this has gone down to some 41 percent. During this same period, local contribution rose sharply from 43.5 percent to more than 55 percent.

During the past year $338 million in school aid, including primary money, was distributed to local school districts by the state for operating purposes. Although this represents an increase of about $34 million over 1961-62, it does not represent an equitable share of the additional revenue needed to accommodate increased enrollments and increasing costs of operation.[28]

In response, the legislature provided $200,000 for an in-depth study of educational finance in Michigan, the "Thomas Report."

The Polley Years (1966-1969)

Under State Superintendent Ira Polley, the department girded itself for its campaign to improve the quality of education in Michigan. State leadership, in the most simple terms, encompassed the identification of policy areas of statewide importance and the utilization of evaluation, analysis, and planning to ameliorate and eventually solve Michigan's various educational problems. In preparation for this drive, the department both raised the quality and increased the diversity of its staff—thus providing an internal capability for more enlightened policy formulation and effective implementation.

Polley's leadership style can be characterized as an administrator-promoter—the administrator concerned with internal maintenance and improvement of the means by which the department seeks to achieve existing goals, and the promoter concerned with restructing the means, establishing new departmental goals, and implementing new ideas. Hence, Polley was responsible for "loosening" the rigid structure of the department, so that innovative alternatives could emerge from within and new ideas could penetrate from without.

Despite his brief tenure (1966-1969), Polley was extremely effective, partly because of his appointed status and previous experience.

His appointment to the superintendency by the state board relieved him of the electoral constraints imposed upon Lynn Bartlett and made him somewhat less vulnerable to environmental pressures.

Dr. Polley received his Ph.D. (Public Administration) from the University of Michigan. During the 1940s and early 1950s he was employed by the National Labor Relations Board in Washington, D.C. and in Minneapolis, Minnesota. Subsequently, he served as regional director and chairman of the U.S. Wage Stabilization Board in Minnesota, state controller in Michigan, and as a faculty member at three universities. From 1962-1966, when he was appointed state superintendent, he was executive director of the Michigan Council of State College Presidents. Possessed of extensive governmental experience and, consequently, a broader perspective of bureaucratic workings, he assumed his position unhampered by the usual attitudes, beliefs, and values acquired through a socialization experience as a public educator.

Under Superintendent Polley's leadership, the *Michigan School Finance*

Study ("Thomas Report") was completed and presented to the State Board of Education. Described by department personnel as a "gutsy guy," Dr. Polley worked diligently to implement and improve the ideas generated in the study.

Research, evaluation, and planning were intensified. Superintendent Polley was noted for asking such difficult questions as—"How much money are we spending and are we spending it wisely? Is it being spent for the improvement of our existing education programs, for initiating new programs, or simply to displace existing resources?" In order to maximize the "new leadership philosophy," Polley recruited key individuals to fill decision-making positions within the department. The Bureau of Research, newly reorganized with the responsibility for needs assessment and establishment of priorities for state leadership, offered an initial avenue for recruitment. Polley went outside the state and hired a cadre of highly talented young graduates with demonstrated leadership potential. While Polley's efforts to strengthen the state department from within were significant at the policy level, he had little impact on the lower echelon individuals responsible for federal programs.

Thus, Polley's efforts (1) to disassemble a sizable research bureau concerned primarily with data processing and assistance to local districts in the collection of information on enrollments, etc; (2) to rid the department of the purveyors of the "service ideal"; and (3) to introduce new leadership and a new authority structure within the department were largely successful. As one would expect, however, polarization and potential conflict over departmental goals resulted.

Selected by a thin majority of the state board, toward the end of his tenure, Polley was confronted by intense conflict within the board itself. He took courageous stands on two major issues which had consumed the entire state: (1) aid for parochial schools; and (2) the replacement of the state board by a superintendent appointed by the governor.[29]

The board split evenly on "parochaid," four backing Polley (who opposed it) and four backing Governor Milliken's proposal favoring aid to parochial schools. For several months the board was deadlocked; consensus was impossible, even on the election of its own president. The situation was described in a book entitled *Crusade in Michigan: The Parochaid Story*, as follows:

In late 1969, the role and involvement of the State Board in the Parochaid controversy was to produce dissention and ultimately to bring about the ouster of the State Superintendent, Ira Polley. The Parochaid Bloc on the State Board appeared to many, as being more concerned with the politics and passage of Parochaid than the affairs of public education in Michigan.[30]

Ultimately, the situation deteriorated to the point where Polley took his second stand, this time in favor of the governor's proposal to abolish the state board. A fifth member of the board joined those who had favored "parochaid"; and three members favored abolishing the board. Shortly thereafter, Polley's resignation came forth in the heat of two of the most controversial issues of his career as state superintendent. However, he had strengthened the MDE in its fight to achieve equal educational opportunity in Michigan.

The Porter Years (1969-   )

An insider and educator, John C. Porter had been in the department for thirteen years and was director of the Bureau of Higher Education. He replaced Polley in 1969 and became the first black in the United States to hold the position of Chief State School Officer.

It should be noted that John C. Porter took this office only months before our investigation. Thus, in our attempt to understand the political dynamics within the MDE, especially in the allocation of federal funds, we are in the position of anticipating his leadership style. This is not altogether speculative, however, since interviews with him and several of his colleagues seemed to indicate the direction the department will take under his guidance, and the style of leadership he will demonstrate in fulfilling his responsibilities as superintendent. From his early actions, particularly as revealed in his restructuring efforts and the quality of his personnel appointments, his leadership style apparently will involve pragmatism, experience, and rational decision making.

Superintendent Porter was perceived as a positive force by those individuals within the department who supported department leadership in educational affairs, and imaginative planning in the conception and implementation of the department's service and regulatory functions. Unquestionably a dedicated educator, his commitment and inspiration are strikingly clear in a brief exerpt of his own words:

But though the conditions of our enterprise may be unsettled and uncertain, the objective remains unchanging—*to provide the best in education for all those entrusted to our care.* To some, this may seem too simple or too obvious to need restatement, but it is, I believe, important to remind ourselves that for every educator at every level, this is, was, and ever more shall be the task, inescapable and unaltered. No difficulties, changing situations, or social upheavals can excuse us from its responsibilities.[31]

Shortly after his appointment, Superintendent Porter sought to complete the job already begun by Polley and to impress his own administrative experience and insight on the reorganization process. At the time of the study, Porter had started to break up various divisions, define new service areas, and to make the department more accountable to the state for its activities. Implicit in Porter's strategy appeared to be an attempt to place responsibility more openly in the hands of the department's staff, and, in the process, to give them more exposure to external interests in education.

For example, the Bureau of Educational Services encompassed several major divisions within the department. It included the five federal programs discussed in this study, as well as curriculum and special education. Strongly biased toward localism and decentralization in services and control, the "line" leadership of this bureau had tenure and extensive political support among local superintendents. In favor of a decisive, aggressive department, Porter set out to dissolve this old-line power structure.

Porter masterfully utilized two strategies to realign the power structure within the department. The first involved isolation, essentially the removal of resources, staff, and whatever else necessary to perpetuate the status quo. As one staff member put it, "In some situations there was a gradual reduction of basic resources until the person in charge was left with nothing more than a desk!"[32] When the reduction of resources or replacement of staff was neither practically nor politically feasible, he employed the second strategy—promotion to staff, rather than line, positions (special advisors, consultants, etc.) with higher status. This enabled him to locate new leadership in key positions throughout the department.

Porter proposed twelve major service areas—four in education; four in management; and four in other department responsibilities. General Education Services, Special Education Services, Vocational and Adult Education Services, and Compensatory Education Services were the four educational service areas. Four management service areas were proposed: School Management Services, Research and Evaluation, Student Financial Aids, and Teacher Certification. Lastly, four other areas mentioned were Higher Education Planning and Coordination, State Library Service, Rehabilitation Services, and Departmental Support Services. As Porter discussed each of these areas, he emphatically stressed their purpose in relation to the needs of children and adults throughout the state. Evidence of his effectiveness with state political leaders and representatives of the education profession could not be ascertained for the present study. It would appear that Superintendent Porter introduced a trenchant style of leadership to direct the MDE toward the fulfillment of the value preferences he brought to his office.

Value Orientations Within the Department:
Traditionalists and Reformers

For the study's purposes, researchers characterized department personnel according to value differences: traditionalists are oriented toward localism and the service ideal; reformers, toward a department that exerts strong state leadership and spearheads a reform movement in education.

Traditionalists. The traditionalists commonly saw the department's role as supervising, determining the eligibility of local applications or proposals, advising, consulting, and engaging in more or less routine matters. Traditionalists hold positions throughout the department, although largely at middle and lower echelons. Directors of the various federal programs examined in this study were seen as occupying lower echelon positions and, in large measure, as oriented toward the traditionalist value system. Although several levels down the hierarchy, they have had a significant impact on shaping the overall priorities of the department.

Because they are able to monitor and control information on their areas of responsibility, the traditionalists have continued to build their own "empires" within the department—thus perpetuating the service ideal. For instance, those in charge of federal programs relate directly to their USOE counterparts. Undoubtedly, they often find more reinforcement in Washington for their bureaucratic expertise in grant administration than they do at home. Once procedures have been established, the traditionalist has a mediative or perhaps ministerial role with respect to the administration of a federally-conceived program.

At all levels of the department, traditionalists are concerned not so much with "policing" their state or federal programs, as they are with assisting local officials to interpret application procedures, guidelines, and other information. Monitoring appeared to be handled as a routine matter, formalized to the point wherein voluminous forms, records, check-lists, and documents are handled by federal, state, and local authorities. The minimum criteria set for state and federal programs are evaluated by individual or teams of consultants who spend at most a week and, typically, one day on site. For all these reasons, the impact of the program on the teaching-learning process receives only limited attention and examination. The traditionalist's perception of the department as a service agency, coupled with staffing and time constraints, impedes the improvement of management techniques, the establishment of new standards, compliance enforcement, and, ultimately, the development of more creative leadership.

Reformers. In Michigan, the reformers typically saw their role as providing the most relevant services to local school districts; they envisioned state department personnel as engaged in continuing evaluation, planning, and the formulation of alternative goals for the achievement of equal educational opportunity throughout the state. Likewise, the reformers were attuned to and challenged by the social, economic, and political problems of the larger society.

The reformers in the MDE believed the department's primary responsibilities to be the identification of policy needs, the resolution of the various attendant problems, and the establishment of performance criteria for evaluating local school districts, as well as their own effectiveness in state and federal program administrations.

In keeping with their beliefs, the reformers attempted to launch a cooperative endeavor with local school districts to assess Michigan's educational progress in basic skills achievement and to develop and eventually measure a range of other performance goals. As would be expected, this statewide assessment program met with considerable resistance within the department and among several local school districts.

Approximately seven months of effort went into the development of the assessment plan. Reformers within the department found support from Governor Milliken who signed Public Act 304 on August 12, 1969. Among other items, the Act required the department to develop a "statewide program for the periodic and comprehensive assessment of educational progress" and the "immediate assessment of certain basic skills . . . during the 1969-70 school year."[33]

The newer members of the department, recruited by Superintendent Polley, particularly those of the new Research and Planning Division, and Superintendent Porter and several members of his immediate staff supported the assessment program. High priority was given to the education of children in poor areas of large cities and suburbs, and in rural towns. Many of the reformers noted that the department's staff was particularly weak in the lower echelon and operational positions. Many felt that lack of accountability was a significant departmental problem. To redress the situation, they recommended structural reform and the establishment of lines of communication with outside constituencies; thus concerned individuals and groups could articulate their demands to those within the department responsible for state and federal programs.

Summary

It is abundantly clear that, on the one hand, the MDE operates in large measure rather independently of the intense external political environment which surrounds it. Education interests, to use Iannaccone's conceptualization of Michigan's situation, are characterized by "state-wide fragmented" structural pattern.[34] State governmental interests had negligible impact on the inner-workings of the MDE, beyond the passage of state education laws. Likewise the department appeared to be insulated from political party leaders within the state. On the other hand, the department is sharply divided within. The continuing effort to recruit and select personnel who adhere to the reformers' value orientation may reverse the tradition of limited external involvement. One could hypothesize that, as the department assumes a more aggressive leadership posture in the state, external pressures from a variety of grass-root sources will emerge to resist. Localist traditions permeate subcultures within, as well as without, education; hence attempts to modify methods of resource allocation and distribution in order to equalize educational opportunity throughout the state will be seriously hampered.

**Federal Aid Administration: A
Title-by-Title Analysis**

ESEA-Title I

Both the Thomas Report and the Guthrie Report (*Schools and Inequality: A Study of Social Status, School Services, Student Performance, and Post-School Opportunity in Michigan*) point to inequities within and between Michigan school districts. Cognizant of these inequities, MDE policy-level staff, in recent months, have seized more initiative in directing the use of ESEA-Title I funds by local school districts. While the state department has taken major steps to improve the quality of Title I educational programs, countervailing evidence suggests the need for substantive changes in program administration.

MDE Title I guidelines stress the assessment of educational needs and the establishment of need priorities. Local educators are to plan special programs for students in schools designated as target areas—i.e., with a higher percentage of poverty-level residents than the average of the district as a whole. They are to consider educational needs and subsequently provide programs and services to enable children from low-income backgrounds to achieve their potential in regular school programs. Local applications must also evidence attention to the social, emotional, and health needs of children from low-income families. In short, each proposed project is assessed by state officials in terms of how well it relates to specified objectives, designed to fulfill educational needs and need priorities.

During the past five years, the total number of participants has decreased substantially; in 1965-66, more than 419,000 pupils participated, but in 1968-69, only 135,000 pupils participated. At the same time, the average amount expended per Title I participant has increased. In 1966, the average Title I expenditure was $80 per pupil; in 1970, $240 per pupil. In Michigan, as in many other states, the projects exhibited great diversity and concentrated on only a few educational problems during the first years of Title I. Title I staff in Michigan commented:

Major Title I users do not devote funds to remedial reading. In 1966, sixty percent of all local Title I efforts strongly emphasized reading, most of it remedial. This year, the thirty-two largest users of Title I are applying about 35 percent of their funds to all language arts, and only a small portion of that to remediation.[35]

Recognizing that a child's chances for successful achievement in school are determined largely during the preschool years, the department has given priorities to Title I projects that serve children between prekindergarten and grade 3. Title I staff estimate that approved projects for 1968-69 with enrollments in grade K-6, total 94,768 children, or approximately 64 percent of the children currently being served by Title I funds. Health services, in-service teacher education, and supportive activities for educational programs social work, food, attendance, and pupil transportation—are increasingly emphasized; more than 30 percent of local district allocations was budgeted for supportive activities in 1969-70. Finally, more money is being diverted from equipment and other hardware to the support of additional staff and salaries to implement Title I projects.

Private school children who should be included in Title I projects represent another objective of Michigan's Title I program. MDE guidelines require local school officials to explain in their proposals how educationally deprived children enrolled in private schools will participate in their project. The local school superintendent has the responsibility to inform, assist, and establish working relationships for the determination of needs and services required by non-public school children.

In Detroit there was some indication that school officials have encountered problems in communication between public and non-public schools. MDE evaluators have recommended that: "A meaningful relationship with private schools for the planning of services to private schools be established."[36] Detroit school officials, in their rebuttal of the MDE site-visit report, however, contend that they have made every attempt to establish contacts with non-public schools; they allege that they have been threatened with audit exemptions for pro-graming too many funds to non-public school children, some of whom Detroit contends were ineligible for funding.

While the report will be discussed later in the section, the Detroit-MDE dispute does highlight ingredients that dilute department attempts to enforce Title I provisions for private school children. For example, Detroit suggests that the problem lies with the non-public school representatives who act more as monitors and liaison persons to the city's Title I program than as individuals determined to: "develop and insure successful programs in (their) schools and to insure the eligibility factor."[37] Detroit also places some blame on the depart-ment, arguing that no specific guidelines on the nature of their relationship to non-public school children have been issued. If the Detroit school system exemplifies a common situation, the department should devote more attention to helping local educational agencies to improve the public-non-public aspects of Title I.

Finally, the thrust of ESEA-Title I in Michigan has evolved to an emphasis on projects sustained for a relatively long period of time. Convinced that "summer only" projects make little impact on the disadvantaged child, the MDE will fund Title I summer programs only if the local district can demonstrate that a comprehensive and sustained local effort will continue the program during the succeeding year.

Resource distribution, concentration and comparability. Title I funds are distributed by the MDE on the basis of project areas with high concentrations of children from low-income families. Local school officials must determine those attendance areas where the percentage of children who come from low-income families per school attendance area is at least as high as the average for the district. Schools are listed in rank order to determine those public schools serving the highest concentration of such children. Sources used include local welfare agencies, Aid to Dependent Children Agency, Economic Opportunity Office (e.g., Headstart data and needs discovered through Community Action Programs), and local school personnel (e.g., principals, visiting teachers, psychologists and guidance personnel).

Expenditure patterns for Title I funds are portrayed in Tables 4-2 and 4-3. Table 4-2 shows large districts spending more for administration and fixed charges and less on transportation, health, food, and building costs. On the other hand, Table 4-3 suggests that the larger districts offer more diversified programs, whereas the smaller districts have allocated slightly more than 50 percent ($262,084 of $515,118) for reading.

Ranking the thirty school districts receiving the largest proportion of Title I funds, Table 4-4 indicates that (1) cities with the largest concentration of Title I eligibles are receiving a proportionate amount of funds; (2) school districts located in highly populated areas have higher concentrations of Title I eligibles, thus receive more funds; and (3) distributions of Title I funds on the basis of

Table 4-2
Title I ESEA Expenditures by Categories

	1967-78 All Districts	1968-69 32 Largest Districts Receiving Over $100,000 Grants Each	40 Districts Receiving Grants Under $10,000 Each
Administration	4.5%	8.%	4.0%
Instruction	71.0	70.	70.8
Attendance	.5	.5	.6
Health	1.6	1.	4.7
Transportation	1.9	1.	3.4
Operation and Maintenance	.5	4.5	7.2
Fixed Charges	13.8	12.	6.8
Food	.8	.5	2.8
Community Services	1.7	2.5	.4
Equipment	3.0	−	.0
Building, Remodeling, Sites and Portables	.3	−	3.0

(Figures may not add to 100% due to rounding.)

Source: Michigan Department of Education, *Federal Aid to Education in Michigan: A Report on Elementary, Secondary and Adult Programs* (Lansing, Michigan Department of Education, August 1969).

Table 4-3

Title I, ESEA Distribution of Instructional and Supportive Services Funds among Activities

	Full Year & Summer		Summer Only	
Instructional Services	32 Districts* Receiving Grants Over $100,000	40 Districts Receiving between $5,000-10,000	32 Districts Receiving Grants Over $100,000	40 Districts Receiving between $5,000-10,000
Cultural Enrichment, Art, Music	$ 675,922	$ 64,612	$ 153,215	$ 5,413
Voc. Ed.-Business Ed.-Industrial Arts	258,820	9,964	8,387	-0-
English-Reading	3,489,487	262,084	476,029	19,151
English-Others	1,182,686	45,718	460,912	2,657
Mathematics	756,790	34,166	144,197	4,984
Phys. Ed./Recreation	99,558	20,062	34,034	5,200
Handicapped	46,395	1,754	6,000	577
Pre-K and Kindergarten	1,390,432	424	78,846	-0-
Supportive Services				
Attendance	323,815	1,300	4,251	650
Food	91,780	17,398	14,640	4,757
Guidance	602,591	12,210	55,487	260
Health-Dental, Medical Psychological	289,460	21,572	20,690	1,260
Library	549,791	700	16,104	350
Transportation	198,973	17,676	10,480	7,688
Social Work	285,136	600	2,240	-0-
In-service Education	1,225,095	4,878	15,200	889
Totals	$11,496,731	$515,118	$1,500,712	$52,934

Source: Michigan Department of Education, *Federal Aid to Education in Michigan: A Report on Elementary, Secondary and Adult Programs* (Lansing, Michigan Department of Education, August 1969).

Table 4-4
Breakdown of ESEA I Funds According to School Districts

School District*	Membership	Eligibles	% of members	% of elig. compared to others	Money Allocated	Regional Type
1. Detroit City	295,907	76,668	26	56.07	9,470,929	Wayne, Oakland & Macomb Met. Core
2. Flint City	47,867	4,174	—	3.05	762,465	South Metropolitan Core
3. Grand Rapids City	34,185	5,087	—	3.72	649,868	South Metropolitan Core
4. Saginaw City	23,433	3,850	—	2.82	475,260	Upper Peninsula Met. Core
5. Pontiac City	24,055	3,029	—	2.22	428,486	Wayne, Oakland & Macomb Met. Core
6. Benton Harbor City	12,190	2,632	22	1.92	341,240	South City
7. Lansing Public	32,184	2,676	—	1.96	338,621	South Met. Core
8. Kalamazoo City	19,384	2,309	—	1.69	280,419	South met. Core
9. Battle Creek City	11,710	1,977	—	1.44	233,048	South met. Core
10. Port Huron City	14,596	1,830	—	1.34	207,118	South City
11. Muskegon City	10,757	1,610	—	1.18	206,872	South City
12. Bay City	15,835	1,162	—	.85	187,697	South City
13. Highland Park City	8,009	1,202	—	.88	179,963	Wayne, Oakland & Macomb Met. Core
14. Jackson Union	14,910	1,138	—	.83	163,895	South City
15. River Rouge	3,785	1,299	34	.95	143,899	Wayne, Oakland & Macomb Urban Fringe
16. Muskegon Heights	4,324	1,021	24	.75	129,378	South Met. Core
17. Hamtramck City	3,345	1,221	37	.89	128,069	Wayne, Oakland & Macomb Met. Core

18. Inkster City	5,087	875	—	.64	124,974	Wayne, Oakland & Macomb Urban Fringe
19. Ferndale City	8,530	982	—	.72	122,951	Wayne, Oakland & Macomb Urban Fringe
20. Mt. Clemens Comm.	6,710	1,045	—	.76	118,557	Wayne, Oakland & Macomb City
21. Monroe City Pub.	8,641	959	—	.70	107,954	South City
22. Roseville City	14,187	801	—	.59	104,859	Wayne, Oakland & Macomb Urban Fringe
23. Ecorse Pub.	4,393	849	—	.62	103,669	Wayne, Oakland & Macomb Urban Fringe
24. Ann Arbor City	18,164	819	—	.60	100,575	South Met. Core
25. Wayne Comm.	20,209	871	—	.64	100,337	Wayne, Oakland & Macomb Met. Core
26. Waterford TWP	17,665	698	—	.51	99,147	Wayne, Oakland & Macomb Rural Community
27. Dear Born City	22,302	842	—	.62	99,027	Wayne, Oakland & Macomb Urban Fringe
28. Royal Oak City	20,201	855	—	.63	91,767	Wayne, Oakland & Macomb Urban Fringe
29. Taylor TWP	19,029	717	—	.52	88,315	Wayne, Oakland & Macomb Urban Fringe
30. Farmington Pub.	15,265	624	—	.46	88,077	Wayne, Oakland & Macomb Urban Fringe

Source: Data compiled for this table were drawn from working papers made available during an interview with the author.

Note: Metropolitan Core—One or more adjacent cities with a population of 50,000 or more which serve as the economic focal point of their environs.

City—Community of 10,000-50,000 that serves as the economic focal point core or city.

Rural Community—a community less than 2,500.

*School districts are ranked according to the amount of money allocated.

high concentration of Title I eligibles resulted in a geographic distribution, as follows: (a) sixteen school districts in the southeastern region (Wayne, Oklahoma and Macomb Counties); (b) thirteen school districts from the southern region of the state (mostly independent, rather than metropolitan or urban fringe cities); and (c) one school district from the more rural area of the upper peninsula. It should be noted that these thirty districts receiving the most funds do not represent a statistical sample of all the districts in Michigan receiving Title I funds, nor does the data reveal the intra-district schools which actually receive funds. Without data on the specific schools, it is impossible to draw completely accurate conclusions about Title I allocations.

The latter issue, actual expenditures for individual "target-area" schools, introduces the question of comparability. This issue had not been completely resolved when the research for this study was underway. In essence, "comparability" required each local school district to demonstrate that comparable services and expenditures, provided with state and local funds, are maintained between Title I project and non-project areas. Then U.S. Commissioner of Education Allen's memorandum on comparability, issued in March, 1970, called for criteria enabling state and federal officials to determine if, in fact, local educational agencies adhered to the comparability requirements.

In June, 1970, Assistant Superintendent Norman Berkowitz prepared an in-house memorandum for State Superintedent John C. Porter.[38] Berkowitz's memorandum attempted to clarify "comparability" standards for Michigan and to suggest possible courses of action in implementing these standards.

Two basic policy recommendations were made to ensure compliance with the comparability provision. In order to increase efficiency and effectiveness, costs in Title I programs, formerly determined on a district-wide basis, would, during the 1970-71 year, be determined on an individual school basis. The second recommendation was to exclude existing state compensatory education expenditures from the base date before determining comparability of expenditures. It was felt that this would preclude the use of state categorical funds to meet the necessary average expenditure per pupil for compliance with federal comparability standards.

In retrospect, resource distribution apparently is based largely on local decisions of need and varies with the types and costs of services in large and small districts. The data also suggest that, geographically, Title I funds are heavily concentrated in the more populated areas and spread rather thinly among the less populated areas of the state. While this geographic distribution reflects the highest concentrations of poverty in the state, it may indicate the need to improve resource utilization and program diversity in the more rural poverty areas.

Evaluation and monitoring. Ninety percent of the Title I projects require additional information or revision upon initial application evaluation. Problems are typically minor and frequently involve numbers of children to be served and further justification of expenditures. Few districts make applications for use of Title I funds for more general activities than specified in the federal requirements. Only one district had not complied with these requirements (as of August 1970-71) and indicated that it would not amend its project. All such projects are considered illegal by department officials and are rejected.

Evaluation has a prominent position in the MDE's Title I guidelines. Pre-, during, and post-project review are advocated, and fourteen possible evaluation procedures are suggested. Yet, the guidelines do not specify nor require the development of objectives for the various dimensions of a project. Rather, if specific objectives based on the identified needs of children have been posed and if the activities of the project were designed to meet these needs and objectives, the extent to which the specific objectives have been achieved should be evaluated. However, on their application forms, local school officials are asked to state two or three specific objectives for each component of the proposed project and to indicate the yardstick that will be used to measure the attainment of the specific objectives. Thus, it can be assumed that if Title I projects are properly executed and monitored, the goals stated in the application could be evaluated effectively.

Considering the logistics and staff required, Title I projects are monitored quite extensively. By 1967-68, MDE staff members had made approximately 1,500 local school visits, and between 1968-70, every local district in Michigan had been visited at least once for monitoring purposes. Follow-up consisted mainly of forwarding letters and reports which contained suggestions and recommendations for the improvement of the projects observed. One MDE official gave the following description of monitoring activities:

There are eight Title I-ESEA consultants in the MDE, and each one will make approximately 25 on-site visits for purposes of quality control this year. The visits range in length of time from one hour for small districts to a week in a large district such as the City of Detroit. Visitations to large districts are on a team basis. Last year the Michigan Department of Education had 16 consultants in Detroit for an entire week. Generally speaking, consultants make visitations on an individual basis getting to one or two schools in a day. They follow up their visits with a written report.[39]

Brief visitation report forms are used for all but the larger districts. Each education consultant must provide at least a half-page of narrative comment and indicate on a rating scale of four items (commendable, acceptable, questionable, and deviations) the suitability of the project with respect to:

> Adherence to target area concept
> Program Coordination
> Class loan
> Dissemination

Equipment Accounting and Utilization
Personnel Utilization
Non-public Involvement
Planning
Number of Students Served
Scope of Program
Selection of Students
Parent Involvement
Evaluation

Since the larger cities have higher concentrations of children from low income families, they merit a more lengthy narrative report, such as the 1970 site evaluation of the Detroit Public School District. The report consisted of general, frequently critical, comments and approximately thirteen recommendations. Eight of these recommendations were directly related to federal regulations. Detroit's lengthy rebuttal clearly illustrates the problem of differing interpretations of federal regulations. In their rebuttal, the Detroit officials contended:

It is difficult to believe that on the basis of a four-day visitation by a team composed of many members that are totally unfamiliar with the Detroit Public Schools, its problems, or its projects, that the great majority of the comments made by the visitors regarding local Title I programs are credited or even true.[40]

Moreover, the Detroit Superintendent of Schools indicated that he was unaware of the department's extensive monitoring activities, nor could he relate follow-up information by department personnel.

With an urban orientation in a largely rural state, and with a bureaucracy larger than the other districts and possibly the MDE, Detroit understandably would feel the need to justify its operations. However, the misunderstandings and differing conceptions illustrate the need for more effective state-local communication and monitoring procedures. Nevertheless, MDE Title I visitation teams do influence a district's actions. In fact, the Detroit rebuttal indicates quite specifically the Detroit school system's attempt to comply with previous state recommendations. The state Title I staff had suggested that funds were being spread too thinly in the Detroit public schools. Consequently, the district withdrew Title I services from some Detroit schools with up to 39 percent of their pupils from low income families and reallocated these resources to schools with higher concentrations of eligible students.

Cooperation and community involvement. The MDE efforts to facilitate cooperation among federal programs at the state level and among school districts and community agencies at the local level have only been partially successful. At the state level, minimal coordination appeared to exist between the Title I program and the various other federal programs. In-service training and equipment provisions have been the principal areas of cooperation, especially with ESEA-III and NDEA-III staff. It was estimated that 90 percent of the cooperative effort of Title I projects involves recruitment preparation and in-service training for professional and paraprofessional staff.

Title I staff have encouraged interdistrict cooperation to ameliorate educational problems shared by educationally deprived children in different districts. The purpose of interdistrict cooperation was to determine if high priority needs could best be satisfied on an interdistrict basis. To avoid unnecessary duplication of programs, local educational agencies are requested to consider existing projects of community agencies, such as the Office of Economic Opportunity.

Finally, in various memos and bulletins, the department stresses the need for community involvement. Reportedly, Michigan parents have been actively involved, both formally and informally, in all phases of Title I projects—in planning, evaluation, lunchroom and playground supervision, and in the classroom, as either paid or volunteer teacher aides. Most of the urban districts maintain formal advisory committees. Despite this participation, state department officials reported a decrease in the number of involved parents, from 19,964 in 1967-68 to 12,599 in 1968-69. To halt this decrease, as of 1970-71, the department will require that a project application demonstrate local district commitment to involve parents of Title I children in an advisory capacity, planning and/or evaluation of the project.

Vocational Education

The Michigan Department of Education has treated vocational education somewhat differently from the other federal programs. While Michigan's vocational education staff has attempted to allow for federal intent, it also has incorporated its own innovative ideas. The Division of Vocational Education has the specific responsibility for administering the state plan. Within the framework of state and federal rules, regulations, and guidelines, the division provides various services to local school districts, colleges, and universities. In addition to the promotion and development of vocational and technical programs, services include evaluation, research support, dissemination of information, occupational advice, and new program development.

Two major goals provide the framework for the vocational and technical education program in Michigan. The first goal emphasizes the development of programs appropriate to the needs of specific groups of individuals, rather than general programs available and applicable to everyone. Vocational educators, therefore, are encouraged to provide diverse programs and courses of study to help individuals with various vocational aspirations. The second major objective emphasizes the development of a skilled manpower pool to meet the needs of Michigan's expanding economy.

Long-range program planning.[41] The MDE's long-range plan advocates continuous study of current and projected vocational education needs. Presumably such constant examination will facilitate the establishment of goals and objectives for future programs. Assessments are made of current and potential students. Programs are projected for occupations in which employment opportunities are available currently, and will be available during approximately a five-year span. Moreover, long-range planning includes the anticipation of ancillary services needed to increase the effectiveness of programs.

On the basis of these assessments of long-range goals and objectives, federal and state funds are committed for both new and on-going programs, for courses of study, and for projects which meet the greatest need of the greatest number of children.[42] As a result of data collected in the various studies, it has been shown, for example, (1) that rapid technological advancement has created demands for a higher level of skills in the Michigan labor force, and (2) that with increasing population growth in the urban centers and out-migration and high unemployment conditions in sparsely populated areas, a multi-purpose vocational program is needed—particularly for the disadvantaged population living in different regions of the state.

The MDE's strategy for dealing with the problems inherent in long-range planning has been to initiate the concept of area vocational centers. The plan for these centers evolved from the department's long-range commitment to continual study of Michigan's manpower needs by geographic regions. Local school districts were assisted in their conducts of manpower surveys to ascertain the need for area vocational centers. With the cooperation of local employment agencies and advisory councils, forty-one studies have been completed. A state report, the result of these studies, and a 1966 Michigan Manpower Study, conducted by the Battelle Memorial Institute, enabled the department to project Michigan's long-range manpower needs.

The Thomas Report on school finance showed the five largest school districts to be located in the Detroit SMSA and southern Michigan.[43] Charts provided in the state plan correspond to these data. Since population increase in the urban centers is associated with an increase in the number of disadvantaged, data on these variables were considered in the plans for area vocational-technical centers. Indeed, there appears to be a significant association between population density, ESEA-Title I eligibles, and projected area vocational-techincal centers. It is important to note, however, that the projected centers are distributed throughout the state.

Specific occupational programs for the various centers were not identifiable in the data considered for the present study. The greatest rate of unemployment is in the northern regions of Michigan, an area that differs markedly from the southern, more metropolitan areas; and the vocational-technical curricula required in the more rural north would probably differ substantially from that needed in the southern region. Some of the eleven proposed centers for the

Upper Peninsula would have an enrollment potential of less than 500 students, necessitating cooperative arrangements among the centers. In sum, it would appear that the MDE has concentrated its vocational funding resources in the areas of greatest need—particularly in the disadvantaged urban centers and rural communities.

Annual Program Planning and Resource Allocation Priorities.[44] Annual program planning is required in the state plan and the Vocational Education Amendments of 1960. The magnitude of the annual program is illustrated by federal and state contributions to the 1968-69 budget. The federal contributions of $9,582,011 were supplemented by state support of $1,950,772. These resources made it possible to devise an annual plan which included such services as instructional reimbursement, construction projects, instructional equipment, and salary supplements for vocational educational staff. Annual program planning by the MDE's vocational education staff involves priority determination within the constraints of available federal resources and federal allocation and distribution criteria.

Constraints imposed by the funding capacity of the Vocational Education Amendments of 1968 were discussed in Michigan's annual program plan. For example, the plan suggested that these constraints would be eliminated only if the programs were funded at the full level of authorization. At lower levels of funding, serious implications for MDE resource allocation would arise. Thus, to allocate resources as accurately as possible, the plan anticipated a reduction in the total amount of funds—federal funds, to $9,105,044; and state funds, to $1,989,004, a net loss of $438,735.[45]

The Vocational Education Act of 1968 earmarks federal vocational education funds in the following manner:

. . . a minimum of 15% of available federal funds *must* be spent for the disadvantaged
. . . a minimum of 15% must be allocated to post-secondary programs
. . . a minimum of 10% must be allocated for use with physically and mentally handicapped persons[46]

Thus, 40 percent of the anticipated federal funds *must* be earmarked for the above-stated purposes.

The desire to continue on-going vocational programs at a level approximately equal to the 1968-69 level imposed an additional constraint on the MDE. Moreover, the vocational education staff recognized that in order to comply with federal provisions and operate within the limitations of the available funds, some programs and projects would have to be supported at lower and less desirable levels; this reduction would make the expansion of existing projects extremely difficult.

Annual program planning involves four major federal criteria which must be considered for determining statewide priorities: manpower needs, vocational education needs, relative ability to pay, and relative costs of programs. One informant indicated that it was almost impossible to devise an effective formula which would adhere to these combined criteria. The formula finally agreed upon by state department personnel consisted of these four criteria and sixteen sub-criteria or factors which were weighed equally in determining priorities and percentage of funding. The four major criteria and the sub-criteria developed by the MDE for determining relative priority of local vocational education applications are:

Manpower Needs and Job Opportunities

1. The local educational agency operates vocational education programs in labor market areas which exceed the state average unemployment rate.
2. The local educational agency operates vocational education programs which have been identified by governmental and non-governmental agencies and institutions as new and emerging occupations.
3. The local educational agency operates vocational education programs which meet identifiable local employment needs.
4. The local educational agency operates vocational education programs which meet identifiable state and national employment needs.

Vocational Education Needs

1. The programs submitted show evidence of meeting the needs of disadvantaged youth.
2. The programs submitted show evidence of meeting the needs of the handicapped.
3. The program gives evidence of the extent to which vocational education is available for secondary school youth.
4. The program gives evidence of the extent to which vocational education is available for post-secondary youth and adults.
5. The program gives evidence of the extent to which vocational education is available for out-of-school youth and adults.
6. The programs submitted provide evidence of meeting the needs of unemployed youth.

Relative Ability to Provide Resources

1. The local educational agency is located in a redevelopment area designated by the Department of Commerce.

2. The local tax effort of the local educational agency exceeds the state average or the average available wealth per student is less than the state average.
3. The school district has been designated as economically depressed, as identified by Elementary and Secondary Education Act criteria.
4. Income, measured by per capita or comparable indices, in the area is less than the state average.

Relative Costs of Programs, Services and Activities

1. Higher construction costs due to variations in price and wage levels incurred by local educational agencies will be considered.
2. Higher instructional cost per student evidenced by a lower than average teacher-pupil ratio will be considered.
3. Instructional salaries incurred by local educational agencies which exceed the state average will be considered.
4. Transportation services as reflected by higher than average expenditure per student by local educational agencies will be considered.
5. Maintenance of plant costs as reflected by higher than average expenditures per student by local educational agencies will be considered.
6. A local tax effort which is equal to or greater than the average local tax effort in the state for all programs, services, and activities will be considered.[47]

A base percentage rate of 10 percent was budgeted for fiscal year 1970 for secondary, post-secondary and adult programs. Local applications were scored, based upon the above-mentioned criteria, and as the score increased from the 1 to 5 factor score needed for the minimum percentage of 10 percent, 3 percent increases were reimbursed to eligible local school districts. Because of limited funds, however, a minimum score of one had to occur in each of the four major federal criteria for local school districts to qualify for new programs. The breakdown of factor scores and reimbursement rates shown below suggest that local educational agencies could receive up to 10 percent beyond the base rate for factor scores of 1 to 5. Factor scores and reimbursement rates are as follows:[48]

Factor Score	Reimbursement Rate
1 - 5	Base percentage
6 - 10	Base percentage plus 3%
11 - 15	Base percentage plus 6%
16 - 20	Base percentage plus 9%

To comply with the federal requirements for programs for the disadvantaged and handicapped, reimbursement rates were established for secondary, post-secondary, and adult programs. Exceptions to all new programs complying to these federal regulations were:

1. A minimum score of one must occur in each of the four major criteria to be eligible for consideration.
2. Those local educational agencies obtaining a total of five factors or more within the two criteria; relative ability to provide resources and relative cost of programs, services, and activities, may receive up to an additional 10% reimbursement over the scheduled rate.
3. In addition, a separate base percentage will be established for disadvantaged and handicapped programs dependent upon availability of funds.

Total Factors Score	Reimbursement Rate
1 - 5	Base percentage
6 - 10	Base percentage plus 15%
11 - 15	Base percentage plus 30%
16 - 20	Base percentage plus 45%

The percentage deviation between the Total Factors Score category will be 15%. Due to the anticipated higher base percentage, the possible additional 10% reimbursement for other new programs does not apply.

The criteria and factors will also be utilized in funding requests for reimbursement of expenditures for construction, equipment, and ancillary services. However, such reimbursement will be considered on a project basis rather than on a state-wide formula.[49]

Clearly, the state plan provides ample operational procedures for allocating federal funds on the basis of the major federal priorities. State and federal criteria developed for determining eligibility and level of funding for the disadvantaged and for new program development suggest consideration of other factors, not always apparent.

The vocational education program director acknowledged that MDE efforts to meet the vocational needs of the disadvantaged were inadequate—a situation, he felt, that was common to other states as well.

Table 4-5, taken from statistics included in the state plan, shows comparisons between (a) percentages of disadvantaged population enrolled in vocational education programs and (b) overall percentages of students enrolled in secondary, post-secondary and adult vocational education. Although in each program the rate of estimated increase in enrollments for disadvantaged is significant, by 1974 involvement by the disadvantaged represents only: (1) 15.9 percent of all disadvantaged secondary (9-12) students; (2) 6.4 percent of all disadvantaged

Table 4-5

Percentage Comparisons Between (a) Disadvantaged and (b) All Secondary, Post-Secondary and Adult Students Enrolled in Michigan Vocational Education Programs

	Secondary		Post-Secondary		Adult	
	a	b	a	b	a	b
Current status (1967-68)	7.0	27.7	.5	4.6	1	2.5
Estimated (1970)	9.0	30.0	1	4.9	2	2.3
Estimated (1974)	15.9	40.0	6.4	5.8	9.3	2.3

Source: *The Michigan State Plan for Vocational Education*

post-secondary (ages 20-24) students; and (3) 9.3 percent of all disadvantaged adult (ages 20-65) students.

It is important to note that state support for vocational education has not increased substantially since the passage of the Vocational Education Act of 1963. While federal funds increased from $2.1 million to $14 million, state and local funds in Michigan only rose from $1.2 million to $1.8 million. Because state support did not increase at a comparable rate to federal funds, total revenues have failed to keep up with program expansion and inflated costs. As a result, the rate of reimbursement has dropped below 20 percent.

Allocations for instruction, nevertheless, have increased when and wherever possible. The Thomas Report recommended that net costs (after deducting state and federal contributions) for vocational education instruction should not exceed the costs of other instructional programs. Estimated allocation of funds for state vocation education programs for fiscal year 1970 underscores the heavy burden these programs place on local resources. Sixty-nine percent of the total funds estimated for fiscal year 1970 would be contributed by local educational agencies; 25 percent would be contributed by the federal government; and the smallest share of all, approximately 6 percent, would be contributed by the state.

It is these fiscal arrangements that have made it difficult to place vocational education programs designed specifically for the disadvantaged and the handicapped higher on the scale of public concern in Michigan. To offset such discrepancies, the MDE has taken a novel approach to vocational education program administration. As indicated earlier in our discussion of long-range planning, Area Vocational Education Centers were designed to enhance the "delivery system" and thus improve the quality of instruction for more children with differing needs. The centers also were designed to encourage more efficient use of fiscal resources. Vocational education staff members would hasten to add, however, that more financial resources must be forthcoming to relieve the strain on the limited budgets of local school districts.

The problem of limited funds more acutely affects the implementation of some of the more imaginative programs conceived by vocational education staff members. Occasionally, new programs and priorities in such areas as vocational counseling and guidance and vocational teacher training have had to be curtailed, especially where there was a special need for programs in previously designated areas, e.g., the dropout problem.

Thus, the limitations imposed by insufficient funds, as well as by inefficient local, state, and federal funding arrangements, seriously frustrate the state department's vocational education efforts. Even if available resources were used more efficiently, the MDE would still find it difficult to comply completely with federal priorities, particularly in those programs involving the disadvantaged and handicapped students.

Advisory councils and cooperative relationships. In compliance with federal regulations, Michigan's State Board of Education has appointed a State Advisory Council for Vocational Education to provide advice and counsel to the department. Although several state department personnel were critical of the actual performance and contribution of advisory councils, advisory committees are required for all vocational-technical programs funded by the department. Underlying these requirements is the assumption that education is a cooperative activity of educational institutions and the communities they serve. These local committees go beyond federal requirements and bring business, industry, and other community representatives closer to the instructional process.

The State Advisory Council participates in the preparation and evaluation of long-range and annual programs. Because the state plan is vague on the composition and activities of the council, this body is used by the State Board of Education to furnish advice and evaluative commentary on an "as needed" basis. More significant are the local advisory committees.

Vocational-technical advisory committees represent various community, educational, business, and industrial agencies. In contrast, occupational advisory committees include persons with a particular occupational background. They provide regular advice and counsel to local school administrators, assist in determining local needs, ensure continuity in local programs, and advise in the development of curriculum content and the acquisition of needed facilities and equipment.

Advisory councils and committees are only one avenue leading toward the creation of a cooperative relationship in vocational-technical education in Michigan. Cooperative arrangements also are sought with the State Employment Service, with state and local agencies concerned with the handicapped, with public and non-public institutions concerned with teacher training, and with organizations dealing with manpower needs. Moreover, representatives for the disadvantaged and handicapped are recruited for membership on advisory committees.

A tangible consequence of this intensive web of cooperative relationships was the tentative plan for area vocational education centers. The plan not only resulted in considerable expansion of federal requirements and a highly innovative approach to meeting the vocational education needs of the state; it also demonstrated the potential of cooperation as a vital educational responsibility of the MDE. Yet, individuals within the state department were divided as to the necessity or effectiveness of these kinds of interrelationships.

NDEA-Title III

NDEA-Title III, like ESEA II, stresses "concrete" assistance to local school systems through the purchase of equipment and remodeling of facilities. Approximately 93 percent of Michigan school districts participate in the NDEA-III program. To an extent, the interpretation and implementation of federal guidelines are left to local officials; however, the accompanying detailed fiscal control and accounting procedures systematize the administration of the program. Thus, NDEA-III staff primarily assume a service role in its administration. As a result, NDEA-III is characterized by a relatively routine administrative pattern. The program director, who had considerable experience in school finance, joined the MDE staff in 1959, when Title III was inaugurated in Michigan.

Michigan's state plan outlines several principles for use in the initial review of local project applications, but they can guide project reviewers in only the most theoretical manner. With one director and approximately ten consultants, there clearly is not the administrative capacity to insure that all applicants conform to these principles. Moreover, lacking precision, these principles at most are parameters within which reviewers can make subjective value judgments.

Use of priorities in determining project objectives. Priorities have been established by the MDE within the latitude provided by federal guidelines and the relative needs of children in Michigan school districts. Accordingly, funds are not allocated solely on the basis of student enrollments. The state plan assigns priorities to the following school districts:

1. Schools that serve low income and disadvantaged communities;
2. School districts (or intermediate districts) that devise comprehensive plans and experimental projects involving multi-funding from various federal and state grants; and
3. Poorer school districts, i.e., with low valuations, high tax rates and the like.

To be approved, programs must be designed to:

1. enlarge the curricular offerings in critical fields;
2. expand or deepen instruction in critical subject fields for students who cannot now obtain that instruction;
3. encourage better use of community and institutional resources in the school system;
4. encourage experimentation and research to find better ways to teach critical subjects;
5. encourage the combination of various resources toward a fuller program including in these resources other available federal and state funds;
6. involve the use of adequate technical and supervisory services in the use of the material and equipment so provided;
7. or encourage the employment of the best qualified teachers and teaching assistants in critical subject areas.[50]

These priorities and program objectives apply specifically to the improvement of curriculum offerings and teaching in Michigan elementary and secondary schools. They provide direction for the MDE and local school district officials to strengthen instruction through the use of new equipment and materials in the ten critical subject areas approved in the federal grant (science, math, reading, economics, civics, geography, modern foreign languages, English, and industrial arts).

Operationalizing priorities for fund allocation and distribution. The department's effort to operationalize its priorities resulted in two very concrete provisions for allocating resources. Michigan's State Plan for NDEA-III makes special provision for educationally deprived children in attendance areas with a high concentration of children from low-income families. Incentive is also given to projects which combine resources from other state or federally funded programs. Thus, the first two priorities for allocating and distributing funds are:

Priority I. Up to 35% of all funds may be allocated for the use of applicant school districts serving areas and districts where economic, social, and other population characteristics create a substantial concentration of deprived students. Reimbursement will be made on a 50-50 basis.

Priority II. Up to 10% of all funds may be used to support comprehensive projects of an experimental nature involving a combination of this program with other federal and special funds. Reimbursement will be made on a 50-50 basis.[51]

The State Plan did not indicate, nor did this study reveal, how concentration of deprived students is determined, nor what specific combination of programs would most likely be approved and/or disapproved. It is believed, however, that ESEA-Title I formula are applied to the first priority.

The third priority sets forth a variable ratio basis of reimbursement which attempts to enforce the relative need requirement.[52] This ratio approximates the ratio of per pupil allowances established by the Michigan School Aid Act. Table 4-6 shows the variable ratio of reimbursement.

Table 4-6

Table of the Variable Ratio of Reimbursement For Participants Under the State Plan For Title III of the National Defense Education Act of 1958

		Fiscal Year 1969-70			
	State Equalized Valuation Per Child in Membership			% of Project Cost from:	
				Local Funds	Federal Funds
Less than	$3,000			38	62
At Least	3,000	but less than	$ 4,000	39	61
At Least	4,000	but less than	5,000	40	60
At Least	5,000	but less than	6,000	41	59
At Least	6,000	but less than	7,000	42	58
At Least	7,000	but less than	8,000	43	57
At Least	8,000	but less than	9,000	44	56
At least	9,000	but less than	10,000	45	55
At least	10,000	but less than	11,000	46	54
At least	11,000	but less than	12,000	47	53
At least	12,000	but less than	13,000	48	52
At least	13,000	but less than	14,000	50	50
At least	14,000	but less than	15,000	51	49
At least	15,000	but less than	16,000	52	48
At least	16,000	but less than	17,000	53	47
At least	17,000	but less than	18,000	54	46
At least	18,000	but less than	19,000	55	45
At least	19,000	but less than	20,000	56	44
At least	20,000	but less than	21,000	57	43
At least	21,000	but less than	22,000	58	42
At least	22,000	but less than	23,000	60	40
At least	23,000	but less than	24,000	61	39
At least	24,000	but less than	25,000	63	37
At least	25,000	but less than	26,000	64	36
At least	26,000	but less than	27,000	65	35
At least	27,000	but less than	28,000	67	33
At least	28,000	but less than	29,000	68	32
At least	29,000	but less than	30,000	69	31
Over	30,000			70	30

Source: Michigan Department of Education

If the total reimbursement to all local educational agencies exceeds the amount of federal funds as a result of applying the variable ratio statewide, the superintendent of public instruction can determine an equitable per pupil allocation for all school districts. No indication, however, was made that such action had previously been taken by the superintendent.

Local school districts can make preliminary estimates by multiplying the total cost of the proposed project by the percentage of local funds indicated in the Table of Variable Ratio of Reimbursement. The amount the local school district must pay and the balance reimbursed from NDEA-III funds may be changed upon completion of the final processing of claims.

Finally, provisions also are made for "unused funds" in the allocation process. At the end of each encumbrance year, any unused funds may be reallocated on a per pupil basis. It was reported that approximately $500,000 fell into this category during fiscal year 1969. Such funds are reallocated to school districts which had been approved for more than originally allocated and encumbered more than allocated.

Specific Problems. Our discussion of specific problems in the administration of NDEA-III should not be considered an evaluation of the staff or the program's administration. As mentioned previously, the director has considerable experience, and the program administration, mainly as a result of detailed accounting procedures, is quite systematized.

The first problem is the lack of sufficient funds. During the past decade, between 462 and 575 school districts have requested NDEA funds. Funds requested by local school districts have been double the amount provided by the federal government. In 1969, for example, the MDE was able to match only one-half of the district requests for equipment.

Secondly, in 1969, 462 school districts serving more than 1,800,000 students (approximately 93.2 percent of Michigan school districts) requested funds. In most instances those not applying were the smaller school districts. For some of these districts, the amount of funds (in spite of the variable ratio of reimbursement) did not justify the local expenditure and the man hours needed for the "paper shuffling" associated with administering the program.

A third serious problem related to the allocation priority concerning deprived students. Although 35 percent of all funds may be allocated for educationally deprived students, the state was unable to secure enough funds for the 50-50 matching basis for reimbursement. Moreover, the use of NDEA funds as a budget supplement has occurred in some school districts. The NDEA-III director attributed these discrepancies to the rigidity of federal guidelines and regulations, but the specific nature of the federal requirements which cause such problems was not indicated.

Finally, despite the very elaborate and detailed provisions for determining the eligibility of equipment and materials, the major means for monitoring and insuring compliance are the program requirements and MDE trust in applications, forms, and validating instruments. On-site visitations, inspection and service are literally impossible with a staff of ten consultants and the program participation of nearly every school district.

Even with these problems, the staff appears very satisfied with the general quality of the program. The program director commented:

With the present economic situation in the State of Michigan and the voter resistance to voting extra allocated operational millage, the elimination of NDEA-III will merely compound the problems in local districts of providing sound educational programs. It is our feeling that NDEA-III is one of the better Federal programs because equipment and programs developed under this Act are financed by the cooperation of Federal funds and matching local funds. The matching of Federal funds by local school districts, I am sure, means that much more effort and thought is given to the need, type and use of equipment in the educational process.[53]

ESEA-Title II

Through the State Board of Education, the MDE has ultimate authority for the administration of Title II in Michigan. The superintendent of public instruction is authorized to submit state plan materials; the state treasurer is legally empowered to receive and hold federal funds; and either the superintendent or the department's fiscal officer may authorize expenditures under the state plan.

While the department is officially responsible for administering Title I, as in many other states, it shares the responsibility with the state librarian. In Michigan, the school library section of the state library is a division of the department's Bureau of Educational Services. However, the program administrator's (school library consultant) association with the state library antidates the initiation of Title II. Administratively, therefore, Title II is essentially a discrete entity—separated from other federal programs both by physical location (at the State Library not the State Education Building) and by immediate administrative responsibility.

The prevailing attitude of those involved with Title II suggests Title II constitutes a relatively uncomplicated program. Federal regulations were perceived as less stringent, and the local districts are able to exercise more discretion. Unlike the other programs, school library resources and instructional materials were conceived as necessary for all schools throughout the state, and, consequently, an attempt is made to distribute funds equitably among the local districts.

Moreover, a Title II staff member suggested that program personnel assume that local districts will purchase authorized materials—eliminating the need for state department personnel to act as "policemen" to insure compliance. Indubitably, the notion of simplicity is reinforced further by the fact that no full-time staff oversees the use of Title II funds. The school library consultant clearly has little time to more actively administer Title II of ESEA. Thus, the department relies somewhat on intermediate school districts of one or more counties and constituent school districts in the administration of ESEA-II.

The staff simply incorporates federal regulations wherever possible (frequently by direct quote) into the state plan and *The Administrative Handbook for Title II*, the official document for local authorities. Written by the program officer in charge, and revised infrequently, the handbook is designed "to clarify federal and state regulations regarding Title II, to interpret the provisions of Michigan's State Plan for Title II, and to provide guidance for participation in this program."[54]

Allocation criteria. The authorization for Title II in Michigan for fiscal year 1969 was approximately $2,140,125. No state or local matching funds are required for this grant. Two main criteria are discussed in the state plan for allocating these funds for library resources, textbooks, and instructional materials. The first, the relative need of children and teachers in the state, is determined initially by the available resources of the local district. The second provides the basis for a four-part program for distributing funds among local education agencies.

The resources of the local district are compared to "standards" set forth by advisory committees; the committee members represent library and curriculum associations, public and private schools, libraries, intermediate and state agencies; and the standards are based largely on American Library Association recommendations. The plan calls for dissemination of these standards through conferences and meetings, as well as mailings. Necessarily, mailings are most often used because of limited staff.

Two other criteria associated with relative need were defined as follows:

1. The special requirements of students and teachers located in schools serving areas of school districts where economic, social and other population characteristics create substantial concentrations of deprived children; and
2. The value judgments of qualified state and local public educational agency personnel as to the urgency of the assistance provided by the plan.[55]

Clearly, these criteria are at most general and even more so when need is interpreted in the state plan as "construed to be in relation to a combination of the factors" mentioned above. There remains some question as to the clarity with which standards are perceived by local officials, not to mention the extent to which they are monitored by state authorities and complied with by local officials. Evaluating the "urgency of assistance" by the "value judgments" of state and local personnel extends further the possible interpretations.

The allocation criteria set forth in the Title II program represent an attempt to clarify and substantiate the concept of "relative need." Forty-five percent of the funds are allotted on a per capita basis throughout the state; 5 percent of the funds are set aside for state administration and some contributions, with local approval, to Intermediate school districts. The remaining 50 percent is to be allocated on the basis of relative need, determined as follows:

1. 11 percent of the funds will be for the use of public and private students and teachers on a relative need basis which will be based on the amount

and availability of existing resources as compared to the standards set forth.

2. 35 percent of the funds will be allocated for the use of public and private students and teachers on a relative need basis which will be based on the special requirement of students and teachers located in schools serving areas of school districts where economic, social and other population characteristics create substantial concentration of deprived students. Deprived students are identified as those from families with $2,000 or less income, from homes with mothers receiving AFDC aid of over $2,000 and those in foster homes. School districts with a concentration of 20% or more or over 600 in a district qualify ·for this part of the grant. Superintendents will be required to certify that these funds are used for materials for the use of students and teachers in buildings with high concentrations of these students.

3. 4 percent of the funds may be allocated for the use of public and private students and teachers on a relative need basis which will be based on the special need for the establishment, continuation or expansion of instructional media centers. The 4% will be distributed in the form of not more than 5 ·special grants to Local Public Agencies as defined in Section 1.27.[56]

Local school districts, including target populations as defined by Title I of ESEA, receive 35 percent of the 50 percent allocated on the "relative need" basis. Presumably, the remaining 15 percent is meant to provide more extensive and concentrated library resources and materials, specifically for poverty pockets in the larger cities and urban areas, and the poorer rural districts.

Selection criteria and proportional expenditures. The MDE has rather extensive criteria for selecting library resources, textbooks, and instructional materials. They range from applicability and utility in the instructional program to the quality of content and format, although it is not defined beyond reliance on "reputable" professional lists. Moreover, the plan explicitly states that "no funds provided under Title II of P.L. 98-10 shall be used for religious worship and instruction."[57]

More important to this investigation is the further stipulation of criteria for allocating funds within the three major selection areas: (1) school library sources; (2) textbooks; and (3) other printed and published materials. The general guidelines adopted was as follows:

1. From 0-100 percent of the grant may be spent for school library resources.
2. From 0-15 percent of the grant may be spent for textbooks.
3. From 0-100 percent of the grant may be spent for other printed and published instructional materials.[58]

The state plan subsequently stated:

It is estimated that approximately 95% of the funds under this Act will be expended for school library resources. Perhaps 5% of the total funds will be spent for basic texts. Some of these materials may go into schools where presently there is not a library, but they will be organized for use in instructional material centers as such centers are developed. It is estimated that expenditures will be about 60% for printed material and 40% of non-print materials.[59]

The existence of a central library facility, quantity and quality of available materials, present per pupil expenditures, and special program needs were among the criteria used to determine the percentage of the grant allotted to each category. To insure the proper use of materials acquired with Title II funds, the state plan calls for in-service education programs in the use and evaluation of school library and other materials. In reality, however, forms, applications, and numerous other written devices far outweigh personal contact between local school and MDE officials.

Maintenance of effort. *The Administrative Handbook for Title II* used by local educators interprets the federal regulation on maintenance of effort (ESEA, Title II, Section 117.24) as requiring local expenditures during the current fiscal year to be at a level equal to or greater than the amount expended for the preceding fiscal year. Local expenditures are derived from an amount allotted for the "same kinds of materials as are eligible to be purchased with Title II funds."[60] Gifts, expendable items and all federal funds are excluded in counting local expenditures.

If their expenditures fall below the previous year's level, school districts may be denied Title II funds and may not be able to participate in the program during the subsequent year. However, there is allowance for "exceptional situations," since local administrators are instructed to provide a written statement (signed by the superintendent) explaining the reason for any reduction in local effort—thus averting automatic rejection of the application.

Coordination with other federal programs. While coordination and planning are only minimal among the various federal programs in the department, Title II does relate to the Library Services and Construction Act and to Title I of ESEA. Informal, monthly meetings are held at the state library, and a proportion of Title II funds are allocated on the basis of the ESEA-I formula.

ESEA-Title III

In Title III of ESEA, the federal government has stressed "innovative" and "exemplary" programs. The MDE has chosen to implement the federal priorities with staff development activities, needs assessment, evaluation and dissemination.

Staff development. The MDE has invested well beyond the average expenditure for ESEA III staff, particularly in areas of evaluation and dissemination. National percentages in the area of staff development may be summarized as follows:

Every State has a Title III coordinator but over 13 percent of the 42 reporting States and outlying areas had less than the equivalent of one full-time administrator for Title III. Despite the emphasis on program evaluation, less than half of the reporting jurisdictions had the equivalent of a full-time evaluator; 11 of the responding States had no evaluator on their staffs. Such States may use non-Title III State department staff members or consultants to fulfill Title III evaluation requirements. There were even fewer disseminators on the State Title III staffs. . . More than half—56 percent—reported fewer than one full-time (or equivalent) disseminator. Seventeen States reported no disseminators on their Title III staffs.[61]

By contrast, during fiscal 1969, Michigan had a full-time staff of 15 people, paid by ESEA-III funds: one administrator, one dissemination specialist, two evaluation specialists, five grants management personnel, two additional professional staff, and four non-professional staff. No part-time personnel were reported.

The department deems the selection and training of state-level Title III staff a high priority. Criteria developed for the Michigan Civil Service System are used and include degree and experience requirements. A dissemination specialist, for example, should have a doctorate and past experience in the use of dissemination techniques and communication skills; in addition, he should be familiar with current education innovations and the techniques for their adoption or adaptation. After their appointment, staff members participate in a thorough in-service program. Exercises in planning and developing projects for the handicapped, evaluation procedures, and strategies for the promotion and implementation of promising educational projects are part of the program.

On the local level, too, the Title III unit conducts staff training sessions in the development and operation of projects. Training sessions have been proposed for public and non-profit private educational and cultural agency personnel. Some of the tentative activities include: (1) effective practices in personnel selection; (2) effective communication; (3) development of local curriculum materials; and (4) periodic local evaluation in terms of locally established goals.

To provide professional in-service education and to heighten public awareness about the goals of Michigan's Title III programs, workshops and conferences are held. Some of these sessions include:

1. Evaluation workshop—training for department staff and project staff in developing an evaluation package for their particular program or project;

2. Awareness conference—providing an overview of operating projects, creating an awareness, and allowing exchange;
3. Critical needs conference—school district representatives examine results of needs study and explore possible ways in which critical needs can be met;
4. Look-see—persuasion conference—focus on demonstrating those projects determined by evaluators as being most effective;
5. Follow-up conferences—focus on the effects of projects in having other districts replicate effective projects; and
6. Project procedures workshop—project directors' meeting for developing and planning procedures for reporting project activities and results, program and fiscal.[62]

The administration, supervision and overall effectiveness of the Title III program in Michigan illustrate that investment in selection and training produces a good return.

Needs assessment. When the MDE assumed total administration of ESEA-Title III funds, the department undertook *A Study of Educational Needs: ESEA Title III.*[63] The study provided an embarkation point for the examination of alternative funding strategies and the development of innovative projects throughout the state. According to Title III staff, department personnel and university consultants collaborated in several planning conferences to design an accurate study questionnaire. The list of educational needs was developed primarily from findings and recommendations of the Michigan School Finance Study, the Michigan-Ohio Regional Laboratory Study, and the Wayne County Survey of Educational Needs.

The schools in Michigan (K-12) were then separated by geographical area, by school grade level, and by school operating expenditure per pupil per year (above and below $510). From this list, a stratified random sample of 340 schools was selected. Questionnaires were sent to four groups of people: (1) superintendents (or their assistants); (2) principals (or their assistants); (3) teachers (building representatives of teacher organizations); and (4) lay persons (officers of parent-teacher organization).

The questionnaire itself was divided into two basic categories: the first, *students having needs*, included ten items. Deprived or poor children, vocationally-oriented students, emotionally handicapped, minority group children, gifted and talented children, and migrant children were among the most frequently mentioned *students having needs.* The second category, *program needs*, consisted of thirty-eight items divided into three sub-categories: (1) *program needs for the learner*, e.g., Equal Education Opportunities, Development of a Student's Positive Self-Concept, Student Relationships with the School and the Community, and Skill Development in Reading; (2) *program needs for the teacher*, e.g., Human Relations and Communication with Students, Staff, and Community, Disposition Toward Chance and Innovation, and Attitude Toward Pupils; and (3) *program needs for the administrator*, e.g., Community Agencies, Increased Professional, Para-Professional and Other Staff, Leadership in Curriculum Improvement, Pre-Kindergarten. Respondents were asked to rank the priority of each of the need items on a six-point scale, with point "7" available for "no response" or "no opinion" item. Blanks also were provided to write in other needs if they were thought to be critical.

In their ranking of student and program needs, respondents representing different groups (i.e., superintendents, principals, teachers, and lay persons) and school operating expenditures demonstrated remarkably great agreement. Table 4-7 shows agreement on three of the four top critical needs included in the "Students Having Needs" category—vocationally-oriented students, gifted and talented children, emotionally handicapped, and potential dropouts; and six of the ten top critical needs included in the "Program Needs" category—state and federal programs for supplementary schools. Moreover, the proportionate differences in numbers of schools between grade level and operating expenditure per child per year varied greatly in the sample. Secondly, operating expenditure was determined on a "school-by-school" basis, and then assumed to be representative of the other schools in the district. Clearly, this usually would not be the case; without additional information, it might be assumed that the sample was skewed in almost any direction—in favor of richer or poorer districts, or even toward the district of average wealth. Finally, the respondents for each school do not appear to be a representative group, either in terms of their relative position in the school's context or in terms of variety of information sources. For example, the building representative of a teacher organization may be more of an expert on teacher welfare than on student welfare, and an officer of a parent-teacher organization may know more about the needs of children from educationally motivating homes than from homes where economic pressures forge different emphases.

To overcome such potential deficiencies in the needs assessment survey, Title III staff reportedly enlarged its sources of information to include diverse Michigan documentary sources, follow-up studies in areas such as vocational education, and further canvassing of community and student views. Hence, Michigan's Title III staff has complied with federal regulations and is seeking to improve substantively its comprehensive and on-going assessment of educational needs. The reorganized Research and Planning Division, strengthened by former Superintendent Ira Polley, provided much of the impetus and data for this assessment effort.

Evaluation. A Title III staff member reported that every project was visited by a Title III consultant at least three times during a fiscal year. Four staff members are engaged in these inspections, and they spend an average of five hours on site

Table 4-7

Listing of the Perceived Critical Student and Program Needs by Schools Having Different Operating Expenditures Per Pupil Per Year

Rank[a]	Expenditure Below $510
	Students Having Needs:
1	Vocationally oriented students (item 7)[c]
2	Gifted and talented children (item 10)
3	Emotionally handicapped (item 12)
4	Potential dropouts (item 6)
	Program Needs:
1	[b]Skill development in reading (item 23)
2	[b]State and Federal programs for supplementary educational services (item 65)
3	Individualized instruction (item 31)
4	[b]Improvement of student's motivation to learn (item 21)
5	[b]Skill development in communication (item 24)
6	[b]Released time for planning and for individual consultation with students (item 39)
7	[b]Mental and physical health of students (item 26)
8	[b]Study habits (item 25)
9	[b]Learning environment: facilities, equipment, and materials (item 42)
10	[b]Diagnostic and treatment services for the physically, emotionally, and mentally handicapped (item 27)

Rank[a]	Expenditure Above $510
	Students Having Needs:
1	Vocationally oriented students (item 7)[c]
2	[b]Potential dropout (item 6)
3	[b]Gifted and talented children (item 10)
4	[b]Emotionally handicapped (item 12)
	Program Needs:
1	Skill development in reading (item 23)
2	Individualized instruction (item 31)
3	[b]Skill development in communication (item 24)
4	[b]Improvement of student's motivation to learn (item 21)
5	[b]Study habits (item 25)
6	[b]State and Federal programs for supplementary educational services (item 65)
7	Diagnostic and treatment services for the physically, emotionally, and mentally handicapped (item 27)

Table 4-7 (cont.)

Rank[a]	Expenditure Below $510
8	Released time for planning and for individual consultation with students (item 39)
9	[b]Development of a student's positive self-concept (item 20)
10	[b]Mental and physical health of students (item 26)

[a]Rankings were based on the mean ratings of superintendents, principals, teachers, and lay persons associated with the schools. The number of schools in our original sample expending less than $510/pupil/year was 193, and the number of schools in our original sample expending more than $510/pupil/year was 147. The percent of these sample schools returning questionnaires from all four types of respondents was 95% in the former category as well as 95% in the latter. It is upon this response that the table above is based.

[b]In the below $510 category and under "Program Needs": the need items ranked 1 and 2 have overlapping 90% confidence intervals; the need items ranked 4 and 5 have overlapping 90% confidence intervals; the need items ranked 6 and 7 have overlapping 90% confidence intervals; the need items ranked 7, 8 and 9 have overlapping 90/ confidence intervals; and the need items ranked 9 and 10 have overlapping 90% confience intervals. In the above $510 category and under "Students Having Needs": the need items ranked 2 and 3 have overlapping 90% confidence intervals; the need items ranked 2 and 4 have overlapping 90% confidence intervals. In the above $520 category under "Program Needs": the need items ranked 3 and 4 have overlapping 90% confidence intervals; the need items ranked 5 and 6 have overlapping 90% confidence intervals; and the need items ranked 8 and 9 have overlapping 90% confidence intervals.

[c]The item number in the parenthese following each need represents the actual number of the item as it appeared in the original questionnaire. In this questionnaire there were a total of ten items dealing with "Student Having Needs," and a total of thirty-eight items dealing with "Program Needs."

Source: Michigan Department of Education: *A Study of Education ESEA Title III* (Lansing: Michigan Department of Education 1969), p. 19.

for each visit. Moreover, during the last fiscal year, university experts who assisted Title III staff spent 295 hours in the field, averaging five hours per project visit. According to one Title III staff member, of approximately thirty-six projects, only 25 percent involved advisory councils and the community in the planning, implementing or evaluating of Title III programs.

The state plan begins with a few basic assumptions for evaluating innovative and exemplary programs. Among the factors to be considered in any evaluation are specified objectives, durability, replicability, and cost. During site-visitations, Title III consultants evaluate projects along the following dimensions:

1. Objectives and Assessments—extent to which objectives are achieved
2. Management and Administration—staffing, equipment, organization and coordination of project
3. Process—conditions which facilitate the processes of change

4. Obstacles—problems encountered
5. Durability—acceptability and probability of continuance when federal assistance ends
6. Reproducibility—ability to be generalized elsewhere
7. Cost—acceptability of cost.

The state advisory council for Title III assists MDE staff in analyzing evaluation reports and determining the overall effectiveness of the program. Members of the advisory council generally are professionals who have taught or worked with community service agencies or churches. Few (none were identifiable) represented low-income groups directly, other than through service agencies. Title III staff is not dependent on this group alone, however, since local project directors contribute to the overall design of evaluation procedures. For example, they are currently collaborating on a feasibility study of educational information services; through their inputs, the MDE staff and local districts hope to learn more of effective evaluation techniques. In short, although the researchers unearthed areas of the Michigan Title III program in need of improvement, the Title III staff have made adequate provisions for the fulfillment of federal requirements for proper evaluation.

Dissemination and diffusion. The Office of Education has been concerned about the only limited effect of Title III-funded programs—supposedly innovative and exemplary—on other educational programs throughout the various states. In Michigan, to appease this concern, the MDE allocated resources specifically for dissemination. During fiscal year 1969, $102,880 was allocated for dissemination, an amount second only to that provided for Title III program administration ($185,001). Michigan has a full-time dissemination specialist as well as a full-time Title III administrator. In both instances, Michigan's effort is stronger than that of many other states.

The Title III staff has written a thorough dissemination program into the state plan. Designed for both the general public and personnel in local school districts, the program utilizes two complementary strategies: broad public support is sought to insure the adoption of new educational practices by local school districts; and assistance in dissemination techniques and methods is provided to local educational agencies with Title III projects. Statewide and regional conferences, state publications, state and local mass media presentations, and Open Houses are some of the activities for implementing the strategies.

To promote the emulation and adoption of successful Title III projects, linkages between individual projects and supplementary education centers, training consultants, and Title III project staffs had to be developed. "Look-see-persuasion conferences" attended by selected organizations and local agencies were used to effect alliances and cooperation at the local level and to encourage interchanges between Title III project staff and local educators.

Project approval and fiscal considerations. To aid local authorities in their preparation of proposals, the Title III staff informs local school districts, prior to proposal submission of the seventeen criteria used in the review. For example, evidence must be shown that the project will supplement the regular program; that it will meet critical educational needs in the area; and that it is economically feasible with a staff adequate both in number and quality.

However, when two projects are found to be the same quality, the criteria are extended and priority is given to the school district making the greater tax effort, in relation to state equalized valuation and average personal income, but unable to meet the critical educational needs in the area; and to school districts which initially planned the project with Title III funds. If projects of the same quality still remain after all the criteria are applied, the Title III staff awards the grants to areas which have persons with the greatest relative need; or which have never had a project.

Fiscal considerations are apparent in the MDE's attempt to comply with the federal regulation that Title III funds will supplement and not supplant state and local funds. The state plan provides the following:

No payment to a state under Title III of the Act for any fiscal year may be made by the Michigan Department of Education to a local educational agency unless the Michigan Department of Education finds that the combined fiscal effort of that local educational agency and the state with respect to the provisions of free public education by that local educational agency for the preceding fiscal year was not less than such combined fiscal effort for that purpose for the second preceding fiscal year.[64]

To assure compliance with this regulation, Title III staff members at the state level review previous programs, conduct on-site visits, and utilize the intermediate district offices to obtain necessary information from local districts. In addition, Title III staff members must review local programs to make certain federal expenditures, other than Title III funds, are excluded from reports of local fiscal effort. State expenditures, on the other hand, are checked to ensure that they have been considered at the same level as the year preceding application for a Title III project. Finally, if any reduction of local effort of more than 5 percent is found for any fiscal year, the school district is disqualified, unless it can demonstrate that the reduction resulted from an unusual occurrence (e.g., removal of property from the tax rolls, etc.). All of these conditions must be certified in the local application for Title III funds.

Lastly, some attempts have been made by Title III staff to coordinate their program with other federal programs. For instance, 15 percent of the funds are set aside for projects designed to meet the needs of handicapped children in cooperation with Title I and Title VI program officials.

Conclusion

Neither education interest groups, nor political parties, nor the legislature or governor exercise much influence on federal aid allocations in Michigan. Thus, the department has been free to move at its own pace, in the direction it chooses. During the past fifteen years of intensive federal funding of education, the pacesetter and pathfinder has been the state superintendent of instruction. In the late 1950s and early 1960s, when federal aid became important, the department's leadership was highly committed to the service ideal—assistance to local districts through an increase in the services offered and the efficiency with which they were provided. This commitment also included great attention to administrative detail and regulatory activities; all of these functions were safe endeavors for an elected superintendent—dependent on the voters for support and office.

Shortly after the Elementary and Secondary Education Act of 1965 became a reality for local and state educational agencies, Michigan's state superintendency became an appointed position. Both of these events affected the leadership role of the state superintendent. Increased federal aid made possible the recruitment of a competent and specialized staff which heretofore the department had lacked. In turn, this more sophisticated, reform-minded personnel provided support for the appointed superintendent's activities within and without the department. Ira Polley, the first appointed superintendent (1966-1969), did not have to be quite as attuned to the voters as had his predecessor, Lynn Bartlett, who owed his office to their support.

Polley strengthened key positions within the department and stressed the setting of priorities, planning, and evaluation. The new personnel who started to infiltrate the department at that time had an orientation different from their predecessors. They advocated reform—equal educational opportunity and better education in Michigan. Their indignation was fueled by the Thomas and Guthrie studies which revealed gross disparities in per pupil expenditures.

To rectify these educational injustices, the reformers have utilized the discretion which the federal acts give to the states in allocating federal funds. They have incorporated the concept of relative need and ordered priorities for districts "where economic, social and other population characteristics create a substantial concentration of deprived students."

Under the current state superintendent, John C. Porter, this reform tendency continues. In order to spread the reform philosophy to the lower and middle echelons of the department where the actual administration of federal programs occurs, Superintendent Porter is reorganizing the department and realigning the nexus of power. A shift has clearly begun within the department from the provision of technical assistance and administration of regulations to an emphasis on research, planning, and public support activities.

But the lack of external political involvement is a two-edged sword: while the department encounters little oppositon, it also commands limited support for its reform efforts. The MDE requires that support in order to effect its reforms and to survive the external forces now beginning to mass.

Notes

1. Three documents were exceedingly important to this investigation. They were J. Alan Thomas' *School Finance and Educational Opportunity in Michigan*, published by the Michigan Department of Education in 1968; Governor William G. Millikin's *A Chronology of Educational Reform in Michigan*, published by the Office of Planning Coordination Bureau, Bureau of Policies and Programs, February 1970; and lastly a draft of the book by James W. Guthrie, et al., *Schools and Inequality* (Cambridge: Massachusetts Institute of Technology Press, 1971).

2. J. Alan Thomas, *School Finance and Educational Opportunity in Michigan* (Lansing: Michigan Department of Education, 1968), p. 196.

3. See, for example, Nicholas Masters, Robert Salisbury and Thomas Eliot, *State Politics and the Public Schools* (New York: Alfred A. Knopf, 1964), Chapter IV; J. Alan Thomas, *School Finance and Educational Opportunity in Michigan*, a report prepared for the Michigan State Department of Education (Lansing: Michigan Department of Education, 1968), 418 pp.; and Guthrie, et. al., op. cit.

4. Nicholas A. Masters, Robert H. Salisbury and Thomas H. Eliot, "Michigan: The Lack of Consensus," in Michael W. Kirst, ed., *The Politics of Education at the Local, State and Federal Level* (Berkeley, California: McCutchan Publishing Corporation, 1970), p. 251.

5. Ibid., pp. 252-263.

6. V.O. Key, *Politics, Parties and Pressure Groups* (New York: Crowell Company, 1958), pp. 11-14.

7. Kirst, op. cit., p. 255.

8. Interview with the author.

9. Data for Table 4-1 were derived from the *Michigan Manual*, an annual publication of The State of Michigan and developed through the Secretary of State's Offices.

10. James W. Guthrie et al., op. cit., Chapter 3.

11. Thomas, op. cit., pp. 325-326.

12. Kirst, op. cit., p. 272.

13. Office of Planning Coordination, State of Michigan, *A Chronology of Educational Reform, Technical Report #1-11* (Lansing, Michigan: Office of Planning Coordination, Bureau of Policies & Programs), p. 2.

14. Thomas, op. cit.
15. Office of Planning Coordination, op. cit., p. 2.
16. Thomas, op. cit., pp. 322-323.
17. Office of Planning Coordination, op. cit., p. 2.
18. Ibid., Appendix D, p. 1.
19. Ibid., pp. 12-13.
20. Ibid., Appendix D. p. 2.
21. Ibid.
22. Interview with the author.
23. Interview with the author.
24. Interview with the author.
25. Michigan Department of Education Staff, "Michigan," in Jim B. Pearson and Edgar Fuller, eds., *Education in the States: Historical Development and Outlook* (Washington, D.C.: National Education Association of the United States, 1969), p. 599.
26. Interview with the author.
27. Kirst, op. cit., p. 267.
28. Pearson and Fuller, op. cit., p. 601.
29. See section on state governmental interests in this chapter, pp. 000.
30. Kenneth W. Carman, *Crusade in Michigan* (Garden City, Michigan: William B. Eerdmans Printing Co., 1970), p. 81.
31. John C. Porter, "The Community School As I See It," *The Community School and Its Administration*, 8, 9 (May 1970): p. 1.
32. Interview with the author.
33. See the Foreword of Michigan Department of Education, *Purposes and Procedures of the Michigan Assessment of Education: Assessment Report Number One*, a report prepared by the Bureau of Research (Lansing, Michigan: Department of Education, 1969), p. iii.
34. Laurence Iannaccone, *Politics in Education* (New York: The Center for Applied Research in Education, Inc., 1967), p. 49.
35. Michigan Department of Education, *Federal Aid to Education in Michigan: A Report on Elementary, Secondary and Adult Programs* (Lansing: Michigan Department of Education, August, 1969), pp. 11-12.
36. *Detroit Public Schools' Reaction to State Department of Education Recommendations*, a rebuttal to the MDE's criticisms stemming from a site visitation March 31 through April 3, 1970, p. 12. (mimeographed).
37. Ibid., p. 15.
38. Norman Berkowitz, "Comparability Standards for ESEA Title I Projects" (an internal memorandum of the MDE from Norman Berkowitz to John Porter, June 4, 1970).
39. Statement by Louis Kocsis in an Inter-Office Memorandum to Richard Barnhart, Curriculum Division, Michigan Department of Education, October 8, 1970.

40. Detroit Public Schools Reaction, op. cit., p. 1.

41. Michigan Department of Education, *The Michigan State Plan for Vocational Education: Part II Long Range Program Plan Provisions* (Lansing: Michigan Department of Education, 1969), 26 pp.

42. See for example studies such as *Michigan Manpower Study*, 1966 Battelle Memorial Institute, Columbus, Ohio; *Michigan Population*, State Resource Planning Program, Michigan Department of Commerce, January 1966; *Projections of School Enrollments*, Research Monograph No. 12, Michigan Department of Education, October, 1967 and several other related statistical reports of the Department.

43. Thomas, op. cit., pp. 312-313.

44. Michigan Department of Education, *The Michigan State Plan for Vocational Education: Part III Annual Program Plan Provisions* (Lansing: Michigan Department of Education, 1969), 33 pp.

45. Ibid., see Introduction, p. i.

46. Ibid., pp. i-ii.

46. Michigan Department of Education, *The Michigan State Plan for Vocational Education: Part I Administrative Provisions* (Lansing: Michigan Department of Education, 1969), pp. 33-35.

47. Michigan Department of Education, *Part III Annual Program Plan*, p. 3.

48. A summary of criteria presented in *Part III Annual Program Plan*, pp. 3-4.

49. Michigan Department of Education, *A State Plan for the Strengthening of Instruction in the Critical Areas*, (Lansing: Michigan Department of Education, 1968), Sec. 3.2.

50. Ibid., Secs. 4.121-4.122.

51. Further elaboration of the Variable Ratio of Reimbursement may be found in Michigan Department of Education, *Instruction for Preparing Local NDEA Title III Projects* (Lansing: Michigan Department of Education, 1969) p. 3.

52. Michigan Department of Education, *Federal Aid to Education in Michigan* (Lansing: Michigan Department of Education, 1969), p. 53. For a brief sketch of activities, trends and new directions of NDEA III, see pp. 53-55, also.

53. Michigan Department of Education, *Administrative Handbook for Title II of ESEA of 1965*, A Handbook prepared by the State Library Division (Lansing: Michigan Department of Education, 1969), cover page.

54. See Michigan Department of Education, *A State Plan for Making Available School Library Resources, Textbooks and Other Instructional Materials*, Section 3.3 Criteria Used in Allocating School Library Resources (Lansing: Michigan Department of Education), Sec. 3.311, nos. 2-3.

55. Ibid., Sec. 3-312, nos. 1-4.

56. Ibid., Sec. 3-4, no. 10.

57. Ibid., Sec. 3.5.

58. Ibid.

59. Administrative Handbook for Title II, op. cit., p. 30.

60. Quoted from an unidentified source concerning background information regarding Title II. The source summarizes financial information percentages of reported expenditures by activity, and the administration of Title II. The report was based primarily on information obtained from State Plans throughout the fifty states and three outlying areas.

61. Michigan Department of Education, *ESEA Title III State Plan for Fiscal Year 1970* (Lansing: Michigan Department of Education, May, 1969), Sec. 2.2.4.2.

62. Michigan Department of Education, *A Study of Educational Needs: ESEA Title III* (Lansing: Michigan Department of Education, 1969), 42 pp.

63. See ESEA Title III State Plan, op. cit., especially Sec. 2.3.11.4 "Evaluation Instrument."

64. Ibid., Sec. 2.3.4.

5

The Politics of Federal Aid to Education in Massachusetts

Laurence Iannaccone

Localism limns the patterns of federal aid allocation to school districts in Massachusetts. The Massachusetts Department of Education scrupulously avoids offending the local education authorities; the LEAs jockey for the power to be masters of their own educational fate. In the match played for federal aid, the MDE king is always checkmated, and the LEAs take home a prize far more valuable than a silver trophy—federal funds.

Three underlying tendencies may be seen in the allocational patterns of federal aid in Massachusetts. First, to avoid depriving any district of the federal windfall, the MDE adopts a policy characterized by vague priorities, superficial review and evaluation and, where it is impossible to reward everyone, a first-come, first-served grant system. The districts also retain substantial freedom in the expenditure of the funds they receive.

Second, although the criterion of need as it affects districts and pupils is a major theme in the federal legislation, in Massachusetts, it is not the dominant design in the pattern of allocation. The desire to share the wealth with as many districts as possible dominates the pattern of aid allocation; need is not a determining criterion.

The third significant pattern in the allocation of federal funds is that urban areas, particularly Boston, do not receive the proportion or amount that population and need would indicate. Relations between Boston and the state have not been notably cordial. Boston is wary of state interference and the state, as a general proposition, has been antagonistic toward Boston in all areas of government—including education.

Research Assertions and Federal Aid in Massachusetts

Assertion No. 1. There will be less involvement and political influence by the governor and legislature on federal aid in comparison with state aid.

This is true in Massachusetts, although it must be a comparison between little involvement and political influence on state aid issues and infinitesimal involvement and political influence on federal aid issues. Massachusetts ranks forty-sixth in the United States in state funding of education: the proportion of state revenues for education is only 21.7 percent. Although it ranked fourth in

193

personal income per child (1970), Massachusetts is twentieth in per pupil expenditure and fiftieth in public school expenditures as a percent of income.[1]

Although the governor appoints the eleven-member board of education for staggered terms of five years each, he exercises no direct or indirect control over the board or the Massachusetts Department of Education.

Both Governors Volpe and Sargent have generally followed the recommendations of the Massachusetts Advisory Council on Education in their appointments. The governor and the General Court exercise so little influence because the local districts dominate both the politics and financing of education.

Assertion No. 2. The influence and impact of the urban school lobby on the state allocation of federal aid will not be significant.

This is definitely true in Massachusetts at the present time. The traditional political alliances and the historical antagonism between the state and Boston conspire to prevent the emergence of an articulate, effective urban lobby. Its lack of influence is evident in the distribution patterns of the five programs studied.

The urban lobby of parents and community antipoverty agencies has not been able to influence the distribution of Title I funds within urban areas. Although PL 90-576, passed in 1968, encourages attention to the vocational needs of socially and economically deprived urban youth, the Division of Vocational Education provides only the minimum support required by the legislation. In 1969, 40 percent of the $5.2 million allocated to Massachusetts under PL 90-576 went to six regional schools, while Boston, with the largest concentration of disadvantaged in the state, got only $13,000. With over 7 percent of the public school students in Massachusetts, the city received less than 1 percent of the PL 90-576 funds. The 1970 allocations show the department's funding of Boston proposals has improved, but its basic priorities have not changed. The urban areas of the state receive no priority in the distribution of the NDEA-Title III funds. In the administration of ESEA-Title II, Massachusetts is still more concerned with being fair to *all* the districts than with honoring the federal priority of relative need which would channel more funds to urban areas.

Perhaps ESEA-Title III will present a different picture. Interviews indicate that the office may have a preference for urban projects; but this priority is not evident in the state plan or regulations.

Change in this state of affairs may be imminent; aided by organizations such as the Center for Law and Education of the Harvard Graduate School of Education, the urban lobby may become a viable political force within the next decade.

Assertion No. 3. As federal aid increases and states have more discretion in allocation, pressures will increase on state government from organized interests.

This is true in Massachusetts. The phenomenon of localism has created a powerful organized interest group in Massachusetts, the local education agencies (LEAs). Although they do not always operate together, the LEAs continuously have the greatest effect on the department's allocation of federal funds. Second in influence is the vocational education pyramid. Local and regional vocational education directors have worked closely with their MDE friends since the first large influx of federal funds after World War I. The MDE's continuing support of traditional vocational education priorities and its grudging minimal compliance with the new vocational education aid legislation emphasize the continued effectiveness of this interest group. The special education interests have an emotional platform unmatched by anything in the politics of education. The Bureau of Special Education now receives millions in federal funds. MDE personnel expect this bureau to follow vocational education in the achievement of divisional status.

Increases in the eligible categories as well as in the amount of federal aid produce new pressure groups which threaten the older established ones. The developing community colleges are a new pressure group whose emergence is largely the result of changes and additions in federal vocational education legislation, particularly the passage in 1968 of PL 90-576. In January, 1970, two of Boston's leading dailies gave prominent headlines and articles to a charge, initiated by representatives of the state's community colleges, that the Division was making illegal payments to certain local education agencies (LEAs) to fulfill "gentleman's agreement" pledges on salaries made prior to the passage of PL 90-576. In continuing to honor these agreements, the community colleges charged, Associate Commissioner Markham was diverting funds from categories, such as post-secondary education, established by the 1968 law. Markham did not protest, but indicated that henceforth his office would abide by the letter of the law. A recent talk with a community college representative indicated that the publicity had helped his client institution. Their allocation for the fiscal year 1970 had increased by 100 percent over the previous year, jumping from $350,000 to $700,000.

Librarians, audiovisual specialists and urban parents are other interest groups who are affected by federal legislation and seek to direct the flow of federal aid.

Assertion No. 4. The state education agency will attempt to minimize political conflict and pressure by using existing state aid formulas for allocation of federal funds.

The programs studied reflect the desire of the Massachusetts Department of Education to "make no waves." Massachusetts allocates federal funds in the same manner as state funds—to make sure that all the districts get funded on a fairly equal basis.

The failure to develop adequate evaluation or review procedures to measure the success of a program also indicates the MDE's desire to avoid conflict; adequate evaluation might point up mismanagement and ineffectiveness—reasons for canceling a program.

Assertion No. 5. Federal aid, except in a manner restricted by federal guidelines or requirements, will flow within a state as it has in the past.

Allocation of federal funds in Massachusetts follows this pattern. Statute determines the allocation of ESEA-I funds to districts. Where there is room for interpretation within the district, Title I aid follows the traditional Massachusetts pattern—except where USOE has quashed it.

Allocation of vocational education aid provides the most obvious example. Even after the passage of PL 90-576, the Division of Vocational Education was still continuing its traditional aid pattern. Although the 1968 act specifically stated that certain categories—post-secondary, disadvantaged, handicapped—had to be included, the division adopted a rather cavalier attitude until publicity and federal intervention forced it to change its position, however slightly.

NDEA-III leaves a great deal of discretion to the state; in Massachusetts this results in a great deal of discretion for the LEAs. In many instances the money has been spent on programs that would have existed without NDEA funds. The state is now beginning to exercise more control because the federal government has threatened to withdraw NDEA funds unless Massachusetts develops a complete plan of needs, priorities, execution, and goals.

The state only considers the criterion of relative need, albeit slightly, in the distribution formula for ESEA II funds because USOE rejected its initial formula which omitted it.

Assertion No. 6. SEA personnel are socialized so that they view their proper role as providing technical assistance to LEAs, not enforcing or policing federal requirements or setting program priorities.

In Massachusetts, where localism is king, this attitude prevails. The ESEA-III administration may prove to be the exception, for in that agency the determination to establish a distribution formula or an evaluation program appears to take precedence over a concern for local prerogatives or a fear of political pressure.

Throughout the other four programs, the MDE scrupulously avoids strong pressure or criticism of the LEAs in their execution of the programs.

The religion of localism has produced an organizational ideology in the department that governs its relations with the local educational agencies. The ultimate phrase which department authorities use to describe the situation in which the state compels local educational authorities to act, refrain from acting, or move in a given direction is "under mandate." State department personnel generally shy away from "mandating" anything, if possible. Certain aspects, such as explicit legislation, they almost apologetically point out, are mandated. So close to a violation of behavioral norms in this activity that personnel emphasized that "federal guidelines are suggestions, not mandates." The connotation of mandate, then, is negative in the typical language of the Massachusetts Department of Education personnel. The word "mandate" is used in contrast to "leadership" and "professional leadership."

There can still be significant change even in this ideology, but it will not come overnight. It will take a determined and continued effort. The initiating role from Washington or other funding agencies needs to be institutionalized in the state of Massachusetts.

Patterns of Allocation of Federal Aid to
School Districts

Except where the federal legislation delineates the categories and requirements, the patterns of allocation in the five acts studied in Massachusetts are determined by localism and uniform distribution rather than by population and relative need.

Under ESEA-I, Massachusetts school districts receive over $15 million annually to provide compensatory services for about 100,000 students. There are approximately 350 school districts in the state and over 430 projects. The way in which Title I is drafted permits a state either to exert strong control of the Title I program or, without violating the legal requirements of the Act, to minimize state activity and play the role of a conduit.

Massachusetts has chosen to play the role of a check-writing conduit.

The 1968 Amendments to the Vocational Education Act changed the matching requirement of overall statewide matching, and specified certain categories, i.e., disadvantaged, handicapped, etc., within which a percentage must be spent. The Law (PL 90-576) clearly indicates that the thrust of the federal effort is to aid economically and socially disadvantaged youth in urban areas. The MDE allots only the mandated 15 percent to the disadvantaged. Moreover, in Massachusetts, the main determinant of the funding level for each program was the number of proposals the department received in that category. In no case did the MDE avail itself of the opportunity provided by and encouraged in PL 90-576 to fund some proposals at 50, 75 or 100 percent. Although the formula is nominally designed to evaluate and to fund each proposal in terms of need, proposals within each category are, in fact, funded at a nearly equal level because the funding level is determined partially on the basis of the number of proposals received, and because the department wants to keep the LEAs happy by treating all proposals equally.

MDE officials were frank to admit that the quality of a proposal and the expertise evidenced in its presentation were influential factors in determining its acceptability for funding. One MDE administrator noted that Boston schoolmen simply did not have the "savvy" of their more competent counterparts in the wealthier suburbs. Some examples taken from the preliminary data of FY 1970 indicate the effect of the allocation system. In the category of programs for the disadvantaged, the only proposal from Boston accepted by the SEA earned 65 points and received $136,215. In the same category, a proposal from Brookline, one of Boston's wealthy suburbs, received 64 points and $109,220. In the secondary school category, Boston received a total of $60,000, while one regional school, Nashoba Valley, with an enrollment of approximately 500 pupils, received over $300,000.

As indicated earlier, distribution among school districts on a rather equal basis is the department's first concern in the allocation of NDEA-III funds. If a truly needy district comes to light, some informal effort is made to encourage that district to apply; but it is clear from the way in which the formula works that the district will *not* get preferential treatment. Districts which seek the Special Project grants tend to be wealthier districts, more adept at grantsmanship and able to engage in projects only partially funded by the federal government.

Under ESEA-Title II, administrators initially rewarded effort—rather than need—thus penalizing a large city like Boston, which suffers from the fiscal problems associated with higher demands for non-educational municipal services. The new formula, instituted at USOE insistence, slightly favors districts with greater need. The formula, however, does not require the districts to give priority to elementary schools, although much research suggests that such concentration is most effective. The desire to give everyone something mitigates against the effect of the need criterion.

The ESEA-III people indicate that they will concentrate on urban areas. Unless the state establishes some specific priorities criteria, however, the pattern of allocation will probably resemble the others—predominantly influenced by LEA demands for equal distribution.

Political Factors Shaping Fiscal and Administrative Patterns

Administrative patterns for the allocation and oversight of federal aid programs are shaped by a number of interacting forces. In Massachusetts, six interacting variables appeared to be most important: constituency, administrative style, focus of the program in the departmental structure, critical events, and key issues. Each of these five variables, however, is influenced and partially reshaped by the sixth and dominant factor in Massachusetts: the political reality of the belief in localism.

The Religion of Localism

The "religion of localism" is a sociological norm requiring that local communities dominate the partnership of federal, state and local government. That norm recurs constantly in the literature[2] and in the language of state education agency personnel.

The implications of this philosophy for the politics of education have been discussed at length elsewhere;[3] however, we shall reiterate certain significant manifestations of this philosophy because the characteristics profoundly affect federal fund allocation in Massachusetts.

Under localism, the local educational authority should be the major determinant of the policies, directions, and operations of schools. The state legislature (composed of local representatives), not the governors' office, will prevail in contests over educational policy making and especially in fiscal support matters. The religion of localism suggests an educational lobby pattern which is heavily imprinted with local and special interests and less marked by a state-wide, broadly concerned educational coalition, as in New York. Most important, the religion of localism characterizes and dominates the operations of the Massachusetts Department of Education (MDE).

Localism must be reckoned a moving force in Massachusetts politics and state government as well as in education. The historical roots of localism grow deep in Massachusetts. In addition, powerful political cultures exist which provide modern support for localism as they interact upon each other.

Edgar Litt identifies as useful constructs four political cultures in Massachusetts: the patrician, managerial, yeoman, and worker, each with a distinct political life style.[4] The Republican commitment of the yeoman and the Democratic commitment of the urban laborer allow the combination of patrician and managerial cultures to play the central role in *statewide* elections and control of the gubernatorial office. This combination operates somewhat akin to a political superstructure for the state. It links the state and federal government. It ties large, modern industry and economic organizations to the state. It is a major source for a general rational, policy oriented, managerial-progressive demand for institutional reform, an orientation shared by the chief officials in USOE during the passage and pre-Nixon era of the Elementary and Secondary Education Act. Beneath this stratum, however, divided on elections for statewide offices because of ethnic, social class, religious and geographic cleavages, a political infrastructure of the yeoman and labor cultures exists. The Republican yeomen and urban Democrats have gained positions of seniority and influence in the middle echelons of the state's political systems. The patrician-managerial influence on the governor's office, and on national offices and affairs is offset by the yeoman-labor influence in the General Court. There, the schisms between the yeoman and urban labor cultures are bridged by their common interest in the retention of political power in the locality. Litt points out that, "the Massachusetts yeomen may seek to formalize their legislative relations with core-city Democrats ... if the central campaign issues are either *quality education*, mass planning, or the development of the suburban belt."[5] He adds, "The Great and General Court, the Executive Council, and *most state agencies* become the union shops for the non-managerial strata."[6]

Nowhere is this seen more clearly than in education. As a result of the traditional lag found so often in the politics of education, however, the MDE reflects the yeoman more than it does the urban laborer and, of course, does not reflect the urban poor at all. The adherents of localism—the yeomen and city workers—appear to be losing ground with the rise of a national corporate and governmental political economy and a suburban middle class. However, the institutions of Massachusetts government and the political processes of the state, especially as these focus upon the General Court, help to maintain the status quo.

The legislature is the central arena for the politics of education in Massachusetts insofar as there is a state politics of education. (Massachusetts, it must be remembered, is more dependent on local funds for education than are forty-five other states.) The Joint Committee on Education is the key legislative unit concerned with the schools, although the Joint Committee on Ways and Means runs a close second. Members of the legislature, including the committee members, gain newspaper coverage by attacking, in every educational crisis, the department's well-documented lack of leadership. In the General Court, some legislators, perhaps reflecting the patrician-managerial views, criticize the department for its weak exercise of the regulatory function. Others, the dominant group which espouse the religion of localism, oppose the MDE's withholding of funds from LEAs even when they violate legislative mandates.

The LEAs constitute the most important interest group and influence on the General Court on educational questions. They do not move as one; each district acts upon the recommendations of its representative. LEA officials play the political game of quietly seeking and receiving departmental services, while zealously attacking the department in public. The personal relationships between such LEA officials and MDE personnel support this pattern and make it difficult, if not impossible, for the commissioner and departmental leaders or the Board of Education to end the practice.

Equally disastrous for general MDE operations are the special interests pursued by various constituencies, especially vocational and special education. The belief that a weak department safeguards both LEA autonomy and vocational education creates a firm bond between ranking members of the Joint Committee on Education and the vocational education constituency. The department is caught between its role as arbiter of state educational standards and distributor of federal aid and its desire to appease the special interest groups and the legislature. If the department tries to enforce even the 180 school-days standard by threatening to withhold state aid, the LEAs run to their representatives who condemn the department.

Constituencies

Localism alters substantially the SEA-client relationship and shifts the balance of influence and initiative in the allocation of federal funds. Four significant manifestations of the situation in Massachusetts are: The client exercises major discretion over the specific program; equal treatment of client requests within program categories becomes the operating rule; advisory groups influence both the definitions of categories and the weight given to criteria variables such as need; and numerous competing educational interest groups have greater influence on the General Court than the department does. The interest that the departmental program administrator views as the reference group, client or, in political terms, constituency, is a major factor in determining who gets what federal funds. When Washington attempts to change programs, it creates serious problems for state department administrators if the changes conflict with the interests of their own reference groups. Moreover, new federal programs which do not find an active influential constituency risk being diverted to established interests, at least until a new constituency sympathetic to the federal interest is formed. The existence of many conflicting constituencies, each linked to its own federal program, diminishes the MDE's opportunity to develop an integrated policy and coordinate program administration. Finally, potential constituencies can provide leverage for more effective execution of federal intent only if they have time to gestate and, more important, if they gain a cadre of support in the department for their programs and federal intent. In some instances, more effective program administration may result from bypassing the department.

Statewide Educational Pressure Groups

There are some statewide educational pressure groups of significance. The most powerful by far is the vocational education pyramid. Both the effects of localism and the long history of access to the federal purse, which has produced enormous professional patronage, contribute to its status. In addition, vocational education is a natural point of accommodation of the yeoman and labor subcultures that compose the Massachusetts political infrastructure.

The special education interests, concerned primarily with programs for the physically and mentally handicapped, have an emotional platform unmatched by anything else in the politics of education. State funding in this area is around $10,000,000. In addition, the Bureau of Special Education receives several millions in federal funding. The area is a political coalition not only of special education, but of mental and public health forces and, therefore, constitutes a significant lobby cutting across many governmental agencies, and segments of the General Court. MDE personnel interviewed expect this bureau soon to follow vocational education in the achievement of divisional autonomy.

The community colleges are a new constituency that is rapidly acquiring political influence and challenging the traditional "company way" of allocations to vocational education. Supported by the public media, this new constituency in 1970 forced the state's vocational education hierarchy to modify its operations and comply more substantially with the federal legislation.

The Massachusetts Advisory Council on Education, established by the state in the Willis-Harrington reorganization, is a potential rather than an actual influence on long-range planning and the formulation of educational policy. Unless the General Court begins to place a higher value on its reports, however, the council and the studies it conducts will have little or no effect on education in Massachusetts.

The state's private colleges and universities are another potential rather than actual leverage point for influencing education. Because they are concerned with a broader area than the state and because they are caught in a conflict of interests when public (i.e., state-supported) education is strengthened, they have not contributed substantially to improving education. Most important, the schools of education, both public and private, could indirectly affect general educational planning and upgrade the LEAs by bringing together the state's school administrators. Competition among these education schools for placement of students, especially administrators, for the sale of field services, and for LEA support in order to attract private, state, and federal grants impedes cooperation.

The Massachusetts Educational Conference Board has the semblance of a coalition, but localism is rampant. Each of its component organizations—PTAs, school board associations, school administrator groups and the NEA state affiliate—continues to operate with its own links to the MDE and to the General Court, not infrequently at cross-purposes. A stronger conference board could help to make a more effective department.

Administrative Style

The personal characteristics and administrative style of MDE administrators who supervise the federal programs appear to be a significant variable in the distribution of federal funds. Three styles with related characteristics and career patterns have been identified in our study of the MDE staff involved in federal programs. The predominant style is designated "check writing." Individuals who display this style try to avoid conflict and the necessity of choosing between program applicants. The formulas which they establish to interpret federal regulations and requirements permit them to make allocations under these circumstances. "Check writing" prevails in Massachusetts in the administration of the ESEA I, Vocational Education, NDEA III, and ESEA II programs.

The MDE administrators of ESEA III have a "social action" style. Clearly, the check-writing syndrome is subordinated to a desire to use the program to work on the major social problems of depressed urban areas. The administrators of this program retain their discretionary power. The risk of conflict between the Title III office and LEAs is not only probable but anticipated by the MDE staff.

Finally, a third style exists in the MDE Research Division, which is largely supported by Title V funds. This is the "research orientation" with a strong emphasis on evaluation. That these people do not appear to have significant roles anywhere in the five programs studied is revealing. Their orientation and style flies in the face of the consistent pattern to avoid comparisons, serious supervision of LEA activities or genuine evaluation of LEA programs.

Locus in the Department

The location of a program, specifically the level of supervision of a program within the department, is a variable with some significance for how that program will be administered. Generally, the lower the program is in the divisional hierarchy, the less interaction there will be between the senior supervisor and his divisional chief; and the greater will be the supervisor's autonomy to administer the program within the limits of a previously established routine. At the other extreme, when a federal program is elevated to divisional status, the program's chief exercises influence over the program and its constituency, influence which extends beyond the department. For example, the development of a statewide network of vocational education directors, with regional vocational units, tends to free vocational education from the control of the LEAs and modifies even the religion of localism.

Critical Events

In each of the programs studied, one or more critical events appeared to give shape to the MDE's subsequent operation of the program and provided a frame of reference for the distribution of program funds. Such crises are the result of federal rejection of an operational plan; the loss or threat of loss of federal funds unless modifications are made in an ongoing program; the federal decreases in funding levels of a given program; and/or a major change in federal regulations which requires the modification of program thrust and MDE routines. We note, however, that these federally initiated crises only become crises when additional stress is produced either by major publicity and/or the protest of a constituency whose interests are favored by the federal action, but jeopardized by an established constituency's influence.

Key Issues

The nature of the federal program itself affects the federal funds. The federal legislation and the way in which USOE applies it are theoretically a major constraint upon the administrative behavior of those who handle the programs for the SEA. Therefore, one could consider the federal regulation itself as an influence upon SEA behavior. Our data on the MDE tend to support this view only in part. Only certain elements in the federal regulations were felt to have made a difference upon MDE operations. Since the ESEA I legislation determines the distribution of funds among LEAs, the within-district distribution provides the key issues in this program.

PL 90-576 raised the issue of distribution of vocational education aid between LEAs. The federal specifications provided funds for post-secondary education, the disadvantaged, and the handicapped. These allocations produced new clients for the vocational education operations. The accommodations which had previously restrained the competition among the LEAs disintegrated.

NDEA III also poses the issue of distribution between LEAs. The issue has been handled relatively low in the departmental structure, by a pattern of equalization and, where necessary, by a first-come, first-served approach which reduces the department's need to play a role in deciding between competitors. A second issue, the required development of state supervisory personnel to upgrade LEA teaching, has, in the main, been handled by not handling it.

ESEA II is concerned with the distribution of funds between school districts and among private schools. These allocations were largely determined by a formula which has provided the framework for subsequent decisions. Other issues, the proportion of funds for books rather than for audiovisual materials, and the control of the audiovisual materials and equipment, still cause some difficulty.

The development of the ESEA III plan raises issues that are not involved in any other program: SEA leadership and the SEA's use of the discretion which the federal legislation allows. Title III raises the issue of inter-district competition. The goals of the people involved in the program and the tradition of the state are at great variance.

Grantsmanship: Not a Major Variable

Differential grantsmanship has not been treated here as a major variable in the distribution of federal funds. This decision was made despite evidence that some members of the department feel it is significant. It seems to us that membership in a given constituency "club" and informal nearness to appropriate MDE supervisors constitute the essence of successful grantsmanship. In addition to the constituency issue, the MDE tendency to avoid picking one proposal over another and to eliminate competition makes grantsmanship the ability to get into the grants category, rather than the determinant of whether one receives a larger or smaller one. In the Bay State, grantsmanship is not simply what you know, but what you know because of who you know.

For practical purposes, the Massachusetts Department of Education has, in effect, transferred its discretion in the administration of federal programs to the LEA. Fiscal control is largely an accountant's or bookkeeper's game, at best. One should therefore expect that, insofar as possible, the Massachusetts Department of Education will engage in *pro forma* regulation of LEA federal programs, protecting itself and the LEA against outright violation of federal regulations, but will avoid looking further into the LEA's activities than is required. The hypothesis must be entertained, although it cannot now be adequately tested, that the system works this way because the participants with political power, especially the General Court, the local school committees, and the organized professional groups, desire it. The department has effectively been prevented from spending even federal funds to improve the administration of federal programs; such prevention reduces further the department's capacity to influence the LEAs, as well as the opportunity to be anything but a junior partner.

The Massachusetts Department of Education

Background

Indoctrinated with the religion of localism, MDE personnel practice an organizational ideology founded on certain basic tenets: the department should not tell local people how to run their schools; and professional leadership is gentle suggestion or guidance to help the LEAs improve what they want to improve. The effective client systems for state department personnel are the LEA or LEA sub-units rather than the state or the school children of the state; similarly, in the administration of federal programs, the LEAs are the perceived client, not the federal government, USOE or the Congress.[7]

At no point in its twentieth century history has the MDE been a coordinated, centrally directed operation.

The Willis-Harrington study of 1965 was much heralded as an effort to upgrade and improve the Massachusetts Department of Education. It is significant for what it attempted; what resulted from it; how little difference it made; and what lessons it provides.

The Willis-Harrington study described the MDE in 1965 as, "a conglomerate historical institution trying earnestly and valiantly to become an organization. The conglomerate had fourteen divisions and offices which reported directly to the commissioner and nine "autonomous" units over which he presided ex officio. The autonomous units "reflected a growing disinclination of the General Court to rely upon the department for new education programs."[8] The Willis-Harrington study identified more than 150 state or regional educational interests in all trying to influence the General Court. The four educational lobbies that were successful emerged as autonomous units or divisions within the MDE.

Most important by 1965 were (1) the vocational education interest established in its division, and (2) the land-use and construction interests secure in the autonomous School Buildings Assistance Commission. The Division of Vocational Education developed its leverage through its long and consistent access to federal funds. As a consequence of the Willis-Harrington report, the department was reorganized and vocational education was reduced to bureau level and placed within a division. The School Buildings Assistance Commission continued its separate and autonomous nature. By 1968, the legislature had again raised vocational education to its divisional status, a testament to the strength of its political constituency.

The Willis-Harrington Report led to Chapter 572 of the General Laws of 1965 to restructure the MDE. The reorganization of the MDE was an effort to rationalize the department according to the policy-oriented, managerial values. The reorganization neither changed the organizational ideology of department personnel, nor the relation of the department to the LEAs. This impasse attests to the continuing power of the religion of localism and its enormous political support.

The political results of the reorganization are most apparent in the *Progress Report, Lincoln Filene Centre Study of Massachusetts Department of Education*, October, 1969.[9] This study, sponsored by the Massachusetts Advisory Council on Education (MACE), was also designed to buttress the department, presumably already strengthened by the legislative outcomes of the Willis-Harrington study. Its tasks were ". . . to identify obstacles to the MDE's effective performance . . . " and to provide, "recommendations for MDE's strengthening its operations and functions." Then, the report stated, "The legislation emanating from the 1965 Willis-Harrington study of public education in Massachusetts set certain goals and mandates for the MDE which either are unclear or have not been implemented." Its memorandum of December, 1969, indicates the MACE report is likely to support the process of regionalization; it recommends six regional offices of the MDE "to provide educational inputs and processes to school systems that demonstrably are providing inadequate education for their students."

The Report tentatively recommends "consistency in applying each and every mandate to all school systems . . . " It continues, ". . . The Department must enforce the mandate and have the personnel and resources to enforce these mandates." Subsequent statements call for support from the General Court, state school board, and LEAs to allow the Massachusetts Department of Education to develop a leadership role.

The "New" MDE

Three boards appear to share responsibility for the MDE's role in education: the Board of Education, generally concerned with education in grades K-12; the

Board of Higher Education; and the Massachusetts Advisory Council on Education. The chief agent of the first board is the Commissioner of Education; Dr. Neil V. Sullivan has held the post since 1968. The Chancellor of Higher Education is the chief agent for the second board and is ex officio on the first. A director of research administers the MACE operations.

The eleven-member Board of Education is chosen by the governor for staggered terms of five years each. The board is given considerable power by law, but is daily dependent upon the General Court for its resources. Despite his appointive power, the governor exercises no direct control over the board or the department. The evidence also indicates that neither Governor Volpe nor Governor Sargent have sought indirectly to influence the board or department, although Volpe strongly supported education requests. The governors have generally followed MACE recommendations in their appointments.

The Board of Education, as created in 1965, is well insulated from the politics of both the executive and legislative branches as well as from the political parties; its influence on the General Court matches its isolation. Further, it lacks public visibility and cannot even use publicity to influence the legislature. Some members of the Joint Committee on Education consider the board politically naïve and ineffective. The passage of time will further weaken its effects on legislation unless the board develops its own political muscle.

Apart from the governor, the executive branch exerts a powerful and significant influence on the MDE through The Department of Administration and Finance. A&F exercises its influence over the MDE through two of the A&F bureaus, the Bureau of the Budget and the Bureau of Personnel and Standardization.

The Bureau of the Budget receives the Board of Education's proposed budget annually. Its review is so completely insulated from the board and the MDE that in February, 1970, the commissioner, while testifying before the Joint Committee on Public Service, was informed for the first time that his budget had been cut, making some of his testimony irrelevant![10] The department must operate in the dark much of the time during the fifteen-month budget cycle on matters concerning nothing less than the next education budget for the state.

More powerful on MDE operations and ideology are the actions of the A&F Bureau of Personnel and Standardization. The key official in this bureau was once a member of the MDE staff. Hostility, suspicion and blurred communication characterize the A&F-MDE relations. A&F's Bureau of Personnel systematically downgrades MDE job classifications for professional personnel and consistently pares the number of jobs requested by the MDE. This process is carried to the extreme. Some federal monies designed to pay for the administration of federal programs are sent back to Washington because the MDE is neither allowed enough persons to administer the federal programs according to the federal intent, nor is it allowed to hire the caliber of staff necessary to do the job as Congress expects. One remedy lies in the "freedom bill," regularly submitted to the General Court by the Board of Education and as regularly rejected. The legislature would still retain budgetary control of MDE operations, but the A&F Bureau of Personnel and Standardization would lose control. Finally, the A&F belief that the MDE job standards should conform to the civil service pattern for all state employees makes it difficult to maximize the employment of specialists trained in educational evaluation—further reducing evaluation or serious supervision of federal and state-funded programs.

The combination of gubernatorial isolation from educational operations, low level of state funding of education, A&F rigidity and insulation, and the General Court's support of this state of affairs maximizes the impact of the religion of localism on Massachusetts education and MDE operations.

More than 600 bills concerning education were submitted to the General Court in 1970. Twenty-one of these came from the MDE. In 1969, the department submitted sixteen, ten of which were killed. The department's win/loss is about 50 percent, the same percentage as before the reorganization. The Massachusetts educational legislative game, even more than in many other states, is a lobby game. The department has tried unsuccessfully for years to combine educational interests around its legislative program. In legislative hearings, MDE officials have not infrequently been treated with obvious disrespect or not heard at all. Once its bills are submitted in the fall, the department as such is virtually out of the legislative process.

The MDE is composed of six divisions, each with a varying number of bureaus. The divisions are: Administration and Personnel, Curriculum and Instruction, Research and Development, School Facilities and Related Services, State and Federal Assistance, and Occupational Education. While our study delved into intradepartmental relations only as needed to understand the five federal programs, some things are obvious. Commissioner Sullivan has achieved some coordination among divisional chiefs to the extent that they sit together in his "cabinet." This is a progressive accomplishment. In most divisions, it is the bureau level which does things, and each bureau within a division tends to work by itself. Horizontal linkages are less important, if that is possible. The mesh of the department is made of personalistic links.

The role of supervisor in education within a bureau is the key to 90 percent or more of the decisions especially on federal programs. The term is a job title. A&F insists on a uniform job specification for that title. Thus the MDE has fifty people with that job title, with the same job specifications, but with very different duties. The published job opportunities for MDE openings—of which there are usually many—communicate nothing. Personnel recruitment is haphazard at best. While the MDE Division of Personnel seeks to give professionals credit for level of education and comparable previous service, the A&F official responsible for the department's requests consistently classifies the jobs much lower on the salary scale. In addition, there is a great lapse of time between the MDE's attempt to engage a professional for a new position in a federal program and the A&F's approval.

The result is that the department is generally understaffed by underqualified, unaggressive people. However, some of the department personnel were clearly better than their salaries indicated.

The state provides supervisors with only meager travel money. One reason federal programs are worth supervising is that these provide travel funds. Even then, long periods fall between the time the money is spent and the department's reimbursement. The implications for the administration of federal programs is obvious. Supervisors do not get into the field enough and cannot look much below LEA paper statements on program activities. Site visits are made, but not often and not for long. Without federal travel funds, things would be even worse.

The Department and Federal Funds

The General Court's reluctance to expand the department or give it the capacity to exert leadership further impedes its growth. Title V funds, which might have helped, were largely used to develop the Research Division. It includes better trained personnel than its current projects demand. The Research Division has been attempting to develop a rational and current set of statistics and programs on the LEA expenditures in order to analyze state aid. Located on route 128 in Woburn, the division's staff is not readily accessible to federal program supervisors located at the department's headquarters in Boston.

The department is responsible for collecting data on public, private, and parochial schools and pupils for financial purposes and depends heavily on LEA reports. The local superintendents often claim that their private/parochial school counterparts do not turn in as complete information as is required of them, and sometimes the norm plummets to the lowest common denominator. Thus there is poor supervision even over allocation of state funds within the MDE as well as to non-MDE agencies. MDE decisions to use Title V to develop an information system are understandable; yet as a result, Title V has had little additional effect in strengthening the MDE.

Our research team discussed the possibility that federal funds might balkanize state departments. The term implies that an existing unity was fragmented by the injection of federal monies. No such unity existed in Massachusetts before federal funding. The MDE, in fact, is largely a product of federal funds. The allocation of federal programs to specific bureaus was the result of historical accident, constituency pressures, and the department's need to spread around the work (and funds). "Empire building" is a phrase frequently heard at 182 Tremont Street. It is used to explain why specialists in one division or bureau seldom work with people in another and why each bureau guards its own federal program. It illustrates how little coordination of federal programs exists. The department is under-financed, and internal competition for federal funds is inevitable. The tendency toward autonomy of divisions, bureaus, and programs exacerbates the divisive situation. An internal departmental fragmentation which parallels the LEA fragmentation is the result.

**Federal Aid Administration: A
Title-by-Title Analysis**

ESEA-Title I

Massachusetts school districts receive over $15 million annually to provide compensatory services for about 100,000 students. There are approximately 360 school districts in the state and over 430 projects.[11]

The program is administered out of the Title I Office within the Bureau of Elementary and Secondary Education, one of the bureaus of the Division of Curriculum and Instruction, one of the MDE's major divisions. In addition to handling the program for low-income children in local educational agencies, the office handles the Program for Children of Migratory Workers, the Program for Children in State Institutions for Neglected and Delinquent Children, and the allocations for children in other institutions for the neglected and delinquent. Beyond this the four-member staff of the office handles the Bilingual Education Act, (Title VII, ESEA as amended), NDEA Student Loan Cancellation Program for teachers in low-income areas, the Follow Through Program, and provides state technical assistance to the Headstart Program.

Theoretically, the office is concerned with the distribution of money between school districts, the distribution of funds within individual school districts, and the assurance of quality program outputs in terms of student achievement. Federal statute largely determines the distribution of funds between districts; and Massachusetts accepts the assumption that the formula sets up entitlements which are not to be revoked or adjusted by any direct or indirect means. It would be possible, pursuant to the legislation and regulations, for the state to insist upon truly high quality project applications (as defined by the federal and state policies) and to refuse to fund those projects which did not meet these requirements. The state, however, never turns an application down. Rather it will suggest and persuade the LEA to make some adjustments in the application before submission, usually to conform to existing or new federal regulations, not to conform to a state policy as to what is a quality project. Then, on the basis of the adjusted application, the office grants approval. These applications are approved usually without the benefit of the evaluation of the prior year's program, since evaluation reports are not yet available, and, increasingly, without knowledge of the amount of the congressional appropriation for the present fiscal year. Appropriation bills tend to be passed months after the school year has started, creating a handicap to the planning by the LEA and the project approval decision by the state. With a staff of four people and over 430 applications, the review of these applications must necessarily be somewhat superficial. The small size of the staff seems attributable to MDE's low salaries and the Title I Office's and MDE's unaggressive recruiting efforts, rather than to lack of funds. A recent study of Title I evaluation efforts at the local level in Massachusetts showed that sixteen of the thirty-seven projects of the sample reported no evaluation design despite the fact the federal regulations require such self-evaluation.

According to state officials this policy is a reversal of the policy the state followed in the first year of Title I, when it concluded the year not having used up all the money appropriated to it because it had denied many Title I applications. Discovery by the press that the state had not spent all the money to which it was entitled caused a public uproar leading to the reversal of this policy, a critical event in molding the operation. State officials still speak about criticism directed against them during that period. As a consequence, the state has relinquished its power to improve the quality of Title I projects through its control of the purse strings.

For most of the five years of Title I's history in Massachusetts, the MDE has left nearly all control of the distribution of funds within the districts to the school officials themselves. Pressure groups other than the LEAs have had minimum impact. The influence permitted to local community agencies and parents has been greatly limited. During the summer of 1966, the local antipoverty agency in Boston, ABCD, complained to the MDE about Boston's self-evaluation procedures and urged that a body of outside, impartial evaluators be established to evaluate Boston's Title I program. The state forced Boston to establish an advisory council of professional educational evaluators from various area universities, with the power to halt Boston's Title I funds if Boston did not cooperate. Its role was to advise Boston in establishing effective evaluation procedures. The council worked with Boston for approximately one year beginning in August, 1966. After much difficulty in working with Boston, after a withdrawal of its power to cut off funds (a power exercised for a brief three-week period), and after failing to achieve its assigned mission, the council disbanded, another critical event. Since that time ABCD has had only limited impact on the Boston Title I program, despite its authority to refuse to sign-off on the Title I application. In 1969-70, ABCD refused to sign-off on the Boston proposal because Boston refused to follow a number of its suggestions. The state nevertheless approved the Boston application.

Throughout most of the history of Title I in Massachusetts, parents have, at best, been informed of what the local officials plan to do and permitted modest suggestions with regard to fringe aspects of the proposals, e.g., the destination of field trips. As with community agencies, the initial federal guidelines on parental involvement have been extremely loose. The original guidelines #36 published in April, 1967, make virtually no mention of parents; and #44 ESEA I Program Guide, March, 1968, requires merely that that the assessment of educational needs be determined in consultation with parents, among others. In July, 1968, the Office of Education issued guide #46 which required the establishment of local advisory committees and suggested that at least 50 percent of the membership of the committee consist of parents. Subsequently in guide #46-A the requirements of #46 were relaxed. The state, it should be noted, still tends to enforce the more rigorous guide #46. Yet this guide does not really detail the degree of parental involvement required, and still leaves parents largely on the periphery of the control of the Title I resources. However, the OEO-funded Center for Law and Education at Harvard Graduate School of Education has been instrumental in bringing together parent groups from throughout the state in a concerted effort to persuade the department to adopt stricter guidelines, guidelines which would give parents a large degree of veto power. The state is in the process of drafting a set of alternative guidelines. Resolution must await further developments.

Indications are that parochial schools have been getting some of the aid to which they are entitled, but that full implications of the federal legislation and regulations have not been realized. Local officials are reluctant to share their limited resources, and private school officials have not really asserted their rights pursuant to the legislation. In Boston, parochial schools have received approximately $70,000 of the $4.4 million given to the city. The state apparently assumes that if private school officials do not complain and if there is minimum compliance with federal legislation and regulations, it is just as well to let sleeping dogs lie. Clearly, also, with its limited staff, the Title I office would find it difficult to inform itself fully of the complete nature of parochial school involvement in the Title I program and to supervise meaningful compliance on the part of the LEA.

As is the case with many other aspects of the Title I program, the federal regulations and guidelines on targeting address themselves to the problem but simultaneously leave room for much discretion at the state level. The regulations (45 C.F.R. 116.17(a)), permit the LEA to use Title I funds on "educationally deprived children" who reside in a project area which contains school attendance areas with high concentrations of children from low income families. These attendance areas are those in which the concentration of such children is as high or higher than the average concentration for the district as a whole. In measuring the level of poverty the LEA may use alternative types of statistics, as in #44 ESEA Title I Program Guide, 1.1 (1968). With the guidelines given, a state has the power to refine and tighten up the method used to determine target districts. In Massachusetts the Title I Office has not been overly strict in this regard, apparently leaving the choice of method up to the LEA. For example, when Boston commenced Title I, it determined eligible school attendance areas on the basis of 1960 poverty income data developed by ABCD. Only in January, 1969, when an HEW audit revealed that Boston's targeting was based on data which was obsolete and not sufficiently broken down to provide accurate measures of poverty in each school attendance area, did the state (at federal insistence) push Boston to develop more accurate methods of targeting, based on AFDC data for each school attendance area. The result of the new assessment was the elimination of several old target areas and the addition of some new ones.

This same relaxed state policy carries over to targeting funds within a particular attendance area. Boston has been permitted to spend Title I funds on all the children within the attendance area on the assumption that all the children within the area were "educationally deprived." The state did not insist upon, nor did Boston on its initiative determine, which of the children within the attendance area were the neediest. There are indications now, however, that the state has become increasingly concerned with this question as the federal government becomes more interested in targeting and the concentration of funds. MDE has sent two special interdepartmental teams into Boston to monitor and review local Title I programs and targeting. The outcome of this review is likely to be gentle state pressure on Boston to improve the targeting of its funds within school attendance areas. Direct orders are rarely, if ever, given to the LEA.

Until the second half of the 1969-70 school year, monitoring and review of the programs were largely restricted to the time when applications were being reviewed and to occasional on-site visits by members of the Title I office. The state has now initiated a new supervision scheme under which larger projects will get more intensive review while many of the smaller projects will not be reviewed at all. The very largest projects, such as those in Boston, in turn will be visited by interdepartmental teams, i.e., teams made up of supervisors from various offices in the Bureau of Elementary and Secondary Education. It may be that this new method of supervision will augur a new and more assertive state role in the control of the LEA projects. The general thrust of the federal policy largely runs counter to the pressures at the local level to spread the money around as widely as possible within the targeting requirements. Although it does encourage localities to concentrate the funds available on the neediest pupils, for the most part, the state has acceded to the local pressures. The state told Boston, when it re-applied, to submit a proposal which provided for a greater concentration of funds (i.e., greater than $125-$150 per child) than in previous proposals. The new Boston proposal concentrated funds at the level of $150 per pupil, virtually no change from the prior proposals. Yet the state approved the plan.

It is clearly the policy of the state to play no important role in controlling the purposes to which the localities devote their Title I money. Thus, the MDE pays nothing but lip service to the goal of persuading the LEAs to devote the largest proportion of their money to improving the educational achievement of students in the primary grades. The state will occasionally suggest to the LEAs that this would be an appropriate way in which to spend the money, in light of the recent research showing that educational deficiencies seem to be cumulative and that money is most effective when spent in the primary grades. As for the kind of program to be developed for these primary grades, the state view seems to be largely that "more of the same" will do the trick.

The state policy in this area grows largely out of uncertainty as to what quality education is. The Title I office has opinions as to what good education is, but is not certain that these opinions are founded on solid evidence. Further the office has stressed the desirability of avoiding uniformity at the local level, i.e., uniformity brought about by state pressure. Apparently uniformity is appropriate if it is a result of the free choice of the localities. Finally, the state office believes that officials at the local level are "professionals" who know their job and that "they should be treated like professionals" and thus not coerced.

The state does not view the Title I program as aimed at achieving certain defined educational outputs which it should try to achieve by manipulation of the inputs. Nor does it make an effort to coordinate its control of the Title I resources with its control over other monetary resources towards specific programatic output goals. The posture of the state is rather to channel the money through to the LEAs in accord with federal legislation and guidelines. Concern with the results obtained—with the efficacy of the money—is something to be left either to Washington or to the LEA. A recent article on public education in Massachusetts notes:

. . . the state cannot determine whether any particular Title I project—or, for that matter, the entire program—met any of its goals. The absence of such data is reflected both in the evaluation forms used by the state and in the evaluation reports themselves. Although the 1968 annual report touches on many of such program goals (aid to parochial students, raising achievement, improving the quality of school offerings in poor schools), it does not provide information that would allow a decision on how well a given project, or the program as a whole, met any of the goals.[12]

Title I legislation provides that the LEAs must at least annually evaluate the efficacy of their programs in improving the educational achievement of the target pupils. In Massachusetts the state provides virtually no regulation of these efforts except an occasional request that a local educational agency beef up its proposed self-evaluation scheme as outlined in its renewal application. A recent study showed that nearly half the sampled districts built no self-evaluation design into the program. Other findings with regard to evaluation were:

1. Pre-test, post-test was most common design used.
2. Control groups were rarely used.
3. No attempts were made to measure any characteristics of the environment that may have a bearing on learning.
4. There was a general lack of communication about Title I students from summer project to winter ones.
5. 74% of the projects used standardized tests to evaluate student progress, achievement batteries being the most popular.

6. Very little testing was done in areas of self-image and attitude change, in spite of the fact that these were prominent aspects of program objectives.
7. Considerable testing did not pertain directly to program objectives.
8. Data collected for evaluation purposes were frequently not utilized; 22 out of 36 projects made little or no effort to analyze data.
9. Evaluation procedures were generally unsophisticated and were not built into the project as an on going process.[13]

It is clear that there is no real effort being made to control educational resources by the rational methods available. State officials feel that it will take time for local school systems to become accustomed to and capable of doing and using evaluations; and until that time the state should not interfere. Furthermore, state officials believe that to mandate the use of standardized tests in connection with an effective evaluation design would provoke uncontrollable resistance from local school officials. Insistence on evaluation efforts which would make it possible to compare the efficacy of similar programs would be politically impossible as well as philosophically undesirable. Finally, there seems also to be some sort of residual faith at the state level that the existing local school systems are basically doing a good job and that what is needed is that those students who are not doing so well should simply get more of the same.

It is clear that the general posture of the Title I office vis-à-vis the various local school systems in Massachusetts is analogous to that of the federal government vis-à-vis the various states. The same caution exists; the same unwillingness to be too directive; and the same tendency to avoid a strong, effective, innovative role. Of the possible pressure groups, only the LEAs had significant impact on MDE decisions concerning the distribution of resources. Neither the governor nor the legislature has any dealing with Title I. Occasionally a member of the legislature will call the Title I office to help grease the skids for a constituent's project application, but beyond this there seems to be little interest on the part of the legislature in the Title I program. The existence of other federal programs seems to have little bearing on the operation of the Title I program. No state-developed effort is made to coordinate the Title I state administration with other federal programs to achieve state-determined priorities. Rather, if funds from various federal programs are marshalled to meet the same needs and goals, this is done entirely on the initiative of the local school district. The Title I office does nothing in the way of educational planning, but merely seems to try to follow its federal orders—as far as it can consistent with the nature of its relationship with the LEAs.

Vocational Education

Unlike other federal programs in our study, vocational education has a very long history and tradition of operations which provide the critical framework for recent developments. The existence of federal support from World War I on has produced, in Massachusetts and elsewhere, a well-established, politically active constituency, and a close informal relationship between local vocational educational directors and state officials. Prior to the 1965 reorganization of the MDE, this constituency found its central point of access to the MDE in its rather autonomous Division of Vocational Education. Passage of Chapter 837 in 1968 once again restored divisional status to this program and testifies to the strength of the vocational education directors' lobby with their allies in agriculture and labor. On the other hand, the passage of PL 90-576 created a difficult situation for this group by opening the program to new participants and new constituencies.

The 1963 vocational education program produced a statewide constituency in vocational education with regional vocational high schools as the key structural units. Thirteen of these schools have been built, and twelve are in various stages of planning. The existing schools are located in predominantly rural areas, serve a number of neighboring towns, and have an average student body of around 700.

The LEAs lost influence to the combined regional vocational high schools as these were developed. The MDE's vocational education program officers played more of a leadership role here than in many other federal programs. The directors in the regions and LEAs are often from out of state and link onto the national vocational education influence structure. Special vocational education regions, in effect, become the operational localities for the religion of localism in this federal program. The key issue then for this area is disbursement of funds between LEAs (the region being the LEA) without generating internal conflict which would wreck the constituency or destroy the division's informal leadership.

Under the 1963 Vocational Education Act, virtually complete discretion was given to the SEA in alloting federal funds. In Massachusetts about one-third was spent on construction and the bulk of the rest on teachers' salaries in the regional schools. Thus the regional development reduced the financial load of the LEA. This minimizes the initial violation of localism, producing a stronger statewide constituency in the long run. The program initially paid 100 percent of the salaries in the first year, 75 percent in the second, 50 percent in the third, and then 25 percent. Such a pattern, in effect, encumbered federal funds four years in advance even though it was not legal to do so.

The 1968 Act (PL 90-576) required a state plan. In May, 1969, the writing of a plan was undertaken as a crash program by the division chief and a few departmental personnel. The 1968 Act had also created the State Advisory Council to watch over the division's activities; it included, with the traditional constituencies, representatives of higher education. PL 90-576 required that funds be set aside for this constituency as well as other new interests—post-secondary, the disadvantaged, and the handicapped. The post-secondary group was in conflict on the council with the established vocational education network which is the prime vocational education constituency. The combination of delay in preparation of a state plan; the long-range encumbrance pattern established under the '63 program; and the demands of new clients produced a crisis and the critical event of the current program.

After refusing the initial plan, USOE approved the revised plan in October, 1969. By that time, and despite the plan, $867,000 was paid out by the MDE on old commitments. The post-secondary group, the community colleges, raised an outcry which was picked up by the press in January, 1970. This was followed by discussions with Washington where the state was told to find a way to fit these payments within the plan. Future operations are likely to see continuation of the post-secondary—regional vocational education struggle within the task forces on the Advisory Council where both interests have access. While the publicity over these events also highlighted the fact that Boston does not share fully in vocational education, the disadvantage provisions of the act are likely to cause less trouble until or unless a significant urban constituency develops.

The Boston School Department's Bureau of Vocational Education is one of the more moribund operations of an ailing system, but the failure to invest more federal money in Boston also reflects an inadequate MDE staff that does not have time to work more with Boston officials; the fact that the higher administrators within the division come from outstate and do not evidence the interest or expertise needed to meet urban problems; and the inordinate amount of pride and effort which the MDE expends on the regional schools. There was also the feeling expressed by one division official that Boston schools receive from other federal programs large sums of money, a fact that must be taken into consideration, he believed, when judging the division's pattern of allocation.

The Division of Occupational Education occupies an entire floor of the Department of Education offices at 182 Tremont Street in Boston. Until the fall of 1970, when he retired, the Division chief was Associate Commissioner Walter J. Markham, a long-time vocational education professional in Massachusetts. Salaries within the division, as in other branches of the Department of Education, are quite low, a fact that has had adverse effects on the general competence of division personnel and on its ability to fill staff positions. One of Markham's assistants estimated that the division currently suffers from a vacancy rate of 50 percent. At one time the division employed thirty supervisors to distribute and monitor $1 million. Today twelve supervisors oversee the expenditure of $8 million. An inadequate staff both in terms of quality and quantity is partly responsible for the division's inability to meet the responsibilities imposed upon it by PL 90-576. For example, the Division's state plan, mandated by PL 90-576, called for the creation of many new jobs within the division, primary among them being directorships of the Bureaus of Secondary Education, Post-Secondary Education, and Disadvantaged and Handicapped. The reorganization was approved by the legislature, but the new positions were not funded. Inadequate staff also results in minimal monitoring and evaluation of local programs, a fact widely referred to and often decried by persons within and without the division. One observer who has worked closely with the division believes LEAs frequently inflate their estimates of the costs of programs when submitting proposals to the MDE for funding. (It was mentioned by one division administrator that their Research Coordinating Unit was working on an evaluation scheme.)

A final example of how inadequate staffing contributes to the subversion of PL 90-576 is found in the fate of several proposals submitted by the Boston schools to fund programs for the disadvantaged in two high schools. The MDE rejected the proposals primarily because they did not include provisions for adjunctive services such as remedial reading and additional guidance services to ameliorate the "disadvantageousness" of the intended clients. The MDE had not told the proposal writer from Boston of these requirements.

There is a discernible desire however, if not yet a trend, for the MDE to supply more in terms of help and direction to the LEAs. One administrator hopes to develop detailed guidelines for developing courses in many occupations that would be disseminated by the state for use by the LEAs. He also hopes to centralize some of the purchasing of equipment through the state office in the belief that better prices could be secured.

Certainly it was felt that PL 90-576 had increased contact between the LEAs and the MDE. "They smell the money," one official noted, "and are curious." It remains a problem, though, to get communities in outlying areas to apply, and some are decidedly not interested in starting new programs with federal funds knowing that in several years they will have to assume the entire financial burden.

Although the 1968 Act (PL 90-576) is slowly and inexorably changing the MDE's traditional priorities, the MDE is complying only minimally in the area intended to be the act's major thrust: the vocational needs of economically and socially disadvantaged youth in urban areas. PL 90-576 requires that not less than 15 percent of the federal funds be spent on programs for the disadvantaged. In Massachusetts, the MDE allocated 15 percent to programs for the disadvantaged. Moreover, by eliminating the project-by-project matching requirement of the 1963 Act, the law meant to permit funding programs in poverty areas at up to 100 percent of cost. Yet, in Massachusetts the main determinant of the funding level of each program was the number of proposals the SEA received in that category. Thus FY '70 allocations reveal that programs for the handicapped were funded at 100 percent because the state received few proposals within this category; programs for the disadvantaged were funded at 90 percent because few proposals were received and because some were disallowed by the SEA. Post-secondary proposals were funded at 33 percent and those in the secondary school category were funded at 25 percent. (This category was significantly larger in terms of amount and proposals received than the others. The MDE provides the minimum required by PL 90-576 to the other categories and then allots the rest to fund programs in the secondary school group.) The 25 percent figure is an average, but in only a few cases did the funding level rise above it and then only to a level of 30 to 35 percent. In no case did the MDE avail itself of the opportunity provided by and encouraged in PL 90-576 to fund some proposals at 50, 75, or 100 percent.

Despite a formula to evaluate each proposal in terms of need and to allocate funds on this basis, the proposals within each category are funded at a nearly equal level because the funding level is determined by the number of proposals received, and the desire to avoid favoritism to the LEAs.

MDE officials were frank to admit that the quality of a proposal and the expertise evidenced in its presentation were influential factors in determining its acceptability for funding. When LEA proposals are received, they are reviewed by either the supervisor for the occupational area, the supervisor of the category the proposal falls within, or by one of Mr. Markham's assistants. At this level the proposal may be rejected or the cost estimate adjusted. The proposal is then put through a process to determine the need for the programs, and it is on this basis that the proposal is assigned a certain number of points. The specific grant is based on the number of points received; the number of proposals considered within the category; the amount allotted to the particular category; and the amount requested in the proposal. Theoretically, need is an important criteria; but in fact, as pointed out above, proposals in each category tend to get funded at a set percentage of the amount requested.

Each proposal and the amount awarded to it is then reviewed by an ad hoc committee composed of representatives of various task forces, each of which represents a specific category, i.e., Adult, Post-Secondary, Handicapped, etc. Though sometimes alterations in the award are made and proposals are rejected in toto, the review by the committees tends to be superficial. The members are not paid, and, coming as they do from positions outside the division, have only limited time to spend on evaluation. The ad hoc committee then pass proposals on to Markham who submits them (strictly a formality) to the State Board of Education for final approval.

The point allocation system which the state uses is one in which they take evident pride and is designed to weigh each proposal according to need. A proposal may achieve 100 points by earning the most possible points in each of the following categories.

1. *Manpower Needs.* From 1 to 30 points are awarded according to the need for training in a particular occupation as determined by state manpower requirement estimates. Thus because the table indicates 5,110 more law enforcement officials will be needed by 1975, a proposal to train them is awarded 24 points, while a proposal to train plasterers receives 6 points since only 224 more will be needed in the next five years.

2. *Vocational Needs.* From 6 to 15 points are awarded depending on whether a program is specially designed for the disadvantaged and/or handicapped (15 points), simply "provides" for the disadvantaged and/or handicapped (9 points), or is a regular vocational program (6 points).
3. *Excess Costs.* (3 to 15 points). If a program is considered to involve especially high costs in construction, rental, equipment and teachers' salaries, it is awarded 15 points. If high costs for teachers' salaries and equipment are projected, 12 points; for transportation, 6 points, etc.
4. *Relative Ability to Pay.* A proposal may receive up to 20 points in inverse proportion to the community's ability to pay. Its ability is determined by dividing the community's equalized assessed valuation by the per pupil expenditure.
5. *Economically Depressed Areas.* A community may receive 3 or 5 points if it is listed as one of 74 economically depressed areas.
6. *High Unemployment Areas.* A community may receive 3, 4, or 5 points if it is listed as one of 61 high unemployment areas.
7. A *demonstration or pilot* receives 10 points.

Although a division document sent to the LEAs states, "The level of funding is determined by the use of a formula as required by the State Plan for Vocational Education," FY '70 allocations reveal funding all proposals within each category at or near a common level, i.e., 25 percent, 33 percent, 90 percent, etc.; thus subjective judgments made at some point in the process serve to equalize the number of points proposals receive.

It is difficult to determine the exact source of the data on which some of the point determinations are made, e.g., economically depressed areas, high unemployment areas, and manpower needs. What does seem clear is that data supplied by the State's Bureau of Employment Security is either inadequate or improperly used by the division. For example, Boston is not listed as one of the state's seventy-four economically depressed areas. Thus when this part of the formula is applied, a proposal from West Tisbury, Massachusetts (pop. 360) receives 5 points and Boston (pop. 697,197), with several ghetto areas, receives none. In the high unemployment area category, a Boston proposal receives 3 points, while a proposal from Mattapoisett, Massachusetts (pop. 1,640) receives 5.

Statistics which determine manpower needs points are, however, the most deficient. Only twenty-nine occupations are listed. (A proposal to train students in a field not listed automatically receives 15 points.) The manpower needs figures are statewide and are not broken down into SMSAs. Thus there may be a local need to train for a specific occupation, but if the statewide need is low, the proposal would receive few points. Furthermore, there is no indication of whether the added number of workers needed in each occupation represents a declining or increasing manpower market. Finally, in ranking occupations according to need, "Sales Workers" and "Waiter/Waitress" stand in first and third places and earn 30 and 24 points respectively. It may be questioned whether vocational education programs are needed in schools to train workers in occupations where on-the-job training has traditionally sufficed.

The new director of the division who succeeds Walter Markham may move from a grudging compliance to a more eager acceptance of PL 90-576. It is too early to tell how well the state advisory council will perform its duty; but if the goals of the council chairman are realized, the council will urge the division to more efficient, appropriate, and effective programs.

The law assumed that the states would go beyond the minimal requirements of PL 90-576 to serve the urban disadvantaged. This has not happened in Massachusetts and perhaps USOE should not expect it. Why would the MDE, which received requests for $24 million in federal aid from numerous Massachusetts communities in FY 70, go beyond the minimum to fund programs in a few urban areas? While division administrators are not clamoring for amendments to PL 90-576 that would require them to spend more in urban areas, it is unlikely that in the absence of such requirements they will do so. This is especially true if, as is the case in Boston, the Vocational Education Department of the LEA is lethargic or is itself not knowledgeable or sympathetic to the needs of the disadvantaged. PL 90-576 does provide an opportunity for funding the proposals submitted by nonprofit private agencies, which sometimes have a greater understanding and drive to serve disadvantaged youth; that they will be used to greater extent in Massachusetts is uncertain.

NDEA-Title III

The NDEA program is handled primarily by one senior supervisor with the assistance of six supervisors located in the Bureau of Elementary and Secondary Education—a bureau in the Division of Curriculum and Instruction. All these people have duties in addition to the administration of NDEA III. The central problem facing these people in the administration of the NDEA program is the distribution of funds between districts and the development of supervisory services over the LEA.

The legislation and federal regulations provide that the state in its plan should set forth principles for determining the priority in which projects will be awarded money. The Massachusetts state plan, the accompanying regulations, and the administrative practices present a rather curious picture of ineptitude and state politics.

The state plan sets forth fourteen objectives which it anticipates will be achieved through the NDEA III program—objectives which taken together amount to at least a minor revolution in the education world. These objectives include (a) a substantial increase of desirable and/or promising practices; (b) intensive local activity in curriculum development; (c) increased opportunity for individual student learning projects; (d) a more intensive program of research in fields pertinent to instruction in the critical subjects; and (e) improved teacher preparation.

All these "principles" must be read in light of the state's formula for distributing NDEA funds and actual administrative practices. The "formula" provides that each district will be eligible for a general distribution grant calculated on the basis of $1 per pupil in the public schools. (NDEA has no provisions for distribution to non-public school.) The remainder of the money available to the state under NDEA will then be distributed in the form of a special project fund. The administrative practice has been one of virtual automatic approval after the most superficial reviews of the project applications filed for money under the general distribution per capita grant. The review which the application undergoes is just to see "what the state is buying," to determine whether the application falls within the categories allowed under NDEA, and if there is a "program" in which the equipment will be used.

If money remains after the general distribution, then the state will consider giving localities grants from the Special Project Fund over and above their grant from the General Distribution Fund. These larger, and probably more expansive, projects may involve the purchase of such items as tabletop computers for use in an advanced mathematics program. These grants are given largely on a first-come, first-served basis: The first applicant will receive an award if its project appears good, even if later projects are better planned and more desirable.

Certain other points should be noted with respect to the state's distribution of NDEA resources. Since not all districts apply for their share of the General Distribution Fund, the amount of money available for the Special Project Fund is enlarged. With the drastic cutback in federal funds (from $1.5 million to $722,000), in this most recent year, the failure of districts to apply for their share was an important factor in making funds available for special projects. If all school districts had applied, there would have been almost no special project funds. Massachusetts feels safe in over-encumbering the funds by 10 percent to 15 percent on the theory that even if districts have applied for funds and received approval of their applications, they often fail to follow through in seeking their justified reimbursement. Apparently it is also possible for the NDEA staff, by shifting money from category to category, in conjunction with the school building fund, to get the school building fund to pay for items otherwise chargeable to the NDEA account, leaving the NDEA account with extra funds.

The original state plan and regulations appear largely to have been the work of a few men within the Department of Education and one man in particular, who at the time was chief of the Bureau of Elementary and Secondary Education. The present implementation of the plan is largely relegated to the senior supervisor in charge of the NDEA program. His subject specialists (known as supervisors) review the applications within their subject area and pass on the reviewed applications to the senior supervisor for approval. He barely reviews the routine applications, but takes a closer look at those applications flagged by the supervisor as out-of-the-ordinary. Although special projects are treated in a similar manner, there is a more extensive review and occasionally an on-site visit to assess the program in which the equipment will be used. These project decisions are never referred to a person higher in the hierarchy; the senior supervisor prefers to avoid referring decisions up the line and discourages the supervisors from seeking advice from either the director of the Bureau of Elementary and Secondary Education or the assistant commissioner for state and federal assistance. No mention was ever made of the associate commissioner in charge of the Division of Curriculum and Instruction in which the Bureau of Elementary and Secondary Education is located. The delegation of the decision making to the lowest professional level within the department evidences the department's desire to avoid conflict with the LEAs.

It is clear from the "formula" used for distributing funds that the primary priority of the department is the spreading of the money among the school districts on a rather equal basis. According to an official of the department, there have been no priorities established that would favor, for example, the urban areas of the state. The flat grant will not change the relative financial position of any school districts and the special grant operation favors the wealthy districts with the capacity to engage in and develop the programs funded by NDEA. The flat grant coupled with virtual automatic approval keeps all the LEAs happy and uncomplaining. The special grant based on a first-come, first-served basis also serves to remove discretionary decision making from the state. This voluntary refusal to exercise discretion, to enhance state developed priorities, reflects the department's unwillingness to exert its priorities over those of the LEAs.

A new demand from the federal government for a new state plan will bring the decision-making process of the department fully into the spotlight. The demand made of the department is that it develop a complete state plan covering the assessment of needs, goals, priorities among goals, the presentation of a concrete program for reaching these goals, and evaluation procedures. Unless Massachusetts submits this plan and it is approved, the NDEA program will be withdrawn from the state. Despite the importance and the difficulty of the task, the director of the Bureau of Elementary and Secondary Education has shown no interest in participating in the development of the plan, nor has he given his official approval to the NDEA staff to take a significant portion of their time for the development of the plan.

The senior supervisor appointed to develop the plan envisions this as a collective decision, participated in by various people at the supervisory level (the lowest professional rank), who will consult with the LEAs before and after the plan is drafted. There is a clear desire for consensus. Agreement on the plan is the key factor—not a rational analysis of the needs, the logical ordering of goals, and the most effective allocation of resources to achieve those goals.

The legislation and regulations call for the state to use a portion of its allotted funds for the expansion and improvement of supervisory or related services in the critical subjects covered by the legislation. The state plan reflects a vast expansion of personnel to deal with this federal mandate. At present, however, there are six supervisors in the ten critical subjects covered by the Act. At this time there is no supervisor in mathematics. The shortage in personnel is due to a shortage in federal funds as well as low salaries. The state plan lists the job of the supervisor as covering eighteen separately listed duties which amount to the following: assisting the localities in developing and planning new curriculum in the critical areas; making on-site visits; reviewing applications; promotional work of various kinds; and participating in research projects. The reality of the situation is somewhat different from that envisioned in the state plan. Basically, the supervisors believe that it is up to the LEAs to develop their own plans (which will probably gain automatic acceptance), and that the state will interfere with a minimum of rules and regulations.

Beyond that, the contact between the department and the LEA is limited to the mailings of application forms and regulations and an occasional site visit. Site visits usually only occur upon request of the LEA. The other occasion for a site visit may be the review of a local program for which the applicant is asking a large amount of special project money. With these exceptions, there have been no field audits largely due to the lack of staff. When field visits do occur, it appears that the evaluation is conducted by "intuition." It is felt the "intuition" is as adequate a way of evaluating a program as any formal method that might be devised.

It is also clear that the relations between the MDE and the LEA are friendly and informal. But, the formal interconnection between the MDE staff and the LEA personnel is also significant. There is constant interaction with professional organizations. Staff members attend the meetings of the various organizations, such as the Foreign Language Association, and the staff has even been instrumental in promoting the establishment of the Massachusetts Association of Science Supervisors. The current president of that organization is the NDEA science supervisor.

The overall impact of this kind of administration can only contribute to a potential abuse of the program and an overall lack of effectiveness. From the local vantage point, it would appear that NDEA is simply considered to be another source to support the regular ongoing program of the school. In other words, the NDEA program has done little to encourage the districts to do anything additional or different. In Boston, the NDEA funds contribute to keeping alive a "Department of Science" which sprang up, just as did the NDEA program, in the aftermath of the Sputnik crisis. This is the only department of its kind in Boston—there are no other such citywide subject departments. The department is largely supported by local funds, but NDEA funds are a handy additional source to use for what it would be doing anyway.

ESEA-Title II

In contrast to Title I of ESEA, the important issue with which the state must grapple under Title II is the distribution of funds between school districts and among the private schools. Title II does not provide a federal formula for the distribution of these funds, but leaves the determination of inter-district distribution up to the state; the only qualification is that the state must take into account the relative need, as determined from time to time, of the children and teachers of the state in public and private schools for library resources, textbooks, or other instructional materials.

Title II is administered out of MDE's Bureau of Library Extension; this bureau is advised by its own Board of Library Commissioners, not by the Board of Education. At the start of the Title II program, the office had been staffed by four full-time professionals. With the cut-back in federal funds, the number of professionals has been reduced. The turnover in the positions which have been filled has been considerable. As a result, the Director of the Bureau is the person most familiar with the details of the overall policy of the state with regard to the administration of Title II. Almost all of the major policy decisions are made by the director of the bureau, aided by the Title II advisory committee—an important decision-making forum in the Title II programs. Unlike Title I, where most of the decisions are made at the office level, under Title II the major decisions are made at the advisory committee level.

The advisory committee is a sixteen-man committee made up of two people from the bureau; several superintendents from public schools; a superintendent from private schools; six librarians from public and private schools; and two audiovisual coordinators. The mixture on the advisory council represents the major contenders for Title II funds—public versus private schools; librarians versus audiovisual coordinators; the combination maximizes the influence of the LEA officials.

Districts which fail to inform the bureau whether they will apply are pursued for a final answer to ensure that no LEA or private school inadvertently neglects to seek its entitlement.

The advisory committee's first attempt at a distribution formula which would satisfy the federal requirements and meet the political exigencies within the state was a two-part grant: a basic grant and a relative-need grant. The basic grant, which covered 50 percent of the money appropriated to the state, was simply a flat grant per child in the school district or private school. The remaining half was distributed on the basis of a complex formula which measured local *effort*. This two-part grant was to be used in the first year of Title II allocations. In the second through fifth years of the state plan, a special demonstration center grant was to be given to the systems in which previous effort had been high and in which centers were already well established. The purpose of these grants was to establish demonstration school libraries or instructional material centers at both the elementary and secondary levels in several regions of the state.

There are a number of points to be made about this initial state policy adopted by the advisory committee. Most important, neither the basic grant portion nor the relative need portion of the grant take into account the relative need of the children and teachers of the state for library resources, textbooks, or other instructional materials. The relative need portion of the grant depends exclusively upon the local tax effort—the higher the tax rate, the higher the amount of the award per child. This tax effort is for support of the entire school program and has nothing to do with the effort the particular district made with regard to supporting libraries or other related services. Moreover, a high tax effort does not by itself indicate relative need. Admittedly, school districts with low property values are often forced to make a great tax effort to raise sufficient money to run the schools, and hence may be considered poor school districts; it is also true that there are school districts such as Boston which are poor despite fairly high property values. While Boston's property values are not the highest in the state, they fall more in the upward rankings; but the number of municipal services which must be supported by those property taxes are significantly larger and more expensive than those in the nearby suburbs. Hence, out of the general tax rate the schools can claim only a small proportion of the total because of the other claims on the tax dollar. Municipal overburden causes Boston to appear to be making a lower school tax effort than many other districts. On the other hand, wealthy suburban districts with high property values and a strong desire to establish a strong school system can tax themselves with a high school tax rate; raise enormous sums for their schools; and in turn be rewarded by this formula for their effort. These are probably the systems with already well-furnished libraries and the systems that will tend to attract the demonstration center grants to boot. Finally, those children who happen to be trapped within a school district that is "lazy," i.e., which makes a low tax effort because the parents prefer to spend their money on private instead of public goods, are penalized by the formula.

Massachusetts developed this formula for a number of reasons. It felt that federal Title II policy indicated maximum participation in the Title II funds, i.e., they should be spread around. Secondly, the advisory council felt it unfair to penalize those who had made an effort to support good library service—a feeling rather contrary to the federal priorities.

USOE rejected this formula and ordered the state to replace it with a formula that more carefully took into account actual relative need for library resources. In response, the advisory committee developed the formula in use since the second year of the program.

Some comments about this formula are in order. First, the proportion of the relative need part of the total grant can vary from school district to school district. In other words, even the relative need portion of this grant seems to operate more like a flat grant than a truly relative need grant. On top of this, those districts which are already well off with high quality services obtain an extra sum of money under one of the categories.

We can only conclude that the advisory council is still more concerned with being fair to all the districts than in really carrying out the federal priority to honor relative need. We must also conclude that since USOE has approved this formula, it also is not taking too seriously the legislative relative need requirement. Under the current formula, private schools are treated the same way as public schools—illustrating once again the advisory council's concern with equality and wide distribution of resources.

ESEA II calls for the state plan to set forth criteria for determining the proportions of the state's allotment which will be expended for library resources, textbooks, and other printed and published instructional materials. The Massachusetts regulations state a series of maximum and minimum percentages which the recipient must follow in allocating its funds. *Not less* than 70 percent of the allocated local funds must be spent on *printed* school library resources or other printed and published instructional materials. *Not more* than 30 percent of the local allocation may be spent on audiovisual materials. *Not more* than 10 percent of the local allocation may be spent on textbooks.

These allocations represent the outcome of a political struggle that has reached into the advisory council. The forces represented on the council clearly did not need assistance to purchase textbooks, because Massachusetts is a free textbook state and the schools are relatively much better supplied with textbooks than with printed library materials and audiovisual materials. Thus the battle for resources was fought to gain money for printed materials or for audiovisual materials. The librarians want most of the money spent on printed materials; if money is spent on audiovisual equipment, they often want that equipment located in the library and under library control. The audiovisual people want to obtain a larger share of the money and to establish separate instructional resource centers controlled and operated apart from the school library. This local battle takes on statewide dimensions as the Massachusetts School Library Association and the Massachusetts Audio-Visual Association vie for Title II funds. (It might also be noted that the audiovisual group is now aspiring to obtain recognition as a profession by sponsoring the passage of a bill which will provide for state certification of the audiovisual personnel.)

The outcome of this struggle in the Title II context has obviously favored the librarians. This outcome is not surprising in light of the fact that the advisory council is largely dominated by librarians (approximately eight) compared with the presence of two audio visual coordinators. Furthermore, it might be noted that the whole Title II administration is handled out of the Bureau of Library Extension and the professional staff working on the program are librarians.

There is an indication that the existing compromise which so heavily favors the librarians may be changed in the future. The direction one important figure on the advisory council (a librarian) would like to take is to indicate that a larger proportion of the local funds may be allocated to audiovisual equipment, after it has been established that the book needs of the school have been satisifed.

As has already been noted, the Massachusetts concept of relative need leads largely to a per capita distribution of funds between school districts and yet the state regulation declares that distribution of funds solely on a per capita basis does not satisfy the relative needs provision. The contradiction resolves itself, however, if one focuses on the word "solely" in the regulation. This clearly leaves room for some distribution on the basis of a per capita allotment. Furthermore, in interviews it became clear that the state would not approve of a local district allocating its resources just to those schools within the district which did not have library service—that is, the state expects the money to be spread around within the district. Thus, the state policy with regard to the internal distribution of resources is one which assumes the distribution of some of the money on the basis of a per capita grant, to be modified somewhat by considerations of need. This same stress on equal sharing is apparent in the emphasis the regulation places upon the placement of the materials in an easily accessible, centralized school library, or instructional materials center. The regulations also stress the desirability of long hours to make the material available to all, and the usefulness of flexible scheduling. Local school officials, superintendents, librarians, and audiovisual people preponderate on the council. People from the local school system clearly would have a political interest in spreading the resources around within the districts as widely as possible.

The between-district formula slightly favors districts which have need problems or make great effort with regard to their elementary schools. The regulations, however, make no mention of the district's making any priority allocation to the elementary schools.

A problem with the Massachusetts approach to the detection of substitution is that it, like other methods, really cannot work.

This program has been captured by the local educational interests (both public and private) in the state. The advisory council is dominated by these interest groups and it is in the advisory council that the major policy decisions are made.

The Division of State and Federal Finance, the Board of Education, O.P.P.C., and, finally, the Office of Education must approve the state plan which reflects the major policy actions that the council must take. The only agency ever to override a council decision was the Office of Education in the first year of the program. These policy decisions tend to favor the wide distribution of money, as might be expected when the interest group being served is itself making the decisions as to who gets what. Similarly, the regulations concerning the amount to be spent on printed versus audiovisual materials clearly reflects the triumph of librarians over the audiovisual people.

In its dealing with the LEAs, the bureau is largely hampered by an extremely small and changing staff. There seems to be little in the way of aggressive leadership. Only the difficult decisions with regard to project application approval reach the director of the bureau, who in turn may consult with the coordinator of federal aid for the Department of Education—the assistant commissioner of the Division of State and Federal Finance. This consultation on a particular project application is also the only degree of coordination that seems to take place between Title II and other federal aid programs. As with Title I, this Title is administered in splendid isolation from the rest of the aid programs.

ESEA-Title III

In contrast to the Title I and Title II ESEA programs, our interest in Title III concerns the future more than the past. It was only in July, 1968, (FY 1969) that the MDE was financially able to establish a Title III office, the Bureau of Curriculum Innovation, to deal with the 1967 amendments to the Elementary and Secondary Education Act. The belated establishment delayed Washington's approval of the Massachusetts Plan until October, 1968. By this date, Washington had already funded a number of projects on its own, thus reducing the state's area of discretion for that fiscal year. The state fully funded twenty-two projects and partially funded four; it had fiscal responsibility for twenty-six of the seventy-five Title III projects in Massachusetts, but all were actually refunded continuing programs. In FY 1970, the state took over 100 percent of the Title III funds allocated to Massachusetts; it became responsible for sixty-nine programs (six others were still directly funded and controlled by Washington). The number of Title III projects has been declining as Title III funding draws to a close. In 1971, only 15 percent of the original programs will still be in operation with Title III funds.

The attrition in the number of programs was illustrative of one of the Title III office's major problems, cutbacks in the level of federal appropriations. As the state's responsibility for decision making increased, its Title III federal funds decreased. In effect, its discretion was usurped by the continuing projects previously approved by Washington. Even after its assumption of the program, the state was, as one Title III official put it, a "junior partner."

What was left for the Title III office to do was to lay its plans and prepare the political groundwork for the time when a strong exercise of state discretion would be appropriate. Primarily responsible for the build-up of the Title III office (known officially as the Bureau of Curriculum Innovation) is its director, John Watson. Mr. Watson has an unusual reputation within the state department; the Title III office is considered the most progressive, exciting, and innovative bureau in the department. Despite the low salary range that the department is able to offer, he has managed to attract to his office a group of approximately a half-dozen people of youth and energy—characteristics that are missing from almost all the other bureaus.

John Watson was also instrumental in hiring the Title III coordinator. The internal operations of the office seem to be informal and cooperative; the Title III coordinator has the major responsibility for the development of the Title III plans, but he frequently consults with the bureau director. In fact, the director and the Title III coordinator are located, together with a third person, in a rather small room so that their desks are in close proximity. This close association is in marked contrast with the relationship that exists between, for example, the Title I director and the director of the bureau of elementary and secondary education, or the director of NDEA and the director of the bureau of elementary and secondary education (BESE).

After the review of the Letter of Intent, notice of approval is sent out. Full proposals are then invited, and the state tells the LEAs that workshops and assistance will be offered to grantees in proposal writing; the stating of behavioral objectives; the development of evaluation designs; and in the dissemination of program design.

The state plan provides for a complicated project approval process.

The associate commissioner of the MDE came from the New Jersey Department of Education in September of 1969. Since that time his primary concern has been "to get hold" of the bureacracy and the bureau chiefs, with the exception of the Bureau of Curriculum Innovation because, in his words, "those people are doing a great job and should not be interfered with." Both the associate commissioner and the bureau believe that the department of education should take a leadership role to encourage new and improved educational services at the local level. This role would be executed through persuasion and encouragement, improved services to the LEA, and consultation and collaboration. The old-line bureaucratic position stresses the role of the department as a check-writer and regulator of the specific minimum legal requirements established by the legislature, e.g., that each school district offer at least 180 days of schooling per year. At this time the check-writers seem to be prevailing, because of the large number who hold key positions, and because of the fiscal constraints imposed by the legislature and the Bureau of Administration and Finance. Coordination with other parts of the department has apparently proved to be difficult. For example, by law, the bureau must assess the critical educational needs of the state. The bureau unsuccessfully tried to gain the cooperation of the Division of Research and Development, but only succeeded when the federal government last spring threatened to withhold $100,000 from the department. This lack of cooperation and coordination is characteristic of relationships among the various divisions and bureaus of the department. Each office pursues its own interests with its own clientele, preserving its "autonomy" from encroachments by others.

The most influential reference group for the Title III Office is the state advisory council which, by law, the state is required to establish. In addition to the usual representatives of the local educational agencies—superintendents, principals, and teachers, the council (as of June, 1970) includes a labor leader, social worker, museum director, a representative from the television industry, two Harvard professors of education, and the executive director of the Massachusetts Council for Arts and Humanities. They, in turn, represent a broader reference group with whom the bureau can work. The Title III office relies heavily upon the council for advice and assistance in developing the state plan. Consultations with some of the more active members of the council are frequent; full meetings of the council are less frequent. The council provides creative input, and its approval of the plan helps to legitimatize the state policies. The office has even gone so far in its use of the council as to get it to lobby successfully in Washington with the state's congressmen and senators for full funding of the Title III program. Reliance on the advisory council has reached the point that the associate commissioner of the division of curriculum and instruction is thinking about urging the office to back away from the close relationship.

The Title III office is apparently politically astute; it hopes to achieve its reform innovations in collaboration with the LEAs, not despite them. Whether the strategy will work remains to be seen. The compromises that have been built into the state plan are obviously reserving many of the difficult political decisions for the future.

In the application procedure, the office sends to LEAs, upon request, copies of the guidelines; the listing of critical educational needs as assessed in the state; and a form and specific directions for the filing of the Letter of Intent. By requesting that the LEA file only a Letter of Intent, the state avoids forcing the LEA into drawing up an elaborate and detailed project application before it has been given some indication that the project will be approved. Following the approval of the project application, the Title III office will negotiate a grant for the first budget period. The initial grant award document will make available the Title III funds needed to support the project for the first budget period. The continuation grant is the amount awarded for the budget period following the initial period. It will be 90 percent of the original grant for first continuation and 80 percent of the original grant for second continuation. The project period is the total period of time, generally not exceeding three years, for which a project may be supported.

In distributing Title III funds within school districts, the state plan considers the control of the funds; the participation of private school children; the marshalling of multiple sources of support; the question of supplementing or supplanting local funds; and the phase-out of federal support. The only real addition to the statute is the state's requirement that the project applications include a plan for phasing out federal support and increasing local support during the life of the project.

The distribution of funds between districts is controlled in part by the Act itself. To implement its requirements, the state has developed a long list of criteria which will be used in evaluating projects. However, there is no real sense of priority given to any of the seventeen criteria, and they are so vaguely described that an applicant could not determine if he had met the criteria without a ruling from the Title III office.

The big political question of "who gets what" has yet to be settled. The office has deliberately avoided developing a distribution formula or a clear set of ordered priorities; in so doing, they have taken not only much discretion, but also many potential headaches. In the long run this can mean, as one Title III official stated, the loss of discretion as the pressures increase from superintendents and their cohorts. If the bureau has a true program of priorities, evidenced in its approval of applications, it can retain its discretionary power. Our interviews indicate the office, in contrast to the other programs, may have a preference for urban projects. This priority does not emerge from the state plan or regulations. However, many of the major political decisions were left unresolved by the Act itself, which merely laid out guidelines without stressing which districts or problems would get priority. The MDE is once again avoiding the responsibility. In two or three years one can expect to find Title III funds spread equally around the state unless the state takes a strong position.

To comply with the federal regulations, the state has planned some ambitious evaluation efforts. They would include "on-site evaluation by a team composed of State Department Supervisors, consultants and, if possible, at least one Advisory Council member. . . . During and following the on-site visitation, the self-evaluation instrument completed by the project staff will be compared with the findings of the visiting team." The evaluation instrument which then appears is a rather loosely drawn document providing for rankings of various items ranging from 1-5 and for comments on strengths, weaknesses, and other aspects of the project. The lack of standards, evaluation by consensus, and the improbability of amassing teams to evaluate all state projects annually are critical. Attempts to work with researchers in the department have contributed little to this evaluation. What remains to be proved is whether or not the state will have the political clout to refuse to renew projects when it finds they are not effective. Given the present state politics and the political muscle of the LEAs vis-à-vis the department, it seems unlikely that the state will have the political power to refuse to renew unsuccessful projects. In this connection, all the elaborate state plans for getting the LEAs to evaluate themselves (as the Act requires) seem a little improbable.

Certainly the Bureau of Curriculum Innovation is different from all the others we have studied. It plans to reform educational practices and casts the state in a far more demanding role than it has played in the other federal programs. The bureau is willing to bear the political pressure in order to preserve the innovative dimension of Title III. It will have to establish and maintain priorities if it is to succeed.

Notes

1. *Rankings of the States for 1972* (Washington, D.C.: National Education Association, 1972).

2. See, for example, the *Willis-Harrington Report* (Boston: Massachusetts Advisory Council on Education, 1965), and Stephen K. Bailey et. al., *Schoolmen and Politics: A Study of State Aid in the Northeast* (Syracuse: Syracuse University Press, 1962).

3. Laurence Iannaccone, *Politics in Education*, (New York: Center for Applied Research in Education, 1968).

4. Edgar Litt, *The Political Culture of Massachusetts* (Cambridge: M.I.T. Press, 1965).

5. Ibid., p. 208.

6. Ibid., p. 209.

7. Willis-Harrington Report, op. cit., p. 130.

8. Ibid., p. 136.

9. Lincoln Filene Center, *Study of the Massachusetts Department of Education: Progress Report* (Boston: Lincoln Filene Center, 1969).

10. This apparently absurd way of doing business has gone on too long and under too many governors as well as commissioners for everyone to assume it is without reason. The present writer offers this hypothesis: That an examination of interest group and constituency access to MDE councils would reveal that a pattern once existed by which such leakage put pressure on the General Court and thence on the Bureau of the Budget. Fear of such leakage and its political effects on the Bureau explains present absurdity.

11. Most of the following information is adapted from "Compensatory Education in Massachusetts: An Evaluation with Recommendations," submitted to Massachusetts Advisory Council on Education by David Jeralum, Director, and Kathryn Hecht, Assistant Director.

12. David K. Cohen and Tyl R. Van Geel, "Public Education," in Samuel H. Beer and Richard E. Barringer, eds., *The State and the Poor* (Cambridge: Winthrop Publishers, 1970).

13. "Compensatory Education in Massachusetts," op. cit.

6

The Politics of Federal Aid to Education in Texas

Michael W. Kirst

Rampant discrimination in Texas federal aid allocations against urban areas and core cities continues unabated and grows more critical with each school year. The Texas population grew by 14.7 percent from 1960 to 1970 (all in urban areas); over three-fourths of its school population is in metropolitan areas. In addition to the decline in the rural birth rate, nearly 245,000 men and women between the ages of 20 and 29 were expected to move from rural areas to urban centers between 1960 and 1970.[1] The number of school age children in non-metropolitan Texas is expected to drop from 750,000 in 1960 to 524,000 in 1980. The 1970 census figures show Dallas and Houston are among the fastest growing core cities in the nation. Yet federal aid in Texas is distributed largely on the basis of 1948 state aid policies, when only one-half of the Texas population lived in sections now classified by the Census Bureau as Standard Metropolitan Statistical Areas.

A rurally dominated legislature; a governor invested with weak formal powers and possessed of unreliable transitory political support; a monolithic professional interest group (TSTA), and a department intent on remaining above politics conspire to create the present inequities.

Research Assertions and Federal Aid in Texas

Assertion No. 1. There will be less involvement and political influence by the governor and legislature on federal aid in comparison with state aid.

This assertion was found to be correct in Texas. State aid issues, particularly teacher salaries, have been a major (often *the* major) issue in Texas politics for the past twenty years. The structural characteristics of Texas government and the traditional politics of education in Texas have precluded federal aid as a significant issue for the governor or legislature. Texas state aid, except for some areas of vocational education, is automatically appropriated once an authorization bill has passed—a procedure which deflects concern from issues not involved in the authorization process. Even in vocational education, federal funds are so merged with state funds as to become indistinguishable as a separate issue. The image of TEA and its commissioner—fair, objective, professional, and above politics—also contributes to the lack of gubernatorial and legislative intervention.

235

Moreover, politicians are loath to question TEA decisions on intrastate aid distribution because they do not wish to tout their pursuit of federal aid. The rural favoritism predominant in most TEA federal aid distribution undoubtedly is, in part, an obeisance to a very rurally oriented legislature which controls TEA salaries and internal budget.

Assertion No. 2. The influence and impact of the urban school lobby on the state allocation of federal aid will not be significant.

This assertion was also confirmed in Texas. The political culture of Texas discourages vociferous examination of federal money. Until a few years ago, no urban school lobby existed. The emerging coalition has concentrated on eradicating the discrimination against cities prevalent in the Texas Foundation program; this almost blatant discrimination was not fully realized prior to the 1968 study of the Governor's Committee on Public School Education. Reapportionment of the Texas legislature must occur if the urban lobby is to amass substantial influence. Moreover, urban districts are reluctant to split with the monolithic interest group, the Texas State Teachers Association (TSTA). TSTA wants to avoid the division of its united front, which would be wrought by favoring urban or rural districts. Overt lobbying is also impeded by the sacrosanctity of the TEA image, since such a campaign would inevitably challenge some of TEA's allocation criteria.

Assertion No. 3. As federal aid increases and states have more discretion in allocation, pressures will increase on state governments from organized interests.

We did not find a significant amount of pressure group activity in federal aid at any stage in its growth and development. TSTA is the only influential interest group, and the executive director, who formerly worked in TEA with Commissioner Edgar, has chosen not to intervene on TEA allocation decisions. TSTA feels that federal aid is "none of our business" unless it involves legislation TEA needs (e.g., Title III ESEA supplementary centers). The leading policy role in federal aid was exercised by TEA Deputy Commissioner Warren Hitt until his death. The department, however, was willing to let TSTA be the initiating and lobbying force in state aid.

There was no evidence of political activities by the NAACP or urban community groups. These groups, however, have brought court suits against the urban discrimination in state aid. Commissioner Edgar and TEA's image have discouraged the use of the state board as a conduit for special interests. The state board is composed of people compatible with local school professionals. The legislature and the governor do not intercede for special interests. In Texas, federal aid allocation is very much a bureaucratic saga with a limited number of important actors.

Assertion No. 4. The state education agency will attempt to minimize political conflict and pressure by using existing state aid formulas for allocation of federal funds.

Wherever TEA had discretion in intra-state fund allocation, actual state aid formulas or a parallel system was used. The vocational education money was merged completely with state aid formulas as was Title II of ESEA, to the extent it was appropriate. ESEA-Title III supplementary centers were based on an earlier state media center program. NDEA-Title III followed the state aid emphasis on small and rural districts, and the formula used for rating and funding projects paralleled the state aid formulas. Title I has a federally mandated formula which is not similar to any state distribution and could not be changed by TEA.

TEA officials would probably not agree that this use of state formulas was based on a desire to avoid political conflict, and not enough data exists to rebut their view. Perhaps it was just simpler and more logical to use an accepted state device like the economic index. Undoubtedly, TEA would have encountered more controversy and resistance if it had attempted to institute changes which challenged the inequity of existing state aid formulas before the 1968 Governor's Committee Report.

Assertion No. 5. Federal aid, except in a manner restricted by federal guidelines or requirements, will flow within a state as it has in the past.

This was definitely true in Texas. Federal aid in Texas shows a consistent lack of specific statewide priorities; priorities have traditionally been left to local judgment. The federal Vocational Education Act of 1968 mandates a certain percentage for the disadvantaged and handicapped which TEA must set aside for special project grant review. The remainder of the vocational education money is plugged into state-aid formulas and concentrations. Before the department was required to set aside 15 percent for the disadvantaged, such programs were only a very small percentage of total vocational expenditures and not marked by large-scale growth. Money for vocational education construction, like construction funds for other state facilities (hospitals, parks, etc.), has been channeled into rural and smaller school districts. It is very questionable whether in allocating vocational education and ESEA II funds, USOE should continue to accept the state-aid economic index as basis of need and ability to pay. NDEA III has followed the state-aid pattern of priority to small and rural school districts. ESEA III was based on a prior state concept of media centers, distributed evenly around the state, with no particular assistance to urban districts. The attempt to initiate statewide comprehensive planning and priority setting was aborted, in large part because of USOE and congressional reluctance to drop categorical aid requirements.

Title I also provides a classic example of this assertion. Until the department saw the U.S. Office of Education cut off funds and demand restitution from Mississippi, program guides #44 and #45 of the basic federal requirements were never sent to LEAs or carefully enforced. The Mississippi example led to a new application form and more detailed monitoring.

Assertion No. 6. SEA personnel are socialized so that they view their proper role as providing technical assistance to LEAs, not enforcing or policing federal requirements or setting program priorities.

The administrative role of TEA staff corresponds to this assertion, although no solid data was collected on the nature of the socialization process. There are very few people in the TEA who would fit even roughly under Iannaccone's classification of "political activist."[2] Some of the second level Title I staff had tendencies in this direction. Impatient with established TEA patterns and ways of operating, they were more concerned with federal intent than the LEAs desired. They also saw the poor as their clients and had close links with Washington Title I staff.

For the most part, TEA staff enforced federal requirements reluctantly and viewed "professional leadership" as helping LEAs get federal money, generating trust from LEAs, and avoiding high conflict situations. Moreover, except for staff in the central evaluation office, there is very little research orientation. This central staff has not been able to use evaluation data as a basis for program or allocation decisions. The department is universally reluctant to overrule LEA judgments on the merits of specific educational approaches or methodologies. Fiscal requirements are enforced to a point, but program leadership is very gentle and slow. In vocational education, it is questionable whether the letter of the federal fiscal requirements on ability and need is being observed by the outmoded economic index.

Patterns of Allocation of Federal
Aid to School Districts

The discrimination against urban areas in federal aid allocation follows the pattern established in Texas state aid allocation.

Texas State Aid: Its Relationship to Federal Programs

Notorious for its discrimination against urban areas, state aid in Texas is now being challenged in several urban-based court suits. The Governor's Committee on Public School Education accurately summed up the situation by stressing Texas now distributes more than $730 million annually in state school aid according to a system which "almost defies comprehension." We will confine our examination of these complex formulas to the parts relevant to federal aid distribution.[3]

The Texas state aid legislation bases need on required teacher units, which in turn are based on ADA. The smaller districts receive more teacher units in proportion to their attendance. They also receive a higher operating allowance in proportion to their needs than do the large cities. Ability is based on an economic index for a whole county. The more widely used assessed property valuation is only employed to apportion ability to pay *within counties*. In brief, the economic index measures economic activity (payrolls, value added by manufacture, income tax returns), and this takes place largely in cities. Cities are penalized for their economic activity in that they receive less state aid. Moreover, the county assessor's office decides which districts within the county are to have the most tax-paying ability. Studies have shown the rural and small town bias of the county assessors office has resulted in overvaluation of city property and undervaluation of property in outlying areas. Because USOE has accepted state aid formulas as an adequate yardstick to measure qualification for Vocational Education and ESEA II funds, state aid formulas must be examined.

The following steps are involved in computing the amount of state aid:

1. Districts with 1,600 or more ADA are allowed one classroom teacher unit (CTU) for each 26 pupils. For each CTU the district receives a salary payment from a state salary schedule.
2. The number of CTUs is multiplied by $600 as an "operating allowance."
3. Transportation costs are computed and added to personnel and operating costs to determine *full* cost of the State Minimum Foundation School Program.
4. Twenty percent of the total program costs for the state must then be distributed among the 254 counties on the basis of the Economic Index.
5. Within each county, the program costs assigned to that county must be distributed to the school district according to the percentage of county property valuations located in each district, as determined by the County Tax Assessor.

The discrimination against large urban districts which begins with the CTU allowance is compounded because other professional personnel are based on the CTUs. The formulas below demonstrate the outcome:

ADA	CTUs
15 - 25	1
26 - 109	2 for first 26 ADA,
	1 for each additional 21 ADA
110 - 156	6
157 - 444	1 for each 24 ADA
445 - 487	19
488 - 1512	1 for each 25 ADA
1513 - 1599	61
1600 and over	1 for each 26 ADA

The federal aid formulas, however, rely on the economic index and the county assessors' judgments as a measure of ability to pay. The economic index is used in only four states; in Texas, it includes assessed property values as well as such factors as payrolls and value added. Data for most components are four or five years old and must be "adjusted." (Everyone agrees that property assessments among Texas counties are far from equalized.) But assessed values must be retained because of inadequacies in the income factors. The income factors, in turn, are justified on the grounds that assessed values are not uniform. The total number of scholastics—which does not bear on a county's final capacity—are also included. Production estimates for agricultural products are based on the 1954 Census of Agriculture. A 1956 study by the Texas Research League still is valid in its conclusion that economic index was no proxy for equalized assessed property values, the intention of the legislature in 1948. Glen Ivy, the staff director for the 1968 Governor's Committee, stressed their data showed that, since economic activity takes place in urban areas, urban schools were being severely penalized by the economic index.

Federal Aid Allocation

Since vocational education and ESEA-Title II funds are distributed on the basis of state formulas, their allocation also discriminates against urban districts.

In NDEA III, the state policy, where possible, has been to channel funds to small or rural districts.

In the case of the supplementary centers—the major recipients of ESEA-Title III funds—the smaller districts have again derived the greatest benefits. Although the twenty centers are dispersed throughout the state and some are headquartered in large cities, the services they provide, such as data processing and media materials, are already possessed by the cities.

Prior to the 1969 administrative changes, even Title I funds were not being targeted as strictly as possible—a construction which would have increased the funds available to inner city schools. Following USOE's punitive measures against Mississippi, department personnel more rigorously examined program qualifications and attempted to channel the funds to the disadvantaged—a policy which increased the flow of federal funds to urban districts.

Political Factors Shaping Fiscal and Administrative Patterns

Rural Orientation and a Political Superintendent: 1900-1947

Texas has about 1,200 local districts enrolling about two and one-half million pupils; more than 800 districts have fewer than 1,600 pupils each. There are 43 districts with more than 10,000 pupils each and about 700 districts with fewer than 500 pupils each. The twenty-one members of the Texas-size State Board of

Education are elected from congressional districts based on the 1930 census. The board appoints the commissioner of education who must be confirmed by the senate. The "political strangulation of the urban areas by a rural dominated state legislature," as noted by MacCorkle and Smith, has also greatly affected the politics of education. Although the 1960 census characterized the state as 75 percent urban (in contrast with 24 percent in 1920),[4] Texas congressional districts were the second most malapportioned in the United States.[5] Until court-ordered redistricting in 1965, the average was one state legislator for every 50,000; this skyrocketed to one to 87,000 in Dallas, and one to 100,000 in Houston. This malapportioned legislature has historically responded to the plight of the rural schools; it has not recognized the impact on the larger cities of recent population migrations and increased urban growth.

At the turn of this century, urban schools were 30 percent to 50 percent superior to rural schools in all areas—expenditures, school facilities, length of term, etc.[6] The first large school aid bill was passed in 1915; directed at rural and small town schools with fewer than 200 students, it provided funds for modern, sanitary schoolhouses.

Formerly composed of a state superintendent and seven clerks,[7] the state department of education increased in size and stature as a result of the rural aid law. The passage in 1917 of the Smith-Hughes Act, with its rural concern, also shaped the orientation of the TEA. In succeeding years, political supporters of rural aid expanded the Act's original goals to include school buses, tuition for high school students compelled to leave their home districts, and a minimum state salary for teachers in eligible districts.

In his campaign for the state superintendency in 1932, L.A. Woods (of Waco) gained political mileage from attacking the discrepancy between urban and rural districts. His departure from the traditional nonpolitical image of the office was described in a recent historical study:

... Woods stumped the state presenting a program of action for education, enlisting personnel support, making promises, and playing politics. The character of the campaign represented a sharp break with tradition. Politics, Texas style, were introduced into the campaign for chief state school officer.

One of the charges Dr. Woods brought against the incumbent, for example, was that the State Department of Education was too remote from the people, and geared to do everything for the city schools, nothing for the rural ones.

This contained enough truth to hurt: the high schools division was large, and high schools were found principally in urban areas.[8]

After his election, Superintendent Woods used patronage to build up a loyal staff. Unlike many politicians, Woods attempted with some success to implement his platform "to bring the state department of education close to the people" by doing everything possible for rural and small town schools—a popular move with the rural-dominated legislature. He placed twenty-four deputies in regions around the state who offered technical assistance to rural schools and helped prepare their local budgets. These regional deputies also were a vital communications link to the state legislators who helped Woods stay in office.[9] Under Woods there was a six-fold increase in rural aid and a large reduction of rural common schools that were under county supervision. His policies, however, led to a situation in which the large urban school systems were left to work out their own problems.

Utilizing everything from radio talks to pamphlets, Woods inveighed against any bill that would enable the state board to appoint the state superintendent. Woods lost on the issue of the state superintendency which was part of a series of finance bills called The Gilmer-Aikin Act of 1948. These acts set for TEA the basic financial formulas, general authority, and orientation in effect today.

A New Image for the TEA

Highly critical of Woods' political orientation, the State Board of Education had commented in 1938:

Leaders in the field of public education in Texas have endorsed the selection of the State Superintendent of Public Instruction by the State Board of Education on the basis solely of educational qualifications and administrative experience. Accession to this office should not be controlled by current noneducational, political issues.

Appointment of the State Superintendent would enable that officer to devote more time to the functions of his office than is possible under the present set up which calls for much political "fence building."[10]

The crucial role of TEA in present federal aid allocation was partially shaped by the reaction against the Woods era. The designers of the 1948 Gilmer-Aikin Act succeeded in establishing a highly prestigious TEA, directed by an appointed commissioner and imbued with an aura of professional expertise "above politics." This situation has provided TEA with great discretionary power and minimal legislative, gubernatorial, and lobby interference. Indeed, one man, J.W. Edgar has been State Commissioner since the passage of the 1948 Act.

With regard to the TEA, one framer of the 1948 Act observed:

We put most of our eggs in the basket of a strong and independent TEA to bring about quality education. If we could elect the state board, we could stop the election of the state commissioner. We investigated other states and discovered very little interest in state board elections. So we came up with the idea of a Texas size state board of 21 members to keep it close to the people's interest.

Then we suggested to local superintendents that they get at least two candidates from each of the 21 districts. These candidates were all local board members who were urged to run by their superintendents. We wanted some competition but not 4 people running.[11]

The chairman of the new state board was Robert Anderson, who had extensive oil and cattle holdings, and subsequently became Secretary of the treasury under President Eisenhower. He arranged a meeting with the key legislators involved in Gilmer-Aikin and proposed a salary of $20,000 to attract a highly qualified commissioner. In 1948, only one school administrator salary in the United States was higher. In the interim period during the summer of 1949, the governor appointed L.P. Sturgeon to be acting commissioner. Mr. Sturgeon subsequently became an assistant superintendent and then head of the only important professional education interest group in Texas—Texas State Teachers Association. He has maintained a very close personal relationship with all the top officials in TEA ever since 1948.

The state board chose J.W. Edgar, superintendent in Fort Worth and a member of the state committee to help pass Gilmer-Aikin. As Pearson and Fuller commented: "Some interpreted his appointment as indicating a swing in the direction of policies favorable to big city schools. This was a justifiable presumption, but a mistaken one. There was to be no continuation of the political atmosphere that had existed in the previous two decades."[1][2]

Edgar's strategy was to reverse the TEA political image and to end overt rural favoritism. He appointed respected educators and utilized extensive study and advisory groups of local school personnel before setting policies. Unlike the flamboyant Woods, Edgar kept very much in the background. Sturgeon was his first assistant superintendent, and Bascom Hayes (now chairman of educational administration at Texas University) was third in command. Warren Hitt, the key man in federal aid, had also been in TEA since 1948, as had the key vocational education staff. An image of a professional department, not ruled by political favoritism, emerged. Dr. Edgar also cultivated a "greater degree of local autonomy of decision making in schools."[1][3] To help small schools seeking to maintain their identity, he established a Small Schools Study and a Texas Small Schools Project in the administrative services division. Literally thousands of professional and lay advisory groups collaborated on the revision of teacher certification requirements. Dr. Edgar has always been reappointed to office and now is serving in his twenty-second consecutive year. His stewardship has led to a substantial influence for the TEA in federal aid allocations. However, TEA influence over federal aid is tempered by Commissioner Edgar's great respect for local control, an attitude that permeates TEA practices and activities.

The Texas State Board of Education

The Texas State Board of Education has not exercised any influence on federal aid distribution. The board members are selected from congressional districts based on the 1930 census. Glen Ivy, head of the Texas Research League, describes the selection process:

We did a little checking—I think out of 50 some odd opportunities for electoral contests there had been half a dozen. People don't run in opposition to board members. When board members get ready to go off the board, unless they die, they generally resign a little early and somebody is picked to replace them. He then runs as an incumbent. Board members are chosen rather carefully from local board members who have been compatible with the local administrators and teachers. I think they have trusted the TEA administrators, and rightly so, because it has been a capable administration. But they, the board, have not done much in terms of questioning the basic philosophy or trying to revise it. In 1972 we will get a new board because a court suit challenged the electoral districts on the malapportionment.[14]

Laurence Haskew of the University of Texas has observed the state board for a number of years and remarked:

The state board scrutinized the vocational education state plan carefully. But they ask factual questions like how much will a certain district get. It is very rare they change Commissioner Edgar's recommendations. Occasionally, they will send something back to TEA for further consideration. Votes do not split in the state board along rural versus urban lines, but in the last three or four years there are more questions raised by the members from the cities.[15]

TEA staff stress that Edgar's image as fair minded and trustworthy influences the board's reactions.

Usdan and his colleagues made the harshest assessment of the state board:

In the opinion of some legislators and university professors, the state board of education is a farce. They claim that it is made up of "well intentioned but incompetent laymen who have been elected, in effect, by local teacher's groups." In fact, the teacher's groups are the only ones who do seem really interested in the board.[16]

Several of the members have been on the state board since Commissioner Edgar came into office. While ad hoc committees consider federal aid proposals, the writer could find no instances where the state board made important changes in federal aid allocation decisions.

The Texas Governor and Education Policy

The formal powers of the Texas governor are among the weakest in the nation. He operates with a very small personal staff, which includes two people who serve as his executive budget division, and his administrative assistants.[17] The governor's limited powers also stem from (1) the election of many important officials (such as the state board which in turn appoints the TEA commissioner) rather than their appointment by the governor; (2) the lack of removal power; (3) the disintegrated and disunited administrative system; (4) the absence of a strong opposition party which makes impossible the governor's exercise of effective discipline in either the legislature or party affairs; and (5) the absence of strong financial powers.

The governor's two-man budget staff receives requests for appropriation and "compiles" them into a document with the governor's recommendations. This "budget" is submitted to the Legislative Budget Bureau. The Legislative Budget Bureau, however, has a larger staff; after a detailed review of agency requests, it submits a separate budget document to the legislature, which the legislature then uses in its deliberations.

The governor's formal prerogatives are even more restricted in elementary/ secondary education. In effect, neither he nor the legislature control the appropriation of state educational aid after an authorization has been approved. The 1948 Gilmer-Aikin Act, at the behest of TSTA, specifies that the commissioner of education calculates the cost of the authorized education foundation program; this amount becomes an automatic appropriation, with first call on the treasury. There has never been an appropriation act for the education foundation program in Texas. The governor and the legislature concentrate on changes in authorization levels, particularly increases in teacher salaries. A close observer of Texas education politics stressed the importance of this process for federal aid:

This automatic appropriation for state aid is why the legislature and the governor are not inclined to look at how TEA is using federal funds. They do not authorize federal funds—the congress does. Since they are not used to appropriating program funds, their review of federal aid is virtually nonexistent. The only thing the legislature looks at is internal TEA funds—salaries and expenses. We even amended the 1948 act to earmark 1/2 percent of the foundation program as an automatic appropriation for TEA salaries and expenses. This is not enough so the legislature looks carefully at salaries, employee classification, organization, and whether TEA is charging enough administrative time to the various federal allocations for administrative expenses.[18]

The governor's total lack of appointive power in the elementary/secondary education area also lessens his potential influence because he cannot reward legislators. In higher education governors have been able to bring about important policy changes by their appointments to the boards. A simple description of formal appointment powers, however, often disguises the real impact of an aggressive politician. The Texas governor was a crucial ally of TSTA in the struggle for increased teacher benefits in the past legislative session. The governor's office helped TSTA draft the bill. He used the high prestige of his office and his influence with individual legislators to obtain passage of the bill. As Usdan and his associates observed:

Even though the office of the governor is weak, it has considerable control over activities of the legislature and . . . over the fate of Texas teachers. Because of the deep involvement of the governor and his staff, the TEA chose not to become seriously involved despite the importance of the legislation at issue.[19]

The governor can veto favorite bills of legislators and no veto has been overridden since 1941.

Traditionally, governors have played a balancing role between the financial demands of the powerful TSTA and the needs of other Texas state agencies. Often the governor has been confronted with so many legislators committed during their campaign to TSTA that he has been worried about financial flexibility for everything else in state government. Even in 1968 the governor only supported about one-third of the TSTA package, in large part, because of his reluctance to show favoritism that would alienate college faculty.

Legislative Politics in Texas

The Texas legislature meets in biennial sessions and the per diem stops after the first 120 days. Although the United States has generally seen a steady growth of executive influence at the expense of legislative, the Texas legislature has held its own,[20] largely because of its refusal to delegate powers to the executive and its insistence on retention of budgetary powers. The biennial session, lack of permanent trained staff, low pay (salary is $4,800 a year), and the end-of-session rush of bills render committees extremely important. In the average legislative session, approximately 40 percent of the members of the House are serving their first terms, and 30 percent of the House committee members are without previous legislative experience in their committees.[21]

Texas committees are largely controlled by the presiding officers who appoint committee chairmen and members. The presiding officer also has extensive flexibility on bill referrals. If the presiding officer is in favor of a certain line of action, he will appoint to the committee only members who share his views. In the 1967 Senate, the lieutenant governor placed one of his closest supporters on twenty-five different committees.

Texas has been dominated by the Democratic party. Two distinct factions have never developed in the party; thus politics has been a shifting vague phenomena of many factions, all under one party banner. The candidates for each office in the Democratic primary usually "stand on their own legs," setting up their own campaign organizations and adopting their own platforms. Consequently, the Democratic party as an organization has not been a significant force on the distribution of federal aid. Lack of party cohesion also provides a good opportunity for TSTA to extract pledges of support in return for its electoral assistance.

TSTA and Politics

The factional one party nature of Texas politics has given a major influence to interest groups. Lockhard classifies the Texas Democratic party as one of "frequent multifactional division."[22] When political parties lack cohesion and a clearly defined policy, legislators must rely more on interest groups for information, endorsements, and political support. Unable to rely on strong party support, the governor must expend more time and effort on political activities and correspondingly less on the oversight of executive departments. These weaknesses enhance the potential influence of TSTA.

After a year as assistant superintendent, L.P. Sturgeon in 1949 became executive director of TSTA and remains in that office today. Sturgeon was an administrator from a rural area near Texarkana. TSTA exemplifies Iannaccone's classification of a statewide monolithic linkage structure between interest groups and the legislature.[23] TSTA holds hearings among its constituent groups (all located in the Austin TSTA Building) and then formulates a legislative package of priority bills. The constituent groups are:[24]

— The Big Seven Council of School Boards (representing seven major Texas cities)
— Texas Association of Secondary Principals
— Texas Association for Supervision and Curriculum Development
— Texas Classroom Teachers Association
— Texas Association of School Librarians
— Texas Elementary Principals and Supervisors Association
— Texas Association of School Administrators
— Texas Association for Continuing Adult Education
— Texas Retired Teachers Association
— Vocational Agricultural Teachers Association of Texas
— Texas Association of County Superintendents
— Texas Association of School Business Officials
— Texas Educational Secretaries Association

The TSTA has made continual increases in state supported minimum teachers salaries its overwhelming goal. Texas currently pays about 80 percent of local school costs with most of the funds devoted to a state salary level for teachers. Indeed, 44.5 percent of all state outlays were used for some facet of elementary, secondary, or higher education; in effect, the legislature is a giant school board. The minimum state salary, incorporated in the Gilmer-Aikin 1948 Act, has been consistently supported by a coalition of TSTA and the rural legislators who dominated the Texas legislature until 1968 and still retain key committee positions. The rural areas tend to pay the state-supported minimum salary, while urban areas pay a differential on top. When the minimum is increased, the metropolitan school districts are pressured to maintain their differential and thereby preserve the overall state average.

Teacher salary bills are usually drafted in TSTA offices; TSTA obtains the support of key legislators before the bills are introduced. TSTA has been consistently successful in extracting commitments from numerous state legislators during their campaigns. TSTA queries each legislator on what parts of the TSTA package he supports and circularizes the responses to its 127,500 members.[25] To insure that legislators honor their campaign pledges, TSTA members attend legislative sessions and committee hearings—a strategy it has employed since 1948.[26] The latest TSTA salary package includes everybody from aides to administrators and ranges from $3,000 to $33,000. In a description of the political maneuvering in the latest teacher salary bill, Usdan et al. emphasize the minimal role played by TEA and the importance of the governor and TSTA.[27] In 1968, after a $1 million study by the Texas Research League, the Governor's Committee recommended school district consolidation and a change in the 1948 aid formulas to put more money in the cities; the additional funds would derive from an equalized property assessment base and a supplemental special urban program. The Governor's Committee report ruptured the united front of TSTA and caused a split between the big cities and the rest of TSTA. Except for the recommended raise in professional salaries, TSTA disregarded the Governor's Committee report, and the legislature subsequently passed only the TSTA-supported recommendations of the committee. This urban split in TSTA has not been formalized, but TSTA was holding hearings on how to make TSTA a "better umbrella for all professional education interest groups in the state."[28] In short, the TSTA has enormous influence on state aid issues, and the TEA does not attempt to influence the course of events once they have started on their way or to dominate salary negotiations.

While TSTA has been the most important continuing force in Texas on state aid issues, it has chosen *not* to become involved in federal aid allocation. L.P. Sturgeon, the executive director, has a close personal relationship with Commissioner Edgar; he has evidently decided federal aid is "not our business" and should be left to TEA. According to Dr. Sturgeon, the last major federal aid issue in which TSTA interfered was under the post-Korean War Lanham Act; in that instance, it fought substitution of federal money for state aid. TSTA is very active in Washington on full funding, but through a tacit agreement with Edgar does not try to influence TEA on its intra-state allocation or administrative decisions. Moreover, TSTA sees no change in its role as long as Commissioner Edgar is there. The only times TSTA gets into federal aid in Texas is if it involves a state legislative bill. For example, TSTA supported the TEA bill to establish Title III-ESEA regional service centers through state authority. TSTA represents so many diverse professional groups and school districts that it will stay out of state aid project decisions that may favor some districts over others. Federal funds also involve the integration issue that TSTA is not inclined to deal with.

Texas Political Culture and Federal Aid

Attitudes, values, and traditions that enhance TEA's discretion have more impact for the oversight of federal aid than do the structural weaknesses of the governor and legislature. In the context of Texas political history, the phrase "federal aid" borders on the obscene.[29] Traditionally, state office-seekers and those already in power at the state level enunciate the states rights philosophy. They argue for a diminution of federal power and the virtues of homegrown government. While the words may be distasteful to Texans, the money obviously is not. No state in the nation, with the exception of California and New York, accepts more money from the federal treasury than Texas. Texans in Congress have discovered that one of the keys to continued success is to bring home the federal dollars. For instance, Texas was an early and large recipient of OEO funds even though the poverty program was a favorite target of politicians.

The myth of the pernicious influence of federal aid has important implications for this study. As one informant remarked: "The lack of public visibility of issues in federal aid to education, including the governor and legislature's low profile, is because we would just as soon not have it widely publicized how much federal aid to education really comes into Texas."[30] As a consequence of this attitude and value system, TEA is free to decide the level of enforcement; the department can determine the amount of pressure to apply to LEAs to insure compliance with federal regulations.

More important, however, is the image of the nonpartisan objective expert, maintained at TEA by Commissioner Edgar and his staff. A governor who wants to intercede in an educational decision, historically TEA's prerogative, is embarking on a perilous venture. As Professor Laurence Haskew of the University of Texas said: "I doubt any governor would exercise much power over federal aid, even if he had formal authority, because of the tradition Commissioner Edgar has established. If there is a state where education is a fourth branch of government, Texas must be it."[31] Vernon McGhee of Governor Smith's staff described their strategy this way:

Federal aid to education has historically been a professional decision. We might go to the TEA and introduce someone from West Texas and say we thought they had a good case for a vocational education project. But if their application came out of TEA with a low priority we would accept this. We know education isn't in the A-95 circular of the U.S. Budget Bureau that gives the governor the right to comment on state plans. . . But if we can't achieve anything significant in federal aid to education, why include it in A-95.

The governor's only significant moves into education allocation decisions are in areas where his office is the logical focus for coordination of multi-purpose federal programs such as model cities, day care, and drugs. A policy planning staff has been established to handle these areas and is just getting started.[32]

This image of TEA also discourages state legislators from intervening on particular projects. The legislature, however, gains a potential lever in project decisions through its control of details of TEA salaries and expense budget.

While all of these political factors provide TEA with potential discretion and leadership, Texas and Commissioner Edgar maintain a strong commitment to local control of schools and to the continuation of habitual ways of doing things. Elazar describes the dominant political culture in Texas as "traditionalistic."[33] Elements in this political culture, according to Elazar, are that it "accepts government as an actor with a positive role in the community, but tries to limit that role to securing the continued maintenance of the existing social order." The TEA, as a change agent using federal funds, would be limited by this kind of value orientation. Although attitudes such as this are hard to empirically document, they do emerge from the interviews. In the establishment of funding priorities, the enforcement of Title I regulations, and the monitoring of projects, TEA conforms to the tradition Elazar posits.

Big City School Districts: The Reluctant Lobbyist

With the exception of federally mandated Title I, all of the categorical title allocation formulas discriminate against the large cities in Texas (particularly Vocational Education, ESEA II and NDEA III). ESEA II and Vocational Education are based on the inequitable state aid formula which has been severely criticized for shortchanging the cities. Although urban school districts are frequent participants on the ubiquitous TEA advisory committees, they have not significantly influenced the course of federal aid allocation in Texas.

Texas city districts have just recently formed a Texas Council of Big City School Districts, but the members stress it is "just getting off the ground." Its functions have been restricted to exchanging information and services. Political action has not been seriously considered. Although the 1968 Governor's Committee on Public School Education Report showed the state aid formula favored rural areas and smaller school districts, the big cities remain under the monolithic TSTA umbrella and have no aggressive legislative lobby group of their own. The cities still work through TSTA, despite TSTA's elimination of all big city aid features in the 1968 state aid bill and TSTA's continued stress on minimum teacher salaries. In part, this is because the big cities, until 1968, had no solid information on the differential impact of the state aid formula. Big city school people concur, however, that TSTA has stayed out of federal aid allocations. As one city superintendent observed: "Warren Hitt of TEA and Sturgeon of TSTA have worked hand in glove for 20 years. The agreement was

Hitt would handle federal programs and TSTA would take the lead on state aid."[34]

Although the big cities are now aware of some of the federal aid formulas that hurt them (particularly vocational education), their lobbying with TEA is minimal on both formula revisions and individual projects. There are two principal reasons for this urban strategy. Until three or four years ago, the general Texas reluctance to highlight or publicize federal aid discouraged the cities from aggressive political action. Urban as well as rural Texans prefer not to acknowledge that they receive or depend on large amounts of federal aid. To fight for federal aid and criticize TEA—a basic break with tradition—would attract statewide attention. Moreover, city school people repeat the commonly held view that Commissioner Edgar and Warren Hitt are widely respected as "fair and above political influence." Thus, it would not be appropriate to use urban legislators to pressure TEA on federal aid. In effect, the TEA image continues to discourage the big districts from applying their growing political muscle.

The Texas Education Agency

Background

The changes wrought in departmental policies and administrative structure by the Gilmer-Aikin Act of 1948 have been discussed previously. Commissioner Edgar, now serving his twenty-second consecutive year in office, has molded TEA into a cadre of professional experts who appear to be neither tainted or swayed by political considerations. This image, Texan attitudes, and state politics combine to give the TEA substantial control of federal aid allocation—a position further strengthened by TSTA's decision to remain aloof from federal aid issues. Dr. Edgar's respect for local control, however, moderates departmental exercise of its prerogatives.

TEA Salaries

Departmental effectiveness in the allocation of federal funds is further hindered by personnel problems. TEA salaries are not commensurate with those of local school teachers or administrators, a disparity confirmed by a 1968 study of the Governor's Committee on Public School Education. Consequently, many TEA administrators resign to return to teaching. TEA only hires people with master's degrees in education and five years of local experience, but an M.A. and five years of experience only entitles beginning personnel to $11,000. There are no step increases, only "merit raises," which require additional legislative appropriations. The top staff salaries are set by a "line item" in the legislative appropriation bill fixing the maximum pay. Table 6-1 illustrates the disparities between TEA and local district salaries. Note the average TEA monthly handicap rises from $194 at the consultant level to $501 at the commissioner level. The *maximum* classified slot starts at $14,800. The Governor's Committee, after a detailed study of TEA salaries, reached the following overall conclusions:

This pay disparity has at least two undesirable effects. It makes recruiting and retention of qualified people much more difficult for TEA. It breeds distrust and friction between the TEA professionals and the district professionals with whom they work. It encourages situations in which the less qualified person supervises the more qualified. . . .

TEA turnover rates are not unusually high, but turnover occurs where it hurts. During a recent 18-month period three persons serving in positions directly responsible to the Commissioner left TEA. Two persons at the highest directorship and two at the next highest level also departed during this period.[35]

TEA currently receives 69 percent of its total administrative funds from the federal government—one of the highest percentages in the nation, as can be seen by Table 6-2.

Table 6-2 also illustrates the variation in total expenditures among the states. New York and California together account for over 20 percent of the total expenditures by all SEAs.

Comprehensive Planning and Priorities

Despite its personnel problems, TEA has been the first state educational agency to attempt comprehensive state planning and priority setting for federal funds; the comprehensive state planning concept was spearheaded by Karl Hereford, the director of Program Planning and Evaluation, USOE Bureau of Elementary and Secondary Education. Dr. Hereford reached an agreement on comprehensive planning with Warren Hitt, TEA deputy commissioner, who was the major actor in federal aid.

Table 6-1
1967-68 Salary Contracts

Position	Average Monthly TEA Salary	Average Monthly Salary by 3 Districts
Consultant	$ 820	$1,014
Chief Consultant	906	1,076
Education Program Director	968	1,135
Director	1,036	1,309
Assistant Commissioner	1,548	1,827
Commissioner	2,166	2,667

253

Table 6-2
FY 1969 Expenditures in Selected State Departments of Education

| State | Total Expenditures | Federal Share | | Expenditures for Planning Development and Evaluation | |
		Amount in Millions	Percentage of Total	Amount in Millions	Percentage of Total
1. Texas	$ 7.6	$ 5.3	69.6	$ .9	11.8
2. Ohio	$ 7.3	$ 4.4	60.6	$ .5	6.8
3. Pennsylvania	$ 11.8	$ 4.8	40.5	$ 1.5	12.7
4. California	$ 20.9	$ 7.5	36.0	$ 1.3	6.2
5. Massachusetts	$ 5.4	$ 1.9	35.8	$ .5	.9
6. Oregon	$ 2.9	$ 1.0	35.7	$ .3	10.3
7. New Jersey	$ 8.8	$ 2.8	32.2	$ 1.0	11.3
8. New York	$ 35.5	$ 7.6	21.5	$ 3.3	9.2
Total for All States	$262.4	$107.6	41.0	$22.9	8.7

Source: Fifth Annual Report of the Advisory Council on State Departments of Education: Table 3, page 15.

With a firm grasp of the mosaic of federal categorical programs, Commissioner Hitt was the key link between TEA, the governor's office, TSTA, and the legislature on all major federal aid issues. The Texas experience under comprehensive planning and priority setting is especially noteworthy because the idea is still widely supported and relevant for concepts such as PPBS and the federal-state Belmont evaluation program.

Assisted by USOE consultants, the department in 1968 started to design a consolidated application form that would be linked to statewide priorities for funding most federal aid programs. The rationale for this effort is outlined in several TEA documents, particularly the consolidated application directions sent to local districts:

In the past the local district has developed a separate plan and applied for each of these federal categorical programs separately. Now the district is asked to "package" them—to consolidate the separate plans into one broad educational plan of the district. . . . Thus, planning encompasses a range of resources, federal, state, and local. . . . "packaging" allows the school administrator more flexibility in utilizing federal funds. He and his staff will be able to plan the use of resources so that they may be brought to bear on areas of greatest local concern—a marshalling of resources on priorities. For example, funds are available for staff development under a number of different federal programs. The situation is now such that the superintendent may have to plan separately for each in-service program utilizing each federal resource. Under a packaged design, he will be able to plan a unified staff development program supported by funds from diverse sources.[36]

The package request must fall within one of the statewide priorities. The priority chosen by each LEA would be posited on a separate local needs assessment and local choice of the most pressing needs.

In order to guide local districts and establish statewide funding, TEA initiated statewide needs assessment that produced nine statewide program priorities. The final document, *Toward Comprehensive Educational Planning in Texas*, includes a few pages of statistical analysis on needs and then sets forth the nine priorities. A participant describes the process this way:

What really happened was Charles Nix, the head of planning in TEA, gathered some good data on educational needs using the usual indicators. But the final decisions were made by 50 or 60 people sitting around a table until they could agree. It did not end up on a strict empirical basis. The state board then approved the nine priorities.[37]

The nine priorities are:

1. Programs for educationally disadvantaged people
2. Educational programs for handicapped children, youth, and adults
3. Language skills development, particularly among children who speak with inadequate command of standard English
4. Vocational education programs as they relate to business and industrial requirements regionally and statewide
5. Early childhood education programs
6. Adult basic education programs, particularly as they relate to occupational skills development
7. Programs for individualization of instruction
8. Comprehensive pupil appraisal
9. School manpower development, both pre-service and in-service.

The document continued: "Immediate targets of highest priority planning in each of these nine priority areas will be the large urban centers of the state."[38]

The packaged application of several federal categorical programs was to demonstrate a link between a package funding request and local priorities that conformed with state priorities. Local districts were advised to organize their planning staffs through a committee or task force "drawn from a range of components in the school's program."

The Texas experiment in comprehensive planning and priority setting for federal funds is still evolving, but the results have not been encouraging, chiefly because of political and administrative constraints at all levels of the federal system. Moreover, the nine statewide priorities, in the words of one TEA staff member, "cover the waterfront." Another TEA staffer said, "We were never able to establish any *low* priorities." The essence of priority setting would be to exclude some kinds of activities from packaged federal funds. Perhaps Texas' problems stem from a respect for local control. One assistant commissioner asserted, "I think the local school districts should decide what is low priority and what is number one priority." Although the USOE Management Review Report (1969) praised Texas for its leadership, it noted:

However, the linkage between the state survey of need and program planning within the agency has not yet been clearly established, either in concept or in fact. Accordingly, the survey of need is not immediately translatable into legislative strategy, and program plans, nor does it lend itself without further development into plans for the agency's own internal for grants management or technical assistance to local districts. The risk the agency runs here is not so much that it will misdiagnose educational needs within the state; rather it runs the risk that those needs will be defined in too general and abstract terms to be addressed directly by planned programs of corrective action that the agency and the local districts could mount.[39]

The TEA, however, presents sound evidence that the failure of USOE to live up to its promises on packaging and comprehensive planning deflated and demoralized their whole effort. Three criticisms stand out: (1) USOE was never able to loosen its requirements for accounting or particular funding criteria for each separate category; consequently, TEA was hindered from packaging funds; (2) the late congressional appropriations and lack of forward funding beyond one fiscal year made local planning impossible and the interrelation of federal funds a farce. If local districts did not receive their funds until midway in the school year, LEAs and TEA had a large task merely to process applications so each federal categorical restriction was observed; and (3) neither the federal or state vocational educational administrators were willing to make a serious commitment to the coordinated effort. As a tragic consequence, the widely-heralded Texas consolidated application form (to cover ESEA I, II; NDEA III, VA; Adult Basic Education, Migrant, and Vocational Education) became in the words of its own administrators, a "pancake application where you turn over one hotcake at a time." The consolidated application is not really a comprehensive planning document. Local school districts merely staple together formerly separate fund applications and attach a cover sheet that summarizes all of the applications. Despite a TEA reorganization that located several federal program coordinators together in a Division of Program Funds Management, TEA still considers separately each part of the consolidated application for each category. As a result, TEA staff still refer to Title I or NDEA as a separate program and decision process. Nor are federal funds and state funds seen as one fund for mutual reinforcement. In short, to reverse the hardening of the federal categories requires more change and effort than Texas and USOE could muster. Initially, TEA was strongly committed to the concept; the department created a separate division of planning and evaluation as well as a new organizational unit designed to interrelate federal categories. However, the collapse of comprehensive planning necessitates, in Texas as in the other states of our study, a title-by-title analysis of federal aid allocation.

Federal Aid Administration: A
Title-by-Title Analysis

ESEA-Title I

Although Texas presumably operates under a comprehensive planning and consolidated application form, Title I administrators report they "quit messing with it after the first year and just consider Title I separately." One of the top administrators described the job of the Texas Education Agency Title I staff:

Our job is *not* to make decisions concerning how effective a particular component is; this is a local decision. Our job is to see if the program meets the federal requirements. If a school district's Title I program does meet the legal requirements, then we have an obligation to fund the program. We do not feel that we are in any position to dictate particular methodologies to schools. The state department might encourage local school districts to choose one of the USOE recommended "best practices," but local agencies should be allowed to do something else, if they can justify that something else.[40]

Title I in Texas amounts to about $70 million annually. In 1969 TEA tightened up its administration of Title I requirements, in part because of USOE's response to the abuses of Title I funds in Mississippi. The Office of Education's willingness to cut off funds and demand restitution impressed the Texas officials. They had first-hand knowledge of the episode because a TEA staff member working for a USOE private contractor had inspected the Mississippi Title I program for USOE. TEA realized that Texas might have problems similar to those in Mississippi. For instance, Texas had never sent out OE Program Guide #44 which outlines the specific criteria USOE expects each applicant to meet. After the staff member related the Mississippi experience, Program Guide #44 was sent out, albeit a year after USOE had distributed it. TEA also took an intensive look at music, art, and physical education projects that could be used for general aid. Several of these projects were reoriented to programs limited to disadvantaged children.

Prior to the development of the consolidated application, the Texas Education Agency had a separate Division of Compensatory Education for Title I. When the consolidated application was inaugurated, the agency was reorganized and Title I, with several other federal titles, was placed under the Division of Program Funds Management. At that time, the evaluation function was separated out from Title I and put into a central planning and evaluation office under an associate commissioner (Charles Nix). Unfortunately, there is minimal use of evaluation data for Title I project approvals.

The Texas AFDC level is so low that TEA decided to allocate funds on the basis of 1960 census tract data for low income families. There are about 1,200 school districts in the state of Texas. In FY 1970, TEA staff reviewed almost

2,000 applications from 1,085 districts. Each application is turned over to one of nine professionals who work in the program review and monitoring section of the division. Consultants review the applications to make sure that the program contents and funding arrangements conform with the requirements of the federal guidelines (particularly Program Guide #44). Revisions in local applications are done by telephone. In fiscal year 1970 there were essentially two application procedures: the first cycle was completed in the fall of 1969; the second occurred after congressional and presidential approval of fiscal 1970 funds in April, 1970. Thus, there is little time for monitoring and servicing of local school districts. As of June, 1970 (the fiscal year ends June 30, 1970), TEA had still not received any guidance from USOE on what to do with fiscal 1970 funds that could carry over to fiscal 1971.

Departmental staff does not provide much technical assistance in the development of Title I programs. Local school districts still come to TEA for program help, but TEA staff is oriented to a fiscal and regulation checking role: Does the program meet federal guidelines? Under the reorganization for comprehensive planning, Title I administrative money is spread throughout TEA. Title I administrative expenses support over 36 percent of the salaries and expenses incurred by the elementary education specialists in the Division of Program Development. Neither this writer nor the Urban Institute team could find significant involvement by these specialists in Title I. The accountants who work with Title I are confined to checking addition because the current local school budget categories defy any other kind of useful analysis.

The changes in the fund concentration requirement illustrate TEA's new policy, initiated after USOE's Mississippi audit. Before 1969, the LEAs could list eligible attendance areas and omit several ghetto districts, and no one in TEA would have known. Since 1969 the LEA must list and rank all attendance areas by poverty criteria; an LEA cannot have any more children in its total program than are in the LEA entitlement. LEAs must also explain if they serve less than the total number of disadvantaged children in an attendance area with Title I projects. Previously, the LEA could spread the funds thinly over several attendance areas with small projects and reach only a fraction of the disadvantaged in any single attendance area. The TEA uses $148.44 per pupil as a guide for concentration of Title I funds. This amount is derived by dividing the total Texas allocation by the total number of eligible pupils. Texas is currently spending $636 (ranks 44th out of 50 states) per pupil for its entire educational effort from local, state, and federal funds.

While specific federal regulations and guidelines are checked, program design procedures are rarely questioned. In a Title I application, an LEA is supposed to identify the educational needs of its students, but is not required to assign priorities. The needs identified are for the entire school district, not necessarily for the target population. The local school district then sets up certain educational objectives it hopes to attain. Finally, it describes the programs it will adopt in order to meet the specified objectives.

Beginning in fiscal 1971, TEA is moving into two new areas of parent participation and comparability. In the past, TEA sent out a notice that parents should be involved in formulating Title I programs, but this was not part of the application, nor did anyone monitor it. In the 1971 application there is an assurance system and a requirement that the LEA "explain how the community and parents will be involved in planning, operating, and appraising the local Title I program."

Department administrators indicated they remain concerned about the extent of general aid in Title I. If an LEA tries to use Title I funds for activities that are outside of the traditional area of Title I activities, TEA will raise questions. The staff will ask for more details to determine if, in fact, the program is targeted for the disadvantaged, or whether the particular activities to be funded are especially relevant to the needs of disadvantaged children. TEA feels projects for art, music, physical education, counselors, doctors, nurses, and media directors are likely to be used to support all children in a school district rather than be targeted for the disadvantaged. A Title I administrator stressed, "School districts have to work very hard to justify funding such programs out of Title I funds."

TEA checks for maintenance of fiscal effort by obtaining the districts total per pupil expenditure and then calculating whether it is not more than 5 percent lower than the past year. For FY 1971, TEA prepared a separate form to check comparability. TEA does not use a dollar comparability test, but relies on comparable personnel, materials, supplies, library resources, etc.

In 1971 LEAs had to list all of the private schools in their district for the first time. In the past, private schools were only listed in applications if they were served. Since TEA officials are now concerned about the use of Title I for general aid, they are asking local public schools to oversee the use of funds in private schools. Like TEA's other new initiatives, its effectiveness is dependent on state monitoring.

TEA monitoring suffers from two major failings. Because it must process close to 2,000 applications a year, the program staff can only spend one or two months on field activities—too brief a period to observe all the programs in progress. Moreover, only compliance with expenditure regulations, not program quality, is monitored. As a TEA evaluator in the Central Office of Planning remarked: "We don't collect evaluation data on program strategy any more. If the program administrators in TEA are not interested in what reading programs are effective, then why should we collect that kind of evaluation information."[41] The department uses the Belmont instruments on a state sample basis for its Title I evaluation plan and design. Title I evaluation is handled by an entirely separate Office of Planning and Evaluation and there are few links between the Title I evaluation and application approval.

As the applications are approved, TEA administrators make a list of questions or issues of concern that ought to be examined and prepare a list of school districts. TEA monitors each LEA about once every three years, but districts on a large special list are given priority. Despite the consolidated application, site visits are made by a number of different sections and categorical program people in TEA. TEA reviews criteria for participation, records of participants, the qualifications and duties of personnel, the rationale for the kind of program, and other factors. If there are discrepancies between the site-visit observations and the district's Title I plan, TEA will notify the local district and ask how it intends to correct the discrepancies. When TEA is particularly concerned, a school district may be visited more than once during the year. At times, the department has threatened fund cut-offs and recovery. The staff stated "in several instances" funds have been recovered on audit exceptions. The TEA head of Title I observed that the disadvantaged are usually the "quiet ones politically" in the school district; consequently, there is a need to insure that categorical aid is targeted to them.

As one would expect, political influence is seldom brought to bear on TEA Title I decisions. The top TEA administrator for Title I could only recall one call from a state legislator and "one or two from a state board member." He said, however, their comparability policy was likely to cause the first united opposition by local superintendents. In sum, it would appear the main pressure to change TEA administration originates at the federal level, and agitation must overcome traditional attitudes about proper state-local relationships in Texas.

Vocational Education

Vocational education is by far the most complex federal aid program in Texas. This complexity has discouraged attempts to evaluate administrative performance or reduce the discretion of the vocational staff in TEA who resisted comprehensive planning and continues to go its separate way. Warren Hitt, the major TEA figure in federal aid, was reported to have remarked shortly before his death that "someday I would like to find out what is going on in the fourth floor vocational division." Other TEA staff refer to vocational education as a "separate barony." Indeed, a separate vocational division has existed in TEA ever since the 1917 Smith-Hughes Act.

Vocational education support from the federal government is indistinguishable in program concept from state aid. Separate accounts are kept for federal audits, but federal funds are a tail on the state aid dog.[42] As Table 6-3 indicates, total expenditures for vocational education have nearly tripled in six years. Most of this growth is attributable to expanding program costs rather than increasing student enrollment (up slightly more than 60 percent). As the Table 6-3 demonstrates, *the state has consistently paid the major share of vocational program costs.*

The pattern of growth since 1963 has been primarily outside the field of agriculture, but, as Table 6-4 indicates, agriculture and homemaking still overwhelm all the other categories.

Table 6-3
Federal, State, and Local Expenditures for Vocational Education in Texas 1959-60 through 1967-68

Fiscal Year	Federal	State	Local	Total
1959-60	$ 2,061,667	$16,482,189	$ 904,828	$19,448,684
1960-61	2,143,785	16,603,227	860,392	19,607,404
1961-62	2,216,849	20,981,989	1,120,594	24,319,432
1962-63	2,249,820	21,680,580	1,247,961	25,178,361
1963-64	2,636,196	22,957,609	1,320,696	26,914,501
1964-65	9,033,178	24,638,135	7,639,767	41,311,080
1965-66	14,105,092	28,753,112	11,815,646	54,673,850
1966-67	15,858,022	28,345,105	13,026,356	57,229,483
1967-68	15,738,533	34,513,382	6,899,722	57,151,637

Source: Texas Education Agency

Table 6-4
Vocational Education Enrollments in Texas

	1963	1968-69
Agriculture	47,476	51,220
Distribution	6,483	12,238
Homemaking	100,966	141,092
Industrial	13,360	31,847
Office	—	8,667

Source: TEA Vocational Education Division

First authorized by the 1963 Act, vocational programs for "persons with special needs" have grown slowly; patterns are not yet established. As indicated in Table 6-5, in 1967 enrollment in these programs by subject area was:

Table 6-5
1967 Enrollment in Vocational Education Programs, By Subject Area

Agriculture	104
Distributive Education	180
Health Occupations	52
Industrial	4,268
Technical	0
Vocational Homemaking	2,404
Office Education	359

Source: Governor's Committee on Public School Education

As this fiscal 1969 data in Table 6-6 indicates, federal funds have been dispersed over the range of vocational programs.

TEA and the legislature have created so complex a web of teacher units and joint federal-state pots of money that detailed tracking of all federal money is nearly impossible. The earmarked amounts in the federal act for disadvantaged (15 percent), handicapped, homemaking, work study, and cooperative education, are deducted first. The remainder is deposited in a joint federal-state fund. Roughly, the fiscal 1970 money in this state-federal fund, which includes most of the federal money, is devoted to these purposes:

$4.7 million to elementary-secondary school districts
$10 million to junior colleges
$1 million to the Texas State Technical Institute
$4.3 million to Area Vocational Education
$1 million to adult education and senior colleges
$2.3 million to ancillary services (research, demonstrations, administration, materials, etc.).

The legislature in line item mandates these specific earmarks in the joint federal-state fund. Most of the $6 million federal increase over FY 1969 for FY 1970 went to secondary schools or four-year colleges and is not reflected in the above figures.

In general, TEA uses the economic index and the inequitable county assessors' judgments as a basis for need and ability to pay. We have already seen

Table 6-6
Estimate of Texas Expenditures for Vocational Education for Fiscal 1969 (in Thousands)

Program Purposes	Total	Federal Funds Smith-Hughes and Geo.-Barden	1963 Act	State and Local Funds State	Local
Secondary	$37,911	$226	$ 3,013	$31,172	$ 3,500
Post-Secondary	8,073	–	3,651	2,325	2,097
Adult	2,433	–	706	1,290	436
Persons with Special Needs	2,930	–	1,315	1,515	100
Constr. of A.V.S.	6,858	–	3,429	–	3,429
Ancillary Services	6,498	–	3,053	2,994	450
Total	67,702	226	15,167	32,297	10,012

Source: Projected Program Activities for 1968-69, (Austin, Texas: Texas Education Agency).

the discrimination in this formula against urban areas, particularly core cities. The junior college allocations are line items in the legislative appropriation bill and are based on enrollment projections. TEA has not attempted to set priorities among junior colleges. The Texas State Technical Institute is located in rural or medium size cities (Waco, Amarillo, Harlingen, and a new one in rural West Texas). None of the allocations at any level are based on reliable projections of manpower needs or trends. The area vocational schools are "area" in name only and do not usually offer the wide range of training opportunities to be expected from the area concept. Political considerations help to account for the continued rural orientation of the funds and the inability to reduce some subject areas like agriculture and homemaking. Our assessment relies heavily on the published data of the Governor's Committee on Public School Education who also stressed that until the 1968 Act mandated 15 percent for the disadvantaged, only minimal funds have been devoted to this group.

High School Vocational Education

Federal funds have been packaged with state funds to pay for functions and objects that state funds are not permitted to support. Federal funds support travel and equipment, construction, teacher training, and instructional materials. State funds support the "hard base" of teacher salaries. Since federal funds are tied to state funds, all the inequities that apply to state funds also apply to federal funds.

Vocational education was incorporated into the Minimum Foundation Program by the Texas Legislature in 1949. The state provides "bonus" teacher units from the Minimum Foundation Program if the school district qualifies for a vocational teacher. Consequently, the rural and small school bias of the teacher allocation formulas are inherent in the vocational education program. The Governor's Committee concluded:

State aid formulas are designed to favor small districts, and combinations [consolidations] sometimes move the resulting district into less attractive brackets. For example, all districts above 1,600 ADA are allowed one teacher for each 26 pupils, while districts below 100 ADA may receive one teacher for as few as 21 pupils (or even one for 15 in the smallest permissible district). Other personnel allotments (personnel, vocational teachers, etc.) are also more generous for smaller districts.[43]

The Texas Research League estimates the cities get one vocational education teacher as compared with four outside the cities, for an equivalent number of pupils. The 1968 federal act required variable local matching depending on the ability to pay. TEA proposed and USOE accepted the economic index as a basis for meeting the federal act's requirements for adjustment of the distribution formulas to reflect need and ability to pay. The 1971 Texas state plan says:

In determining the taxpaying ability of each school district, the State Commissioner of Education, subject to the approval of the state board of education, shall calculate an economic index of the financial ability of each county . . . and shall constitute for the purpose of this [Federal] Act a measure of one county's ability to support schools in relation to the ability of other counties.[44]

The state plan goes on to include the county assessors' judgments as the method to determine school district ability to pay within counties. Ample evidence has been produced in prior sections of this chapter to show the discrimination of this formula against urban and large districts. It is incredible to the writer that USOE could accept this Texas formula as meeting the requirements of the 1968 Act. According to TEA officials, USOE requested more information on the state foundation formula, but was satisfied after reviewing the details of the economic index and intra-county assessment.

TEA uses a complex system of vocational base units and bonus units with federal funds devoted to each. The maximum number is derived from classroom teacher units which, in turn, depend on total ADA. A district's "base units" are the total number it has applied for and had approved in the past through specific projects. For instance, Amarillo could have ninety-three eligible vocational units but only fifty-three base units have been applied for and approved. TEA never changes the base or attempts to reduce it. TEA reviews new unit requests through an in-house team within the Vocational Education Division. Each unit request is reviewed as a separate project and may be eliminated on several criteria such as low quality of proposal or inability to meet local manpower needs. The TEA vocational education staff decides on the overall mix of vocations (agriculture, office, etc.) for all districts to be supported in the coming year. The various specialized teacher groups have a chance to lobby for their specialty within TEA.

The Governor's Committee was particularly critical of the survey techniques used for assessing local manpower needs. A school district is required to make an occupational survey of its "labor market area," a term which has not yet been defined in state survey instructions. The Governor's Committee asked the Texas Employment Commission for an interpretation of "labor market area" and using their definition analyzed seventy-nine local occupational surveys on file at TEA. Twenty-three of these surveys had been used to justify federally funded Area Vocational Schools.

Using the Texas Employment Commission Research Director's definition, only 29 of the 79 surveys applied to a "labor market area." Fifty of the surveys concerned only a small-to-medium sized community and took no notice of job opportunities outside the district making the survey. Many of these districts are in communities with a static or declining population; yet surveys take no account of out-migration trends or follow-up records of former students. They make no mention of redirecting existing programs from areas with declining job opportunities in the local community. Of the 79 surveys examined, only two indicated collaboration by two or more school districts, although the surveys are intended to justify "area" vocational schools. . . . They contain no estimates of the number of out-of-school youth or persons with special needs who must be eligible for federal programs.[45]

These Texas manpower surveys have been done by amateurs (usually with the help of the chamber of commerce or a civic club) who interview local business firms about anticipated job opportunities. The Governor's Committee stressed "the basic fallacy" of designing localized educational programs to fit local needs in an era of rapid metropolitan growth, rural decline, and high population mobility. A 1968 university-based study of 250 high school sophomore boys (100 white and 150 black) in three rural east Texas counties revealed that 61 percent of the black and 12 percent of the white boys expected to live in a large city; conversely, 35 percent of the black and 73 percent of the white boys expected to live in the suburbs of a city.[46] The Governor's Committee found substantial labor shortages, particularly at the skilled level, in the rapidly growing Houston and Dallas areas. Yet they estimated no more than 60,000 in 1966—or less than 1 in 10 attending high school in all Texas were taking vocational education courses which might help them to obtain a job in an urban environment.[47]

A significant amount of federal money goes into area vocational high schools (AVS). These "area schools" supposedly attract students from more than one district, but in 1967 ten schools visited by the governor's committee staff had a total of twelve transfer students. As reasons for their low number, the committee cited no provided transportation; the reluctance of small school districts to encourage pupil transfers because the resulting drop in average daily attendance may cost them a teacher under state aid; interference with a student's extracurricular activities; and, for the most part, the lack of very broad or attractive programs that would provide an incentive for transfers.

On this latter point the governor's committee compared Texas and Ohio area schools. Under the Texas state plan, only five programs are required in order to qualify as an AVS, drawing 50 percent reimbursement for construction and equipment costs. Of the sixty-four area schools in Texas, only twenty-three offered more than ten courses in 1966, and the average capacity was 255 students. An Ohio study concluded that a minimum of twelve programs serving approximately 500 students are required for a reasonably comprehensive vocational program which satisfies current needs. Pennsylvania's guidelines (like New York's) call for a minimum of ten shop-laboratory activities with a suggested enrollment of 2,500 pupils.

Programs for the disadvantaged and dropouts are restricted to the earmarks required in the federal law. TEA handles the $1 million—(102[b]) disadvantaged program on a project basis, evaluated internally by TEA staff. With respect to the various priorities in the federal act, the 1971 Texas state plan urges "special or particular consideration":

Programs, services, and activities which can serve the greatest number of persons in areas of the state where manpower needs and job opportunities will be given consideration for highest priority.[48]

Special consideration will be given to the approval and financing of programs and services in those areas within a school district, variously described as ghettos. . .[49]

Particular consideration will be given to those local education agencies whose proposed vocational education programs are best designed to (1) fulfill current or projected manpower needs . . . (2) fulfill new and emerging manpower needs.[50]

The state plan outlines the approval process for these many projects:

A review by a committee composed of consultants [TEA staff], area supervisors, and head state supervisors . . . The review committee may utilize the services of personnel from the Advisory Council, local and state agencies, and other departments of the state education agency to evaluate information provided in the application. . .[51]

In sum, the system for distribution of vocational education at the high school level is exceedingly complex. Researchers in Texas who have talked with local school officials, particularly those in cities, contend this complexity made it difficult to change the old ways of doing things. It is easier to add a new unit than to reorient old units; as of 1969, Houston still had 30 percent of its teachers in vocational agriculture.

Post-Secondary Vocational Education

Both junior colleges and four-year colleges receive federal funds. Vocational education at this level is a relatively new effort. The structural and coordination problems were highlighted by the Usdan et al. study:

At present, the vocational-technical function overlaps both elementary-secondary and higher education but its structure is something of an enigma. At the present time, vocational-technical education is being administered through TEA while the junior colleges are under the Coordination Board for the Texas College and University System. Such organization is explainable since there is vocational-technical training in the secondary schools, but the structure does not appear to be workable. It has been suggested that the TEA contract with the Coordinating Board to coordinate all vocational-technical education. Such an arrangement would serve both groups better financially as well as administratively.[52]

The state legislative appropriation completely merges state and federal funds. Funds are allocated on the basis of local demand for student contact hours for various types of vocational courses.[53] Different occupations receive different rates of pay for each contact hour. For example, data processing may be reimbursed at $1.70 per student contact hour, and agriculture, at $0.30. The state pays about 60 percent of each contact hour. The legislature earmarks appropriations for each junior college based on past contact hours and TEA estimates of contingency for new enrollment. There are no statewide priorities; funding levels depend on what types and amounts of vocational training the locality requests. If a junior college has had a welding program, it can be increased merely by adding students and thereby having more contact hours. Junior colleges are reimbursed on certified figures for the prior year's contact hours. If a junior college wants to move into a new occupational area, their request is reviewed by internal TEA staff. Each request is rated by TEA's specialists, admittedly, on a "subjective basis."

In compliance with the 1968 Act, the federal funds for the disadvantaged and handicapped are set aside and handled on a separate project basis. Obviously, under the contact hour system there is no way to target money to particular areas of the state or target populations. An in-house committee also evaluates these special projects for the disadvantaged.

The coordination problems are highlighted by the Governor's Committee's example of vocational education programs in Dallas. The Dallas Independent School District is building a new Science-Technical High School at a cost estimated to exceed $16 million. Meanwhile, the Dallas Community College has already opened its El Centro campus in Downtown Dallas and plans an eventual seven-campus complex. At least from their descriptions, a number of programs to be offered by the school district and the community college are very similar.

Dallas I.S.D.	El Centro College
Data processing (keypunch to basic computer)	Data Processing 130 (keypunch)
	Data Processing 131-2 (Basic Principles)
	Data Processing 135 (Introduction)
Dental Assistant	Dental Assistant
Radio-Television Electronics	Electronics Technician
Vocational Drafting	Drafting and Design Technology
Vocational Office Education (including prerequisite courses)	Secretarial Science (one-year program)

Federal money also provides $1 million in general aid to the Texas State Technological Institute. TSTI is a part of Texas A & M and is 100 percent supported by federal or state money. The location of the various institutes—none near a large city—appears to be determined primarily by political considerations and the availability of facilities.

The Advisory Council on Vocational Education

Texas created a lay advisory council before the federal act required it. Although the council has made one report, it has not dealt with the intrastate distribution of funds or reforms in the state foundation program. Its major concern has been the lack of sound data on labor market needs or on evaluation of the effectiveness of the training programs. Until this information is furnished by TEA, the council will be hampered in its formulation of specific policy recommendations. An excerpt from its March, 1970, report, *A Concerned Texas*, reveals the council's frustration:

The council has found little evidence that there is a serious and consistent commitment by public secondary schools as to placement of students or follow up to determine their success or failure, and the subsequent redirection of school programs to correct deficiencies. Further, the council has not found a requirement by state government or the Central Education Agency that the local school system collect and report such data on all students graduating from or leaving school . . . Texas does not have a labor market information system that provides sufficient data for planning educational activities to meet the needs of employers and the economy.[54]

The advisory council on Vocational Education is now studying the construction program of area vocational schools. Their figures show over $27 million in federal funds have gone into constructing the area schools during the past six years. Over the same period, post-secondary institutions have received $14.5 million; secondary institutions, $12.6 million for construction under federal aid. The TEA state plan uses fifteen factors as criteria for "determining relative priority of construction projects." Not really priorities, several of the criteria are contradictory. Overlapping and wide-ranging criteria leave maximum flexibility for TEA. A long-time observer of Texas politics remarked:

The rural legislator is particularly interested in any facilities since they are very visible in small or declining communities. They see area vocational schools as a big asset. We see the same rural distribution pattern in most state facilities— hospitals, parks and so on. In the past, the malapportioned legislature meant the cities had very little clout. City legislators were also not as interested. The legislature sets TEA salaries and controls their internal budget. Their influence may be more covert than overt.[55]

Perhaps the legislature influences the location of vocational education schools, since its rural orientation has affected the location of many other state facilities.

NDEA-Title III

From the outset, TEA administrators have controlled the allocation and criteria for NDEA-III. A deliberate attempt was made to favor the small (usually rural) schools with the allocation formulas. As a TEA administrator emphasized: "We wanted to use our formulas to build these small schools up to minimum professional standards in libraries, instructional equipment, and materials. Our top priority has been to give kids in small schools an equal chance with the kids in big school districts." The NDEA director in the department has been in federal program administration since 1958. He formerly was a chemist for a corporation and a high school science teacher in a town of 20,000. He stated that he sometimes visits school districts to find out "what they feel their needs are and how it is going."

Since 1959, NDEA III has provided about $5.3 million in Texas annually, until the cut-back last year to $2.3 million. When the federal appropriations were larger (around $90 million for the U.S.), Texas distributed three-fifths of the money on an ADA basis and two-fifths on the basis of "priority areas." First, the total state NDEA-Title III allotment was divided by the total Texas ADA. This calculation provided a ceiling for all districts to submit projects under NDEA. If all districts in Texas had requested their ceiling amounts there would have been no money left for TEA reallocation to other districts. Over the years, however, only about 60 percent of the total has been claimed leaving about 40 percent for state reallocation to "priority areas."

It is with this 40 percent reallocated money that TEA has attempted to build up the small and rural schools. First, priority was given to those districts with 500 ADA or less. All requests, however, had to be in the general program priority areas that were formulated by the TEA subject matter specialists in science, math, racial studies and so on.

Examples of these equal criteria for project approval are:

a. Equipment and materials which contributed to individualizing instruction
b. Equipment and materials used in language skills development
c. Equipment and materials used in establishing industrial arts programs
d. Materials for use in pre-school and kindergarten programs where they were an integral part of the elementary school.[56]

After requests for districts with 500 or less ADA were approved, priority was given to smaller applications in dollar amounts. TEA assumed the smaller dollar requests would most likely be from smaller school districts. Applications were grouped in this order of priority:

1. ADA of 500 or less
2. Applications of $25,000 or less
3. Applications from $25,000 to $50,000
4. Applications from $50,000 to $100,000
5. Applications over $100,000.

When the federal cutback came in FY 1969 from $5.3 million to $2.3 million, TEA staff wanted to end the allocation based on ADA and approve all the money on the basis of small district and program priorities. The funds did not arrive until more than nine months of the fiscal year had passed, so TEA used the ADA formula and, with $800,000 left for reallocation, applied partial funding to each applicant, as shown in Table 6-7.

Table 6-7
FY 1969 Allocation of NDEA III Funds to School Districts

Number of School Districts	Amt. Requested	% of Fund Request Approved
139	$2,000 or less	100
38	$2,001-$5,000	30
26	$5,001-$10,000	20
21	$10,001-$17,500	15
8	$17,500-$25,000	10
11	$25,001-$50,000	9
11	$50,001-$100,000	8
4	$100,000 and over	7

ESEA-Title II

After the 1965 passage of the Elementary and Secondary Education Act, TEA convened a fifteen-member advisory committee to discuss an allocation formula for Title II. Chosen from large, medium, and small districts, the committee included seven superintendents and principals and eight librarians. It is noteworthy that the Governor's Committee criticism of the economic index was not published until 1968. Until that time neither large or urban districts—nor the TEA staff—had any solid information on the impact of the economic index.

After meeting for over two days, the advisory committee recommended the following components for the distribution formula. The economic index should be counted as the crucial "need factor" and receive a 50 percent weight, or as much as all other factors combined. All districts should receive 60¢ per child based on current ADA. It was estimated this would consume 20 percent of the funds. The three following factors, relating more specifically, would receive a 10 percent weight each:

1. *Book Inventory.* The formula rewarded past effort or districts who had tried to build up a library. This was computed by a count of the books in the library. TEA administrators stated they required the copyright dates in order to prevent poor districts from counting books that were given by a "retired General"—10 percent weight.
2. *Sparsely settled districts* were given another 10 percent.
3. *Library Standards.* A bonus of 10 percent was given to schools which

could meet the national standards for number of librarians compared to the number of teachers, books, and children. A district might also receive a 10 percent bonus for high standard library facilities.

The damage is compounded by the unreliable county tax rolls that determine local district shares within each county. The Governor's Committee describes the procedure:

Most county governments in Texas are still rurally oriented. As a rule the county tax assessor "borrows" the tax rolls of incorporated municipalities—particularly the large ones—and copies the assessed values at some reduced rate as the basis of county valuations. For property outside the city limits, the county assessor is more likely to accept the value as rendered by the property owner, often without question. In most cases, property outside the city is rendered as though it were all "undeveloped"—with no buildings or improvements.

Conversion of the county tax roll into a tool for distributing state school aid burdens the county tax assessor with record keeping duties which have nothing to do with the primary functions of his office. For county tax purposes, it makes no difference where separate installations might be located in the county. . . . Every time the assessor for Harris Houston and environs and Dallas County revalues a segment of the county and shifts one percent of the reported value from one district to another, he shifts more than $200,000 in state aid.[57]

The Governor's Committee conducted a special study of these intra-county tax allocations and "verified that city school districts in Texas are being cheated in the distribution of state school aid because county tax rolls favor rural areas."[58] They found, for example, the assessor for Tarrant County was reporting about 7 percent more taxpaying ability for the Fort Worth School District than its actual values would justify. This difference alone meant more than a half million dollars in lost state aid each year. Nobody has calculated the lost federal aid, but TEA has proposed and USOE has accepted the Texas state aid formulas as a basis for "adjusting for need" in vocational education and Title II. The Governor's Committee stated bluntly:

The big urban districts of Texas, with most of the children (especially those with educational handicaps) and heavy competition for tax resources from municipal governments, are hit by two-way discrimination under the Minimum Foundation Program. Both the measurement of need (for personnel and operating funds) and the measurement of ability are heavily weighted in favor of rural districts.[59]

Table 6-8 illustrates this by comparing state aid per ADA to market value of property per ADA—by district size group.

Texas also presents a clear pattern of discrimination by size of districts in the effective tax rates, as shown in Table 6-9.

This formula was transmitted to USOE, which sent it back for revisions that would favor poor schools. After some negotiations, OE insisted that ADA be

Table 6-8

1968-69 Comparison of Foundation Program Costs and State Aid Per ADA to 1966-67 Market Value Per ADA, by School District Size Group

School District Size	1966-67 MV/ADA	1968-69 State Aid/ADA	1968-69 MFP/ADA
Less than 500 ADA	121,000	$318	$415
500-1,599	79,000	271	346
1,600-2,599	51,000	258	318
2,600-4,999	48,000	255	312
5,000-9,999	43,000	232	304
10,000-39,999	28,000	242	290
More than 40,000	36,000	219	287
State Totals	47,000	$245	$309

Source: Texas Research League

Table 6-9

District Size and Effective Local Tax Rate

Dist. Size Group	Total 1966-67 Market Value	Total 1968-69 LFA	Avg. Effective LFA Tax Rate
Under 1,600 ADA	$ 39,263,800,000	$ 37,930,000	$ .096/$100
1,600-4,999	21,516,100,000	26,270,000	.122
5,000 and over	50,320,100,000	89,323,000	.178
State	111,100,000,000	153,523,000	.138

Source: Computed from data compiled by the Governor's Committee on Public School Education

multiplied by 1.43 as a "need" factor and the other factors decreased accordingly. This was accepted by TEA and as one administrator stated, "the program has been run by a computer ever since." The revised (1967) state plan says there will be "a reassessment of the relative need criteria" in the federal law. If such a reassessment was carried out it has resulted in no changes (despite the devastating evidence produced by the Governor's Committee on the economic index).

The state plan gives minimal guidance to LEAs on priority expenditure of the funds. The two significant clauses follow:

It is the responsibility of professionally qualified school personnel within the boundaries of a district to determine the relative need of pupils and teachers in the various schools for materials from the three categories (Library Resources, Textbooks, and Other Printed and Published Instructional Materials). . . .

Under this [state] plan all children attending school in a district will be treated equally and shall be considered as having the same relative need for materials.[60]

Since Texas provides textbooks on a statewide basis, the state plan states: "It is anticipated that a lesser percentage of the funds," up to 15 percent, can be used for textbooks and a ceiling of 15 percent is also imposed on "other printed and published materials."

TEA auditors check on maintenance of effort through a state plan provision that: "per pupil expenditures of that district and of all schools in that district for the types of materials eligible under this act will increase or at least remain at the same level as that of the two most recent years for which information is available."[61] TEA staff stated some money had been recovered from school districts under this provision. Extra-large library book purchases, however, may be listed under capital outlay rather than operating expenses which TEA audits for maintenance of effort.

In short, after 1965 TEA has enforced the letter of the federal law and the state plan, but no significant revisions in the state plan have been made since 1965. The adjustment of the formula to correspond to relative need has not been challenged by OE since the first year.

ESEA-Title III

Administration of ESEA-Title III in Texas was in part shaped by some earlier state legislation establishing media centers. Well organized in the State Association of Audio Visual Directors, the media educators, assisted by the media expert at the University of Texas, lobbied for a new state-funded program of media centers. TSTA endorsement was secured, and, after several years of trying, the media lobby was successful in 1967. It was envisioned that these media centers would provide films, filmstrips and other audiovisual materials, with state matching of local funds up to $1 per child. TEA did not take the initiative in the media center bill and played no significant role in its passage.

The first year of Title III of ESEA included several multi-county projects, many with university involvement. In 1967 the TEA office of planning and particularly the deputy commissioner, Warren Hitt, reasoned that ESEA III money could be used for transform the media centers into comprehensive regional service centers. The state media legislation did not establish any incentive for the local matching. TEA persuaded USOE to put up $67,000 in planning money for each supplementary center, to refine the concept and stimulate local interest. TEA convened an advisory council to draw up boundaries for the supplementary centers. The commission and TEA originally came up with thirty-two districts based on the ease of mail deliveries for media and materials. After further deliberation, the U.S. Census Standard Metropolitan

Statistical Area or access to a university became the determinant. This latter formula produced sixteen service areas, but TEA as well as several commission members thought some of the regions were too big; ultimately twenty centers were founded. Five years after the regional service centers were initiated, two-thirds of Texas Title III money remains committed to them. During the era of USOE control of the Title III program, each center was allocated $125,000 base and $1 per ADA. This distribution pattern has not changed since the initial year of funding. In 1967 Warren Hitt decided to seek state legislative authority for the supplementary centers. He drafted the bill and lobbied it through with TSTA endorsement. Hitt conceived each center to be locally oriented and locally based. Consequently, the legislation provided for joint committees of local superintendents who would elect a lay board of seven members.

The service centers provide a number of functions based on local needs. No one center offers all the following services, but the following list indicates the range: curriculum development, data processing, driver education, in-service training, instructional techniques, media, migrant education, planning, pupil appraisal, and special education. Almost all centers provide services in data processing and special education. One regional service center director was interviewed, but there was no attempt to assess their impact or performance.

All TEA personnel interviewed mentioned that the largest cities, Dallas, Fort Worth, Houston, and Corpus Christi, have received very little benefit from the services offered by the centers, since they already possessed their own processing services and media programs. Indeed, Fort Worth donated their media library to the Title III center. Superintendent White in Dallas never accepted the concept, and his district participated only minimally. The medium size centers— Amarillo, San Antonio, and El Paso—did benefit more from the centers. The state legislation gives the centers status as a local school district so they have applied for and received Title III project grants on top of their basic allotments.

There are two statewide bodies to oversee Title III centers. A Texas Planning Council, composed of twenty service center directors, meets monthly with TEA staff. There is also a once-a-year meeting of the lay board of directors called the Texas Commission for Service Centers. This body is recommending a state base of financing to replace Title III sometime in the future. The last Texas state plan includes only the vaguest requirements for a regional supplementary center, thus leaving the specific programs to local decisions.

The allocation for ESEA III projects, other than service centers, is an academic issue in Texas because of a lack of uncommitted funds. All of Texas' share of the $8.5 million for Title III has been used by the supplementary centers. One new project has been funded since TEA gained control of the funds from USOE in 1968. TEA has not even been able to support up to 100 percent of USOE commitments under the central cities project to Fort Worth, Houston, and Laredo. TEA has been reluctant to circulate guidelines or establish project rating schemes until there is money available. It is impossible to speculate how

TEA will handle open competition for Title III projects. In FY 1969 the federal share was allotted to projects that were previously funded.

The 1968 Governor's Committee Report (Vol. IV) raised three important issues with respect to Title III: (1) variations among the regions in size (from less than 40,000 to more than 400,000) and percentage Latin (from 0 percent to 78 percent) and black (from .4 percent to 36 percent); yet each is allocated a flat base of $125,000 plus $1 per ADA as a "need" factor; (2) the degree to which services now centralized in TEA could be offered more efficiently from regional centers; and (3) political responsibility of the governing boards of the centers which are chosen indirectly by the administrations of the participating school districts. Although they have substantial state and federal funds to expend, they are outside the chain of publicly elected representatives and their actions are never subject to popular vote.[62]

Conclusion

The structural and procedural factors of Texas government are important in determining who influences federal aid allocations. The automatic appropriation of Texas state aid tends to deflect gubernatorial and legislative interest in the administration and distribution of federal aid. Texas politics of education revolves around authorizations, particularly teacher salaries. Both the governor and legislature have concentrated on teacher salary increments—a major issue in Texas politics for the last twenty years. Impeded by a small staff, no budget control in education, no important appointive powers and factional one-party politics, the governor's office has not even attempted to keep track of the flow of federal aid to education within Texas, and the top staff were uncertain as to the differences among major federal categorical programs.

Composed of part-time members who meet once every two years, the legislature has little professional staff and has evidenced no particular interest in federal education aid. Although TEA's administrative budget is subject to legislative scrutiny, the writer could find no one knowledgeable about federal aid. The high turnover of legislators inhibits legislative ability to tackle the complexities of federal aid or to acquire the caliber of experience and staff used by the U.S. Congress to oversee USOE administration performance.

TSTA, the only influential interest group, has chosen to avoid federal aid issues and concentrate on state issues, particularly teachers salaries. Preserving a united front among all education groups, TSTA presents a unified program to the legislature. An influential force in electoral campaigns, TSTA has been extremely adept in acquiring support of key committee members before its bills are introduced.

The lack of involvement in federal aid issues of the governor, the legislature, and TSTA has left the state department of education relatively free in its allocation decisions. This freedom has been increased and buttressed by the image of objective professionalism, cultivated during the twenty-two years that Dr. J.W. Edgar has been in office. Despite this aura of objectivity, federal aid allocation, like state aid in Texas, clearly and substantially discriminates against urban school districts. This rural orientation in funds for education had its origin in the early twentieth century, when rural districts were at a disadvantage. However, lack of concrete data (except for the 1968 Governor's Commission on Public School Education) and the persistence of a malapportioned, rural-dominated legislature have permitted the rural favoritism to continue at the expense of the growing urban districts. Until recently, the large cities did not attempt to alter the patterns of allocation because of insufficient data and a reluctance to confront TEA; however, during the past few years, they have formed a coalition and instituted several court suits which are currently pending decision.

Notes

1. *Report of the Governor's Committee on Public School Education.* (Austin: Texas Education Agency, 1968), p. 19.

2. Laurence Iannaccone, "Federal Program Administration in Three Styles," unpublished paper prepared for a meeting of this research team in Syracuse.

3. For a more complete analysis, see the five volumes of the Governor's Committee on Public School Education, 1968. For the Texas system of finance viewed in its Constitutional significance, see Joel S. Berke, et al. "The Texas School Finance Case: A Wrong in Search of a Remedy," *Journal of Law and Education*, I, vol. 3 (1972).

4. Stuart A. MacCorkle and Dick Smith, *Texas Government* (New York: McGraw-Hill, 1968), p. 2.

5. Ibid., p. 5.

6. Jim B. Pearson and Edgar Fuller, *Education in the States: Historical Development and Outlook* (Washington, D.C.: NEA, 1969), p. 1203.

7. Superintendent of Public Instruction, *Biennial Report*, Austin, 1909, p. 57.

8. Pearson and Fuller, op. cit., p. 1207.

9. Ibid., p. 1208.

10. Texas Board of Education, *Fifth Biennial Report, 1936-1938*, Austin, 1938, p. 15.

11. Comment in interview with the author.

12. Pearson and Fuller, op. cit., p. 1212.

13. Ibid.

14. Comment in interview with the author.

15. Comment in interview with the author.

16. Michael D. Usdan, David Minar, Emanuel Hurwitz, Jr., *Education and State Politics* (New York: Teachers College Press, 1969), p. 155.

17. Ibid., p. 156.

18. Comment in interview with the author.

19. Usdan et al., op. cit., p. 156.

20. See MacCorkle and Smith, op. cit., pp. 72-82.

21. Wayne Odom, "The Function of Standing Committees in the Texas Legislature," paper presented at the Southwestern Social Science Association Convention in Dallas, March, 1967.

22. Duane Lockhard, *The Politics of State and Local Government* (New York: Macmillan, 1964), p. 177.

23. Laurence Iannaccone, *State Politics and Education* (New York: Center for Applied Research in Education, 1967).

24. Texas State Teachers Association, *Texas Schools* (Austin: June, 1970), p. 1.

25. See, for instance, *TSTA Legislative Survey* for April, 1970.

26. Rae Eiles Still, The Gilmer-Aikin Bills (Austin: The Steck Co., 1952), pp. 71-73.

27. Usdan et al., op. cit.

28. TSTA, *Texas Schools*, p. 1.

29. See Fred Gantt, Jr. et al., *Governing Texas: Documents and Readings* (New York: Thomas Y. Crowell Company, 1966), Chapter 5.

30. Comment in interview with the author.

31. Comment in interview with the author.

32. Comment in interview with the author.

33. Daniel Elazar, *American Federalism* (New York: Crowell, 1966), p. 97.

34. Comment in interview with the author.

35. *Report of Governor's Committee on Public School Education*, op. cit., Vol. III, pp. 145-146.

36. Texas Education Agency, *Guide for Completing Consolidated Application for Federal Assistance* (Austin: June, 1968).

37. Comment in interview with the author.

38. Texas Education Agency, *Toward Comprehensive Educational Planning in Texas* (Austin: 1968), pp. 7-11.

39. U.S. Office of Education, *Report of the Texas Education Agency: Management Review* (Washington, D.C.: Government Printing Office, 1969), p. 10.

40. Comment in interview with the author.

41. Comment in interview with the author.

42. New federal programs, like cooperative education and work study, are handled as special project grants.

43. *Report of the Governor's Committee on Public School Education*, op. cit., Volume IV, p. 25.

44. Texas Education Agency, *Texas State Plan: Vocational Education for Fiscal Year 1971* (Austin: 1970), pp. 58-59.

277

45. Ibid., pp. 98-99.

46. William P. Kuvlesky and W. Kennedy Upham, *Social Ambitions of Teen-Age Boys Living in an Economically Depressed Area of the South: A Racial Comparison* (Texas A&M University, multilith), pp. 12-20.

47. *Report of the Governor's Committee on Public School Education*, op. cit., Vol. II, p. 102.

48. Texas Education Agency, *Texas State Plan: Vocational Education for Fiscal Year 1971*, p. 50.

49. Ibid., p. 74.

50. Ibid., p. 61.

51. Ibid., p. 51.

52. Usdan et al., op. cit., p. 160.

53. A student contact hour is one hour in which a student has contact with an instructor.

54. Advisory Council on Vocational Education, *A Concerned Texas* (Austin: 1970), pp. 6-7.

55. Comment in interview with the author.

56. Texas Education Agency, *Annual Narrative Report: NDEA-Title III* (Austin: Fiscal Year 1969), p. 4. In earlier years priorities were more specific, such as electronic equipment for junior high foreign languages.

57. *Report of the Governor's Committee on Public School Education*, op. cit., Vol. V., p. 49.

58. Ibid., p. 52.

59. Ibid., p. 54.

60. Texas Education Agency, *A State Plan for Title II of PL 89-10* (Austin: 1967), pp. 12 and 14.

61. Ibid., p. 16.

62. *Report of the Governor's Committee on Public School Education*, op. cit., Vol. IV, p. 51.

7

The Politics of Federal Aid to Education in Virginia

Edith K. Mosher

After decades of neglect that put its schools near the bottom of all interstate comparative ratings, and a brief but traumatic period of defiance to the desegregation edict of the United States Supreme Court, Virginia took unprecedented measures during the 1960s to repair its educational reputation. This objective was contemporaneous with the increase in federal categorical school aid programs; and the subsequent meshing of joint efforts was pursued according "to the way of doing things that is Virginian." Jean Gottman describes this condition in *Virginia in Our Century:*

. . . . Virginia stands out as a highly individual state in the nation, not only because of her past, but also because of her present, not only because of a set of economic features all her own, not duplicated elsewhere, but also because of a way of doing things that is Virginian . . . The past and present of the Old Dominion testify both to the power of psychological isolation in shaping a region's behavior and the inability of such mental attitudes to keep away indefinitely the pressures of the environing world. It is perhaps the unique combination of these two trends in Virginia, one making for change, the other resisting it, that contributes to lend a special personality to the state.[1]

If the state were entirely unique, Virginia's experience with federal aid to education would not provide a comparison with the response of other states. However, Virginia's recent rapid evolution is congruent with and even more marked than that of the whole South.[2] Coexistent with a unifying sense of identity is an intrastate regional diversity matched by few states of the same size. In his study of the implementation of the Civil Rights Act of 1964, Orfield points out that the presence in Virginia of several well-defined regions with distinct histories and sets of attitudes made possible the viewing of a spectrum of responses to the Act almost as broad as can be found in the entire seventeen southern and border states affected by this legislation.[3]

Economic growth, population shifts (including increasing metropolitanism and in-migration), and increased black political participation and influence characterized the milieu in which we tested our research assertions. Like the political setting in which it is embedded, federal aid to education is influenced simultaneously by an established and honored Virginia past and the promise of an undefined and unpredictable future.

Research Assertions and Federal Aid in Virginia

Assertion No. 1. There will be less involvement and political influence by the governor and legislature on federal aid in comparison with state aid.

With the exception of the indirect influence of the negative attitudes that most state officials had toward federal grants-in-aid in general, this assertion applied without qualification to fiscal administration until Linwood Holton, a Republican, took office in January, 1970. Governor Holton has expressed his intention to see that the state exploits all potential federal grant resources.

In Virginia, the governors have traditionally dominated legislative action on state school aid. Now that the Democratic General Assembly must deal with a Republican governor, this subservience may be less marked; but the legislature has yet to have much independent impact on *either* state or federal school aid. As befits their leadership role, all recent governors have been involved in the explosive issue of school desegregation. When the prospect loomed that Virginia would forfeit federal aid because local school divisions failed to comply with Title VI of the Civil Rights Act of 1964, both Governors Godwin and Holton spearheaded negotiations with federal officials.

Assertion No. 2. The influence and impact of the urban school lobby on the state allocation of federal aid will not be significant.

Until very recently, there was no vestige of an urban lobby on any issue. As the present fiscal crisis of the cities intensifies, a new group, the "Urban 12," may be able to exert some influence on the state's educational decision makers. To do so, they will have to overcome what appears to be the conviction of many officials that urban areas are already better off than the other areas of the state.

Assertion No. 3. As federal aid increases and states have more discretion in allocation, pressures will increase on state government from organized interests.

There has been a virtual absence of pressure group activity with regard to state allocations of federal aid. The most active Virginia groups concerned with educational policy have been those attempting either to promote or hinder school desegregation. They have dealt with local school officials or made representations to the governor, but they have left the state department in unquestioned control of the decision making involved in federal grant administration. The state's new community college system does not yet constitute an "organized interest," but it may in time strive to wrest a greater share of vocational educational funds from the state department of education.

Assertion No. 4. The state education agency will attempt to minimize political conflict and pressure by using existing state aid formulas for allocation of federal funds.

Virginians like and respect familiar practices, especially Virginia practices. Thus the state department of education may have been guided by tradition, rather than by any conscious desire to avoid trouble or conflict, when it determined the distribution of federal grant funds. Whatever the reasoning, dependence on state aid models has been obvious, notably the adoption of the practice of compensating 60 percent of local salaries according to the State Minimum Salary Scale for vocational education teachers and guidance counselors. The procedures adopted for Title III of NDEA and Title II of ESEA exemplify the well-established use of per pupil allocations, with some limited attention to equalizing the resources of needy districts. In a larger sense, the state department minimized political conflict by staying clear of the controversies over school desegregation caused by Title VI of the Civil Rights Act of 1964. Local school officials were responsible for achieving federal approval of their compliance with Title VI provisions.

Assertion No. 5. Federal aid, except in the manner restricted by federal guidelines or requirements, will flow within a state as it has in the past.

Past policies have led Virginia's local school officials to expect that "nobody will be left out" in the distribution of grants-in-aid. The administration of NDEA-Title III indicates that the state department of education tried to satisfy these expectations, in preference to greater targeting of funds to needy districts. The 25 percent for post-secondary vocational education from VEA funds appears to have become a firmly fixed policy. There has also been considerable continuity in the funding of the Title III projects.

Assertion No. 6. SEA personnel are socialized so that they see their proper role as providing technical assistance to the LEAs, not enforcing or policing federal requirements or setting program priorities.

The Virginia experience partially supports and partially refutes this assertion. Much emphasis is given to maintaining a rather passive, technical assistance role *vis-à-vis* the local school divisions; yet many Virginia Department of Education personnel perceive the state's required fiscal procedures as a very valid, desirable method to ensure orderly compliance with recommended types of performance, even those promulgated by the federal government. The tradition of fiscal accountability is extremely strong throughout the state government; it is reinforced by the General Assembly practice of appropriating the anticipated revenues from federal sources, so that they are subject to the strict controls imposed by the state. The localities receive their federal monies on a reimbursible basis; the possibility that they will be denied payment for non-conforming expenditures is ever present. The imposition of state fiscal controls on the administration of the department itself is doubtless an influential constraint on staff members who might wish to move outside the safe confines of established precedents.

In general, the department personnel do not *appear* to be aggressive in setting program priorities for the LEAs. But many school divisions look to them for information and guidance in fulfilling the federal requirements, and traditional "ways of doing things" in Virginia support compliance with higher authority. For example, the Title I staff has seen to it that some of the more specific federal priorities have been implemented. The Division of Vocational Education also reports that it has successfully brought about statewide changes in emphasis among its programs.

Patterns of Allocation of Federal
Aid to School Districts

State Fiscal Aid to Local School Divisions

Virginia's method of dispersing state school aid has been an important guide for departmental decisions on the intrastate distribution of federal categorical grant funds.

Virginia has 136 separate local school divisions; 95 are coterminous with county governments, 35 with cities, and 7 with towns. One county and city are classified as "non-operating" because they transfer their students to neighboring divisions. This simplified pattern of school organization, with relatively few local units, reflects the historical practice in several southern states of delegating responsibility for public education to the civil subdivisions.[4] At present, the designation of "county" and "city" does not clearly delineate the rural or urban character of a school division, since "cities" may be created for areas having as few as 5,000 inhabitants, and several Virginia counties are highly urbanized. Consistent with the wide dispersal of population centers throughout the state, most regions have school divisions of various urban-suburban-rural types and sizes, except that those in southwest and Southside are smaller and less urbanized, and those in northern Virginia are all suburban in character.

A more useful basis for comparison of the characteristics of the school divisions of the state is achieved by the separation into SMSA and non-SMSA categories. The six SMSAs include the Virginia portion of the Washington, D.C. complex, Richmond, Norfolk-Portsmouth, Newport News-Hampton, Roanoke, and Lynchburg and environs. Further, because of the diversity and growing metropolitanism of the state, the subclassification of the SMSA school divisions into "Metro Central" and "Metro Other" categories, and those of the non-SMSAs into "Emerging Metro" and "Non-Metro" reveals significant differences. It is also desirable to analyze separately the data on the six Northern Virginia counties. They are distinctive as part of an interstate metropolitan complex, and they have socioeconomic characteristics which distort summary statistics relating to the state as a whole or to its SMSAs.

These subclassifications appear in Table 7-1, which presents comparative data derived from a stratified sample of sixty-nine school divisions.[5] From this table it is apparent that the six school divisions of Northern Virginia are, on the average, notably richer, spend more on schools, and have lower black enrollments than those in the other SMSA areas. When they are excluded from the sample, the state's "Metro Central" school divisions show up, on the average, as

Table 7-1

Comparison of Virginia School Divisions in Metropolitan and Non-Metropolitan Areas by Social and Economic Characteristics

Virginia Sample,[1] Classified by Metropolitan and Nonmetropolitan types, and separately for Northern Virginia portion of metropolitan areas.[2]

Variables	State Sample N=63	SMSA N = 20			Sample Excluding Six School Divisions of Northern Virginia SMSA					Non-SMSA N = 20		
	State Sample N=69	Total	Metro Central N=7	Metro Other N=13	State Sample N=63	SMSAs N = 14 Total	Metro Central N=7	Metro Other N=7	Northern Virginia Only N=6	Total	Emerging Metro N=11	Rural Areas & Isolated Cities
Mean Per Cap Income	$2478	$3085	$3151	$3049	$2380	$2905	$3151	$2658	$3506	$2230	$2455	$2162
Mean Dist Wealth	$32M	$86M	$74M	$92M	$23M	$66M	$74M	$58M	$131M	$11.2M	$17M	$9.5M
Total ADA	727,588	514,132	195,720	318,421	559,198	345,742	195,720	150,022	168,399	213,456	76,094	137,362
Total Operating Costs[3]	$379M	$282M	$102M	$180M	$269M	$173M	$102M	$71M	$110M	$96M	$36M	$60M
Mean Cost/Pupil	$520	$549	$521	$566	$481	$499	$521	$469	$652	$451	$470	$440
Mean ADA	10,544	25,707	27,960	24,493	8876	24,695	27,960	21,431	28,066	4356	6917	3614
Mean Bk Enrollment	2303	5518	11,316	2,181	2386	7067	11,316	2818	1438	1048	2066	754

[1] Sample, constitutes 50% of total number of school divisions, includes all which have an ADA over 10,000, and accounts for 75% of all school enrollment in 1967-68.

[2] Category definitions are based on ELSEGIS I national sample. (*Statistics of Local Public School Systems*, OE-22027-68 p. 2) and on those utilized by Donald C. Dixon in *University of Virginia Newsletter*, March 15, 1968.

[3] Computed by multiplying cost/pupil ADA for each Division. Capital outlay and debt service which amount to approximately 25% of all local expenditures, statewide, are not included in cost/pupil.

having greater wealth and spending more on schools than the school divisions in their environs. They also show a much higher proportion of black students than appears in any other category. Not surprisingly, the average for school divisions of the "emerging metropolitan" category reveal that they are similar to those in the SMSA areas in several respects.

The non-SMSA school divisions of the isolated cities or rural areas fall farther below them, as well as below state averages, on nearly all the indicators, (wealth, size, school expenditures, and racial compositions). However, diversity in this category is quite extensive. Virginia counties vary widely, for example, in their proportions of non-white inhabitants. The *majority* of poor, rural residents are white.

The system of school governance in Virginia is one which greatly minimizes local community participation and school board autonomy. Appointed school boards are the rule, accomplished in most counties by a three-stage process: circuit court judges, themselves appointed by the General Assembly, appoint school trustee electoral boards whose sole function is to appoint the members of the school boards. The locally-elected boards of supervisors are responsible for raising local school revenues and approving school board budgets and expenditures. This mode of operation practically guarantees that a political organization which can control the state and local legislatures will dominate educational policy. Under the regime headed by Senator Harry Flood Byrd for more than three decades, the schools visibly suffered from both the state's firmly entrenched conservative fiscal policies and public apathy in many localities.[6]

The state remained aloof from the tendency of many other states to redesign their school aid distribution formulas. In 1965, the *Washington Post* reported as follows:

The amount of public school revenues coming from state sources is lower in Virginia than in any of the other ten Southern states surveyed by the National Education Association in 1963. Receiving this minimal aid, the local cities and counties must decide for themselves whether to have quality education. In a rich urban district, the answer is "yes." In a poor rural county the answer can only be "no."[7]

The urban and suburban areas suffered doubly because their local taxes supported most of the improvements in their own schools, while the individual and corporate taxes collected mainly from these areas provided the bulk of the state's general fund revenues. Critics of the Byrd organization contended that the state school aid allotted from its general fund was so inadequate that it scarcely mattered how it was distributed.

The major state contribution purports to take account of factors of local need and effort. To be eligible for the state grant, a division must put into effect the State Minimum Salary Scale (which for the 1970-71 biennium begins at $5,000 for holders of collegiate certificates) and provide from local sources not less than 30 percent of its total expenditures, excluding capital outlay and debt service, for school operations.[8]

The average percentage contribution of the state to the operating costs of the local school divisions in 1968-69 was 38 percent, with a range of variation from 60 percent to 16 percent.[9] Since over 80 percent of the state funds distributed to the localities were uniformly determined on the basis of numbers of teaching positions and size of ADA, the general effect of the formula is to provide a per pupil allocation, with relatively small adjustments for wealth or size of district.[10] The contribution of the state (including that for retirement benefits) amounted to only 33 percent of *total* school expenditures, since the localities bear the entire costs for debt service and almost all the costs for capital outlay.[11]

The formula for state aid takes little account of the realities of actual school costs or of the diversity of local wealth and effort. For example, in 1969-70 all the school divisions had beginning salaries higher than the $5,000 of the State Minimum Salary Scale, and 120 had starting salaries above $6,000.[12] Furthermore, most school divisions have class size ratios lower than those used to compute state aid.[13] The actual average classroom teacher salaries vary widely across the state, with only 21 school divisions exceeding the state average of $7,328 in 1968-69. The average salary for the highest ranking county, $9,097, was 53.8 percent higher than the average for the lowest, $5,912. The local ability to support education, as represented by amount of property taxable for school purposes per pupil, varied from $77,995 to $12,843, and the amount of local funds invested per pupil, from $665 to $79. As for local effort, determined by the true tax rate on each $100 of property taxable for school purposes, the variation was from $.45 to $1.64. Only 33 localities equaled or exceeded the state average of $1.00.[14]

As would be expected from the nature of the formula, the correlations of amounts of state grant funds with ADA and district wealth (true value of real estate and public service corporations) are uniformly very high, while those with per capita income and total cost per pupil, are either low or negative. It appears that state funding accounts for a greater share of school support in the non-SMSA school divisions, which have the lowest mean per capita income, the lowest enrollments, and lowest mean cost per pupil. These are, in general, the localities which are unable or unwilling to provide additional school support from their own resources. The Virginia formula is not one, however, which would reward local effort or initiative for school divisions in any of the categories.

Early in 1970, a study of state school fund distribution, which had been authorized by the General Assembly, was submitted by a commission chaired by Delegate George N. McMath and composed of state legislators, local government officials, and professional educators.[15] Concluding that the present plan was unrealistic and too complex, they recommended that the General Assembly establish the cost per student of a basic program of education, the costs of which would be shared equally by the state and the *combined* localities of the state. Special funds were recommended only for capital outlay and pupil transportation. The commission also stated that further attention should be given to the problem of added state aid to school systems having high proportions of educationally disadvantaged children. The commission proposals entailed an estimated increase of $35 million for 1970-71, including $11 million for capital outlay; they failed to receive significant official attention or support from the state department of education, the outgoing or the newly-elected governor, or the members of the General Assembly. Instead, the state department of education recommended and the General Assembly approved a modest increase over 1969-70 funding levels under the existing plan, making slight upward adjustments of the minimum salary scale ($300 per year) and of the per pupil allotment for other operating costs ($15 over two years).

Whatever its other limitations may be, the present school aid distribution scheme has some political utility in the Virginia context. In the first place, the funding requirements can be projected with considerable accuracy, a feat which the state department of education and its long-time fiscal chief, J.P. Blount, performed so efficiently that their estimates were accepted with confidence by the General Assembly. Secondly, it permits cautious bargaining, within narrow limits, as to overall appropriations for state aid.

Thirdly, the plan reserves a considerable measure of fiscal and program initiative to the state policy makers. It is ironic that Virginia's accretion of numerous special grant funds for localities perpetuates the fragmented forms of categorical aid that the state officials so roundly criticize in the federal school aid programs. The underlying rationale is the same in both cases: to offer inducements to the lower level of government to implement specific program priorities set by the higher level. Virginia's subventions to its localities are, in general, less flexible than those of the national government.

Apart from the McMath Commission criticisms of the present distribution scheme, there have been other evidences of restiveness with state policy. Bath County, Virginia, instigated an unsuccessful suit, similar to those in several other states, charging that the system of financing school aid denied equal protection of the law to the children of the county. On May 23, 1969, a three-man federal district court denied the plaintiff's suit while noting "their beseeming earnest and justified appeal for help."[16]

The Scope of Federal Funding (1966-1970)

Table 7-2 lists the amounts allocated to Virginia under various federal grants programs for the period July 1, 1966 to June 30, 1970. Actual expenditures are somewhat lower than these authorizations. Because of the cash accounting

Table 7-2

Federal Fund Obligations to Virginia for Selected Programs, 1966-70 (in thousands of dollars)

Programs	1966-7[1]	1967-8[3]	1968-9[5]	1969-70[5]
ESEA I	$24,225	$29,277	$27,229	$31,466
ESEA II	2,132	2,076	1,057	910
ESEA III	3,892	4,136	3,568	2,498
ESEA V	426	518	604	604
NDEA III	2,336	2,018	2,003	925
NDEA VA	559	557	382	324
VOC ED	7,216	6,967	6,770[6]	9,905
PL 874	27,964	32,880	35,705	35,182
PL 815	968	33	3,590	635
Adult Basic Education	877	951	1,133	1,272
School Lunch and Milk	5,715[2]	6,093[4]	8,309[6]	5,775[8]
Appalachian Commission (Sec. 211-214)	4,296	1,379[4]	2,066[6]	1,419[7]
MDTA	1,330	1,020[4]	1,028[6]	1,703[8]
Total	$82,000	$88,000	$93,000	$93,000

Sources:

[1]U.S. Office of Education—Office of Budget, Mimeo. Summary.

[2]*Annual Report of Virginia State Superintendent of Public Instruction 1966-67*, p. 179.

[3]U.S. Office of Education,Budget Division, Mimeo. Summary.

[4]*Annual Report*, op. cit., 1967-68, pp. 194-95.

[5]*Congressional Record*, August 19, 1970, p. E7853.

[6]*Annual Report*, op. cit., 1968-69, pp. 191-92.

[7]*Budget Exhibit*, State Board of Education, 1970-72, p. A-59.

[8]Commonwealth of Virginia, *Budget 1970-72*, p. 236.

method used in Virginia, whereby disbursements are charged to the fiscal year in which they are made rather than to the years in which they become available, there are some difficulties in reconciling reports of federal fiscal authorizations and state disbursements for the same fiscal year. During the initial start-up period for the ESEA programs (April, 1965, to June, 1966) the annual reports of the state department of education show disbursements well below federal allocations in the case of Title I and Title V. However, by the academic year 1966-67, the state was spending its federal grants at close to the currently authorized levels.

Table 7-2 indicates that 60-70 percent of the state's total allocations are accounted for by Title I of ESEA and PL 874 funding. Next in magnitude have been the allocations for the vocational education and school lunch and milk programs. The $11 million increase in the state total over the five-year period largely consists of the greater amounts going to these programs, with declining amounts for Titles II and III of ESEA and for the NDEA titles.

Since the federal government is responsible for allocating funds to the local school divisions under PL 874, PL 815, and ESEA-Title I, state discretionary authority in this regard applies to a minor portion of the total state subvention and particularly those programs which call for state matching of the federal funds. The manner in which the state carried out these varied but basically limited responsibilities with regard to several of the federal grant programs will be described in Section V.

Differential Impact of the Federal Aid
Programs (1967-68)

In order to study the impact of federal funding as a whole, as well as of individual grant programs, on the different types of Virginia school divisions, data for the year 1967-68 (Fiscal Year 1968) for a sample of sixty-nine districts were compiled and analyzed. The definitions of variables, classification of school divisions, and correlational methods were the same as those employed to compile Table 7-1, thus providing the basis for comparison of the impact of federal funding with that from state and local sources. It was found that the funding from both state and total federal sources correlated with all the indicators of local division characteristics in a highly similar manner. That is, both sets of correlations with ADA and district wealth for all types of divisions tended to be uniformly high and those with per capita income and cost per pupil to be either low or negative. Some exceptions occurred with regard to the "Metro Other" category (excluding northern Virginia divisions), and these may, in some degree, reflect such dissimilarity among the suburban areas.

When correlations were computed between the total amounts of federal funding for the localities and the amounts they received under several of the separate federal grant programs, considerable variation was found both with regard to the separate grants and the various categories of school divisions, reflecting to some degree the differing eligibility and allocation requirements of the federal legislation. The lowest correlations are those for the non-SMSA areas and the funding for PL 815, PL 874, and vocational education. Funding for Title I of ESEA showed a high degree of correlation with the total federal funding for all categories of districts, when the northern Virginia divisions are analyzed separately. The pattern is less consistent when these divisions are combined with the other suburban divisions of the state.

Correlations were also computed between amounts granted under the separate federal programs and the amounts of funding from both state and local sources. Except for the "non-SMSA" and "Metro Other" categories (excluding northern Virginia), the correlations were positive and fairly high. In the case of Title II of ESEA, vocational education, and PL 815 and PL 874, school divisions were closely comparable with regard to all three sources of revenue. However, except for northern Virginia, Title I funding correlates less markedly with funding from local sources than it does with total federal or state funding. This would confirm an equalizing effect of the unique Title I allocation formula.

When grants under Title I of ESEA were correlated with those of the other federal grant programs, the correlations with amounts for vocational education appeared to be highest in all the SMSA school divisions. Correlations were positive but lower with the amounts for Titles II and III of ESEA. The negative correlations found between amounts for Title I and PL 874 in the non-SMSA school divisions may be explained by the fact that PL 874 funding goes almost entirely to SMSA school divisions.

The intended equalizing effects of Title I were found to be uneven with regard to the various categories of school divisions. Correlations of Title I grants in relation to measures of personal income were predictably high and positive for the "Metro Central" areas, and negative for the "Metro Other" and non-SMSA areas. Amounts for Title I also correlated less highly with the measure of district wealth in the case of the non-SMSA areas. However, it appeared that the large, wealthier school divisions in the "Metro Central" and "northern Virginia" categories were also receiving proportionately large amounts of Title I funding.

Political Factors Shaping Fiscal and Administrative Patterns

The Heritage of Traditionalism

A strikingly Janus-like political milieu surrounds present educational policy-making in Virginia. A statewide political system, that dates back to Revolutionary days, for a long time successfully blunted and contained pluralistic and external influences, even in the face of changing circumstances. During the Revolutionary era, Virginia was distinguished because of its historical seniority among the colonies, the size of its population and territory, and the emergence of an elite which demonstrated exceptional qualities of leadership. The state developed what Elazar defined as a traditionalist political culture "rooted in an ambivalent attitude toward the marketplace coupled with a paternalistic and elitist conception of the commonwealth . . . It accepts a substantially hierarchical society as part of the ordered nature of things, authorizing and expecting those at the top of the solid structure to take a special and dominant role in government."[17]

Elazar further considered the maintenance of Virginia's cultural patterns to be the norm or issue involving the greatest internal unity of the state vis-à-vis the federal and other governments, and he ranks the state with the other southern states as possessing the highest relative degree of intrastate unity.[18]

Yet significant diversity within the state is also recognized by Elazar and Gottman. While Elazar classifies the state's political culture as predominately traditional, he also indicates that an "individualistic" culture characterizes northeastern Virginia and that the southwest and central valley regions show what he defines as a strong "moralistic" strain.[19] Gottman shows, for example, how the recent economic development in the state has been manifold and differentiated from area to area, with rural pursuits still being carried on and well protected by legislation, as in the cases of tobacco, peanuts, and other products.[20] He considers that the dispersion and variety of industrial concentrations which developed in Virginia by 1967 help to account for its resurgence on the national economic scene.

Before examining in detail the unifying and durable political influence on state educational policymaking, it is thus necessary to describe briefly certain basic features of its locale and population, economic growth, and urbanization.

Regionalism and Race

Although regionalism and local differences divide the state's population, the deepest and strongest demarcation lines are etched by race and color. The state's white population is fairly homogeneous, descended mainly from English settlers, or, in the western part of the state, from Scots and Germans. Blacks, who constituted about 40 percent of the population by 1800, were estimated to account for about 19.6 percent in 1966.[21] The largest black populations are in the Southside and Tidewater regions where opposition to integration and federal influence has been strongest. Blacks in Virginia have for some time been more urbanized than in other southern states. As in other parts of the country, during the last three decades, the proportionate number of non-whites in ghettoized central-city areas has increased. Increasing urbanization, civil rights legislation (including the Voting Rights Act of 1965), and the removal of the poll tax have made the black vote a political force to which Virginia politicians must pay increasing attention. Historical relationships between race and party affiliation have proved to be highly significant and very durable. In 1960, Democratic strongholds were still to be found in the slaveholding areas of a century ago, while Republicans were relatively strong west of the Blue Ridge, where slaves had been scant.[22]

Population Growth and Urbanization

The preliminary reports on the 1970 census show a total population of 4,543,249, a gain of 573,000 persons over the 1960 figures, but a slowing down of an annual average rate of increase of over 2 percent to 1.45 percent for the decade of the 1960s.[23] Rural areas either lost population or made very small gains, while the metropolitan areas in the northern and eastern parts of the state boomed.[24] Three of the major population groupings (northern Virginia, Richmond and the emerging Petersburg complex, and Hampton Roads-Newport News) are growing toward one another on major highways and have recently become known as the state's "urban corridor."[25]

Both demographic and economic analysts expect Virginia's total population to reach six million by 1985 and to show further metropolitan concentrations.[26] It should be noted that statistics on state growth do not reflect the relationship which the suburban counties of northern Virginia bear to the Washington, D.C., central city complex. Any analysis of political trends requires special attention to this region, the initiator of many innovative educational programs and the seedbed of opposition to the state's traditional politics.

The state's upsurge in population and urbanization is accompanied by rates of industrial and economic growth which have exceeded national averages. The 1964 reapportionment of the Virginia General Assembly to provide more adequate representation of the growing metropolitan areas of the state was an acknowledgment of the cities' influence and increasing importance.

The Legacy of Massive Resistance

The 1954 decision of the U.S. Supreme Court outlawing de jure school segregation on racial grounds led to an era in Virginia which became known nationally as "massive resistance"; it lasted for about five years. The historical origins of massive resistance lay in the governmental system which had permitted Southside and rural conservatives to dominate the state leadership, state legislature, and state school policy since the 1920s. The "Old South" ethic of Senator—formerly Governor—Harry Byrd was also important in its ideology. Although overt racism and heated political debate were strikingly at odds with the Byrd style and organizational practice, the architects of massive resistance went to extreme lengths to court the state's most stubborn segregationists. In part, this was an effort to recoup some of its political power, lost during the five years preceding the Supreme Court decision; during those years, internal and external critics constantly assailed the Byrd organization's monolithic power and the low levels of services which it provided for a growing economy.[27] The federal ruling offered an opportunity to divert attention from these conflicts and to win transient support with the emotional appeal of Virginia as the champion of states' rights.

Massive resistance cannot be explained, however, entirely in terms of its obvious appeal to racists or its presumed benefits to the political power structure. Its support also derived from values long held by other influential segments of the population: for example, the free-enterprise ideology of state industrialists, which included resistance to federal regulation; and the espousal by the state's social elite of private school education for their own children. In Virginia, the most favored agencies for this purpose were the schools under control of the Episcopal church or those organized as military academies.

The struggle over compliance with the federal rulings thoroughly convulsed state educational policy; the repeal of compulsory attendance requirements, mandated school closings, and, following a statewide referendum, amendment of the State Constitution to permit state payment of tuition grants for private schooling were the results. (Such payments were declared to be contrary to the U.S. Constitution in 1968 and were discontinued in June, 1969.) The state leadership even prevented school districts from complying with federal regulations if they wanted to do so. However, when the doctrine of interposition espoused by the massive resisters was rejected by court decision, a shaky coalition of legislators and citizen groups, more interested in the public schools than in maintaining segregation, finally prevailed. Implementation of the Supreme Court ruling proceeded in many parts of the state without disruption of the schools.[28]

Although the failure of the massive resistance movement signalled the end of the "old politics," it had a lasting influence on the educational policy making of the 1960s. The energy and leadership resources which were devoted in other states during the 1950s to school planning and improvement were dissipated in Virginia by a bruising struggle which exacerbated already critical deficiencies. It led to more intense polarization throughout the state between citizens who favored implementation of civil rights legislation and meeting other new demands of the times and those who saw the maintenance of segregated schools as the overriding concern. Furthermore, massive resistance had been fueled not only by traditional views on race relations, but also by an historical reserve toward, even suspicion of, the national government. Although voicing of overtly racist opinions became unacceptable among the majority of Virginians, objections to any federal influence on educational programing were widespread and undiminished.

The subsequent implementation of the Civil Rights Act of 1964 intensified these attitudes, enabling extremists, opposed unconditionally to the provision of racially-integrated schooling, to make highly inflammatory statements by cloaking them in "anti-fed" rhetoric. Sensitized by the massive resistance debacle to the potential explosiveness of racial issues, consensus-minded state politicians and education officials sought in every way possible both to localize and to minimize their implications in all matters of school policy.

The Changing Politics and Education in the 1960s

In January, 1962, Albertis S. Harrison succeeded J. Lindsay Almond, Jr., the beleaguered governor of the massive resistance period. Educational administrators at the state level tried cautiously to conduct business as usual. With the exception of vocational and technical education and the nationally recognized educational programs, developed independently by a few rapidly growing local school divisions in northern Virginia, few educational strides were made in these years—a period which on a national level produced the early Great Society programs, including the Civil Rights Act of 1964 and the Elementary and Secondary Education Act of 1965.

Virginia educators were beginning to implement these novel and, for most of them, disconcerting legislative enactments when Mills E. Godwin, the incumbent lieutenant governor, was elected governor in 1965. His performance for the four years that ensued is the political saga of a dramatic and successful break with the past. Governor Godwin's broad-ranging activities and personal leadership were crucial to Virginia's response to the growing federal presence in its educational affairs, as well as to the upgrading of its educational system.

Ironically, during the 1950s Governor Godwin was an official spokesman for massive resistance; he demonstrated great dedication to fiscal stinginess and other tenets of Byrd politics. In the early 1960s he was anathema to Virginia liberals. However, his position as lieutenant governor during the Harrison administration provided an ideal climate for him to develop a more moderate position, since there were no issues on which he had to take a stand; moreover, his position as lieutenant governor permitted him to mingle with important Virginians on a congenial basis that had been impossible at the height of the massive resistance conflict.[29] He is credited with doing what a man of less orthodox credentials could not have done in Virginia—dismantling many of the very traditions he had worked to sustain.

Governor Godwin correctly assessed the realignment of voter support created by the elimination of the poll tax, substantial in-migrations, legislative reapportionment, and especially by the accelerating urbanization and economic expansion. This ability had enabled him in 1965 to forge a coalition which included black and labor groups to defeat Linwood Holton, the Republican candidate. After his election, it enabled him to accomplish a program of sweeping legislative measures with a minimum of obstruction.

Cognizant of the voters' desire and need for increased public services, he engineered the enactment of the sales tax which the Byrd organization had blocked for years. This tax, now levied at 4 percent with a minimum of 1 percent earmarked for schools, yields more than $280 million annually. A successful public referendum in 1968 on an $81 million bond issue was another fiscal innovation—in sharp contrast with the unbending pay-as-you-go policy of the Byrd era. Not only did this bond issue alleviate the pressing capital needs of the higher education and mental health institutions, it also paved the way for new constitutional provisions which now permit broader borrowing powers.

By Virginian standards, activities in Richmond began to move at a frantic pace. There were program advances in all sectors of state government.

The most durable achievements of the Godwin years may well be those related to constitutional changes and educational development, especially higher education. The two are closely linked, since the 1970 state constitution strengthened the articles dealing with public education and incorporated concepts, such as the assurance of education "of high quality" to all children, a far cry from earlier mandates. Another innovation of the Godwin era was the provision for a statewide network of twenty-two community colleges, expected to make post-secondary education available within commuting distance in every section of the state during the 1970s. State support for higher education was doubled; expenditures for elementary and secondary schooling rose from $177 million in 1965-66 to $264 million in 1967-69. For the first time, grants were made for kindergartens and other types of categorical aid to encourage local effort. The state superintendent of instruction developed a nine-point program of needed reforms, largely measures for the improvement of teaching; it was adopted by the State Board of Education in 1965 and funded with new generosity by the General Assembly in 1966 and 1968. The State Board of Education authorized in 1967 an Advisory Commission on Raising the Levels of Education, composed of state and local educational and other officials and chaired by William M. Turner. A number of its key proposals were subsequently implemented by the state department of education.[30]

The developments at the state level are an important background to the study of the impact of greatly expanded federal aid in Virginia during this period of ferment. However, these changes proceeded in isolation and aloofness from national events, with few exceptions. At best, state personnel would probably have had little inclination to seek out assistance or to collaborate on programmatic concerns emanating from official Washington. The problems of implementing the Civil Rights Act of 1964 further intensified the old hostilities.

School Desegregation in the 1960s

Following the collapse of massive resistance and de jure school segregation in the early 1960s, Virginia relied on a pupil placement board established by the General Assembly to carry out a form of token integration of schools. However, several communities in Northern Virginia exercised their option to end control by the board and adopted some kind of modified geographic assignment plan.[31]

The response in Virginia to the passage of the Civil Rights Act in 1964 and the subsequent implementation of the U.S. Office of Education guidelines are indicative of the diverse forms of educational policy making at local and state levels.[32] Predictably, the most stubborn resistance to school desegregation was to be found in the Southside and Tidewater areas with large black populations. The statewide political support mobilized for massive resistance was by no means quiescent, but the growing diversity and wealth of the state exerted counter pressures against further defiance of federal action.

The most powerful persuasion for compliance, however, was the prospect that further resistance might jeopardize the increased amounts of federal funding which became available in the mid-60s. Only one sizable school division, Henrico County, held out for long against this threat; and it was, perversely, a suburban area of Richmond having a low black enrollment. It has also a politically active minority of residents with extremist racial views.

A dichotomous response to the federal civil rights legislation on the part of state-level bureaucrats and politicians might have been predicted from a knowledge of the state's recent past. The first task of the Office of Education under the 1964 Act was to obtain a civil rights compliance pledge from a gun-shy state department of education. After the rejection of the first two pledges, the State Plan was finally approved in May, 1965. Except for one brief mention of the Civil Rights Act in the *One-Hundredth Anniversary Report* on the development of the Virginia public school system,[33] one finds no references in recent annual reports of the state department to the implementation of desegregation plans by the local school divisions.

While it is difficult to assess the progress made in school desegregation by Virginia's 135 school divisions, as of February, 1969, 48 divisions were reported by USOE to be in compliance with Title VI under Forms 441; 22 were operating under court order; and 65, under voluntary plans. Of the 65, 10 had federal funding terminated, and three have been cited for hearings. Problems of federal enforcement have been fewer than in many of the southeastern states and, until the urban busing controversies intensified in 1970, less visible on the national scene.

Elected officials could not stay on the sidelines on so crucial an issue, however. During the first year under the federal act, when no official standards had yet been issued to guide local officials, Governor Harrison utilized the services of the prestigious law firm of Battle and Battle to assist Virginia school divisions in their negotiations with the federal officials. William Battle was a new breed of Virginia Democrat who had managed the Kennedy campaign in Virginia in 1960. He dealt directly with top executives at the U.S. Office of Education and was able to win concessions which took account of the special problems some school divisions were encountering. In spite of much confusion, and the pressure federal officials exerted to get plans adopted which went beyond "freedom of choice," all the divisions submitted plans acceptable under the initial guidelines, and no funds were withheld.

However, the second set of federal guidelines, issued in early 1966, "raised the price of federal aid from token integration to a restructuring of the entire educational system on non-discriminatory lines."[34] Their requirements for percentages of black enrollment and faculty integration were a basic threat to the status quo in Virginia; the guidelines reactivated a political struggle between the conservative remnants of the Byrd organization and a political grouping farther to the right, the Conservative party, on the one hand; and, on the other, several effectively organized groups of blacks, long involved in the court fights for civil rights and greatly strengthened by the removal of poll tax and other restrictions on black registration and voting. Neither faction commands more than a minority of voters, but their strength is sufficient to make elected officials aware of the hazards of making too many concessions to either. Thus politicians with statewide constituencies began to pursue a zig-zag course between extreme positions on the federal intervention in educational policy making.[35]

The results have confounded political analysts. Although Governor Godwin owed his election partially to his unprecedented but successful appeal to labor and black groups, he demonstrated his opposition to the 1966 guidelines for school desegregation. He traveled to Washington to confer personally with HEW Secretary Gardner; he supported the other southern governors in protesting to President Johnson; and he released public letters that challenged specific federal actions.[36] At the same time, he urged moderation and encouraged the application for federal funds.

Conservative party defections and liberal support are credited with effecting the election in 1966 of William B. Spong, a moderate Democrat, to the U.S. Senate; Senator Spong defeated the incumbent, Willis Robertson, a stalwart of the Byrd organization. The new senator had gained statewide prominence and a lasting interest in education when, as a state senator from Portsmouth, he had chaired the Commission on Public Education in the Commonwealth in 1959-60, appointed by the General Assembly. Even a committed segregationist like Harry S. Byrd, Jr., who was appointed to Virginia's other senatorial seat when his father retired from office late in 1965, attempted to keep the race issue out of his own campaign in 1966. The liberal tide in voting, plus redistricing of a large sector of northern Virginia, is also credited with the 1966 toppling of veteran congressman, Howard Smith.

In spite of Godwin's remarkable record in loosening the hold of traditionalism on the state government, he was unable to transfer his power and influence to the Democratic nominee for governor in 1969, William S. Battle, who was defeated by the Republican, Linwood Holton.[37] The Republicans won the governorship, but two moderate Democrats were elected lieutenant governor and attorney general.

Educational Issues of the 1970s

Governor Holton did not give educational improvements especially high priority during his first year in office, but he pledged general support to the reform program of his predecessor, especially to the community college and vocational education programs. Both before and after his election, he strongly supported the adoption of the new state constitution, issuing joint statements with

Governor Godwin, and singled out the strengthening of the education article for special endorsement. In his appointments to the state board of education, he added representation from northern Virginia and urged that the board take strenuous steps to rebuild public confidence in the schools.

To meet the commitments he had made to black supporters, he appointed a capable black educator as a race relations advisor on his staff. Governor Holton's position on school desegregation was rendered anomalous, however, by his obligation, as a Republican endorsed by Nixon, not to criticize, though not necessarily to support, the various policy shifts of the Nixon Administration. What appeared to be a softening of the federal enforcement effort was, of course, well received by Virginia segregationists.

It became evident in the summer of 1970 that four of Virginia's biggest cities—Richmond, Norfolk, Roanoke, and Lynchburg—were to be ordered by the federal courts to achieve greater racial balance in their schools (in most cases, by greater use of busing). Over one-quarter of the state's black children live in these four cities, which were among the state's twenty-seven school divisions that had not desegregated by 1969. The situation has changed from that of five years earlier in that controversies over desegregation in urbanized Virginia are beginning to resemble those of the larger metropolitan centers elsewhere.[38]

The most violent opposition to the expected court orders came in the Richmond area, where KKK groups again unleashed their extremist rhetoric, playing on the fears of white and black parents alike for the safety of their children. By November, 1970, the Richmond school board had taken an extraordinary action to obtain a broader base for integration of 65 percent black enrollment. Over opposition from the Richmond City Council, it requested the federal court to order its consolidation with the counties of Henrico and Chesterfield. Subsequently, the state department of education became a defendent in the court action. In January, 1972, U.S. District Court Judge Robert R. Merhige, Jr., issued the landmark ruling that the state has an "affirmative duty" to eliminate all vestiges of segregation and cannot ignore the duty by pleading for local control of schools or by insisting on traditional boundary lines. The Fourth U.S. Circuit Court of Appeals set aside Judge Merhige's schedule for establishment of the consolidated district, pending action on the defendant's appeal, but ordered the state department of education to continue with necessary preliminary planning activities. By the spring of 1972, the Richmond court decision had sparked a national furor over the issues of district consolidation and increased use of busing to bring about school desegregation.

The rancor this court action engendered, indicating complete lack of concern with the growing crises in urban education, even in areas not directly affected, may be judged from editorial comment in the November 17, 1970, edition of the Charlottesville *Daily Progress*:

We hope Henrico and Chesterfield will be able to protect themselves in this unfortunate situation and we are confident that they will. Richmond's action, in seeking to drag two other school systems into its own troubles, is far from commendable and deserves to meet with defeat.

Governor Holton's response to the pressure for state intervention in 1970 was a marked contrast to the behavior of the state leaders of the late 1950s. After receiving pledges of help from federal officials, he refused to intervene and urged a "calm, reasoned approach," and obedience to federal decrees. He entered his own children in the predominatly black schools in the area of the governor's mansion, an act which was praised by J. Sargeant Reynolds, then Democratic lieutenant governor, indicating that bipartisan support for rational handling of racial issues existed at the highest levels of state government.

Neither the short-range nor long-range effectiveness of this appeal to the reason of Virginia citizens can yet be evaluated. The results of the November, 1970, elections for the U.S. Congress are paradoxical. Senator Harry Byrd, Jr., running as an independent with former Governor Godwin as his campaign manager, polled 54 percent of the vote. The election results were a reversal of the tide that had been running against the Byrd organization since 1964, and perhaps can be explained by the Virginia penchant for clinging to the familiar in times of stress and uncertainty. Byrd's heavy suburban support suggests that voter turnout and segregationist sentiment have both increased in these locales. Senator Spong, a seasoned observer of Virginia education, has expressed concern over the upsets arising from the numerical comparisons of the racial composition of urban schools, feeling they have brought a change in public mood which may hurt future prospects for school support. On the other side of the ledger, it should be noted that strong statewide majorities approved new state constitutional provisions which departed from the Byrd fiscal philosophy and strengthened the authority of the state board of education to require a locality to provide its share of funding.

One must conclude that the state's eventual emergence from its political past is a process still in the making, and that the future of its educational politics remains speculative. However, certain clear conclusions which affect federal grant allocations may be drawn. The first is that all aspects of state-federal relations are likely to awaken tender political sensibilities. The second is that many Virginians have come alive to the need to improve their schools and are willing to accept—even welcome—federal aid to this end, in spite of the sometimes galling constraints it imposes.

The Governor

The foregoing discussion of educational policy developments illustrates that the governor is at the center of Virginia's political life. Authorities identify the Virginia governor as one of the strongest state executives in the country, both with regard to his formal powers and the manner in which many of the incumbents have performed since the 1920s, when Harry S. Byrd, Sr., served as governor. In Virginia, the governor has control of budget development and execution; direction of the state's personnel system; and extensive powers to appoint departmental officials, regulatory boards, and their staffs. Only three statewide officials are elected, and there is no effective opposition to gubernatorial authority from within the executive branch. Virginia's governors have predominated as legislative leaders, utilizing their powers to call special sessions and their annual budget and "state of the state" messages to structure the agenda of the General Assembly with regard to major statewide issues. The possibility of unwelcome legislative action is further reduced by the governor's formal powers of item veto and executive amendment. Few policy recommendations of any import, including state educational policy, have been initiated or adopted except as part of the governor's program. When the governors were penurious in their budget requests, state provision of resources for education remained minimal. When Governor Godwin advocated expanded programs, the General Assembly gave him all he requested.

Although the 1969 election and Republican victory augured changes to come, the pace has been moderate as befits the Virginia pattern of action. Governor Holton moved deliberately in his task of making more than four hundred appointments, including the reappointment of the state superintendent of public instruction, Dr. Woodrow W. Wilkerson. The most obvious explanation for the circumspect tactics, adopted by a man whose personal style is far from stolid, is the need to develop a distinctive, but viable, legislative program and biennial budget for 1972-74. With heavy Democratic majorities in both houses, this can be accomplished only by adhering to the patterns of continuity and consensus-building acceptable to Virginians. How well Governor Holton will succeed is open to question, since the legislature, normally so dependent on executive initiatives, began in the 1970 session to organize and strengthen its resources for independent action.

The Legislature

Until the advent of Governor Holton, a Republican, the state legislature was exceptionally compliant with regard to the leadership of the governor and its own presiding officials. Regular biennial sessions are limited to sixty days, and neither individual legislators nor committees are provided the salary, quarters, or staff support that would encourage them to linger in Richmond. Virginia's documentation of legislative activity is relatively parsimonious, reflecting to some degree the tendency of its political officials to operate through personal acquaintance and modes of communication. The development of a legislative agenda on matters of statewide concern such as education has frequently depended on the utilization of interim ad hoc study commissions whose membership may include the governor's appointees, members of the legislature, representatives of state and local government, and knowledgeable laymen. They employ consultants, conduct hearings, and issue reports similar to those prepared in some other states by legislative committees and their staffs.

The distinctive nature of Virginia's local government also affects the nature of legislative activity. It provides for a large measure of decentralization of detailed decision making in what is, at the same time, a highly centralized statewide system, susceptible to control of major policy by a relatively small elite group of officials.

The Influence of Interest Groups

Educational policymaking in Virginia has been devoid of the sharp cleavages between public or professional interest groups and of the highly combative campaigns which have been waged in other states to influence the state legislature and bureaucracy. For example, the professional groups coalesced on urging Governor Holton to reappoint Superintendent Wilkerson. The NEA affiliate, the Virginia Education Association, dominates the professional scene; its representations to the General Assembly are almost exclusively directed to welfare measures. The Virginia School Boards Association has grown and gained new strength in the past decade. Its agenda of suggestions for state legislative action includes a number of comprehensive and forward-looking, though by no means revolutionary, policy and program proposals. The school division superintendents meet annually with the state superintendent, and periodically in regional groups, but these sessions are devoted to mutual professional concerns.

In the spring and fall of 1970, a group of the larger Virginia cities and counties, led by the city manager of Richmond, organized themselves as the "Urban 12"; they presented to Governor Holton and interim General Assembly committees their pleas for financial relief at the 1971 session of the legislature. Their key requests are for authority to levy an additional 1 percent local sales tax and for more state welfare aid in 1971. They constitute a notable effort to bring the state's usually fragmented urban power to bear on common goals, including those for education.[39]

Organized interest groups have thus far been little concerned about the state role in the allocation or administration of federal grant funds. When queried as to whether the VEA had conducted any research studies of federal school aid in Virginia or developed any policy positions on the matter, the organization's executive secretary stated that all available information could be obtained from the department—indicating acceptance of the department's posture of cautious neutrality. The prospect of new funds for aiding desegregation efforts under the 1970 Emergency School Assistance Program raised publically for the first time the question of why Virginia had never applied for funds under Title IV of the 1964 Civil Rights Act. On August 26, 1970, the *Richmond Times-Dispatch* stated that Governor Holton was expected to do soon what his Democratic predecessors declined to do—prod the state department into setting up such a unit. In December, this move was actually made. The State Board of Education requested $56,000 in federal funds to establish a one-year project to help local school divisions with their desegregation problems.[40]

Thus, unofficial interests have had little independent impact on educational decision making. The monolithic system of educational governance which combines (1) a strong governor, (2) an understaffed if not subservient legislature, (3) tight fiscal controls, (4) a scrupulously honest and unaggressive state educational agency, and (5) fiscally dependent local school boards militates against such influence.

Local Views of Federal Aid

In the fall of 1968, Senator Spong (D.-Virginia) surveyed Virginia school superintendents, school board members, and other local educators to obtain their evaluations and suggestions for improvement of the various federal aid programs, as well as their opinion of the school divisions' greatest needs. One hundred and thirty school superintendents and 270 other respondents returned the mail questionnaires. The superintendents' major criticism was directed at the late, inconsistent funding of the programs; some also felt that the programs were too rigid or categorical, subject to too much federal control and/or required too much paper work. ESEA II, which allows great state flexibility and loose federal supervision, was the favorite program. NDEA III, which also allows great state flexibility, was second. There was almost universal agreement, even by the northern Virginia counties, with the decision to turn funding of ESEA III programs over to the state.

State department personnel almost uniformly comment that constructive changes have occurred in the attitudes and operations of the local school divisions since 1965. Even some of the most obdurate resisters of federal aid now believe that, since the money came out of the state in the form of federal taxes, they would be derelict not to recoup what rightfully belonged to their localities. The administrative experience gained by local federal aid coordinators has been invaluable, giving them new skills which they bring to superintendencies to which several have recently been promoted.

Local coordinators' criticisms of state department operations are generally low-key, such as the differing requirements for federal and state fiscal reports or the lack of systematic coding of the instructional memoranda from Richmond.

Growing awareness of their common problems and interests has led the coordinators to form a loosely organized group which meets in conjunction with the annual meeting of the Virginia Education Association. Such an organization runs counter to the general departmental attitude that federal aid adminstration is an inseparable part of the local school administration.

The Virginia State Department of Education

Background

In Virginia, the children of privileged parents were traditionally sent to private schools, and the state's leadership was slow in making provisions for free public education. Long wedded to localism in governmental affairs and later bankrupted by the devastation of the Civil War, the state did not establish an educational agency until 1869. The early superintendents of public instruction struggled hard for survival, and their successors were expected to operate unaggressively on the most abstemious of budgets. The Virginia State Department of Education of the 1960s reflects in many ways its historical ethos, as well as the more recent influences and events recounted in previous sections. For example, in the 1960s the state's political leaders became the spokesmen for the state's opposition to federal policies, and the local communities were responsible for compliance with the federal civil rights legislation. Thus the state's educational bureaucracy was able to deal at arm's length with their federal counterparts in a climate of relative neutrality.

The political context which shapes the department's operation tends to nourish and reward the type of professional conservatism which has also characterized many other state educational agencies.[41] Like the Virginia legislature and the closely-articulated machinery of the Byrd political organization, the state department of education has been characterized by low visibility, a high degree of continuity in office, and a reputation for integrity and economy in the conduct of operations. As is generally true in state government, the office of the governor does not closely supervise departmental operations. However, in Virginia, financial operations are highly centralized and rigorously audited.

Organization

The state board of education consists of seven members, appointed by the governor, subject to confirmation by the General Assembly, for overlapping four-year terms. It is also designated as the state board of vocational education. The superintendent is similarly appointed and confirmed, but his term is coincident with the governor making the appointment. Promotion to all the policy-making positions in the department has almost universally been from within; the present superintendent, Dr. Wilkerson, was formerly director of secondary education. Dr. Wilkerson manages the department with the assistance of a deputy superintendent, two assistant superintendents, two special program assistants, a director of public information, and the six directors of the "operating" divisions: Teacher Education, Special Services, Educational Research and Statistics, Secondary Education, Vocational Education, and Elementary and Special Education.

The departmental staff was reorganized and enlarged in response to the educational initiatives of the Godwin years and the advent of greatly increased federal funding. In FY 65 its personnel strength was reported as 273; FY 66, 349; FY 67, 381; FY 68, 385; FY 69, 347.[42] It is apparent that federal funding accounts for the lion's share of the department's staff expansion after 1965. Expenditures for its own operations in 1968-69 totaled approximately $5 million, 80 percent of which was from state sources and 20 percent from federal sources. This represents less than 2 percent of all the funds for which the department is responsible.[43]

Administration of State and Federal Aid

The department controls the disbursement of all state and federal funds except those granted under PL 815 and PL 874, which are distributed directly to the treasurers of the local school divisions.[44] Since 1965, funding from all sources has greatly increased; at the same time, the *relative* contributions from state and local sources shrank as the volume of federal aid rose after 1965.[45]

While state funds increased from $151,551,000 in 1964-65 to $264,226,000 in 1968-69,[46] they dropped from 34.5 to 33.1 percent of the total. Similarly, local funds increased from $256,335,000 in 1964-65 to $446,373,000 in 1968-69, but the percentage of the total for the same time dropped from 58.3 to 55.8 percent. During the same period, federal funds increased from $31,636,000 and 7.2 percent of the total (in 1964-65) to $88,570,000 and 11.1 percent of the total in 1968-69. However, the percentage of contribution of federal aid had exceeded national averages even before the passage of ESEA, because of the large number of Virginia school divisions receiving impact aid under PL 874. The virtual doubling of total expenditures for education during this recent period of "catching up" exceeded the national average rate of increase and has greatly improved Virginia's comparative position among the states.[47]

The department has a relatively autonomous form of program operation, circumscribed by unusually comprehensive statewide administrative regulations. Virginia is one of only two states which handles its fiscal transactions on a reimbursible basis. Thus, local school divisions advance from their own resources the amounts required for their current operating expenditures, and their requests for reimbursement from state or federal sources of funding are subject to pre-audit in the state department of education, prior to authorization of payment by the state comptroller and the state treasurer. In view of this pre-audit sanction, the value which the state has long placed on frugality and strict accountability in fiscal transactions, and the large share of the state budget allocated to education, it is not surprising that the position of assistant superintendent of administration and finance is one of great power and prestige. Until his retirement in 1971, the incumbent, J.C. Blount, Jr., was informally known as "Mr. School Finance." He was held in respect, even awe, by all who were subject to the thoroughness and "Blountness" of departmental fiscal procedures. He did not hesitate to impose requirements tighter than those of the federal government. For example, the Tydings amendment to the long-delayed Office of Education Appropriations Act for FY 70 permitted "carry-over" of funds to June 30, 1971. Mr. Blount established December 31, 1970 as the cut-off date for the Virginia school divisions.

A federal official who worked with the state education agencies on the early implementation of ESEA I recalls that the Virginia agency was notably less preoccupied than other states with the novel programing provisions of the Act. Instead, their initial questions were: "When will we get the money?" and "When will the auditors come?" Much as program development officers may deplore the central importance accorded to fiscal management in Virginia, the federal auditors are given little basis for faulting the state's performance.

Two other state agency officials play leading parts in administering federal funds: the special assistant for federal programs and the director of the Division of Vocational Education. The former supervises directly the administration of ESEA I and III; coordinates the overall planning of ESEA V; oversees the administrative aspects of ESEA II; and keeps records on the amount of funding that localities receive directly from PL 874 and PL 815 grants. The latter is in charge of all the vocational education, school food, and manpower training programs. Responsibility for the operations of other categorical federal programs is lodged within units of several other divisions.

While involvement in the federal programs is widely diffused throughout the agency, staff members tend to regard the programs as quite distinct from the continuing state functions. This attitude may be due not only to the practice of earmarking the positions supported by federal funds, but also to the manner in which program controls are administered. Preliminary to the departmental fiscal pre-audit discussed above, the various units in charge of state plan administration or program supervision for each of the federal grant programs review all local school division requests for reimbursement, to determine whether expenditures were made in accordance with prior authorizations and agreements. A separate, detailed record of transactions for the federally supported programs or projects is maintained in each unit.

The recognition and independence accorded to the divisional specializations tends to compartmentalize the agencies. It appears that program coordination and planning depend largely on the activities of the assistant superintendents for instruction and for administration and finance in their respective areas, together with "cabinet" meetings and other contacts among the top divisional personnel. There is no central planning staff and limited evidence of cross-divisional collaboration at lower levels, except of a short-range operational nature. The special assistant for school evaluation and planning does not have the statewide planning responsibilities which his title might suggest. The function of this position is to assist local school divisions in strengthening their programs, utilizing the assistance of teams of state department personnel.

The additional funds earmarked for planning activities, which became available to the state in FY 70 under Section 402 of ESEA, may enable the department to give more attention to the long-range, broad, and coordinated type of planning which has been minimal in the past. Federal officials, familiar with the caution, even reluctance, which Virginia's educational establishment initially showed in accepting the ESEA-funded programs, express the opinion that the state department "has come a long way in the widening of its horizons" since 1965.

Recognizing that a foundation for acceptance of change has now been laid, Governor Holton is promising strong support for greater and more innovative activity. He is said to have delayed the reappointment of Superintendent Wilkerson until he was certain that the superintendent could provide this type of innovative leadership. Dr. Wilkerson will be near retirement age when his present term expires; hence he is free of the inhibitions which might be expected to influence gubernatorial appointees. Thus, the departmental potential for moving away from "tried-and-true" forms of educational programing has been greater than at any time in the last decade.

**Federal Aid Administration: A
Title-by-Title Analysis**

ESEA-Title I

Title I of ESEA is one of the two federal school aid programs for which the department's federal programs office, headed by the special assistant to the superintendent, has complete responsibility. In 1965-66 the Title I staff initially consisted of its present director, an educational grants advisor who is still on the staff, an accountant, and three secretaries. Subsequently, five assistant supervisors and another accountant were added to the staff; four of the supervisors, one of whom also has special responsibility for the program for migrant children, serve in field liaison positions; one is in charge of evaluation and dissemination activities. All of the professional staff except the grants advisor have state educational certification. The latter pre-audits local applications for compliance purposes. There has been very little turnover of Title I staff, and, as of 1970, they constitute a very knowledgeable and experienced group.

In FY 1969, 131 LEAs participated in 228 projects, an increase over FY 1968, in which 24 LEAs participated in 196 projects. In both years all the approved projects were completed. Table 7-3 shows the extent of the Virginia Title I program in Fiscal 1969, as compared with 1968.

In the regular session, 51 percent of the students were white; 47.8 percent, black. In the summer session, the reverse was true: 46.9 percent of the students were white, 53.2 percent were black.

Since the school districts are coterminous with the boundaries of the local governmental jurisdictions, Virginia had a comparatively simple task of computing Title I entitlements at sub-county levels. All the city and county data required for the Title I formula, which is provided by the U.S. Office of Education, is directly applicable to the state's local school divisions, except in a few instances where cities had annexed adjoining county territory subsequent to the 1960 census. There are still some school districts, in addition to the few who have had all funding denied for non-compliance with the 1964 Civil Rights Act, who do not take full advantage of their Title I entitlements. This is due in part to feelings of "defeatism," i.e., that the amount of money does not justify the work involved.

Staff members stated that at first local school divisions experienced some difficulties in financing expenditures for Title I on a current basis. Now most cities and counties plan for these anticipated revenues as part of their annual budgets, just as they do the state-aid funds. However, the cash reserves of some cities have recently declined so that the reimbursement policy of the state for grants-in-aid programs is beginning to cause them some hardship.

Table 7-3

The Extent of the Title I Program in Virginia Fiscal Year 1969, as Compared with 1968

	1969	1968
Projects Approved	228	196
Projects Completed	228	196
Number LEA's Participating	131	124
During Regular Term Only	18	
During Summer Term Only	9	
During Both Regular & Summer Term	104	
Number Pupils Participating In		
Regular Session	140,034	136,573
Summer Session	56,404	80,315
Unduplicated Count of Pupils Participating	148,310	163,878
Cost Per Pupil	$170.06	$170.18
Total Funds Spent in Virginia at LEA Level	$25,355,773	$27,888,969

Source: Fiscal Records as of November 1, 1969 for C Projects Low Income Groups.

The office schedules extensive, frequent visits to the local school divisions—a practice they feel is absolutely essential to keep track of the use of Title I funds. Required commitments such as targeting, use of equipment, and community participation are prone to receive varied interpretations and opportunistic modifications; they can only be monitored on the basis of direct observation.

Because the Title I requirements were so novel, changeable and complex, and, in some communities, rather unpopular with school clientele, many local school officials had to learn to avoid non-conforming actions. Such federal policies as those relating to use of Title I funds for construction, or to the funding of early childhood projects did not prove especially difficult to implement. On the other hand, the sophisticated Title I requirements for project evaluation have taxed the present competency of Virginia educators. The attention paid to student achievement data is a novelty in a state where publicizing such information has not been an accepted policy.

Many divisions tend to operate their approved projects year after year until they become a fixture of the school program. They do not make sufficient effort to extend successful programs on a system-wide basis, using local resources, or to try out different types of projects. Great difficulties are involved in withdrawing Title I services from target areas or groups once they have been initiated. The targeting requirements are apparently more easily met in the summer programs.

Department officials state that they regard Title I as a *local* program. They say, "The school divisions take full responsibility for their actions when they sign the required assurances. We are a service and stand ready to help the divisions willing to be helped." A great deal of informal communication and negotiation goes on between local officials and the staff of the Richmond office in connection with the development and modification of project proposals; thus, a formal, outright rejection of an application is seldom required.

While the Title I staff does maintain the personalized relationships with local school officials so characteristic of the Virginia style of administration, the posture of a purely voluntary collaboration is not quite accurate for at least two reasons: (1) Title I federal funds also become state appropriations to a special fund and are subject to state fiscal controls, including disbursements of funds already "earmarked" for the localities on a reimbursible basis and under rigorous pre- and post-audit practices; (2) the state must satisfy its own assurances as to "affirmative findings" that the local Title I projects meet federal criteria. The statute also mandates important statewide reporting, evaluation, and dissemination responsibilities.

In fact, the state's relations with the local school divisions evidence differentiated modes of operation including reliance on established procedures, friendly persuasion, and potential use of fiscal exceptions for non-conforming expenditures. The larger, better-staffed school divisions apparently do carry out their responsibilities with a considerable degree of independence; the smaller divisions, lacking their own personnel resources, lean heavily on the Title I staff for assistance with virtually every facet of local programing—delineation of target populations, design and evaluation of projects, preparation of applications, selection and training of personnel, initiation of the project advisory groups. The state has not considered it necessary to issue its own Title I guidelines; it has apparently found that the local officials who seek assistance want and need verbal explanations and interpretations of Title I requirements.

How are the approach and effectiveness of the Title I staff evaluated by others? One federal official commented that the reception accorded to Washington "people and paper" is quite reserved, but that the Virginia staff makes a conscientious and intelligent effort to obtain local school division compliance with national criteria. Only two incidents of public questioning of the program were reported; the first came from parochial school interests in the Tidewater area, who enlisted the help of their state senator to enlarge the participation of such students in Title I projects. The second was an appeal by mothers on welfare to gain clothing allowances for their children from Title I funds. The latter was apparently part of a widespread and successful lobbying effort which led to changes in the national guidelines.

A recent development exemplifies a policy of greater initiative in the deployment of Title I funds on the part of the state department of education. During 1970-71, the department stimulated and monitored an experimental program in performance contracting which involved 2,250 students in seven school divisions.

Virginia state officials do not wait for the required HEW audit of local projects under Title I. Instead, they have gone ahead with state audits and, in a few scattered instances, required local divisions to repay funds improperly expended. While the Title I grants, with all their red tape, are not received with open-armed southern hospitality, apparently Virginia has avoided public controversy and zealously preserved its traditional attention to correct procedure.

Vocational Education

Associated with Virginia's post-war industrial development has been a rapid expansion during the past decade of state programs in vocational and technical education. A legislative commission appointed in 1962 made an extensive review of the state's needs and drew up a program of broad recommendations for program improvements both in the public schools and at the post-secondary level. In 1964, the General Assembly made a biennial appropriation of $3,000,000 for vocational education, with emphasis on experimental programs for youth with special needs; the upgrading of technical institutes and area vocational schools; vocational guidance institutes; vocational training centers for high school youth and adults; and the establishment of a program of technical education to be administered by a new Board of Technical Education. These developments coincided with increased federal funding made available under the Vocational Education Act of 1963. In 1963, Virginia also inaugurated the Manpower Training Program and established an additional service in the Division of Vocational Education to coordinate and plan the construction of local vocational centers. The construction of facilities has progressed rapidly throughout the state; a target date of 1975 has been set for attaining the planned levels of adequacy in both the secondary school divisions and community college systems.[48]

Vocational education programs in Virginia are under the direction of the Division of Vocational Education, an integral sub-division of the Virginia Department of Education. The division is organized into major vocational program fields or "services": agricultural education, business education, distributive education, home economics, and trade and industrial education.

The size of the division's staff in the "state plan" services is approximately 60-65 professional and non-professional employees, which is just about the level of 1964-65; however, divisional management positions have been expanded more adequately for new planning and coordination duties. The division has made formal agreements covering its working relationships with a number of other state agencies. For example, current and projected manpower needs and job opportunities, particularly new and emerging needs and opportunities on the local, state, and national levels are identified in collaboration with the Virginia Employment Commission, the State Division of Industrial Development, the State Division of Planning, and the Statewide Cooperative Area Manpower Planning System (CAMPS).

The creation of a system of community colleges in Virginia required the development of effective new collaborative relationships between the department and the state board for community colleges. An agreement between the superintendent of instruction and the chancellor of the state board for community colleges was made in 1967 to earmark 25 percent of the federal appropriations for vocational education expenditure by the community colleges. During 1968-69 this amounted to $1.45 million, and $1.58 million was requested for 1970-71. In June, 1969, specific responsibilities relating to the requirements of the 1968 VEA amendments articulated: Under the agreement, the state board for community colleges would:

(1) Assure adherence to the provisions of the Vocational Education Amendments of 1968 and the State Plan for Vocational Education, including the use of 10% of these funds under part B of the Act for programs of activities for the handicapped, and use of 15% of these funds for the disadvantaged.

(2) Cooperate with the state department of education in providing for supervision of the vocational-technical education programs within the community colleges. The state department of education has the responsibility for seeing that the state department of community colleges provides effective supervision of the programs and activities under the State Plan.

(3) Cooperate with the state department of education in the determination of the qualifications of vocational-technical education faculty, and the joint approval of such faculty participating in the State Plan.

(4) Advise the state board of education with respect to the proportion of the designated funds to be alloted for each category such as instruction, equipment and construction in the vocational-technical programs in the community colleges.

(5) Submit application for appropriate vocational and technical education programs, services, and facilities to the state board of education through the state director of vocational education.

(6) Submit claims to the state board of education through the state director of vocational education for reimbursement and disbursement of federal funds for community college vocational and technical education in compliance with the requirements as established by the laws of the Commonwealth; the Vocational Education Amendments of 1968; and the provisions of the Virginia State Plan for Vocational Education.

(7) Provide for an exchange of curriculum materials between teachers of occupational courses in the community colleges and teachers of trade preparatory and occupational courses, in the secondary schools in order to promote more effective articulation. This procedure of exchange is coordinated through the articulation committee made up of three members of the staff of the state department of community colleges and three members of the staff of the state department of education.

The long-established Virginia formula for distributing federal-state vocational educational grants followed the model for basic state aid. That is, 60 percent of the salaries of eligible teaching and supervisory positions in the regular day schools of all districts were reimbursed, with a somewhat different schedule of percentage reimbursement applied in the case of teachers of adult classes. In 1968-69 these two types of salary payments accounted for nearly $9 million of a total budget of vocational education grants amounting to $16.9 million. Another $1.9 million was distributed to localities for equipment, $1.6 million for construction, and $2 million in Appalachia Commission funds on a local project or geographical area basis. When the state plan was revised in 1969 to incorporate the variable funding requirement established by the 1968 VEA amendments, only a slight adaptation of this basic formula was made. It was determined that amounts of federal funds would be allotted to local school divisions on the basis of relative wealth per pupil, per capita income, the dropout percentage, the percentage of unemployment, the manpower needs, and the vocational education costs.

The school divisions are now ranked under each of these six factors and, based on their rank, in relation to other local educational agencies, they may be given a 1, 2, 3, 4, or 5 rating. The total of these ratings is calculated and a combined control factor value assigned. Those with the highest control factor value are the ones with the greatest needs and their applications will be given high priority. The total control factor for each school division is used to determine the percentage of Part B federal funds the school division will receive.

Table 7-4 shows the grouping made of the actual school divisional ratings, which ranged from a composite of 10 to a high of 28. It may be noted that the percentage variation in funding is 8 percent, with a difference in only one point in the control factor allowing for a 1 percent difference in the rate of reimbursement for districts falling in the 18-20 range.

The same 8 percent range is applied with regard to all the allowable categories of expenditure under Part B of the federal act, including salaries of local instructors and supervisors. The effect of the formula is to give federal

Table 7-4
Classification of Virginia School Divisions by Control Factors for Distribution of Federal Funds for Vocational Education, by Location in SMSA and Non-SMSA Areas (Cumulative Percentages for Each of These Factors is Shown)

Total Control Factor	Number of School Divisions SMSA	Number of School Divisions Non-SMSA	Sub-Totals	Percentage of Reimbursement	Cumulative Percentages SMSA	Cumulative Percentages Non-SMSA
28	0	1				
29	0	0				
26	0	3				
25	1	3				
24	0	5				
			13	Base + 8%	4%	12%
23	0	7				
22	1	6				
			14	Base + 7%	8%	25%
21	1	7				
20	1	10				
			19	Base + 6%	16%	38%
19	1	14	15	Base + 5%	20%	50%
18	3	11	14	Base + 4%	32%	64%
17	4	8				
16	1	3				
			16	Base + 3%	52%	75%
15	2	3				
14	2	13				
			17	Base + 2%	68%	90%
13	6	4	10	Base + 1%	92%	94%
12	1	4				
11	1	3				
10	0	1				
			10	Base	100%	100%
Total	25	103	128			

matching on this item a range of 22 percent to 30 percent, while the state will continue to allot a flat 30 percent to all classes of districts. Because salaries account for so substantial a part of the grant total, the degree of equalization is quite limited. Table 7-5 illustrates this effect.

The reimbursement procedures favor the non-SMSA districts. For example, only 20 percent of the SMSA divisions receive as much as the base reimbursement plus 5 percent, while 50 percent of the non-SMSA divisions are ranked at that level.

The allocation of federal funds under Part B of the Act to state colleges and universities providing post-secondary and adult education programs is based on labor market demands and need for the program. All the state colleges and universities are ranked on a 1-5 scale on both these factors, the highest total score indicating the greatest need for funds.

For those vocational education activities under the Appalachian Regional Development Act, the percentage of federal funds available under Part B to be used as reimbursement on construction projects, including initial equipment, is determined for each project under the state priority needs for aid and the requirements of the Appalachian Act. Exact percentages are established for each project and are included in the approval of the project by the Appalachian Commission and the U.S. Department of Health, Education, and Welfare.

Community college enrollments are growing even more rapidly than predicted and the staff of the board of community colleges is caught up in the challenge of its new enterprises; thus it is not surprising that some tensions parallel the formal agreements with the long-established Virginia Department of Education, whose operations are characterized more by caution than by fervor. The staff of the community college board look at the larger share of federal vocational education grants which several other states allocate to post-secondary and adult vocational education and think they can make a good case for enlarging its present 25 percent allocation. Some have urged stronger collaboration in program planning, in order to bring benefits to the state from various other federally-aided activities which the department may not have fully exploited, as well as to avoid duplication in facilities and programs. The departmental vocational education staff, on the other hand, consider that advance planning has minimized the possibility of duplication and that there are excellent prospects for local school vocational education programs to complement, rather than replicate, those of the community colleges. The staff are also aware that Governor Holton and the General Assembly gave generous support to the community college program for the 1970-71 biennium. These diverse viewpoints do not present any serious barriers to effective future collaboration, but they do show that negotiations for federal support of vocational education are becoming more competitive.

During the past two years, the development of the new state plan required by the Vocational Education Act Amendments of 1968 has been perhaps the

Table 7-5

Identification of Value of Total Control Factors for School Divisions for Distribution of Federal Funds Under Part B of the Act

Total Control Factor	Percentage of Reimbursement	Number of School Divisions	Construction	Equipment	Salaries & Activities for Programs for Handicapped or Disadvantaged	Vocational Planning Projects & Related Activities	Salaries Local Instructors & Supervisors	
							Federal	State
24-28	Base + 8%	13	50%	75%	100%	100%	30%	30%
22-23	Base + 7%	14	49%	74%	99%	99%	29%	30%
20-21	Base + 6%	19	48%	73%	98%	98%	28%	30%
19	Base + 5%	15	47%	72%	97%	97%	27%	30%
18	Base + 4%	14	46%	71%	96%	96%	26%	30%
16-17	Base + 3%	16	45%	70%	95%	95%	25%	30%
14-15	Base + 2%	17	44%	69%	94%	94%	24%	30%
13	Base + 1%	10	43%	68%	93%	93%	23%	30%
10-12	Base Percentage	10	42%	67%	92%	92%	22%	30%

most demanding exercise in coordinated forward planning ever carried out by the Virginia State Department of Education. The division director responsible for this task, Mr. Sandvig, regards it as a highly significant step toward strengthening the state's programs in vocational education. He also expresses concern about the difficulties associated with attempting to modify the attitudes and practices of school officials and educators at all levels; he states that it will take time and much effort to bring about the desired shift from their previous, almost exclusive preoccupation with specialized short-range operational activities.

NDEA-Title III

The original state plan for NDEA III was approved in 1959; during the 1964-65 school year a revision was prepared in response to new federal regulations requiring expanded local supervision. In March, 1965, Virginia created the new position of supervisor, and Henry B. Brockwell, a professional educator with relevant previous experience, was appointed to organize, administer, and coordinate the state-level activities. Several field supervisors in the divisions of elementary and secondary education assisted in the development of the revised state plan, the guide for making applications, and other facets of the program. They were originally supported by NDEA III funds, but in 1967-68, payment for the services of these supervisors was transferred to ESEA V programs. The additional professional personnel are mostly subject matter specialists formerly affiliated with the local school divisions; the oversight of the NDEA III program is, of course, only a part of their broader field supervision functions. The NDEA III instructional materials and forms which the state provides for local personnel are very specific, complete, and familiar; thus much of the field work is concerned with advice as to relative equipment needs, most effective timing of application, and monitoring of the use of the equipment provided. The state government has not made any special funds available for NDEA matching, except for an appropriation of $250,000 for the 1964-66 biennium to assist the localities in strengthening and improving instruction in science, mathematics, and modern foreign languages.[49]

The local popularity of the program, confirmed in the Spong Survey, might have several explanations: its visible, concrete payoff in the form of new equipment, the funding formula, the assistance rendered by the state NDEA coordinator and the supervisory staff members, the personal contacts made possible by the small number of school divisions, or even the familiarity stemming from the program's eleven-year history. Inaugurated at a time when the state finally began to upgrade school quality, this federal subvention was not accompanied by unfamiliar, unwelcomed intrusions into local educational programing. In any case, its administration is less characterized by anti-fed rhetoric and appears to be less isolated from departmental functions than other federally funded activities.

Mr. Brockwell describes the operation as "a real partnership between the state and the localities." While this perception of intergovernmental collaboration certainly plays down the federal contribution of practically all the matching funds, it indicates that considerable affinity has developed between those who allocate the funds and the benefiting localities. The genuine friendliness and mutual confidence that permit them to arrive at gentlemen's agreements to ease procedural and other hang-ups are, of course, buttressed by the state's policy of reimbursible funding. The localities can be quite certain that they will have to pay the entire cost of any non-conforming types of equipment from local funds.

The distributional decisions made at the state level relate not only to assuring conformity with federal and state requirements for project and equipment specifications, but also to attaining desirable and equitable spread of available funds (1) among the various critical subject-matter areas eligible for funding, (2) between the elementary and secondary levels of education, and (3) among the competing school divisions. The informal processes of advance consultation ensure that a highly "improper" or indefensible application is not very likely to reach the stage of formal submission. The use of matching funds for minor remodeling and for projects in the subject matter of economics is not included in Virginia's state plan. Otherwise, the state distribution of approved projects among the subject matter areas adheres closely to the national pattern, with the exception of somewhat higher than average allocations to English and lower ones to mathematics and reading.[50] The percentage of funds approved for all elementary school projects varies from year to year, but generally runs from 15 percent to 30 percent lower than the allotments for the secondary school projects.

The Virginia state plan permits a variable percentage for matching local funds, but the consistent rate paid has been 50 percent. Participation by the Virginia school divisions has been very widespread each year, with regard to both submission of applications and the approval of at least a minimal amount of funding for each division. To determine the relative size of the grants, a choice is made on the basis of several interwoven factors such as school division size, need, and subject matter priorities, that are difficult to state as general rules. The decisions are made by Mr. Brockwell and the state department supervisors who are well acquainted with the localities and have a reputation for fairness. There is doubtless some rivalry between the subject matter specialists, but the co-ordinator is also guided by the priority which the local superintendent may assign to his own requests.

While relative size of division enrollment is one overall consideration, the five or six large, wealthy divisions "that can get the equipment anyway from their own funds" are not permitted to pre-empt too large a share of the total amount available. A school division may have its funding application for an unusually large amount of equipment approved at the time a new building is being completed; but it will then have lower priority assigned to subsequent requests until the needs of some other divisions are met. No advance stockpiling of equipment or substitution for approved items is permitted.

While the needs of economically disadvantaged districts are considered, there does not seem to be any particular priority given to projects directed to the needs of disadvantaged children. Because full funding of projects for this clientele is available under Title I, the NDEA III officials are likely to recommend and local officials are likely to seek needed equipment from that alternative source. Long-range planning has been made difficult by uncertainties as to levels of funding and to timing of NDEA appropriations at the federal level; these uncertainties also affect short-range operational scheduling that would permit equipment to be ordered and received at the time it is most needed. Both state and local officials suffer from these shortcomings, and no other serious complaints, apart from chronic shortage of funds, appear openly to mar their "partnership."

ESEA-Title II

State responsibility for the implementation of Title II of ESEA is rather sharply divided along administrative and professional lines. The special assistant for federal programs has handled the allocation procedures, negotiations with federal officials, and state plan development, while the staff of the school libraries and textbook service of the division of special services provides technical librarian services to the local school divisions. Since this staff has similar responsibilities for state-aided library programs, the possibilities for efficient employment of the department's professional resources are excellent. Personnel time assigned to the ESEA program is reported as the equivalent of one professional and two non-professional staff members. Virginia has annually expended virtually its entire allotment of Title II funds, with average amounts per child varying from $.88 in 1969-70, the lowest year of national funding, to $2.20 in 1966-67.

Originally worked out by Mr. Wingo, the formula for allocating funds to local school divisions is as follows:

(a) Not more than 49 percent of the total state allotment shall be made on the basis of the average daily attendance for the previous year.
(b) Not less than 60 percent shall be made to school divisions by use of a formula based on the following factors:
    1. The number of books per child in ADA for the preceding school year as an index of *need for library resources.*
    2. The amount of money expended per child in ADA during the preceding school year for library materials and audio-visual aids as an index of *local effort.*

3. The locally taxable wealth per child in ADA as an index of *economic need*.

   Each of these three factors will be converted to standard index numbers with an average of 100 and a standard deviation of 10. Each of the three factors will be given equal weight. Since each factor must be treated inversely, standard index numbers for the reciprocals of each will be computed. The totals of these standard index numbers (composites) will be converted to standard index numbers with an average to be determined by the amount of funds available per child in ADA for the preceding year. The exact standard deviation to be applied in the computation, which will fall within the range between 15 cents and 35 cents, will be determined on the basis of the funds available.

(c) Not more than 10 percent shall be made for the establishment and maintenance of demonstration libraries in different parts of the state to provide examples of excellent library programs and services.

(d) Not more than 5 percent of the total amount of projects approved will be allocated for state administration.[51]

The effect of this formula is to allocate Title II funds in a manner which correlates very closely with the distribution of total state and local funding. Division size of enrollment is the basic determinant, with a limited degree of equalization for those with lower levels of taxable wealth and more limited library resources. The standard deviation actually applied in computing annual entitlements has been the lower figure, so that the range in amount per child between the larger, wealthier divisions and the smaller, poorer ones has been only about $.30 for two-thirds of the total number of school divisions.

During 1967-68, the Virginia state plan was changed to give the local school divisions wider opportunities for selection of materials and responsibility for ordering them; new guidelines were distributed by the state department of education. The only difficulties have been in timing, in receipt of funds, and in delivery delays of orders from suppliers. Otherwise, local school divisions apparently have nothing but praise for the Title II program, which the Spong Survey found to be the favorite of local school division superintendents, perhaps because they receive predictable amounts of funding and have more autonomy than in the other programs. While the definition of "need" in the state formula does not strongly reflect the wide disparity in school resources throughout the state, the practice does not appear to be especially controversial. It is likely that few state or local officials are fully acquainted with the details of the formula and see little reason to question an objective computational procedure which does not diverge from familiar practice.

The department has allocated 10 percent of the state's annual Title II entitlement to establish nine demonstration libraries, three each in elementary schools, junior high schools, and senior high schools. These demonstration libraries were located in schools which, in the judgment of the department, already had good libraries. The intent was to increase their quality by means of the additional Title II funding so that they could serve as truly outstanding examples which educators could conveniently visit for ideas and inspiration. The state officials feel that this objective has been successfully met, since hundreds of persons visit the various libraries annually, and many local school divisions have recently increased their own funding for school libraries.

ESEA-Title III

Responsibility for the conduct of Title III of ESEA in Virginia was assigned to the federal programs office during the 1965-66 academic year, but the first supervisor of program activities was not named until the following year. Subsequent to the state's assumption of greater program authority, the staff has been enlarged by two additional professional employees. The Title III staff now constitutes a separate organizational unit within the federal programs office. The Title III office is headed by Anne Tucker, previously an assistant supervisor who was promoted to the position of supervisor when the first incumbent resigned. Both women were professional educators, as are the two other staff members, both men. One has special responsibility for evaluation activities: the other, for dissemination.

As of June, 1967, twenty-six applications had been approved by the U.S. Office of Education, and projects were either in operation or at the point of implementation. In addition, nineteen planning grants of $25,000 or less were approved. The department pointed out in its *Annual Report* of that year that the projects were well distributed geographically and were representative of school population densities. Perhaps the most notable of the early projects was a laboratory center, established at Newport News, for children who experience difficulties in reading. In 1968, it was included in the national sample of forty successful Title III projects which was analyzed by Benson and Guthrie.[52]

During the 1967-68 school year, thirty-six additional applications were submitted, of which eighteen were approved for funding and implementation in the 1968-69 school year. At that time, fifty divisions with approximately 65 percent of the state ADA were participating in Title III programs. During 1968-69, the first year of state management, thirty-six projects were in operation and no new projects were funded. The next year, thirty projects were funded, of which sixteen were new. With rare exceptions, the school divisions which have received federal grants have been able to continue the projects with local school division funds when the grants were terminated.

During 1968 and 1969, the Title III staff issued state guidelines, modeled closely on the similar federal instructions, in two sections: *Proposal Procedures* and *Manual for Administration*. An advisory council was appointed and has met periodically since. Its role at the outset was apparently somewhat passive, perhaps because most of the projects already approved continued in operation. The state plan was submitted to the U.S. Office of Education in June, 1969 and received tentative approval, pending completion of the statewide educational needs assessment mandated by the ESEA amendments of 1968. This study, funded for $167,000 and conducted in close collaboration with the special assistant for federal programs, the Title III staff, and a department-wide committee of the division heads, was completed by the Bureau of Educational Research of the University of Virginia in February, 1971.

The Title III staff are heavily involved in developmental work with local school officials; they stress the design of varied, geographically dispersed, and creative projects for multi-year funding, projects which will have a good chance for eventual absorption into the school division's regular program. A self-report evaluation form, developed by the staff, is completed each year by project officials; and the state conducts a project visitation program, manned by university and departmental personnel. Summary reports of the visitation team evaluations are prepared and transmitted back to the school division.

The Title III staff are thoroughly committed to furthering the innovative thrust of this program, a situation which sometimes puts them at odds with personnel from the other divisions of the state department "whose recommendations on some projects would draw out the very creativity Title III is supposed to encourage." While working relationships remain viable, Title III obviously imposes unique purposes, legal mandates, and funding arrangements which represent a distinct and not universally applauded departure from customary state department practices.

Conclusion

The administration of federal aid to education in Virginia occurs within a changing political landscape—a landscape molded by forces uniquely Virginian and, at the same time, marked by regional and racial disparities. From within and without, winds of change are sweeping away the residue of traditionalism; gradually, more liberal, progressive attitudes and actions are replacing it. A larger, more diverse electorate, increasing urbanization and industrialization, and federal legislation and litigation have instigated the changes. A lengthy period of educational decay and a brief period of defiance to the U.S. Supreme Court have been succeeded by the current educational era—a period in which both state and local interest and expenditure in education have increased.

As in all other areas of government, changes in education take place in a manner and at a pace that is Virginian. At every stage, the governor's role is pivotal. Mills Godwin, the Democratic governor from 1965-1969 was instrumental in upgrading the caliber of education in Virginia, through increased legislative appropriation, a bond issue, and the ultimate strengthening of education in the revised State Constitution. Although he took issue with USOE's edicts for Virginia's compliance with Title VI of the 1964 Civil Rights Acts,

Governor Godwin realized that federal funds for education were too important a source of aid to be ignored or forfeited. Linwood Holton, his Republican successor, has continued and extended Governor Godwin's policy on federal aid. However, a new turbulance has arisen in the Virginia educational atmosphere as a result of recent court decisions requiring district consolidation and busing to further school desegregation.

According to a survey conducted by Senator William Spong (D-Virginia) of state and local superintendents and officials, ESEA II and NDEA III are the most popular federal programs. In both instances, the department has been relatively free to follow its own dictates as to formula and fund allocations. Where it has been possible, the state has also used its traditional formulas in vocational education. However, the new community college system, initiated during Governor Godwin's term, is a likely contender for an increasing share of vocational education aid in the future.

To date, no urban lobby has exerted any great pressure on federal aid allocation; however, the recent formation of the Urban 12 may produce changes in this situation.

The department personnel emphasize that their relations with local divisions are informal and congenial, characterized by suggestion and persuasion rather than by demands and interdictions; however, Virginia's policy of reimbursable funding vastly enhances the department's persuasiveness.

In short, the politics of federal aid to education in Virginia is characterized by orderly and consensual decision making. A strong and astute governor, a relatively compliant legislature, low profile interest group activity, and an unassertive educational bureaucracy interact to produce a politics of conciliatory tone, deliberate pace, and deep regard for continuity.

Notes

1. Jean Gottman, *Virginia in Our Century* (Charlottesville: University Press of Virginia, 1969), pp. 557-58.

2. Ibid., p. 563.

3. Gary Orfield, *The Reconstruction of Southern Education* (New York: Wiley-Interscience, division of John Wiley and Sons, 1969), p. 208.

4. Herbert Jacob and Kenneth N. Vines, *Politics in the American States* (Boston: Little, Brown and Company, 1965).

5. The category definitions are derived from the ELSEGIS I national sample of school districts. See *Statistics of Local Public School Systems*. OE-22027-68, p. 2.

6. J. Harvie Wilkerson, *Harry Byrd and the Changing Face of Virginia's Politics* (Charlottesville: University Press of Virginia, 1968), Chapter 2.

7. *The Washington Post*, July 21, 1965.

8. *Computation of State Aid to Localities in 1969-70*:

First, for each school division two amounts are added together to obtain the total cost of a "minimum program", which constitutes the measure of "need":

(a) the total cost of its "state-aid" teaching positions, using a ratio of 23 students in ADA in high school and 30 students in elementary school and the appropriate steps of the State Minimum Salary Scale for the incumbents of such positions;

(b) an allowance of $115 per student in ADA for other operating costs.

Secondly, from the total cost of its minimum program are subtracted two amounts: a "local share" or "effort" represented by 60 cents per $100 of the 1968 true values of real estate and public service corporations; and a "basic state share" amounting to 60% of the total cost of salaries as computed in the preceding paragraph.

Thirdly, if the combined local and basic state shares are less than the total cost of the schools division's minimum program, the state adds a supplementary share equal to the difference.

In addition to the above grants from the basic school aid funds, the state also makes categorical grants under a number of special funds such as those for transportation of pupils, guidance counselors, local supervision, special education, teachers' sick leave, summer schools, twelve month employment of principals, etc. The practice of reimbursing 60% of salary costs from the special funds is generally followed. The state pays 100% of the costs for the state retirement plan for teachers and for the contributions to the Federal Social Security program. In 1969-70 this amounted to about 15% of the total state-level expenditures and it is not reported in the category of "aid to localities."

9. Virginia State Department of Education, *Facing Up: Statistical Data on Virginia's Public Schools*, January, 1970. Table 8.

10. For a complete description of the Virginia plan see Thomas L. Johns, ed., *Public School Finance Programs*, Washington, D.C.: U.S. Office of Education, 1969), (OE-22002-69).

11. The state has no provision for aiding school divisions with regard to expenditures for construction except for the limited availability of loans from the State Literary Fund. According to the 1968-69 *Annual Report*, debt service and capital outlay accounted for 35 percent of the expenditures of the local school divisions (Table 42).

12. *A New Plan: Report of the Commission to Study the Formula for State Aid to Public Schools* (Richmond: Commonwealth of Virginia, Department of Purchases and Supply, 1970) pp. 9-10.

13. *Facing Up*, op. cit., Table 4.

14. Virginia Education Association, *Virginia's Educational Disparities*, Research Service, VEA R-111, February, 1970.

15. *A New Plan*, loc. cit.

16. For a discussion of the issue, see Advisory Commission on Intergovernmental Relations. *State Aid to Local Governments* (Washington: Superintendent of Documents, April, 1969) p. 43. The Virginia litigation was one of the precedents cited in *Serrano v. Priest*, the California case in which the Court ruled in favor of plaintiffs who sought relief on similar grounds.

17. Daniel J. Elazar, *American Federalism: A View from the States* (New York: Thomas Y. Crowell Company, 1966), pp. 92-93.

18. Ibid., pp. 17-18.

19. Ibid., p. 110.

20. Gottman, op. cit., p. 467.

21. Ibid., p. 566.

22. Wilkerson, op. cit., p. 207

23. U.S. Department of Commerce, Bureau of the Census, *Population Counts for States*. Preliminary Reports P C (P.)—48, July, 1970.

24. Wilkerson, op. cit., p. 102.

25. A.E. Dick Howard et al., *Virginia's Urban Corridor: A Preliminary Inquiry*. (Charlottesville: Center for the Study of Science, Technology, and Public Policy, University of Virginia, March, 1970).

26. Division of State Planning and Community Affairs, Commonwealth of Virginia, *1980 Population Projections for the State of Virginia*, Statistical Information Series No. 70-1, March, 1970.

27. Wilkerson, op. cit., p. 153.

28. Several detailed accounts of the massive resistance movement are available including: Gates Robbins, *The Making of Massive Resistance*, (Chapel Hill: University of North Carolina Press, 1964) and Benjamin Muse, *Virginia's Massive Resistance* (Bloomington, Ind.: University of Indiana Press, 1961). See also Wilkerson, op. cit., Chapter 5.

29. See Wilkerson, op. cit., Chapters 10-13 for a detailed account of Godwin's rise to power and the early months of his administration.

30. "Historical Development of Virginia's Public Education System, 1870-1970," *Public Education in Virginia*, Winter, 1970, pp. 34-38.

31. Civil Rights Commission *Public Schools, Southern States*, 1962, pp. 207-208.

32. A thorough study of the Virginia experience, on which this summary is based, was made by Orfield, op. cit., Chapter 5.

33. Ibid., p. 33.

34. Ibid., p. 229.

35. Details concerning political alignments and contests during the period from 1964 to 1967 are reported by Wilkerson, op. cit., Chapters 11 and 12. See also the analysis of recent Virginia election results by Professor Ralph Eisenberg

published in several issues of *The University of Virginia Newsletters*, especially those dated April 15, 1965; January 15, March 15, May 15, and June 15, 1967; February 15 and May 15, 1970.

36. Orfield, op. cit., p. 232.

37. Battle was hurt by his previous association with the Byrd organization and the failure of the liberal wing of the State Democratic party, led by Senator Henry Howell of Norfolk, to close ranks in the general elections. Howell had been strongly supported in his primary fight with Battle by labor and minority groups and especially by voters in the central cities. In 1971, Howell was elected Lt. Governor (as an independent) to fill out the term of the moderate, J. Sargeant Reynolds who died.

38. "Four Virginia Cities Writhe over Pupil Edicts," *Washington Post*, August 23, 1970.

39. *Washington Post*, November 30, 1970.

40. Ibid., December 12, 1970.

41. *Emerging State Responsibilities for Education* (Denver: Improving State Leadership in Education, 1970), Chapter 2.

42. Data reported by the U.S. Office of Education: in: *Reinforcing the Role of the States in Education*, OE-23050, Appendix B and Table 22; *Focus on the Future: Education in the States*, OE-23050-68, Table 18; *The State of the State Department of Education*, OE-23050-69, Table 16; and *The Federal-State Partnership for Education*, OE-23050-70, Chart 3.

43. Amounts estimated from data for this period in Commonwealth of Virginia, *Budget, 1970-71*, pp. 237 and 243, by subtracting total operating expenses for "Aid Benefitting Localities" (377 million) from grand total operating expenses for the Department ($382 million).

44. Under state law all other expenditures of federal grants are contingent upon legislative approval, by inclusion in this biennial appropriation act. They are designated as "special funds" and are subject to all state fiscal controls.

45. Table 45, pp. 234-235, *Annual Report*, op. cit., 1964-65.

46. Table 42, pp. 211-212, *Annual Report*, op. cit., 1968-69.

47. National Committee for Support of the Public Schools, Fact Sheet #11, March, 1969.

48. Historical Development of Virginia's Public School System, 1870-1970," op. cit., p. 33.

49. *Annual Reports*, op. cit., 1964-65, Table 41, and 1966-67, Table 39.

50. *The Federal-State Partnership for Education*, op. cit., Table III-5.

51. Virginia Title II State Plan, Section 3.31. The local school divisions are also responsible for determining and reporting to the State the ADA of the non-public schools in their districts.

52. Charles S. Benson and James W. Guthrie, *A Search for New Energy*: ESEA Title III, *An Essay on Federal Incentives and Local and State Educational Initiative*, (Washington, D.C.: George Washington University, 1968).

8

The Politics of Federal Aid to Education in New York

Frederick M. Wirt
with the assistance of
Anthony M. Cresswell
and Paul M. Irwin

In a nation that measures quality by quantity, New York has much going for it on both counts. New York's size, wealth, and intellectual reserves constitute enormous resources for the achievement of any public goal it pursues.[1]

As early as the 1780s, New Yorkers deemed quality education such a goal. New York appointed the first state superintendent of instruction (1812) and provided the highest salary for him (1966). Whether measured by per capita state aid to local schools or by its innovative capacity, New York has sought to maintain the pre-eminence of its schools.[2]

Education in New York is directed by the regents, their appointed commissioner and the New York State Department of Education. The department is second in size only to the California State Department of Education and has a staff greater than the U.S. Office of Education. Similarly, the commissioner has the opportunity to exercise far more extensive power than his federal counterpart. Commissioner James E. Allen, Jr., and his successor, Ewald B. Nyquist, have exercised that power in the establishment of priorities and coordination of planning for federal aid allocation.

However, diverse other forces—including department personnel, the legislature, and the colossus of New York City—also seek to design the patterns of federal aid allocation in New York and to affect the programs that result.

Research Assertions and Federal Aid in New York

Assertion No. 1. There will be less involvement and political influence by the governor and legislature on federal aid in comparison with state aid.

While this hypothesis was supported in New York, two important conditions should be noted. The state has far less control over the allocation of federal funds than of state aid, and more important, federal funds are a much smaller amount. If the funds from the two sources were similar in size, there would likely be equal involvement.

Within the confines of lesser amounts and greater restrictions, significant

325

involvement and influence by both the governor and the legislature on federal aid were found to occur. Because of the more public nature of the transactions, legislative involvement is easier to document. Especially with ESEA-Title I, the legislature is concerned with the distribution of federal funds, the particular projects, and project evaluation and effectiveness. It recently passed detailed legislation requiring the joint evaluation by school districts of Title I projects with the state urban education projects. The Decentralization Act also mandated that the allocation of Title I funds among New York City's community districts parallel the state's method of allocation of Title I within counties. The legislature's budget staff considers, informally of course, federal funds in conjunction with state aid to education in determining how much state aid is needed by the school districts.

While the governor is much more involved with higher education than with elementary and secondary education, he does concern himself with the latter. His interest there is probably less in federal than in state aid, but not as little as the small amount of federal funds would imply. Through his budget office, the governor exerts at least as much, if not more, control over education than the legislature does. Special concern is taken in the areas of educational finance and innovation. Our conclusion is that more federal funds and greater innovation through federal programs would increase the involvement of the governor.

Assertion No. 2. The influence and impact of the urban school lobby on the state allocation of federal aid will not be significant.

This assertion was also found true for New York. The general lack of impact seems to be caused mainly by the position of New York City in the state's political milieu, particularly the political hostility of the rest of the state toward it. Two other reasons exist for this lobby's inefficacy in the state politics of allocation. First, the cities already receive most of the largest federal aid program (Title I) without needing to engage the state level. Second, the political battlegrounds of this lobby lie elsewhere, within the cities.

Because the federal guidelines specify the distribution of Title I funds among counties and because the New York City school district is coterminous with five counties, the state has no discretion in the allocation of 70 percent of New York's Title I funds. This is the amount for which the New York City school district is eligible.

Political conflicts over Title I funds do occur, however. At the school board level, especially in New York City, urban interests disagree on the distribution among the city's schools and various programs.

The urban school lobby has had some impact on ESEA-Title II allocation decisions and is striving for more in vocational education where its influence is almost non-existent. The lack of impact does not necessarily reflect on the influence of school lobbies. Rather, it may reflect the impotence of *all* urban lobbies vis-à-vis other organized interests in the state. A new situation may be emerging, however. During the past few years, other urban districts throughout the state have joined forces with New York City in the "Big Six"; this united front undoubtedly will increase the impact of the urban lobby in all areas, including education.

Assertion No. 3. As federal aid increases and states have more discretion in allocation, pressures will increase on state government from organized interests.

Although a number of recent events indicate that pressures from organized interests have increased, it is not clear that the increase is the result of greater federal aid and state discretion in allocation.

Federal programs pre-dating ESEA have not expanded in recent years; indeed, they have become so routinized that no pressure short of total fund cut-off seems able significantly to change these programs. That leaves only ESEA, especially Title I, for consideration. The critical decision the state would make on Title I, if it could, would be how much of a share New York City would receive. Because this is decided in Washington, no pressure is needed on the state government. Some increase in pressure has come from the UFT in New York City, but it seems more reasonable to attribute this to the growing militancy of all unions in that city, not to increases in federal aid to education. It may well be that federal aid has increased the militancy of all unions, but the attempt to establish that is beyond the scope of this study.

As indicated in Assertion No. 2, the real political battles over Title I have taken place at the school board level, where unions and administrators have been fighting continually during the past five years. Some of these battles have extended into the state legislature, but usually after all hopes for change at the local level have expired. The Educational Conference Board took its first stand on federal aid in its annual statement of 1970. This should not be attributed to increased federal aid, but rather to an attempt by the State Teachers Association (an ECB member organization) to compete with the growing influence of the UFT (which is not represented on the ECB). Furthermore, tighter budgets at the local level have caused all members of the ECB to pay more attention to federal aid, no matter what the amount. Therefore, while the assertion is well supported, the causal implication seems tenuous.

Assertion No. 4. The state education agency will attempt to minimize political conflict and pressure by using existing state aid formulas for allocation of federal funds.

In New York, patterns emerge which challenge the assertion. Rather, urban schools get more under federal than state formulas. The existing state aid formula distributes 31 percent of its funds to the six largest cities, which have approximately 39 percent of the state's enrollment. However, this formula is not used in the allocation of any of the federal funds in this study. The state has no flexibility in its allocation of ESEA-I funds among counties, which means most of it goes to cities. It does reserve some of these funds for predominantly rural areas by using a 10 percent low-income criterion rather than a 100 percent AFDC standard; as one department official said, "Rural poor have their problems too, you know." ESEA II is distributed by a complicated formula wherein the six largest cities receive funds larger, not less than, their percentage of state aid.

No formula exists for ESEA III in New York, and the distribution is complicated by the allocation of one-third of the funds to regional centers. But overall, disproportionately more funds are allocated to the largest cities. On the other hand, vocational education has no formula, but the cities receive a much smaller percentage than they do from state aid. Neither is NDEA III distributed by formula, although the state's "enrichment" priority definitely favors above-average students. But the six largest cities in the state receive a larger percentage of these funds than they do of state aid, (39 percent as opposed to 31 percent). In short, where the state is allowed discretion, federal aid is distributed in this state at least with lesser bias against the large cities than in state aid. Clearly, existing state formulas have not operated when these federal monies were allocated.

Assertion No. 5. Federal aid, except in a manner restricted by federal guidelines or requirements, will flow in the same manner as state aid.

This assertion was also found to be false for reasons presented in the discussion of Assertion No. 4. That is, within the discretion allowed by federal guidelines, federal aid is distributed with a bias toward urbanized areas, possibly even greater than the state aid bias toward non-urban areas. Two qualifications should be made, however, which point to parallel federal-state operations. First, a number of federal guidelines and regulations originated in, or were copied from New York, thereby making the state in "compliance" before it was necessary. Second, while the distribution of state aid shows bias against the largest cities, "traditional" patterns of educational administration in New York also include large doses of innovation which help the cities.

Assertion No. 6. SEA personnel are socialized so that they view their proper role as providing technical assistance to LEAs, not enforcing or policing federal requirements or setting program priorities.

This assertion seems to be true in New York, at least among the personnel who communicate directly with the school districts about federal program affairs. The vocational education personnel are the only partial exception to this; they exert strong leadership over the school districts, but only in the establishment of state priorities, not in the enforcement of federal requirements. The assertion is not true for personnel in the more academically inclined areas of the department, e.g., the research and evaluation section.

Political Factors Shaping Fiscal and Administrative Patterns

Several major allocational institutions in New York have traditionally operated to produce a system of state educational politics. Some of these are formal organs of educational administration; others are the constitutional branches of government; still others are the informal "political" combinations of parties and interest groups which come together in changing patterns over time. Underlying the components of the system and determining their mesh are distinctive sets of attitudes and values about how the state and schools should interact.

The Formal Educational Apparatus

In 1784, barely six months after the British had evacuated New York City, the New York legislature sowed the seeds of the state's public education system. The legislators created the Regents of the State of New York to govern King's College (later Columbia). A decade later the legislature provided funds for common schools, to be also supported financially by local districts. However, in the years after 1795, the legislature gave only fitful financial support to this program. Finally in 1812, the basic outline of the present public education system was laid out in the Common School Act. Towns were divided into school districts, to be controlled locally by a board of trustees—state agents with authority over tax levies and school matters. The state contributed to teachers' salaries while local contributions covered other costs. A Department of Public Instruction under a state superintendent was established to coordinate state and local efforts.

Applied to elementary education at first, this pattern was extended in 1853 to include secondary education, thereby precipitating a half century of conflict. The regents remained to supervise higher education and private academies; the superintendent oversaw public elementary education; and both came into conflict over control of high schools. Not until 1904 did the legislature resolve the issue by designating the regents the governing board for all education in the state, public and private. The superintendent (now the commissioner) became its executive officer as well as administrator of the department of education.

The regents—no less than nine (now fifteen)—are elected by the legislature for fifteen year terms, are unsalaried, and meet monthly. The sweep of their authority is enormous. As observers have summarized it:

It has sweeping power over public schools and lesser but still highly influential power over private schools through its right to charter and register (which implies its right to visit and to require periodic reports from the institutions). The board continues . . . to license and regulate specified professions, to maintain and operate the State Library, and to charter and have general governance of public and private libraries in the state.[3]

The commissioner of education and the department of education (NYSDE) implement regental standards. The regents' appointee, the commissioner, has large formal authority in shaping the direction and details of education. His authority extends to creating and enforcing regulations which have the effect of law, such as devising standards for and certifying professional school personnel and setting student examinations. He is responsible for educational planning and its implementation; for allocation of state funds (not on his own, as we shall note); for providing innumerable supplementary services for local schools; and for arbitrating school disputes. While the position contains a latent capacity for leadership—with the public, educators, legislators, and governor—the commissioner must develop it.

The New York State Department of Education's supervision of education is part of an administrative complex. Its oversight and leadership contributed to the school consolidation movement which swept New York after the turn of the century. The dramatic results are seen in the declining number of school districts in New York—from 10,651 in 1904 to 997 in 1965—and about 500 when the master plan is realized. The system of supervisory districts, created by statute in 1912, facilitates further the department's oversight. Counties are formed into supervisory districts, headed by superintendents who are in law and fact intermediate officers for the NYSDE's supervision of school districts. With local consolidation, these supervisory districts also declined, from 207 in 1912 to 47 in 1972.[4] On that date, Boards of Cooperative Educational Services (BOCES) were created as rural regional service centers under district superintendents.

The NYSDE allegedly has a high degree of independence from the governor. Unlike departments in other states, the governor has nothing to do with the appointment of its authorizing body—the regents—or its top administrator—the commissioner. The legislature, however, exercises considerable authority over operations of the educational apparatus.

Both the analysts outside and participants inside agree that the New York educational apparatus has traditionally had special influences, if not independence, unlike that found in other states. Stephen Bailey et al. could conclude in 1962:

It may be fairly stated that for most of the period since 1800 the regents have been, in many respects, a fourth branch of government—effectively independent in many of their roles of governor, legislature, and even court . . . Nothing is surer to raise the hackles of professional schoolmen and state educational officials than to suggest any diminution of this independence. . .

[Indeed it] enjoys independent . . . power of such scope as to bring into question the consonance with American constitutional principles of separation of powers and checks and balances.[5]

Recent events, however, suggest that a new configuration of power may exist.

The Governor and the Legislature

At the basic level, New York's constitution is the fundament for all schooling in that state. The governor is formally divorced from much broad policymaking, except in financing—not a minor consideration, as we shall see.

In matters affecting federal aid, the governor primarily has limited his office to urging higher levels of such assistance for all school programs. In most recent years, his formal initiative in policy matters has been quite sketchy, although his informal influence within the NYSDE may be worked into its actions.

The legislature is formally far more important in educational decision making, partly for its role in finances but also for its weight in authorization of new education programs. These formal interactions may be seen in the urban education thrust of 1968-69.

Under pressure during the 1960s to increase state aid both to big cities and to all districts, the legislature attempted to respond to both these demands. By the 1968-69 legislative session, many lawmakers were convinced of the need for special assistance for educationally disadvantaged children. Recognition of that need had existed much earlier in the commissioners' minds. Governor Rockefeller in the summer of 1968, expressing concern for the urban crisis, asked the NYSDE to develop school programs as part of his urban package. In interviews for this study, we found credit for the original law being claimed by Republicans and Democrats, NYSDE, and regents. Whatever the truth, the NYSDE budget requests sought an increase of $110 million. This was reduced in the governor's budget to $50 million, and the legislature found bipartisan support to pass it. The bulk went to the Big Six City districts.

Increasingly, however, suburban and rural areas, heavily Republican, have opposed expanded big city school aid. Although the 1969 legislature appropriated the $50 million for each of two years, in 1970-71, the legislature opposed regental desires to double the amount. The Republicans have also been under pressure to drop the urban education appropriation from those who favor return to the state aid formula which favors upstate schools. Critics of the Urban Education appropriation contend that it overlaps the compensatory education provisions of ESEA I.[6] In 1970, Republicans demanded that urban education be evaluated in conjunction with ESEA. These recent demands indicate that the legislature views its own allocations in light of federal programs. In this thinking, federal aid is coming to be conceived not as an addition to state programs, but as a substitute for them.

It is important to understand the reasons for this new and significant legislative involvement. First, although relatively small, New York's share of federal aid has become an important part of its budget, particularly in New York City. In 1969-70, the state received $237 million, including $170 million which came from ESEA I; the latter included $120 million for New York City—6 percent of its school budget. When tight budget years come, as they have, that fraction takes on a larger importance among local officials. It also moves some legislators in Albany to think of reducing state aid to New York City.

A second reason for this shift of legislative interest arises from internal changes in the legislature itself. After action in 1969, the legislature now has considerably expanded staff for overseeing executive agencies. This implements the longer-standing strong staff for the Ways and Means Committee of the Assembly, responsible for initiating fiscal legislation. The Ways and Means

Committee has the largest and apparently most effective staff organization in the legislature; its secretary is traditionally the Speaker's right-hand man and a powerful figure in the legislative process. He is considered a fiscal expert and is involved in the negotiations which result in the final budget. Other major persons on the staff include a director of budget studies and a staff professional for each of the major substantive areas, e.g., education. The last is a key link between the Committee and the NYSDE, enabling the legislature to maintain close contact with its daily operations. Too, the budget analysts assume the responsibility of taking an active part in the formation and administration of NYSDE policy—on federal aid and other issues.

Ways and Means budget staff men also maintain close contact with Washington to track developments in federal aid legislation for education and other fields. Like the commissioner and his federal relations assistant, they must be closely attuned to the changes and projections in the flow of federal dollars to the state. In interviews with the authors, they indicated that federal revenues enter into the budget calculations for state expenditures and are part of the planning integral to the budget-making process. But they were quick to add that the required maintenance of state effort is closely adhered to and that federal monies are never used for substitutions. The amount of funds committed to the urban education program, over and above ESEA I expenditures, was cited as evidence of good faith on this account. But it was clear that at this level of planning there is considerable coordination of funds among the federal programs and with the state budget.[7]

Within the past several years, legislators have expressed increased interest in the NYSDE administration of federal funds, an interest evident in at least three items of legislation. Two became law; while the third passed only the Assembly, it is expected to arise again. All three involve the administration of ESEA I, by far the largest and most controversial of federal programs. All three legislative actions came as a direct result of *unresponsiveness* by those in charge of these programs to initiatives from legislative leadership.

The term *leadership* is key here. There are frequent attempts by individual legislators to assert control over some operation of the NYSDE or a school district. This is particularly true of New York City legislators, who dispair of a satisfactory response from the administration of their city's schools. However, such attempts are stifled by the legislative leadership, usually in committee, *provided* the NYSDE remains sensitive to its demands. Because the amount of conflict involving these federal programs is likely to increase, the extent of legislative involvement is expected to do likewise.

The Role of Interest Groups

The traditional influence of regents, commissioner, and NYSDE is also reflected in political party operations. In New York, support of education and its finances has until very recently had the qualities of a "given" among political parties. The strong party competition in the legislature (so intense that party voting is taken for granted and clerks often read out merely a few names of each party before boredly announcing the vote for all members) breaks down in votes on school assistance. Interparty agreement most often prevails because of behind-the-scenes accommodation of potential divisions, resulting in an open vote that is nearly unanimous.[8]

The weight of interest groups is both more important for understanding educational politics in New York and more complex. than that of party. As a rough rule of thumb, there exist more or less permanent combinations of what Bailey once termed "schoolmen and their friends."

Building upon the fundamental concerns of parents and the citizenry at large for adequate education, pro-school interests can be divided broadly into four groups. First are the educational academics who fashion in the first instance plans for school aid and form the intellectual core of the movement. Second come the officials in state government, sometimes leaders in state departments of education, sometimes officials with other responsibilities, who adopt the school cause. The third group consists of the professional educators—teachers, superintendents, principals—and their lay supporters, school board members, PTA's, and school betterment groups and the coalitions which those interests strike. Finally, there are the "surprise" actors, individuals and associations engaged in pursuits not normally aligned with public schools but which for numerous and subtle reasons make common cause with the schoolmen.[9]

Of these, the "scribblers" have played an enormous role in placing on the political agenda ideas on finances, curriculum, testing, etc.[10] This innovative function—by such men as Paul Mort at Teachers College, Columbia University, and Alfred I. Simpson of Harvard—reshaped financial aid programs all over the nation and specifically in New York after World War II. That tradition continues today in an interesting way; each of the regional urban blocs on school policy now emerging has a "scribbler" cohort from a university in its domain.

Such men lack political clout, however, to move their conceptions into public policy, so officials in the educational and governmental systems—regents, the commissioner, the NYSDE, the governor and legislators—must be enlisted if authoritative action is to take place. Regents provide reinforcement, particularly when they can play upon the notion that they represent a nonpartisan, general interest for better education. They can invite innovation by creating a study commission (which has a politique of its own) to testify before legislative and public forums; they can encourage the commissioner and the NYSDE to new directions.

Just as possible, it is true, the relationship may be reversed so that the regents become "sympathetic responders to the executive and administrative officials they oversee." In New York in recent decades, commissioners like Allen and incumbent Ewald B. Nyquist (long-time deputy to Allen) have provided the stimulus to innovation and support in governing organs and with the public. This they do by different means:

> ... working on party leaders to have their aims recognized in party platforms, joining hands occasionally with other interest groups, doing staff work for legislative and executive branches alike. But most typically, the procedure has been to persuade governors and key legislators to espouse their cause.[11]

In such efforts to achieve legitimacy, however, they most often must rely upon those interest groups which can mobilize support by articulating relevant needs—an effort directed ultimately to the formal decision-making process. Under the rubric of "educational associations and their satellites" are those professional educators and lay supporters which can stimulate local attentive publics or pressure local legislators.

In New York, since 1937, such allies have been coordinated by a statewide coalition, the Educational Conference Board (ECB). This has provided a holding company which could be mobilized for educational programs which its key operators—executive secretaries in affiliated groups, NYSDE officials, teachers, and school boards—agreed were vital to meet schooling needs. Both Bailey's and Michael Usdan's study of the ECB,[12] at about the same time, gave it a central, if not dominant, role in shaping New York's school finances for many years. One official interviewed in the present study, who has worked intimately with the ECB as a scribbler, claimed that this influence was exaggerated, although it may have had such importance shortly after World War II.

Like all such coalitions, the ECB contained potential divisions—which were widened severely by events during the sixties. The growing "militancy" of the United Federation of Teachers (long only an occasional participant, but most often a critic of the coalition) pushed the State Teachers Association toward enlarged demands. These were increasingly opposed by the School Board Association, whose local members balked at providing larger resources to meet such teacher demands. Too, voter resistance to increasing property taxes, as well as an economic recession, had by the end of the decade combined to demand that the state either cut back school expenses and/or increase the state's contribution to those expenses.

These forces generally supporting school programs confront rather regularly other groups consistently opposed to such measures. Bailey and his associates found in the northeast that the Roman Catholic Church, popularly believed to be firmly opposed to increased state expenditures for public schools because of the "double taxation" imposed upon its communicants who support parochial schools, actually did not take such a stance. On the other hand, neither had its hierarchy taken a lead in seeking more state funds—although individual Catholics had done so. More obvious in the opposition have been business groups preoccupied with the tax structure and its incidence upon them. Whether opposing all taxation which seems unfair to them, or just certain ones, they emerge as a consistent force in all states in the union.

In New York, as is evident from even a glance, this depressant force has fought a losing fight. In 1966 New York was sixteenth highest of all states in contribution to local school costs, while in 1900 it had been thirty-eighth.[13]

One should not ignore the anti-school program force which under various guises represents the pull of localism. For Bailey and his associates, rural localism was seen as "the most pervasive and persistent of depressants on state school subsidies."[14] This force has a particular intensity in New York, however, because the most basic factor shaping state politics—whether over school or any other policy—has been the split between urban and rural constituencies. If the development of education in New York may be seen as centripetal—one long effort to centralize structure and policy, then the thrust of rural localism has been centrifugal, and it has been buttressed by political clout in the legislature.

The downward pull of the ideology of "local control" may be more illusory than real, but it has influence. It acts as a first barrier to any innovation which centralizes power in Albany. It shapes the discourse even of the regents, who in reality head one of the most centralized school apparatuses in the nation. But it conceals a contrary reality, as Bailey observed:

The language falls pleasingly on the ears of local school board members, superintendents, teachers and parents; and it may well be a barrier to arbitrariness at higher levels. But the term "local control"—powerful as it is as a political shibboleth—flies in the face of the fiscal and administrative realities of state and federal grants in aid and the standardizing effect of professionalism upon public education across the land. This struggle between shibboleth and reality is one of the political anomalies of educational finance. Part of the political tension which surrounds and infuses contemporary educational finance controversies derives from the fact that in a highly interdependent, technological world, the myth of local control of educational policy is increasingly unrealistic.[15]

Another facet of this rural localism is partly demographic, partly status-oriented, partly political—and greatly value impregnated. This is the division between city and country. In reality, however, this urban-rural split has historically been one between sprawling, bawling New York City and the rest of the state.[16] In recent years, this city has been joined on some educational concerns by other cities upstate (the "big six" grouping noted earlier). But there still prevails in the state's politics a sense of New York City versus "the other guys."

But the nature of this geographical split changed during the sixties. Enormous urban outmigration, particularly from New York City, has brought new strength to the suburbs. This, accompanied by more nearly equitable reapportionment compelled by courts, has increasingly joined rural to suburban opponents against large city demands.

The Process of State School Politics

The process by which school policy emerges from the interplay of these agencies and forces yields few generalizations, partly because of its variations and partly because of its mutability. Standard descriptions by Bailey and Usdan emphasized the influence of school interest groups, particularly the ECB. This view is strongly questioned today in light of new influences by the governor and legislative committees during the sixties. We can analyse this shift by noting the stages in which policy is initiated, support built, and authorization secured.

In New York since World War II, the initiative for the most significant school policy—financial aid—has rested with school lobbies, particularly the ECB. Since its origin, it has regularly analyzed prevailing financial conditions, defined needs, and recommended alternatives. The support-building functions have been diffused through other school groups. "Grassroots" efforts to mobilize local support directed toward local legislators have been continuous by the School Boards Association. Locally prominent, projecting the mythology of being less self-seeking than teachers when requesting more state aid, these school boards have the potential access, status, and skills for mobilizing local sentiment.

Such support mobilization is joined to Albany-based school lobbies acting within and around the official arenas of decision making. Interacting with the governor and key legislators, members of the ECB have for decades played a direct hand in transmitting their preferences to significant lawmakers.

Yet more recent analysis has questioned the current significance of such groups. Focusing upon who controls access to the New York legislature, Robert E. Jennings now finds other factors have diminished that influence educational groups may have once had. Summarizing events since 1920, he concludes:

Results indicate that the rise of a strong governorship, dominating the legislature, reduced conflict in the legislative process. Party discipline was enforced in the legislature, particularly as the governor obtained new powers, such as the executive budget, which put legislative initiative in his hands. Later, as the governor was able to take control of his own political party, and integrate it into his role as the developer of statewide programs, conflict with party practically disappeared. Finally, the office of the governor increasingly began to reach out for problems and assign them for solution before they reached a stage of severe political repercussion. All of these developments reduced the number of effective points of access to the legislative process.

Co-optive political strategy, developed earlier by the educational interest groups for influencing a more co-equal legislature in the matter of state aid, was then utilized to induce the governor to modify his policy proposals. Basically, the groups attempted to generate pressure from local jurisdictions and through the legislative leadership so that the governor would either modify his program or establish a committee to examine the problem. The education coalition would then try to co-opt the committee, knowing that the governor would be identified with its report. Thus, the committees became the effective access point for a co-optive strategy. This approach, too, had its limitations. The governor, by simply selecting or electing to deal in dollar amounts for the given year instead of adopting proposed formula changes, put the groups in the position of having to renew their legislative effort each year.

Major changes in educational policy for the state, particularly in finance, must now be proposed or have endorsement through the governor's office. The structural and functional framework of the legislative process has been changed in such a manner that other access points are relatively ineffective. Co-option, as practiced by the educational interest group, may have run its course. . .

Other forces are at work changing that picture, including collective negotiations, the rise of teachers' militancy, incipient dissatisfaction with the schools among several socioeconomic groups. There are indications that these are contributing to the slow breakdown of the [ECB] coalition as much as its inability to change its political behavior to meet the changes in legislative process.[17]

Some evidence that educational lobbies may be currently misperceiving their influence has been provided by Jennings and Mike Millstein. Their interviews with Albany lobbyists and legislators in 1969 sound as if two contrasting realities were being reported. School group leaders believed the governor to be the key access point in the policy-making process because of his statewide influence, party leadership role, and program direction for the legislature through executive program and budget. Too, schoolmen believed it more important to focus in the legislature upon its leaders, and less important to influence legislators back home. Schoolmen also thought their most important influence lay in the information they provide decision makers.

Legislators, however, report another world of policymaking and influence. First, 78 percent of those polled stated that school legislation was not treated in any way different from other policy, despite the allegedly special aura surrounding education. However, they did see it being influenced by those enduring forces noted earlier which also affect any policy—the urban-rural split, the conflict of the state with New York City, and party differences. Second, legislators felt the governor's influence was not as great as schoolmen perceived it; 41 percent said they gave his position little or no attention when voting. Rather, legislators found influence coming from elsewhere, as seen in Table 8-1.[18] Further, where schoolmen thought one element of the governor's power lay in his closeness to legislative leaders, only 9 percent of the legislators felt their leaders were important in the governor's program.

Another set of contradictory perceptions lay in schoolmen's belief that it was most important to focus in the legislature only upon the leaders. But note in Table 8-1 that only 6 percent saw their party leaders in the legislature as important and 9 percent saw them of little importance in oversight of the governor; hence they could hardly be influential with him. Schoolmen saw that body as highly centralized in part because party discipline was so tight; hence their view of the importance in dealing mostly with party leaders. But the legislators were of another mind; only 38 percent saw this world of party

Table 8-1
Factors "Very Important" in Influencing New York Legislators' Views about School Policy, 1969

Factor	Percentage Rating Very Important
Experts in the legislature	55
People in the districts	48
Education committees	39
Educators back home	34
Educational Interest groups	25
Legislative staff opinions	24
Committees other than education	14
Executive department agencies	8
Party leaders	6

discipline operating, while another 16 percent thought it depended upon the issue.

Finally, as to schoolmen's view of their most important asset—the provision of information—three out of four legislators said their most important source of information on legislation was their own legislative research agencies. The next mentioned source was indeed interest groups, but only 24 percent mentioned this source. Here is evidence of a quite recent tendency in this legislature, the development of larger and more sophisticated staff support and data collection sources. As an experienced legislative staffman put it to the author:

Up until three or four years ago, Howard Goold and Arvid Burke (State Teachers Association and officers of ECB) could sit down with members of the governor's office, staff representatives of the fiscal committees, and special legislative commissions on education to work out the state aid formula. But public objection to school costs and those local levies created terrific pressure upon all legislators. The old demands of the school people to get more for their constituents couldn't be endured any longer. Now the legislature turns inward for staff work, developing its own professionals like_____who know where to get information and how to get it from the bureaucracy and who can talk with the governor's guy.[19]

Indeed, this staff performs not only functions of data collection and alternative clarification; both majority and minority staff have been actively engaged in informing legislators what the school aid formula means for each district. However, that service comes in part from the commissioner's initiative in developing a computer capability to assist them. Designed to free legislators in part from the domination of information by executive agencies and the governor, these alternative staff and consulting sources may counter or supplement the alleged role played by schoolmen's supply of facts.

It may not be surprising, then, that Jennings and Millstein found in this 1969 group of legislators a diminished view of education's power, well behind the most powerful; the power ranking was labor (79 percent), education (54 percent), and banking-finance-insurance (32 percent). Equally damaging of schoolmen's views of their influence is the finding that legislators rated their most powerful education group the newly militant wing of organized teachers—the Empire State Federation of Teachers/UFT (54 percent). Well behind were the associations of school boards (26 percent), state teachers (23 percent), and the ECB (only 5 percent). This is especially surprising in light of the fact that the UFT focuses its efforts locally, especially in New York City, while the others, particularly the ECB and other teachers group, maintain large operations in Albany.

The disparity of views between legislators and schoolmen is not unique to New York. Comparable studies of Massachusetts, North Carolina, Oregon, and Utah in 1968 found much the same differing views about schoolmen's special power.[20] In each state at least 81 percent of the legislators found their chief source of information on school matters to be their colleagues, not school lobbies.

Legislators' reported perceptions must be used carefully, however. To say one relies upon lobbyists for assistance in his official duties runs counter to his public image of representing only his district. Too, the report of receiving information from one's colleagues begs the question of where *they* received their information.

The opposing perceptions of the power of organized schoolmen may well arise from a kind of cultural lag among the latter; however, some state educational leaders interviewed by the author for this study point out that schoolmen's influence may have been exaggerated even earlier. Bailey and Usdan studied events of a decade ago, but since then immense new forces have entered the educational scene—taxpayer revolts, desegregation challenges, widespread complaints about educational outputs and the difficulties of achieving educational accountability, and a more demanding and less quiescent generation of teachers. Any one of these was enough to disrupt traditional relationships between educator groups and state authorities. But to have them all at once, especially when magnified by the special distorting effort of New York City, goes far to explain differences between earlier and newer accounts.

New Forces in School Politics

From this analysis of the educational politics of New York State emerges the conclusion that this political matrix is currently undergoing new and great strains generated by the challenging of the expertise of schoolmen at every level of society. For example, the influence of the regents, arising ostensibly from their independence of the governor, becomes questionable when the legislature upon which they depend financially is dominated by the governor. When, as with Dewey in the late forties and Rockefeller in the early and mid-sixties, a governor used party resources and command of knowledge to obtain significant legislative clout, what he decided about budgetary matters affecting schools became definitive. In 1962, Rockefeller could override the preferences of the ECB on total school finances and distributional formulas. In effect, he ignored ECB's characteristic rural bias in order to meet growing urban needs.[21] Yet, in that period, the role of the NYSDE in developing new ideas for policy leadership was very strong. One of its staff wrote the author that

... from the inception of the Diefendorf formula to the present, most of the innovative ideas enacted by the Legislature originated in the Department: to cite only a few, they include racial imbalance, urban aid, high tax aid, ceiling changes, changes in BOCES aid, school breakfast, STEP, ABLE, Pre-kindergarten, etc. In fact, most of the significant financial additions of money to the Diefendorf formula have been developed and/or recommended first by the (NYSDE). . . .
It should be noted, too, that the only other significant change in finances has been the nonpublic aid. The Bundy aid was recommended by the department, and the nonpublic aid for elementary and secondary was initiated and developed by the Governor, not the Legislature.

By 1968-69, however, the governor seemed to have relinquished his domination of the school aid formula to the legislature. Since then, according to legislative staffmen, no significant proposal on the issue has come from the governor's office, and the legislature has become the key arena. However, the governor did appoint the Fleischmann Commission to study the financial aid problem; it recommended in 1972 that the state assume the full funding of local school costs. While at this writing that issue has still not been fought out in the legislature, the governor will have played an important role in whatever changes come from the Commission report. Meanwhile, the NYSDE continues working on finances by preparing legislative programs. As one of its staff wrote, commenting upon a draft of this chapter:

Last year [1971] the Legislative proposals would have simply frozen the high tax aid, giving it to districts receiving the aid the previous year and in the same amount. The inequities of this are obvious. Department officials working with others in the field concerned with legislation were able to force reconsideration of this stand-pat approach so that those districts having the highest rates received the high tax aid.

What had developed in New York, then, by 1972 was a state educational politics in which schoolmen are divided by their competing claims for resources, while the governor, in close alliance with the strengthened legislature, has come to exert greater influence over that most basic of school policies—financing.

The old divisive forces in that kind of politics still remain, however—localism, city vs. country, religion—although modified. The rural bias against cities has become the rural-suburban bias, and upstate urban areas have made efforts to league with New York City.

During this decade, the tremendous growth of the suburbs has brought in its wake reapportionment changes and greater suburban clout in the legislature. State formula aid has hence come to provide these districts with special advantages. But Albany officials see this as merely an extension of the rural bias of old, for residents in both locales still view city life with distaste. However, urban concerns are reflected in a legislature still dominated by representatives from outside the city. Since 1968-69, about $50 million a year has gone into a special Urban Education Program, about 85 percent for New York City.

The urban-suburban divisions today arise over several issues. Suburbanites particularly resent the local share of school costs raised by property taxes and pressure Albany to increase the state's share. In 1970, when all state programs were being cut, the legislature increased aid to suburban Nassau and Suffolk counties. Urban centers are less exercised over this issue, partly because the state picks up a larger share of their costs already (but proportionately less than for suburban and rural districts) and partly because they were just unable to do much when their delegates were all Democrats. Measures of distribution of state and federal aid based on AFDC population in a district are also resented by suburbanites. Because they have few such children, they feel the formula discriminates against them. But this outlook may change in the seventies. There is just emerging an awareness that big suburbs touching on borders of the cities of America are coming to have many of the same problems of those cities.[22] In May and November, 1971, the *New York Times* reported the dismay of officials in Suffolk and Nassau counties at signs of the social crabgrass of suburbia—increasing welfare, crime, and poor education.

In all this, rural power has not disappeared, but merely allied with the suburban—usually Republican—legislators. A group of a dozen self-named "apple-knockers" in the Assembly organized to prevent rural areas' aid from being reduced. In 1970 they declared they would not vote on school aid unless they were in on the decision; the thin GOP margin in the Assembly magnified their influence. They blocked elimination of a "size correction" aid formula which helped fund small rural districts; they succeeded in freezing assistance to the previous year's level.

Accompanying these changes has been a more basic one. The forum for decisions about school program and moneys has been altered. That no longer lies in a once monolithic coalition of schoolmen, which first internally resolved conflicts among its parts and then presented the product to a complaisant legislature, while the governor idly watched.[23] Such a description may not have been accurate at any but the briefest times in the past.

As internal divisions among schoolmen became no longer containable, the governor and legislature took on new interests, resources, and direction in shaping school policy. The regents, commissioner, and department officials may well be increasingly professional and competent. Their program interests may be more varied and their innovations broader than in the past or than in other states. But as all programs must ultimately operate with funds, schoolmen must face the constraints and preferences of those who allocate funds. These have increasingly been found across the street from the education buildings in Albany, in the legislature's Victorian rockpile and the executive offices. A key legislative assistant put it to the author in terms of the new questions being asked about education in New York and all over America:

Until 1968 or 1969, educators' claim that more money for education meant better education went unchallenged. The two were synonymous. Since then, the legislature and governor are asking questions. How does more money mean better education? How do you educators support this linkage? Can you prove it? There is no question about the quality of education in this state now, but the costs are also so very high—salaries, fringe benefits—maybe best in the country. So the legislature now says, "We've done our part in elevating education, but what do we get for our next $100 million in education? What if we don't even change the formulas upward? Did you know that without such change the money available for aid would *still* increase by $75 million next year and $185 million by 1972-73? What are we getting for all this?"[24]

Such unsettling questions for the NYSDE are paralleled by local complaints about taxation. These culminated in the 1972 recommendations of the Fleischmann Commission, conducting a decenially required review of the state's state of schooling. It called outright for *total* state assumption of public school financing, with funds from a statewide property tax plus general revenue. Administration would devolve onto eleven regions, in each of which a BOCES would service local districts and supervise such special programs as vocational education and that for handicapped and gifted children. At this writing, the outcome of the recommendations is unknown, but local publics' and high courts' rejection of the existing fiscal scheme are major forces moving the state toward total assumption.[25] In that event, yet another shift in New York's school allocational politics will take place.

The New York State Department of Education

Under the direction of the regents and their designated commissioner, the NYSDE supervises education in New York. Its external relationships with the governor, legislature, and interest groups has already been examined. The department must be conceived, moreover, as a structure of decision making and influence in its own right, with linkages to its local district components. While overt expressions of concern about "local control" abound, the history of education in New York and other states has been one of increasing centralization. This has come either through state legislature or the SEA's imposition of professional norms of educational quality—with each feeding on the other.

In New York, the department's statutory power is augmented by several other sources including its size, its history of extensive involvement in local schools, and its pattern of growth in the period of increased federal involvement. Perhaps more important, however, as explanations of the NYSDE's power, are its relationship to particular reference groups and its emphasis on the norm of professionalism.

Size, History, and Patterns of Growth

Largeness of size is a special component of power in a nation where bigness counts. In both relative and absolute terms, the NYSDE is big. As of June, 1970, there was 3,823 full-time, permanent employees listed, over 1,500 of whom were in professional ranks. The largest department in the state's government, the NYSDE is second in size only to California's State Department of Education. Only part of NYSDE's growth can be attributed to the infusion of federal funds. As far back as 1960, the department personnel already exceeded 2,000, with less than 100 positions federally funded. Since 1960, new federal funds have accounted for only about one-fourth of the new slots (excluding the nearly 300 vocational rehabilitation positions funded in 1970 which operate outside the public school system). The five programs included in this investigation include only 262 positions, less than 7 percent of the total, which administer nearly 95 percent of the federal revenues (again excluding the vocational rehabilitation program).[26]

Second, the size and degree of the NYSDE development reflects the history of large-scale involvement of the state in local school administration and finances. The NYSDE administers almost half the total revenues of the public school system.

New York pioneered in the formation of regional administrative units for certain aspects of the school program (known as Boards of Cooperative Educational Services, or BOCES) funded directly from the NYSDE. Furthermore, the state has a history of categorical programs for special activities (transportation, district consolidation, integration, achievement testing, construction, vocational education), in addition to the usual programs for curriculum, teacher certification, and handicapped children. Such state involvement leads, of course, to large state administrative staffs. A large research component is maintained as well, partly under an associate commissioner's office and partly in the finance division. In sum, the NYSDE's state level functions are large and well-established relative to the federal component.

Reference Groups

A key to understanding the NYSDE's power and its administration of federal programs lies in its relationship to special groups. These are less "constituencies" than "reference groups." To say that state staff respond to a constituency implies that an individual makes decisions on behalf of some specified group without being a part of that group, neither emotionally attached to nor accepting its motives and values. A reference group, on the other hand, is one with which the person identifies. "The process of identification," it has been noted, "refers to his emotional ties with groups of the same or superior power to which he turns and to which he may defer."[27] However, constituency relationships imply also an element of quid pro quo between group and representative. Reference group responses, on the other hand, suggest that a state official's actions are not so much based on tradeoffs with local districts as they are on his perception of membership in the same professional group as the local administrators. Recruitment policy reinforces these relationships. The personnel section expressly seeks out district employees for NYSDE positions which parallel their former duties. They therefore identify with the milieu of the administrators in the field.

Academic background is another link between the department and its reference group. When the 1969-1970 school year opened, *eight* with the rank of assistant commissioner or above had received their doctorates from the same institution—Teachers College, Columbia University; New York University claimed three more of these administrators. Since the reign of Paul Mort, Teachers College has also been closely associated with the Educational Conference Board. From Teachers College, Professor Mort had supervised the doctoral studies of at least four of the high-level staff. At the same time, he directed the research of the ECB, largely through the State Teachers Association's research committee based at Columbia.

The relationship between the NYSDE's evaluation division and the academic community is an example of a department-reference group relationship. The close linkage between the evaluation division and the academic community is illustrated by the selection of doctoral candidates from nearby universities, usually SUNY-Albany, as temporary employees to assist in screening project proposals during the peak periods. Further, faculty members are chosen by the division to advise and participate in site visitation and monitoring functions. For example, evaluation teams which perform the required examination of ESEA I projects include professors, NYSDE personnel, and local district representatives. The evaluation division has also developed a catalogue listing most of the state's resources for review of educational programs. Included here are the names, addresses, fields of interest, and consulting fees for the state's university experts on educational evaluation.

Other arrangements link the NYSDE to advisory committees and related groups. For example, the assistant commissioner for education of the disadvantaged meets regularly with the State Committee on Equality of Educational Opportunity, consisting of representatives of major school groups (PTA, State Teachers Association, School Boards Association). Advisory committees for library programs, vocational education, and others, also serve the state as forums for input from the "field," as well as transmission belts for information to it. Membership on these is a good indication of which organizations must be "checked with" in the formulation of policy in a program area.

It is important to note here, however, the discrepancy between the views of state personnel and school staffs on the importance of contributions from these committees. Program and finance administrators emphasize the importance of their contacts with the field. No major decision, they claim, is made without careful consultation with selected representatives of the local districts. Such consultations were described as learning experiences for NYSDE staff, enabling them to correct and modify their preliminary plans. Administrators in the field, however, report that their participation in these groups is largely pro forma ratification of decisions already made by state administrators. One school superintendent called in regularly for "advice" seriously questioned whether state officials would be prepared to handle any disagreements from the advisory committees, so unexpected would it be. The fact that this selection of local administrators is made at the discretion of the state administrators is central. In our interviews with state officers, the most frequent description of this selection process indicated an attempt to overcome objections of and generate support from the key local administrators.

The NYSDE has other important local linkages. Where large or significant changes in state policy on a federal program are in prospect, the message is delivered directly to the grassroots. Regional meetings are organized across the state, and the responsible state officers make the rounds. For programs which change from year to year, such as ESEA I, the administrators spend much of their time in regional meetings. These meetings with school administrators and occasionally board members are with the groups that are served and identified with by most state program administrators.

Professionalism

Another source of NYSDE influence lies in its members' norms. Professionalism characterizes the overall operations of the agency; by it the NYSDE's operating strategies are interrelated. Only certain specific manifestations of professionalism are of interest here. They are best described as (1) norms related to the decision-making styles, and (2) reference groups characteristic of the NYSDE staff. They tell initiates how to make decisions and who their peers are in the world of school politics. Professionalism in decision-making norms includes:

1. Avoidance of "politics" and "special interests" as an influence.
2. Reliance on consensus and conflict avoidance.
3. Reliance on academic, preferably certified, expertise for substantive decisions.

These are not so much hard-and-fast rules for action, but rather the framework of guiding principles which the NYSDE staff uses to define "good" and "bad" organizational behavior.

Like all such well-maintained behavioral norms, professionalism is a source of power for the organizational members. Contrasts are clear between the norms of program administrators and those of evaluation personnel as well as between their reference groups relationships. Styles of operation reflect these differences. Program administrators spend much time consulting with their local school reference group. They rely on consensus and individual school-by-school negotiation, as among peers. They seek their advice on program policy. The local autonomy theme characterizes their norm; basic questions of educational policy are matters for the local board and administration. The implied purpose of the NYSDE is to assist the boards in accomplishing their objectives, not to follow some state purpose. Local "professionals"—or "peers"—are thought to be the ones to make important decisions on local programs. Conflict with local school districts is carefully avoided and is considered evidence of failure to communicate.

By contrast, the state evaluation professionals devote much time to concentrating on technical problems in cooperation with professionals in the academic community. They view the evaluation of district programs as a monitoring function, not a cooperative venture with the district. Among the evaluators, conflict is evidence that careful evaluation has turned up a problem in the program involved; they have an established procedure for conflict resolution.

For administrators, "professionalism" in these terms extends to the allocation of responsibility for administrative decisions within the NYSDE as well. Program administrators defer review of proposals and evaluative reports to the subject-matter specialists within the department. These specialists review only that portion related to their specialty; they do not see the whole picture. For example, reading program proposals are reviewed by NYSDE reading specialists, recruited from the ranks of reading specialists in public schools. They spend much time in direct contact with their local counterparts in program development in what are called "cooperative review" sessions.

These state reading specialists also have the responsibility for review and evaluation of proposals under ESEA I and New York's own Urban Education Program. Furthermore, the same personnel who review and comment on proposals and applications are responsible for site visitation and evaluation. Since they are considered "professionals"—that is, above any conflict of interest or shortage of objectivity—it is only fitting that they should evaluate as well as allocate. The implications of this pattern of operation for the allocation of federal aid are twofold: (1) although new offices were set up to administer federal programs, the actual responsibility for allocation decisions was spread through the department in the same pattern of operation that existed prior to federal funding, and (2) the norms characteristic of this process reflect a "professionalism" based on close identification with local peer groups.

Important exceptions to this generalization exist, such as the reference groups of the evaluation division which are located in academia, not the schools. A more important deviation from this pattern is found in New York City, whose former relationships with Albany have obviously been disrupted by decentralization. Prior to the division of New York City into its present 31 administrative units, its central board of education was considered the sole, responsible, "professional" agent for the city. Federal funds were turned over to the city board to dispose of as it chose, with little or no intervention from Albany. But now there is no longer a single board and superintendent to speak for the city schools; there are 31 of each plus the powerful voice of the UFT. The cacophony of voices for various interests within the city's schools drowns out attempts to achieve a rational, "professional" consensus.

At this time, no stable new pattern seems to have emerged. The resulting inability of the NYSDE to respond to legislative initiatives led to the three separate forays by lawmakers into the administration of federal funds, two of which related directly to decentralization. The only clear outcome of this conflict at the NYSDE level has been increased monitoring of the allocation process for ESEA I funds to New York City and a reorganization of the department to place that title and the urban education program under the same officer. In addition, the legislature has mandated that (1) both programs be evaluated jointly by the NYSDE in its report to the legislature, and (2) the allocation of funds within New York City must reflect the formula by which the city's portion was determined. The effect that these provisions will have on the administration of the programs remains to be seen.

Coordinating Priorities and Planning for Federal Programs

The diverse ways in which the American states regularly decide to allocate their funds for education are unlikely to disappear when federal money becomes available. As this book attests, when Washington seeks to standardize programs through a state mechanism which itself must reflect the diversity of its local constituencies, the federal thrust is particularly blunted.[28] Federal efforts to induce each state department to create statewide priorities of needs, to relate its resources to those priorities through planning, and to evaluate local district compliance are colored by each state's political culture.

Even a glance at the chapter on Texas will show the differential impact of state's political culture on the coordination of priorities and planning. How much an SEA spends on this priority-planning-evaluation syndrome relative to its total expenditures (including federal grants for this purpose) should indicate roughly the extent of its determination to achieve coherence. Pennsylvania shows the largest effort; 12.7 percent of all its SEA expenditures went into this task. But the successively smaller percentages show a curious order—Texas (11.8), New Jersey (11.4), Oregon (10.4), Massachusetts (9.3), Ohio (6.8), and California (6.2). New York appears about at midpoint—9.3 percent.[29] In short, what a state has attempted with this federal objective is not a function of such quantifiable matters as size, complexity, or available resources. Rather its emphasis on formal planning activities is determined far more by the attitude taken by the SEA, hence from its state culture.[30]

The planning function thrust upon the NYSDE by federal aid programs was hardly new. Indeed, some of New York's practices have set standards which USOE has adapted as models for other states. It had gone through the coherent planning schemes of PPBS and PARD from their earliest emergence upon the national school scene. Neither, however, provides the user a definition of his program needs, and this function had to flow from determinations by the regents, the commissioner, and the NYSDE. Clearly, ESEA demanded that urban school needs, particularly those in the most disadvantaged areas of the cities, have highest priority. Within that quite broad rubric, however, Commissioners Allen and Nyquist focused upon the need to remedy the glaring deficiencies in reading which characterize urban school products all over the nation. Further, this need could best be remedied by application of funds to elementary education. Research had shown—and post-ESEA research would confirm—that dollar for dollar a greater effect could be achieved in a child's early years of learning attitudes and basic skills.[31]

Across the gamut of ESEA titles and NDEA III, it was possible to emphasize these priorities to obviously attendant districts. According to NYSDE officials, the early days of ESEA saw little local effort to determine priorities and to plan on such a basis. In a process familiar elsewhere, the NYSDE spread the word through meetings, reports, and project guidelines after 1965. Not surprisingly, districts complied by submitting projects to meet exactly those needs. By 1970, around 40 percent of all projects submitted to the state for categorical aid had a reading component. Applications with the reading component as only one part of the package would find only that component funded and the others deleted or cut. Officials even today insist they "cannot mandate priorities" but instead only "emphasize certain educational values." However, when this is backed up with quite detailed instructions to districts on how to apply for funds, including concern over these priorities, or when the NYSDE reports on "successful" projects which are heavily larded with those priorities, a district's project officer would have to be surpassingly stupid not to grasp the message.

Coordination of priorities across categorical programs is different from their articulation. It can be achieved by three administrative models. One would be not to attempt it at all, and this book suggests that this may be the prevalent model. The second would be to devise a centralized office which attempts coordination in some pre- or post-audit fashion. A third model would be to forge a connecting link between old-line departmental agencies and new program priorities. Then Commissioner James E. Allen, Jr., and his deputy Ewald B. Nyquist utilized the third model. Combining Title V with that small percentage of each title appropriation which a state can employ for internal administration, Allen and Nyquist tightly managed these funds to create an articulated two-part staff mechanism. One, the title administrator's staff, dealt with problems of planning, research, and evaluation. The second and larger group, specialists for categorical programs, were funded within other NYSDE divisions. This two-part staff design permitted both vertical and horizontal transmission of state priorities. The specialists could review any district project, sent them by the title administrator. This review, coordinated through the title administrator, projected the commissioner's needs priorities back to the local level. Cabinet meetings provided the mechanism for the commissioner to coordinate the efforts of his title administrators.

The commissioner could also transmit his priorities laterally into the old-line agencies of the NYSDE through these specialists. For example, a specialist in reading located in the curriculum division could apply professional standards to applications on such matters as the number of staff needed to expand a Title I reading program for the disadvantaged. Others in audiovisual education sections could pass on the library and reading materials aspects of the ESEA II or NDEA III portions of that application. In the process, these title specialists working within their divisions necessarily interacted with their non-title colleagues to transmit information on needs, plans, programs, etc., which reflected the commissioner's priorities.

The special role of Commissioners Allen and Nyquist in this matter must be noted. After ESEA's passage, Deputy Commissioner Nyquist became coordinator of all federal aid programs and the single, focused, "clear channel" to Washington from the NYSDE. That single channel arrangement was the first major impact of these federal laws. Besides day-to-day contact between title administrators and their counterparts in USOE, there is Washington contact on major policy matters between Nyquist and the USOE commissioner, as well as with Nyquist's assistant for federal affairs, who spends several days a week in Washington. These internal budget arrangements were not reviewed by the regents or the legislature, thereby giving the commissioner considerable independence.

However, that independence is now coming under the eye of the state bureau of the budget. That agency must technically authorize such internal expenditures by issuing "certificates of approval." In the past, the bureau had ignored its potential power to examine these programs; it had concentrated on state expenditures, and its small staff proscribed further forays. But, as state school finances have come under ever heavier pressure, the bureau has become active in seeking out ways to cut costs or transfer funds—measures which can affect administrative arrangements.

Too, federal monitors in 1971 increased their objection to this articulated administration. They preferred, particularly for Title I, that there be a single office whose members would be put in the field to monitor programs directly. Whereas the present structure emphasizes pre-audit, that which the USOE calls for would be more a program audit. "They want us to go into the field and actually count whether the books the application called for are actually there," said one dissatisfied NYSDE official. "And that arises all because some district— particularly New York City—has fallen so far behind in its post-audit statements or any kind of evaluation of its work."

Two major problems have attenuated NYSDE efforts to set priorities and coordinate the programs to achieve them. First, the amounts of money thrown into the educational deficiency attacked—reading in urban schools—were insubstantial. While New York State secured the largest dollop of such federal funds, it was inadequate for the problems of education in the big six cities. No amount of clever management of priorities and resources in Albany by the most professional staff under the best leaders could do more than microscopically narrow the schooling gap. The world's best engineers could bridge the Grand Canyon's narrowest width of 4 miles—but not if given only enough steel for 1 mile.

The Distorting Effect of New York City
on Planning and Coordination

The second problem lies in the phenomenon of New York City with its 1,100,000 students, thirty-one school districts, $131 million in Title I funds alone in 1970, and numerous community groups whom the NYSDE must socialize to bureaucratic norms, and the echelon of administrators at 110 Livingston Street, too.

The legislature sought to alleviate New York's schooling problems by special financial programs, e.g., in urban education, and by decentralizing a bloated city administration into thirty-one community districts. In the process it provided the funds and instruments which have aggravated that city's educational politics.[32] The commissioner and the NYSDE appear to have a minimal administrative role, for the routine administration of applications and approval of programs has little or no impact on the allocation of Title I funds within New York City. Neither do the state guidelines include specific regulation of the allocations within the city. Attempts at influence appear instead to be more informal, through the consultation of state officers with central board and administrators at 110 Livingston Street. The most direct intervention of the state in this city's allocations is the Decentralization Act itself. Observers of its drafting and passage have described it not so much as an example of a statewide decision as a battle, in the legislature, among interested representatives from New York City. The Act could be viewed, therefore, not as a new, state-level initiative to influence Title I allocations within New York City but as a shifting of the locus of decision making to the legislature.

In general, state administrators view the New York City school system as a hopeless mess whose problems and complexities are to be avoided as much as possible. The state officers appear to comply with the board's actions in this and other ESEA matters. Unclear answers were given as to how well New York City schools met state standards of priorities and planning. The very fact that the city's federal funds had been withheld briefly by the commissioner for failure to render evaluations suggests the difficulties of securing compliance with an important aspect of a coherent process. Because the available constraints the NYSDE can employ are seldom considered seriously or its regulations and planning phase strenuously enforced, the planning function cannot be said to be effective for the largest school district in the state and nation.

It might be argued, however, that this is not necessary when state and city have parallel interests in the reading needs of the urban poor. It may be a mark of their concern that the Martin-McClure Report, denouncing the host of improper Title I expenditures in the first year of that act's life, mentioned New York only once—briefly, and in reference to the school lunch program.[33]

But parallel interests are not the same as a coherent planning function related to a needs priority schedule. They do not provide consideration of federal programs as a single fund interrelated through priorities, so that they reinforce each other or state funds for the same educational objective. The unusually long delays of New York City in reporting evaluation results clearly vitiates coordination efforts. In mid-November, 1971, the city had just turned in its ESEA II report for 1967-68, and that was improperly done (on handwritten ledgers and not machine statements) and due to be returned.

In sum, then, the priorities and planning thrust of federal legislation has had a mixed record in New York. While it fostered professional and public thinking about urban school needs of the poor, the inadequate funds and the centrifugal weight of New York City prevented achievement of the conditions explicit in the PPBS models. The bulk of federal funds (Title I) went in one lump to one site—New York City—over which the NYSDE had little control under federal law (and that exercised lamely) and only somewhat more under state law (and that muzzled by local political intricacies). Despite these legal and political limitations, however, the NYSDE did make a strong effort to do what the federal legislation attempted. At the very least, the effort has produced a wider interest among school districts in thinking about priority and planning coherence, as well as in building the administrative structure—particularly regional structure—to make the whole work. That is not a minor victory.

Federal Aid Administration: A Title-By-Title Analysis

ESEA—Title I

In New York, the enormous concentration of disadvantaged children in New York City results in the allocation of 70 percent of ESEA I dollars to those boroughs. Thus, there are two worlds of ESEA I in New York. For a minor proportion of such funds—outside New York City—Albany strives to introduce new concerns for urban education and accountability. But the major share of these funds goes down the Hudson virtually unaffected by the NYSDE. There they become a political resource impressed upon the existing contest among central board, UFT, and community boards.

The early days of ESEA I were hectic for NYSDE title administrators such as Louis Pasquini and Irving Ratchek. The first task was not major but laborious: determining the number of AFDC and low-income families upon which each county allocation rested. Other and more troublesome issues concerned them as they began to work with their federal counterparts: the need for specific guidelines to augment vague program goals; implementation of evaluation requirements; and the NYSDE's relationships to the private school system now eligible for public funds and to the required advisory community councils. These state and federal professionals were excited over the sudden availability of that aid to education so long discussed and desired. One noted,

So many matters those days were exploratory, so we had to pool our judgments. It wasn't a case of representatives of two governments standing glaring at one another. There wasn't the taking of sides, my view versus your view. Rather, it was more like, "What is your view of this?" That is, not a master-slave relationship then—or now.[34]

Little of all this entered the state's politics of education. The regents were aware of ESEA I, of course, from briefings, but no authorization was needed from them; they might make recommendations, but could be little involved technically. Little was heard from the governor's office or the legislature while the professionals were hammering out their first *modus vivendi*. ECB interest groups were involved, however, primarily at the NYSDE's initiative; as early as 1965, the department used their meetings to disseminate information on the new law. That first year, with about $65 million to be spent in a great hurry, required quick word to these reference groups.

Subsequently, it all got very involved. First, the low income and AFDC criteria expanded with amendments in 1966-67, adding foster children and neglected and delinquent children. Beginning in 1967-68, district allocations were based on factoring the 1966-67 allocation. A year later, the formula was (1) 60 percent of last year's allocation, (2) neglected and delinquent children, and (3) AFDC. In 1969-70, it was 70 percent of the previous year's allocation and criteria (2) and (3); in 1970-71, it was 80 percent of the previous year and the two children criteria. By late 1970, NYSDE officials in the divisions of educational finance and the disadvantaged were calling for use of only the AFDC figure.[35] This single factor would drop from funding twenty-three districts without any AFDC, increase funds to those with many, and decrease them to those with few. In short, this was a call by those closest to NYSDE's administration of ESEA I to move more funds into the big cities.

Other state groups have been drawn into allocation decisions in recent years. Teacher contracts are now appearing with the right granted to require their approval for ESEA I contracts. The legislature has become involved since 1969 with the question of richer districts getting some—or too much—funds from a law explicitly designed for poor districts. A first-class row developed when it was discovered that the far-from-poor Garden City school district had received $37,000 (in 1971-72 it was still getting $11,000). A bill was immediately filed in the State Legislature to insure that such funds be issued only on the basis of AFDC, but the obvious urban bias doomed it in a body dominated by rural-suburban interests.

In all this, the traditional administration of the NYSDE was learning new skills. Its characteristic rural—and now suburban—orientation was being pressured by new urban interests. These came from the title administrators, from the urban education program thrust, from new regents with urban concerns, like university administrator Stephen K. Bailey and psychologist Kenneth B. Clark, and from the Title I-mandated citizens advisory councils. Under OEO and ESEA programs, councils were to provide suggestions, oversight and administration for new urban service. They and the professionals had different definitions of citizen cooperation. For the schoolmen, it was the model PTA of middle-class white America which they sought to impose, i.e., to restrict its role to one of reinforcement of professional direction. For the citizens, however, the model was one of "accountability" of everyone and everything connected with a school system which was deemed to be destroying their children. The schoolmen saw these groups in many districts *demanding* that funds be used for anything, while NYSDE officials were charged to ensure that money went only for categorical programs for special services.

The effect of NYSDE oversight through these years cannot be determined with any clarity. Much in the existing school system worked against that effort. There was still within its walls an uncertainty about dealing with the complex problems of urban education. There was the decision, noted earlier, to decentralize its approval of ESEA I projects throughout its structure instead of utilizing such personnel as field monitors; this could be seen as a reflection of the traditional deference to local control and professional courtesy. Too, the NYSDE never demanded that a negligent district return its misused funds. And there was always the confusion and frustration of having to deal with New York City.

The federal legislation required evidence of a program's effectiveness. The NYSDE did develop and regularize the application process, incorporating an evaluation system which may last far beyond the life of ESEA. Concern to find out what programs really made a difference in improving the deficiencies of the disadvantaged caused the ESEA I staff to demand that more rigorous standards of evidence of effect must be applied. The ESEA I office generated highly detailed guidelines and instructions for grant application which—by an emphasis upon behavioral definitions of educational goals—compelled many district leaders to think beyond educational generalities. Consultants, themselves often principals and teachers, working in collaboration with university staff, developed these forms, check lists and other mechanisms for operationalizing the general goals of the law.

Previously, universities had provided models for schoolmen in matters of curriculum, teacher training, and administration which they adopted and modified to fit immediate circumstances. But little of this training proceeded as if the educationally disadvantaged existed or there was a need for models of effective evaluation.

Much of this work crystallized under the associate commissioner for research and evaluation and his division of evaluation and bureau of urban and community programs evaluation.[36] All districts were informed in detail how to prepare requests for categorical grants in behavioral terms. This was supplemented by continuing reports on what other districts were doing, particularly with successful projects;[37] consultants were told explicitly how site visits were to be made to monitor projects.[38] But most important, Albany officials went to great lengths to explain how to set up for evaluation when planning a project—complete with model forms, checklists, approved behavioral definitions, etc.[39] Too, because of problems of non-comparable data and differing reporting sources, they have been leaders in developing the "Belmont System" of standardizing information on school input and output variables. The results would facilitate evaluating the delivery of education.[40]

Staff in the NYSDE evaluation agencies seem deeply excited about the value of their work, as well as intrigued by the intellectual difficulties of developing it. Albany's approach to district schoolmen is to claim that they are supporting them by such evaluation. The locals feel threatened by the new skills being demanded, and they fear that the end product will be sanctions for those poorly evaluated. So Albany offers itself as a supplementive service, seeking to provide the locals with improved ways of doing their job as clearly and effectively as they wish. But the districts must relay the data back to Albany for the evaluation procedure to be effective. Frequently, this is not done—or done poorly—a situation not restricted to New York.

A recent report noted that of 1,200 evaluation reports from around the nation which a private agency was called in to analyze, only 326 reports of purportedly successful projects were in a form which made controlled evaluation possible—and only 10 showed the projects were effective.[41]

The ESEA I office in Albany does produce annual reports showing educational gains from these funds; they are not large, but are nevertheless gains.[42] Yet, title directors admit the difficulty of knowing clearly whether programs have succeeded educationally. Too often, despite NYSDE urging, different testing instruments are employed across districts. At the approval stage, certain instruments may be required and accepted by Albany, but if the evaluation several years later employs others, the state thrust has been blunted and the question of effect further muddied. Nor is the task facilitated when federal funding is often delayed by belated congressional budget approval for ESEA I. Well-conceived programs, planned for September, which cannot begin until December when the funds finally come in, are off to a bad start—both educationally and methodologically.

New York City and ESEA I. New York City's size and complexity generate relationships which not even the next biggest city in the state knows. But because of its weight (70 percent) in ESEA I funds, some remarks are in order about how that city dealt with its allocation problems, not only with this title, but with the state's Urban Education Program; both serve much the same groups and have similar problems. These, in turn, bring in the issues of decentralization and UFT contracts.

Superimposed on the latter two legal and political issues is the problem of compensatory education. Much of the city's recent school politics is a controversy over the need for, nature of, and control over compensatory education. In the early sixties, there was a steadily growing realization that the achievement levels indicated a massive failure of the city's public school system. Much of this awareness can be attributed to the growing militancy and sense of community in the black and Puerto Rican areas where the children were so poorly served. The stress thereby engendered pressure for changes both in school operation and resource allocation, and moved various actors in the system to compete for influence over compensatory education.[43]

At first, integration was the focus of the struggle by many minority and other educational interest groups, but to little avail because of school system resistance.[44] However, the UFT interest in compensatory education began with the initiation of special service schools and their subsequent modification. These were poverty area schools which received extra staff complements to reduce class size—a major UFT objective.

Frustrated with unsuccessful integration and propelled by the momentum of Black Power and other ethnic movements, many groups pressured for community control of schools, particularly for the districts' right to operate their own compensatory programs. However, disagreement on such reorganization among the board, UFT, and communities led to bitter conflict in the 1968 and 1969 school years. Teacher strikes and political battles in the city and the state legislature resulted in the Decentralization Act in 1969. As of June 1970, community districts were to be run by boards elected locally. Within this framework of conflict and reorganization, the central board, the UFT, and the community boards competed for *control* over the manner in which ESEA I funds were to be allocated.

ESEA–Title I and Urban Education Programs. Before ESEA, programs for compensatory education had been negotiated ("mandated") between the central board and UFT, e.g., special service schools in the early sixties. After an agreement in 1963 among the board, the UFT, and the school administrators association, the innovation known as MES (More Effective Schools) was adopted; its expansion has been an issue for each subsequent contract. Reduction of class size, necessarily increasing the professional positions, is the predominant feature of MES. Thus, maximum pupil/teacher ratios are written into the contract for K-6 in each MES school; assorted specialists and administrators are required to man it; and extra preparation periods (when teachers have no teaching responsibilities) are written into the contract as well. Expansion of MES, therefore, means more teachers in the schools and less actual teaching time for each teacher, interests of UFT.

The MES schools were located in poverty areas in 1964-65. With ESEA funds in 1966, the number of MES schools was raised to twenty-one, and the funding shifted completely to that title. The actual number of MES schools was not expanded in the following year, but a new program in Five Primary Schools (5P) was begun. The grades and program were much the same as MES; but even smaller class sizes were mandated, and the school day lengthened. In 1966, the MES concept was enlarged again and the Strengthened Early Childhood (SEC) program appeared in the UFT contract; it mandated expansion of staff positions in other early childhood programs, predominantly in poor areas.

In the summer of 1967, the UFT sought an expansion of MES to forty-one schools which the board rejected. It believed that recent evaluations of the program did not justify doubling its per pupil expenditures through reallocation of another $9-10 million of ESEA I. However, two new items appeared in the ESEA I budget that year—SEC and 5P. Although it concentrated on pre-kindergarten through grade 2, the SEC formula was the same as that for MES—an allocation of $8.3 million went for small class sizes and more teacher aides. Five primary schools (5P) were also selected for $1.1 million funds for increasing staff much as with MES, in the same grade levels, and with mandated pupil-teacher maximums. Although not called MES schools, these new programs were roughly equivalent.

Clearly then, compensatory programs were being defined and federal funds used in terms of increased professional staffing. Funds for MES, SEC, and 5P grew from $7.9 million in 1966 (12 percent of ESEA I for New York City) to $51.3 million in 1971 (49 percent of ESEA I there). Simultaneously, community boards funds increased from none in 1966 to $16.2 million in 1970-71 (15 percent of New York City's ESEA I allocation). Although the trends in the relative influence of the central board, UFT, and community districts seem clear from such figures, the picture is more complex.

Another pool of resources for compensatory education became available to the city in 1968. Several state programs of this kind were consolidated, with an appropriation for two new categories of urban services: (1) Community Education Centers (CEC), and (2) Quality Incentive Programs. New York City's share of this first appropriation was $44.5 million, with which twelve CECs in different poor districts and an Experimental Elementary Program (EEP) were established. The CECs were administered by community boards, the EEP by the central board. Like MES and SEC, EEP is based on a union contract which mandates smaller class sizes and greater use of specialists and teacher aides.

Two key points characterize the allocations of these ESEA I and urban education funds. First, until the beginning of fiscal 1971, the central board had almost complete discretion over allocation of both pools of resources. So both the UFT and community boards were in competition for these resources—the UFT in mandating more staff and the community boards in pressing for more decentralized funds. The central board is under no legal command to use ESEA I funds for the mandated programs, but trapped between UFT demands and fiscal pressures of the city budget, it would be expected to use any available non-local resources to satisfy these demands.

Second, the allocations made reflect this board discretion and resource competition rather than the formulas or objectives of the legislation under which these funds come to the city. Eligibility for ESEA I city funds was determined according to objective poverty criteria, but the internal allocation was based on mandated programs and the board's approval of district applications. Urban education money followed the same pattern. Part of it went to programs defined and located in negotiation with the UFT, and part to the CECs in certain districts based upon their application. However, the Decentralization Act brought this competition to a head, affecting the current use of federal and state funds.

Effect of the Decentralization Act. The Act requires that funds allocated *to* the city on the basis of a formula be distributed among the districts within the city by a scheme which (1) reflects that formula and (2) is developed in consultation with the community school boards. By this provision the legislature stepped directly into the competition between the UFT and the community boards. It is a partial victory for the latter in that their consultation is required and the amount of discretion which the central board is able to shift to the UFT in negotiations is restricted. But the satisfaction of this requirement will also mean redistributing funds and disrupting programs of community boards as well as those mandated in the UFT contract.

Indeed, the central board cannot at the same time fulfill the Decentralization Act and its contractual obligations to the UFT. If ESEA I funds were redistributed, many MES, SEC, and 5P schools would be forced either to close down or switch to tax levy funding. But the union is unlikely to tolerate the former, and the school budget cannot tolerate the latter. Furthermore, it can be argued that the legislation voids any mandate the central board has to operate these UFT programs, and so the community boards are free to use those allocations for other purposes. Such redistribution would decrease urban education budgets in districts now using them. At the same time, maintenance of both mandated and existing urban education programs will result in an allocation pattern which clearly violates the law.

Predictably, the action in mid-1970 by the central board was a compromise, undertaken without community board consultation. Its key feature was to shift competition for control of these resources from one in which the board itself is in an intermediary position to one where the UFT and the community are in direct conflict. This was accomplished by distributing ESEA I money for 1970-71 in two parts: (1) Most districts with mandated programs in the current year would receive two-thirds of the projected cost of these programs; (2) ESEA I funds remaining would then be distributed according to each district's number of pupils eligible for free lunch.

Those districts receiving less than the previous year would receive an amount somewhere between the two, but still an overall reduction. The other districts would receive an increase in their decentralized allotments. But that allotment will not be all discretionary. The two-thirds funds must be used to carry one-third costs of mandated programs (MES, SEC, 5P), but: "it is within the prerogative of each district to determine the *exact* amount of money to be used for the program in so far as the district's plans do not deviate from the basic guidelines."[4][5]

By this, the central board committed ESEA I funds to cover two-thirds of the projected costs of mandated programs without regard to the formula by which those funds had come to the city—in partial disregard of the Decentralization Act. At the same time, this is only a partial commitment to the UFT contract. However, the community boards are expected to make up the rest of the commitment, although left the choice of the "exact amount." The community boards, of course, did not participate in the contract negotiations which produced the mandated programs, nor are they required under the federal or state regulations to use their ESEA I money to fulfill these mandated requirements. As a result, the district boards are squeezed between community demands to develop and control their own programs and threats of a UFT strike if the contract provisions are violated.

In New York City, the politics of allocation of state resources seems to apply to federal resources as well. Further evidence is found in the use of a ESEA I contingency fund to cover the outcome of negotiations in 1970 with the UFT paraprofessionals. In a central board budget release to community boards was an entry "Reserve for Innovation and Experimentation" for $6.8 million. But community board members were told that this "reserve" was in fact to cover an anticipated salary increase for paraprofessionals. While ESEA I funds were used here, the practice existed before with state funds. Because budgets must be published before salary negotiations are complete, the board must find some way to provide for anticipated increases and also conceal it from the UFT.

The role of the NYSDE in this process at the administrative level appears to be minimal. That is, routine processing of applications and approval of programs have little impact on allocation of ESEA I funds *within* New York City. Neither do the state guidelines include specific regulation of allocations within the city. Attempts at influence appear instead to be more informal, through NYSDE consultation with 110 Livingston Street. The most direct state intervention in city allocations seems the Decentralization Act itself. But its origins reflected the city's own political in-fighting, a struggle merely transferred to the legislature. The tendency for NYSDE and other government officers to remain aloof from the intra-city allocations does not seem to be substantially altered by this event.

Use of these federal resources could be constrained by enforcing the various guidelines and regulations, but these constraints are seldom considered seriously. The NYSDE tries, of course, but little effect is noted; suspending further ESEA I funds was tried once but did little good. Nor is the influence of the USOE much greater; some in Albany complain that Washington misperceives the complexity of New York City, treating it like Keokuk.

Vocational Education

Of all the federal school programs in New York, vocational education (VE) has been most free from federal control, most resistant to urban claims, and most protective of its long-established autonomy within the NYSDE. Much of this syndrome can be illustrated in the recent New York City report, *Washington to Albany to New York: The Games That Governments Play*, (hereafter cited as *WANY*).[46]

The Office of Occupational Education's (OOE) Albany staff is not very large for an agency disbursing about $275 million in 1970-71 (see Table 8-2). The small size is, in fact, the result of decentralized administration (but not control) resting in 73 centers, 37 community colleges jointly sponsored with local governments, 6 agricultural and technical colleges, 5 inner city centers, and 1,420 secondary programs.[47] All these enrolled over 622,000 students under about 20,000 teachers in that year; by 1975, OOE foresees over 882,000 students and almost 25,000 teachers. In 1971, VE funds financed 12 construction projects and over 5000 programs. Their gamut is astonishing, from the rotting core of New York City to rural backwaters, from secondary education to continuing programs, from the handicapped to the Indians.

Although the 1946, 1963, and 1968 vocational education amendments

Table 8-2

Estimated[a] Allocation of Federal Funds for State Vocational Education Programs, New York, 1970-71

Program/Purpose	Total Funds	Federal Funds	State Funds	Local Funds
Part B State Programs				
1. Secondary	138,253,312	2,753,312	63,500,000	72,000,000
2. Post Secondary	45,109,580	3,109,580	21,000,000	21,000,000
3. Adult	29,000,000	2,000,000	18,000,000	9,000,000
4a. Disadvantaged	15,109,580	3,109,580	6,500,000	5,500,000
4b. Handicapped	5,073,053	2,073,053	1,500,000	1,500,000
5. Construction of Area Vocational Schools	21,000,000	5,000,000	9,000,000	7,000,000
6. Guidance and Counseling	3,110,000	310,000	1,500,000	1,300,000
7. Contracted Instruction		b		
8. Ancillary Services (Total)	17,375,000	2,375,000	8,000,000	7,000,000
a. Administration and Supervision		2,160,000		
b. Evaluation		-0-		
c. Teacher Training		140,000		
d. Research and Demonstration Projects		-0-		
e. Curriculum Development		75,000		
Total	274,030,525	20,730,525	129,000,000	124,300,000
Section 102(b): State Programs				
Disadvantaged:	-0-	1,145,363	-0-	-0-

aEstimate of expenditures as projected in accordance with the policies and procedures in the State Plan.

bContracted instruction charged against local program purposes identified through local project applications.

Source: NYS VE Plan, 1970-71 Office of Occupational Education (Albany: NYSDE, 1970), IY, 119.

emphasized the drastically changing occupational context, in New York they have not had sufficient clout or credibility to move the OOE as far as the cities claim they were designed to. As New York City complained in the *WANY* report, "The Congress has made clear in the law that priority consideration for funds must first be given to economically depressed areas having large numbers of unemployed and educationally disadvantaged persons."[48] The commissioner and OOE do not see it that way. For the city, it is simply a matter of equating its state share of VE funds with its share of the poor and unemployed. For the OOE, however, this is a "simplistic" basis for allocation, as well as ignoring the city's reluctance to follow state and federal regulations. The two cannot even agree on the amount the city receives, as Table 8-3 shows.

Basic to understanding this conflict is the attitude in OOE about its program leadership. Those we interviewed said that after the 1963 amendments they had initiated regional assessment of VE needs, leading in part to the creation of BOCES; 40 percent of these groups' teaching time is currently used in VE courses.[49] One official, asked about OOE's main constituency, did not say "students," but "district superintendents," who are the directors of BOCES, none of which is urban centered. OOE's position was that it was free to use funds according to its own priorities, developed in turn by VE regional planning agencies. Of these nineteen, New York City is but one; even if the other five

Table 8-3
New York City and State Claims of City's Share in VE Funds

Program	NYC Claim Fiscal Year			NYS Claim Fiscal Year		
	1970	1971	1972	1968	1969	1970
1. Secondary	21.1%	33.3	32.1	11%	21	21
2. Post-secondary	0	0	0	25	14	20
3. Adult	29.6	31.5	26.5	17	21	30
4. Handicapped: Socioeconomically	68.2	50.0	42.8	29	27	43
Physically- Mentally	39.6	36.2	34.5	0	0	40
5. Private	0	0	0	0	0	0
6. Guidance	0	0	0	138	58	0
7. Construction	0	0	0	0	0	0
8. Ancillary Services	0	0	0	0	0	0
Total Percentage	19.2	19.8	21.9	13	13	19
State Total Allocation (millions)	$20.7	$22.7	$24.8	$16.8	$17.0	$20.7

Source: *WANY*, 47, 57. Abstracted from each government's figures.

large cities could bespeak only urban interests, the urban voice in these planning councils would still not be large. Nor can it be when the state advisory council lists only ten of its thirty members from that city, and only one from its school system (only five from state schools). In short, this oldest of federal aid programs has developed in the state an orientation that is either indifferent or inimical to big city problems.

This sense of vested interest is reflected also in OOE attitudes toward federal pressure. Because Washington provides only about 10 percent of New York's VE funds, a OOE official concluded, "this is administered as a state program without federal influence." He judged federal contacts were made only about once every six weeks—with the regional director. He thought too many regulations came with the federally mandated 15-15-10 percentages; this, he said, "shows distrust of the states' ability to do the job." He saw the federal presence as too often merely complaints over "picayune" details of accounting, and never of programs; he could recall no federal program objection since the 1963 amendments. He saw the problem as not Washington, but regional officials located in New York City; they lack "expertise and understanding needed to make pragmatic judgments and Washington's concerns can't get through this regional block."

This official asserted that his is not a federal but a state office, and the function of federal law is to "reimburse the state for expenditures it made" under its own criteria.

New York is one of 5 states which reject—and quite firmly—any disbursement formula for the 6.5 percent of these national funds they have been receiving. As Table 8-2 shows, state funds emphasize quite strongly VE in secondary schools; federal funds have been used for more diverse programs. Much of that stems from the 15-15-10 percent of federal funds which must be set aside for programs 2 and 4 in Tables 8-2 and 8-3.

The operations of OOE with VE funds have "closed system" symptoms. This has been noted in its perception of its constituency—superintendents. It may be also seen in who is involved in OOE's decisionmaking.

Thus, the state advisory council plaintively requested regents to "utilize more fully [its] potential" and that "before the regents prepare a position paper on occupational education, they call upon [it] to make recommendations." As much as one-half to one-third of its members are regularly absent, possibly because of a sense of not being wanted. Certainly the one of 30 members to represent New York City schools did not feel it important to attend many meetings, and none on the state plan—the council's central work.[50]

Similar signs of a closed system are seen in the regents' mid-1971 policy statement on VE. Emphasis in short-range plans should be on continuing what exists already, and

... less upon initiation of costly new programs than upon continuation and acceleration of existing trends in program redesign, more efficient and effective use of available resources, and greater understanding and support of occupational education among students, parents, educators, and the general public. The Regents do, however, recommend immediate action to close gaps at the elementary, secondary, and adult levels which inhibit development of and access to an occupational education continuum.[51]

Of the fifteen objectives of their long-range program, in only two do the words "innovative" and "initiate" appear, and both are part of other less change-oriented qualifiers. Indeed, these objectives are replete with system-maintenance words like "continue to," and "strengthen."

But the key closed quality is OOE's refusal—despite federal and city pressures—to change the allocation formula so as to send more money to the big six. The federal law [Sec. 123 (a) (5)] requires the state plan to show how these funds will equitably meet the four major needs which precipitated the 1968 amendments: manpower and VE needs, state and local ability to support VE, and VE's relative cost. New York City's complaint describes two distributional processes, informal and formal.

Informally, the local agencies submit their various programs to the staff of [OOE]. Following a series of informal conferences, an allocation is provided by the state, and the local agency is responsible for establishing its own priorities to come within that set allocation, or the local agency may try to push the state for additional funds if it can convince state officials of their program priorities.[52]

Thus, when New York City submitted $11 million for VE in 1971-72, the OOE approved all its programs, but allocated only $7.35 million. When the city commission sought to ascertain why, OOE's Director Robert S. Seckendorf was reported replying that he did not know; his staff determined it. He did claim guidelines operated—degree of innovativeness, an increase in enrollment in VE programs, and submission of long-range plan to the state. But the city report complained, "These elements somehow play a role in the amounts allocated to local agencies, but to what extent and how exactly they are applied is again not known or made public."[53]

While this may determine actual allocations, a formal procedure also operates, laid out in the state plan in extraordinary detail.[54] Local budgets are submitted in relationship to the state long-range plan and to area manpower and VE needs. Priorities seem to involve weighing the relative wealth of the district and its plan's costs. Yet in none of this is there what the *WANY* report calls a "numerical or formula weighting system to determine how, in fact, a particular program is rated." They thus charge that decisions are based on state officials "rather subjective and arbitrary judgments."[55]

While New York City residents admitted recent increases in VE funds (*WANY* reported it had nearly doubled since 1963),[56] they felt more the enormity of VE needs in their population. Against 20 percent of VE funds, the city commission reported in their borders: 49 percent of all jobs in the state; 39

percent of secondary school students; 58 percent of high school dropouts; 70 percent of educationally disadvantaged; and 62 percent of economically disadvantaged. In addition, costs in New York City were abnormally high and income frozen; 80 percent of its property tax (already over 99 percent of the state constitution limit) was committed to non-school purposes vs. 64 percent in other cities and 48 percent in the rest of the state. Teacher salaries were well over the state average; costs for school sites per acre were $193,376 versus $3,047 elsewhere in the state.

With such data before them, the city board of education appealed to Commissioner Nyquist in late 1970 for "an objective formula" for allocation which would provide it $8-10 million more annually. In blunt words, supported by his version of law, data, and events, the commissioner rejected the claim on several grounds.[57]

First, the law did not require percentage matching of local VE spending, nor a weighting or formula distribution plan. Other states had retained after 1963 the old formula of reimbursing local VE costs on a pro rata basis. But New York shifted to direct grants for new programs, rather than supporting continuing ones, with resulting expanded services to those not reached before. The state underwrote start-up costs, but the district picked up costs once underway. Formula ideas stemmed from the USOE's, reflecting older ideas of financing, and, the commissioner claimed, these were designed to evade prohibitions against them in the 1968 amendments. He noted that his state had resisted strong federal pressure to revise its state plan to include a formula; other states were trying untested formulas just to get their plans approved, even though reporting problems with them. Second, because of the variance among areas and districts in their needs, an equitable formula could not be devised for the eight VE programs noted in the tables above. Third, the city had not met state standards; it had not drawn an acceptable long-range plan; sought to expand enrollment with what it had; or showed strong effort to meet its vocational needs. A subsequent meeting between these two levels merely reaffirmed their opposition, although they agreed to work more closely thereafter.

The *WANY* report concluded with a condemnation of the program's "failures . . . which are the responsibility of officials at every level of government." The federals had not pushed enough their statutory objectives and had permitted different allocational devices. The state lacked a "systematic" means of allocating aid. The city showed the lack of effort which the commissioner had pointed out, as well as failing to take the state to court. It concluded:

In the end, the most disturbing fact is that if a federal program like VE with all of its law, guidelines, policies, and criteria can be distorted by those who implement the law, then surely other more significant programs can be similarly distorted. The purpose of this law, as with others, is not to serve the subjective interests of government employees or officials at whatever level they may exist; it is to serve the needs of those who must have such assistance in order to cope with this society.[58]

NDEA-Title III and ESEA-Title II

NDEA III's long-term charge to improve academic courses and ESEA II's thrust to provide library materials for the educationally disadvantaged have recently been joined in New York. For both, the Bureau of School Libraries now provides project criteria, sets application guidelines, and approves and evaluates funded programs. Since the NYSDE coordinates the two programs in much of its funding, NDEA III and ESEA II should be examined jointly.[59]

NDEA-Title III. When it was founded in 1958, the New York NDEA III operation was a small unit; the office spent its efforts in "final claim audit," i.e., auditing claims for reimbursement submitted by a district after expenditure. No concept of program direction of such claims seems to have entered the picture.[60]

With the coming of ESEA, NDEA became part of a new federal aid office. It still remained within the finance division where it had been since 1963. Claims were handled seasonally; consultants, working for about two to three months, would dispense with the claims; certainly no monitoring was done except for the largest outlays. By 1968, however, NDEA III leaders Richard Shilling and Frank O'Conner had developed two priority schemes. "Priority one," reimbursed at 50 percent, went for resource programs of "enrichment," while "priority two," reimbursed at 40 percent, went for less effective programs, such as mass purchases for the film library. Because of the competition for these funds, usually only the first priority programs could be funded. Consultants looked for plans which could be implemented quickly (would make an immediate difference); which students could use and touch (unlike lecture materials); and which involved little remodeling.

At present, NDEA awards are competitive, based on the merit of the application, and emphasize high quality programs; the state must match half the project amount. The objects of such awards are "for the purchase of prior approval equipment, materials, and minor remodeling for strengthening education programs in [nine specified] academic subjects. . ." Those eligible are public schools and regional BOCES. Priority currently is on programs emphasizing reading, redesign (devising model schools), and drug-environmental education. Evidence of comprehensive planning is urged, while seven criteria specify desirable expenditures. All these focus on the enrichment of the nine critical academic subjects. But the NDEA III administrators also emphasize another quality which does not appear in printed guidelines. They wish these funds to go to the "better than average student who needs assistance just as much as the disadvantaged," as one put it to an interviewer. Whatever the criteria, no special urban bias could be seen in the allocations as late as fiscal 1969. The big six schools' 39 percent of the enrollment received 39 percent of Title III's $4.3 million.

ESEA-Title II. The original ESEA II allocations were per capita by district. But when these were heavily criticized for falsely assuming equal needs for each student, allocation shifted to funding major library resource needs.

These funds are dispersed in two ways. Basic Grants, approximately 70 percent of the allocation in 1971-72, are based on a "relative need" formula: "the degree of financial need . . . the degree of reading achievement deficiency, and the number of public and private school students in a district." There are priorities for elementary school libraries (particularly where weak or absent) and for reading-motivation programs. Divided equally between written and audio-visual materials, the entire grant must go for school library resources.

The remaining 30 percent of the funds are dispensed through Special Purpose Grants for developing "exemplary library media centers." The Special Purpose Grants were a New York innovation in ESEA's first year. USOE fully approves and encourages the concept in other states, half of which now use them. Grants are competitive, and available only to public agencies (including BOCES), although "available on loan in an equitable amount" to private schools. Priority is on centers with the highest librarian standards that involve new resource uses to enhance learning and focus on critical schooling needs that a district identifies. To that end, the ESEA II office highly values grants reflecting "community planning for educational redesign" of the local district; specific guidelines help further define this goal. If such pre-planning is not undertaken, then the office values programs that focus upon two statewide needs—reading and drug-environmental abuse. Twenty specific criteria detail what this office has in mind.

These two grant types have mostly benefitted large urban districts. Thus, in fiscal 1969, the big six districts—with 39 percent of the enrollment—received 49 percent of the $4.1 million ESEA II funds, but only 31 percent of state revenue. The Basic Grants were then limited to 200 out of the 600 districts then in the state. This provided more concentrated funds for urban districts with the greatest needs, deprivations, shortages of library resources, and numbers of students. Of the many criteria the guidelines suggest, emphasis has shifted from, first, elementary school libraries, then in 1969 to library programs for special target groups, including linguistically disadvantaged, ESEA I eligibles and the handicapped. Most recently the emphasis has shifted again, to library materials concentrating on the arts and humanities and on reading programs.

Administration by NYSDE's Title II office is assisted by a state advisory committee, although it is not required by law. Represented here are varied interests—New York City and parochial schools, librarians, audiovisual experts, superintendents, and minority groups.[61] Interviewers report, however, that the director makes most critical decisions, although both director and advisory council still reflect a strong urban bias. Thus, while the minimum grant allowed was decreased in 1970 to $1,500, there has been no disposition to spread the funds among all districts. Too, the state office has strictly forbidden distribution of the Basic Grant monies within a district on a per capita basis.

In 1970-71, NYSDE combined NDEA III with ESEA II to give both a library resources orientation. The "unigrant" was developed to encourage planning and to streamline application processing by combining two or more programs of grants.[62] Competitively, a district's unigrant has higher priority than its application for a separate ESEA or NDEA grant. Titles I and II of ESEA at one time had combined personnel and resources grants. When USOE tightened the comparability requirements, ESEA II funds could no longer be used if a librarian was to be funded with ESEA I or other federal sources. In 1970-71, 117 unigrants were approved as well as 248 separate NDEA III grants. No figures were available, but officials thought a majority of all grants now seek combined federal aid for educational programs. If so, the union of the two programs is going far to achieve its primary purpose—a program rather than shopping list approach for NDEA III. Instead of using its money like an item veto, the office could now use it to stimulate districts to plan for their needs in course materials.

In this marriage, the role of the state commissioner was not unlike that of the father with the shotgun. His rearrangement of priorities, his shift from per capita to program funding, and finally his combining the two under one direction reflect the discretion allotted the NYSDE under the law. In comparison with the definition of objectives and funding in the national law or the federal guidelines, NYSDE has exercised strong direction in the establishment of goals, methods, and funding alternatives.

This direction was not achieved without a political context, one element of which is the federal presence. In the early days there was far more supervision of NDEA III than at present. One official in the Division of Finance recalls that the "fed" used to analyze NDEA grants, claim-by-claim; a year or two later, USOE would issue a list of grants exceptions. There ensued a negotiation game, partly with the local district (whose money was long spent and which never was required by Albany to return funds) and partly with USOE. The latter engaged in a paper debate for as much as two to three years, but as a state official put it, "These things just melted away like a tired old soldier." Most recently, however, USOE has shifted interest to encouraging programs, like the union with ESEA II or the unigrants. Now USOE recognizes the problem raised by paperwork delay. But its management suggestions are still being resisted except for accounting procedures.

Similarly, ESEA II administrators note that USOE involvement was "more regulatory in tone than now." Thus, Washington first resisted and then approved programs for exemplary library projects. But it has also been opposed to per capita formulas which dilute ESEA II effects, and it has forced the shift to the relative needs formula. As one Albany source put it, "They were right in there on top of us in devising that formula but since then they have been reasonable in reviewing our work." The Basic Grant is "highly political," said another, because its proportion of all ESEA II grants can be shifted by the state. Hence the office is under pressure to allocate it in a way which satisfies the big six districts, especially New York City. There is evidence that this office has had to increase grants to the latter because the city's political pressure—or at least highly publicized complaints—got too strong.

There is yet another political dimension—local districts and the evaluation process. There is evidence that little evaluation has been done and that districts are not questioned extensively on their use of funds. In ESEA II, most review goes to the largest grants; on minor grants, "We take the district's word on it. On Special Purpose Grants, the office can get some sense of the difference made over a period of years by the introduction of library resources—one clue is whether the district adopts "hot" ideas of innovative instruction *after* the grant is made. Control can operate in the approval process, of course, by application of detailed criteria; in 1970-71, about 150 of 350 grant applications were approved.

But post-audit is scanty at best. Evaluation forms are provided, of course, but they are delayed by many factors, some discussed earlier for ESEA I. When, as in 1970 for New York City, funds are held back, it is only to enforce reporting requirements and not to affect program contents. Also, in both NDEA III and ESEA II, state officials shrug and say that it is hard to do much when the money has already been spent. Certainly few site inspections take place, about fifty in 1970-71 for ESEA II and a tenth of that for NDEA-Title III, and only then for large cost overruns. Yet, despite these limitations of control, as one ESEA II official stated firmly, because of this program "I can walk into any school in this state which has had large dollops of Title II and see kids carrying out a specific, individual learning task." Or, as an associate of the commissioner noted to a reviewer, "The districts must have bought the materials, because after all, the stuff got into the schools and is still there." Nevertheless, the state's deference to local districts—through the gentlemen's agreement of state and local professionals—blurs any clarification of what happened educationally afterwards.

ESEA-Title III

ESEA-Title III's purpose of creating supplementary centers and services for educational planning has been met in New York by a system of sixteen "regional centers," the absence of any clear formula for dispersing the funds (but an urban bias), and some effort to use the money to stimulate intradepartmental thinking about state priorities. Unfortunately, no good measure exists of their effectiveness.

The program developed amid already existing regional systems for educational services, the Boards of Cooperative Educational Services. These BOCES fought for survival with the regional centers and finally merged in many aspects. The allocations over time clearly favor the centers. While local districts of BOCES share ESEA III funds with the centers, the latter's share has increased from an original one-fifth to a present one-third. That increase represents an implicit peace treaty between the centers and BOCES. The boards could have obtained all the funds when the program began, as they already provided cooperative and supplementary services for districts. They did not monopolize the funds, however, because the program's sponsors feared BOCES would be dominated by traditionalists, while new ideas were needed. Too, BOCES had no urban base, so new organs had to be created for the cities. In short, the regional centers provided new alternatives and an urban thrust.

Part of the allocation decision may have reflected Commissioner Allen's desire to stimulate local planning with an organization not identified with past programs. Allen saw ESEA III as a means for decentralized dissemination of the results of demonstration programs. Too, money could be put into the development of ideas that preliminary research had indicated were promising. Whatever the reasons for their separation, however, both centers and BOCES have increasingly been melded under the office of district superintendent. The increasing ESEA III funds for the centers suggests that future allocations will more strongly emphasize regional administration.

The Title III allocational formula is among the vaguest found in this state survey. Clearly, equal distribution among districts is down-graded and on-going projects are up-graded. Clearly, too, there is an urban bias; while New York's dollar totals dropped between fiscal 1969 and 1971 from over $13 to about $9 million, the big six urban districts have received about 50 percent of the funds, although they have 39 percent of the state's enrollment. Those interviewed talked not about a formula but "rules of thumb"—concern with how much New York City should receive; with how to maintain an equitable mix among regions (while ignoring intra-regional distributions), and with how to allocate between small projects (some being the most innovative) and large urban ones (having the greatest need). Occasional thought has been given to a single vast project, but nothing has yet materialized.

The funds provide for planning both in Albany and locally. The regional centers currently are restricted to "provide services not available through the BOCES." In practice, this means they assist the state ESEA III office in various ways: dissemination of project information; original screening, preparation, and coordination of fund applications; evaluation of on-going projects; assessment of local needs; and more recently guidance of BOCES or districts in comprehensive planning.

Within the NYSDE, funds have gone for the administration of planning and innovation for the whole state. This is linked directly to the elementary, secondary, and continuing education sections of the department, and the ESEA III staff also has direct access to the deputy commissioner in charge of these sums. The staff provide part of the stimulus to needs planning discussed earlier. A state advisory council, drawn from urban, suburban, and rural schools, as well as industry and universities, assists in the establishment of state priorities, reads project proposals from all agencies, and performs some site evaluations. The

ESEA III staff reports a close working relationship with the council and takes its recommendations.

The staff, along with the regional centers and council, had devised various lists of priorities and needs that have been the source of continuing friction with the USOE. The controversy has been over the proper scope of activities. The NYSDE wanted the entire department to undertake such needs assessment, consonant with the earlier noted interests of Commissioners Allen and Nyquist. In addition, the ESEA III office wanted to apply its innovations throughout the department. Washington sought to limit both activities, but seemingly in vain. This needs assessment activity, incidentally, was a model grassroots operation; meetings were held in all sixteen regional centers, leading to eighteen "critical needs."

Need perception and priority of this kind can be illustrated from the 1970-71 work. As one observer noted, "Not all the centers put 'more money' at the top of the list." Highest priorities were given reading programs (we earlier noted how this permeates other programs), New York City decentralization, and "redesigning of education." The last involves planning the redesign of school districts in terms of four prototypes including increased parent-student participation in school planning. Yet again, the process of translating such priorities into fund allocations is not clear. At any rate, the realities of a retrenching financial scene have currently restricted most funds just to on-going projects.

The evaluation of state and local planning functions under this program reveals once again general reluctance to do much of it. Little of the state office's time and energy goes to monitoring and evaluating local projects. It is assumed that the latter are not in trouble unless they ask for help. Rather, the state ESEA III staff claims it is assisted in this function by others—NYSDE's divisions of finance and evaluation, the advisory council, and regional centers. Office of Education and state department officials think this is abrogation of the Title III office's duties; the Title III staff sees it as a highly important way of disseminating innovative educational ideas and programs. Also, staff members believe that by involving others they have to some extent achieved coordination with similar state and federal programs, as well as exerted influence on the entire education sections of NYSDE.

In sum, New York's ESEA III office considers its objectives to induce innovation both in the local district and NYSDE. Despite some USOE objections about the breadth of these goals, federal funds continue to be used in this way. Certainly NYSDE's highest officials think that much of the department's recent consideration of needs assessment and priority planning stems from this office's efforts. The Title III office's local thrust, on the other hand, has been to foster regionalism as an alternative to state control, as well as to stimulate district assessment and planning functions.

What have been the results? The program's input has been into the cities. The commissioners' flexible interpretation of ESEA -Title III's purpose has been the key force providing strong leadership for planning. Yet it is also fair to say that the evaluation of such effort, whether at Albany or locally, does not exist, so that one cannot determine how well the interpretation has worked out. Clearly, it has worked to co-opt local professionals into district, region, and state-level decision making, a reflection of the reference group orientation laid out earlier. This lack of evaluation is unfortunate; it would be quite valuable to know whether this innovative, decentralized application of centralized encouragement to adopt new behavior has worked. Once again the failure of evaluation has lost some important information to the whole system.

V. Conclusion

In New York, Commissioners Allen and Nyquist attempted to establish priorities and coordinate planning for the allocation of federal aid. Increasingly, however, the legislature has intervened in the NYSDE's administration of federal funds. The Decentralization Act specified that the distribution of ESEA I funds within New York City's community districts must parallel the state's method of allocation of Title I funds within counties. With its vocal rural group, burgeoning suburban faction, and strong anti-New York City sentiment, the New York legislature has sought to use federal aid as a possible offset for state aid, since the urban areas receive only 31 percent of the state aid. This view of federal aid is evident in the legislature's insistence that the state's Urban Education Program be evaluated jointly with ESEA I.

While New York has introduced many innovations that have been praised and adopted elsewhere, it is difficult to measure the effectiveness of the programs or the achievement of the objectives because evaluation procedures are neither coordinated nor enforced. This situation exists for three reasons. First, the particular relationships between NYSDE personnel and their reference groups militate against a rigorous examination of projects. Second, the districts do not always gather or transmit the data requisite for effective evaluation. Third, is the problem presented by the position that New York City holds in the allocation of federal funds. Since it receives such a large proportion of the federal funds, its inability or unwillingness to collect essential data impedes evaluation; through such action (or inaction), New York City erects a barrier that the NYSDE and its evaluation procedures have yet to penetrate.

Notes

1. That finding emerges after careful statistical controls; see the macro-analysis studies cited in Ira Sharkansky and Richard I. Hofferbert, "Dimensions of State Politics, Economics, and Public Policy," *American Political Science Review*, 63 (969), 867-79.

2. On innovation, see Jack L. Walker, "The Diffusion of Innovation Among the American States," ibid., 880-99. The salary ranking is found in Edgar Fuller and Jim B. Pearson, *Education in the States: Nationwide Development since 1900* (Washington, D.C.: National Education Assn., 1969), 102. New York's per capita aid to local schools rose between 1900 and 1966 from $3.7 to $283 million, an increase from 11 to 44 percent of local school costs; see ibid., 178-80.

3. Edmund H. Crane et al., "New York State Department," in Jim B. Pearson and Edgar Fuller, *Education in the States: Historical Development and Outlook* (Washington, D.C., National Education Assn., 1969), p. 864.

4. Consolidation figures are from ibid., 867-68, and commissioner's office.

5. Stephen Bailey, et al., *Schoolmen and Politics; A Study of State Aid to Education in the Northeast* (Syracuse: Syracuse University Press, 1962), pp. 8-9, 27.

6. The New York program does have more of an adult education component, however.

7. At lower levels, relations between the NYSDE and the legislature also remain close. In fact, much of the bill drafting for financial items is handled by the Division of Finance and Research. At the request of the legislature, experts in this division do cost projections for major bills with fiscal implications, clearly an assistance to the committee in its decision making.

8. In the 1970 Assembly, all but one legislator voted for the state school aid formula bill; in 1971, somewhat more, but still a small minority, broke the consensus.

9. Bailey, et al., op. cit., 22-23.

10. See the seminal work in Paul R. Mort, *State Support for Public Schools* (New York: Teachers College, Columbia University, 1926). For an excellent review of this history, see R.L. Johns, "State Financing of Elementary and Secondary Education," in Fuller and Pearson, op. cit., ch. 4.

11. The quotations above and below are from Bailey et al., op. cit., pp. 27, 30.

12. Michael D. Usdan, *The Political Power of Education in New York State* (New York: Teachers College, Columbia University, 1963), and his revised view, *The Political Power of Education in New York State: A Second Look* (New York: NYS School Boards Assn., 1967).

13. For rankings in New York, see Johns, op. cit., 180.

14. Bailey et al., op. cit., p. 47.

15. Ibid., p. 11.

16. For a popular review of this force, see Warren Moscow, *Politics in the Empire State* (New York: Knopf, 1948).

17. Robert E. Jennings, "State Political Process Change and Educational Interest Group Political Behavior," paper presented to the American Educational Research Assn., 1971, pp. 11-12.

18. Robert E. Jennings and Mike M. Millstein, "Perceptions of the Educational Policy-Making Process in New York State: Educational Interest Group Leaders and State Legislators," paper presented to the American Educational Research Assn., 1971, p. 13. They received responses from 60 percent of assemblymen and 47 percent of senators.

19. Interview with the author.

20. Harmon Zeigler and Michael Baer, *Lobbying* (Belmont, Calif.: Wordsworth, 1969), pp. 117, 195.

21. The change added 7 percent in state aid to the operating costs of the "big six" city school systems.

22. See Frederick M. Wirt et al., *On the City's Rim: Politics and Policy in Suburbia* (Lexington, Mass.: Heath, 1972).

23. On this and other patterns of school lobbies, see Lawrence Iannaccone, *Politics in Education* (New York: Center for Applied Research in Education, 1967); Michael D. Usdan, "The Role and Future of State Educational Coalitions," *Educational Administration Quarterly*, 5 (1969), 26-42.

24. Interview with the author.

25. Between August 31 and Christmas of 1971, courts in three states overturned the local property tax as unconstitutional for depriving children of equal funds for their schooling. These were: *Serrano v. Priest*, 40 U.S. Law Week 2129 (California Supreme Court); *Van Dusartz v. Hatfield*, 40 Ibid., 2228 (Federal District Court in Minnesota); and *Rodriguez v. San Antonio Independent School District*, No. 68-175-SA (W.D. Texas).

26. However, that 7 percent is larger proportionately than the 4-5 percent which federal provides of the state's total public school expenditures.

27. Daniel Katz and Robert L. Kahn, *The Social Psychology of Organizations* (New York: Wiley, 1966), p. 286. On the role theory urged here, Norman Luttberg, ed. *Public Opinion and Public Policy: Models of Political Linkage* (Homewood, Ill.: Dorsey, 1968), pp. 1-10, Parts V-VI, and literature presented there.

28. For a historical review of this resistance, see V.O. Key, Jr., *The Administration of Federal Grants to the States* (Chicago: Public Administration Service, 1937).

29. Calculated from data in Fifth Annual Report of the Advisory Council on State Departments of Education, Table 3, p. 15. Rank order correlation coefficients show no relationship of this ratio to total expenditures for SDE operations (0.00) or to size of the federal grants to SEA operations (−.09).

30. On other evidence of the effect of differing political cultures on school policy, see Frederick M. Wirt and Michael W. Kirst, *The Political Web of American Schools* (Boston: Little, Brown, 1972), ch. 7.

31. See *Title I ESEA, Annual Report 1968-69* (Albany: Division of Evaluation, NYSDE), p. 50.

32. For school politics in this city, see Martin Mayer, *The Teachers Strike*

(New York: Harper & Row, 1968); David Rogers *110 Livingston Street* (New York: Random House, 1969); George R. La Noue, "The Politics of School Decentralization," paper presented at the American Political Science Convention, 1970, to appear as part of LaNoue and Bruce Smith, *The Politics of School Decentralization* (Lexington, Mass.: Heath, 1972); Nancy Bordier, "An Eastonian Systems Approach to Analysis of Education Politics," Ph.D. dissertation, Columbia University, 1971; and Boulton H. Demas, *The School Elections: A Critique of the 1969 New York City School Decentralization*, (New York: Institute for Community Studies, Queens College, 1970).

33. *Title I of ESEA: Is It Helping Poor Children?* (Washington, D.C.: Washington Research Project and NAACP Legal Defense and Educational Fund, 1969).

34. For a broader review of this first year in the nation, see Stephen K. Bailey and Edith K. Mosher, *ESEA: The Office of Education Administers A Law* (Syracuse: Syracuse University Press, 1968).

35. Section 116.4.

36. The current officers are, in order, Lorne H. Woollatt, Alan G. Robertson, and Leo D. Doherty.

37. See Bureau of Urban and Community Programs Evaluation, *Preparing Program Objectives* (Albany: NYSDE, April, 1971). Other examples are Division of Evaluation, *Title I ESEA, 1968-69 Annual Report* (Albany: NYSDE, n.d.) and Division of Education for the Disadvantaged, *Federally Funded Educational Programs for Disadvantaged Children and Youth*, ESEA Title I 1968-69 (Albany: NYSDE, n.d.).

38. See Bureau of Urban and Community Programs Evaluation, *A Primer for Making Site Visits* (Albany: NYSDE, August, 1970).

39. See Office of Research and Evaluation, *Assessment and Evaluation Handbook*, Title I ESEA (Albany: NYSDE, n.d.).

40. Federal/State Task Force on Education Evaluation, *An Overview* (printed pamphlet without origins given).

41. Figures from report cited in Michael J. Wargo et al., *Further Examination of Exemplary Programs for Educating Disadvantaged Children* (Palo Alto: American Institutes for Research, 1971). Sec. 1.

42. Division of Education, *Title I ESEA, 1968-69 Annual Report*, Part IV and Appendixes.

43. The Eastonian framework of analysis is most helpful in giving coherence to what occurred; for such analysis of these events, see Bordier, loc. cit.

44. The methods of delay are found in Rodgers, loc. cit.

45. Letters from central board June 15, 1970, and another n.d. but after June 26, 1970. Emphasis in original.

46. Commission on State-City Relations, *Washington to Albany to New York: "The Games that Governments Play"* (New York: City of New York, Oct. 3, 1971). Hereafter this is cited as *WANY*.

47. See Office of Occupational Education, "A State Plan for the Administration of Vocational Education under the Vocational Education Amendment of 1968," (Albany: NYSDE, May 22, 1970), Parts II-III, pp. 64-66, 119 ff. Hereafter this will be referred to as "State Plan."

48. *WANY*, p. 4.

49. Ibid., p. 52 note, is the city's figure, however.

50. Ibid., Tab C, 10.

51. Regents of the University of the State of New York, *Occupational Education*, (Albany: NYSDE, May, 1971), p. 14; the proposals referred to below are at ibid., pp. 15-16.

52. *WANY*, p. 13.

53. Preceding quotations are from ibid., pp. 13-14.

54. "State Plan."

55. Preceding from *WANY*.

56. "Double" figure is from ibid., p. 17; other data from ibid., p. 17-18.

57. Commissioner Nyquist's full reply is at ibid., Tab G.

58. Conclusions are amplified in ibid., pp. 21-22.

59. In this section, all quotations, except when tied to a person, are drawn from Bureau of School Libraries, *Planning Guide, ESEA II-NDEA III*, (Albany: NYSDE, 1971-72 ed.).

60. An excellent brief evaluation of the program in this period found great decentralization; effects hard to ascertain; no federal controls; and little local evaluation of moneys spent. See Bureau of Department Programs Evaluation, *NDEA Title III, An Evaluation of the Program in New York State*, (Albany: NYSDE, n.d., but c. 1965).

61. The UFT requested, but was denied, membership by the then ESEA II director because, he asserted, the union had no special claim to knowledge of library programs.

62. Including the Special Purpose Incentive Grant for "elementary school library media centers in existing [schools] without such facilities and programs." This totals 5 percent of the state's allocation, with no grant over $20,000, and all grants competitive according to six detailed criteria.

9 Intergovernmental Relations: Conclusions and Recommendations

Joel S. Berke and
Michael W. Kirst

In the course of our studies, we have investigated both the fiscal allocations and the administrative practices that determine the distribution of federal aid to education. In designing our research we have sought to maximize the yield for decision makers, the interested public, and scholars who want to draw upon the experience of the past in order to improve existing programs or to design new policies for federal assistance to education.

Accordingly, we focused our major energies on the areas of important policy relevance about which there was the least available knowledge. The first such question we sought to answer was: "What kind of districts are benefiting from the federal programs and in what proportions?" The second major question was: "What is the role of the state political and organizational factors in determining the patterns of allocation to those districts?" The first eight chapters have described much of what we learned on those topics.

Our purpose, however, was more ambitious than to answer those questions alone. In this chapter we have placed the states in their federal context by putting more emphasis on the vertical dimensions of their relationships. We turn first to a discussion of the dynamics of intergovernmental relations among federal, state, and local administrators. Then we shall isolate some of the problems that occur at each level. Finally, we shall attempt to summarize the major conclusions of the study and discuss the major policy recommendations which our studies have suggested to us.

The Dynamics of Intergovernmental Relations

As this study has shown, the major federal categorical programs are administered in substantial part by the states.[1] ESEA, for example, was founded on the basis of "creative tension" between federal administrators wielding general guidelines for local categorical programs and state departments of education with sole power to approve specific local project proposals. For the first time, big city school districts were confronted by state departments of education with federal money sufficient to support an effective staff capability.[2]

USOE exercises control through its regulations that have the force of law and the guidelines that interpret the "legalese" in the regulations. Guidelines also include a mixture of USOE advice and suggestions which are legally non-binding. Some USOE programs employ periodic and supplementary program memoranda which presumably clarify regulations and are effectively legal mandates. These three different instruments of federal control—regulations, guidelines, and memoranda—confuse SEAs and LEAs. This confusion permits slippage and evasion, especially when supplementary federal program memoranda have changed longstanding policies.

In short, the limits of USOE legal muscle are unclear. Since funds are almost never withheld, there is virtually no court precedent on the "gray areas" in binding or non-binding guidelines and program memoranda.[3] Occasionally, federal auditors recover funds where SEAs and LEAs have violated explicit regulations. More often, suspected or actual violations are negotiated informally among professional educators at local, state, and federal levels. The outcome of the negotiations is usually similar to the Federal Trade Commission's "consent decree"—a promise not to continue the questionable practice with no penalties for prior actions.[4]

If federal influence were widespread and highly effective, state and local responses would tend to be uniform. As we have seen, this is not congruent with our findings. On the other hand, states do respond in a general manner to federal influence. Most money is spent for specific categories under NDEA or vocational education. Federal results have come gradually in such areas as concentration of Title I funds and parent involvement. There is still a considerable distance to go but recent USOE actions on audit exceptions under Title I promise more progress.

Except for Title I ESEA, large federal categorical programs are administered through state plans. Since 1917, when the Smith-Hughes Vocational Education Act inaugurated the use of state plans, USOE has never denied any vocational education plans, although several have been delayed until suitable corrections were made. State plans consist primarily of a repetition of the federal regulations. They contain little specific information on the intra-state allocation of money, the preferred educational programs thrusts, or criteria for approving or rejecting LEA proposals. Consequently, the state plans reveal little about the operation or funding criteria of a federal-state program.

The negotiations between the state and local levels reflect varying degrees of the "religion of localism." LEAs frequently try to reword their own priorities so that they fit loosely within the federal categorical regulations. Open conflict with the SEA is rare, and substantive disagreements can be ironed out among professionals. Some states go beyond the federal guidelines in a positive fashion of additional requirements to target aid to disadvantaged pupils; others do not even bother to enforce basic federal regulations. Although states are distributed all along this continuum, federal policymakers often act with one end or the other in mind.

One of the difficulties in funding results from what David Porter calls "multipocketed budgeting."[5] Federal aid must be seen as an integral part of the local district's entire funding structure. School districts have multiple sources of revenue, including bonds, property taxes, several categories of state aid, and numerous federal categories. As the number of income sources increases, the ability of any single supplier to trace the impact of his contribution decreases. Administrators tend to use those resources with the greatest number of restrictions first, and save those with the fewest restrictions until last, i.e., a propensity to conserve all-purpose resources.

Federal policy makers often assume implicitly that local administrators plan their "local programs, fund them, and then turn to funds available from the federal government." Any federal programs undertaken, in this view, are added only after the local budget has been obligated. In reality, however, this procedure is usually not followed. As Porter and Warner demonstrated, more often local administrators follow the strategy of multi-pocketed budgeting. They plan their programs and then review all their income sources, including federal grants, to find the needed resources. This latter procedure tends to promote local priorities at the expense of federal ones.

The substitution of local priorities seems to be encouraged by such concepts as packaging or "program budgeting." Districts plan ways to shift their flexible resources to other uses as categorical grants become available. For instance, Porter cites a suburban school district in the Southwest that devotes as much federal money as possible to salaries because salary support is the hardest money to find from other sources.

When all of the local, state, and federal income sources are aggregated, few school districts have less than fifteen different sources; large districts have close to one hundred. One large district in Porter's survey had twenty "project directors" in the superintendent's office just to handle the categorical aid programs. As the total number of income sources proliferates, the apparent restrictions imposed by a particular source become less and less stringent. If a federal categorical grant is restricted to an area in which the district thinks it is doing an adequate job, it will work out a procedure where at least part of the funds are "symbolically allocated"—e.g., a federal grant releases local funds which would have been used in the federally aided program. The complex and Byzantine nature of school accounting makes difficult the discovery of these symbolic allocations.

Intergovernmental Bargaining in
Educational Administration

In an article on Title I ESEA, Jerome Murphy has examined a number of the crucial constraints within intergovernmental administration.[6] In his discussion he questions why USOE has not been more aggressive in managing the program and following up on the audits. He enumerates several reasons: (1) limited staff and a service orientation, (2) pressure to get the program moving quickly and to bring about good working relationships with the states (both leading to a tendency to overlook alleged misuses and accentuate the positive), (3) a fear that if USOE pushed too hard, Congress would replace categorical programs with general aid (in which case USOE would have even less influence), and (4) a tendency for congressmen to abhor waste except when OE accuses officials in their districts of misusing funds, in which cases state prerogatives and local control become convenient congressional justifications (and USOE needs congressional support to survive).

A final reason is expressed by Murphy:

USOE's behavior has in part been adapted to take advantage of its strategically weak bargaining position. It is virtually impossible for USOE to cut off funds which the states view as their rightful entitlement under law. The states know this and so does USOE; thus, orders or demands by USOE are bound to be ineffective since they cannot be backed up with action. Furthermore, demands might alienate the states and result in a loss of communication. Since USOE's influence comes mostly from the power of persuasion, and since it is presently almost totally reliant on the states for information about local programs, it is absolutely essential that USOE maintain cordial relations with the states. Under these bargaining conditions, the states are in a position to exact a price for their good will. . . . USOE's problem, then, is not simply the lack of will or lack of staff, but lack of political muscle. [7]

Moreover, SEAs existed before USOE and have a longstanding power base . . . Consequently, it has been impossible for USOE to create a state agency ally as has been the case in newer areas of state endeavor such as welfare and urban renewals that were initiated by federal grants.[8]

Parent and Student Participation

Educators have traditionally asserted their "expertise" as justification for a very restricted role for parents in devising educational programs.

The concept of parental influence runs counter to the traditional closed system government of education. This closed system magnifies the power of professionals and relegates lay participation to the school board, PTA, and occasional aggressive parents. PTA is the country's largest voluntary organization, but it is aptly described as an "irrelevant giant" or a "cookies and coffee group" when observers assess its policy impact. A review of recent articles on curriculum design found scant notice of parental participation—it was not considered relevant or appropriate.[9] Student governments were even more powerless.

All of this has been changing in recent years with a substantial assist from the federal government. Education, however, has lagged behind such other policy areas as model cities and the Community Action Program. Parent participation was not explicitly included in any USOE legislation except in subsequent amendments to Title I. In 1965 parent involvement in Title I and other poverty-oriented programs was presumably to be exercised by the required CAP checkpoint procedures. CAP never could get a leverage point on Title I, and Congress eliminated the CAP role in 1967.

Murphy's description of the tortured history of parent participation in Title I ESEA exemplifies the built in federal-state-local resistance to this alien concept.[10] The first set of basic criteria was issued on April 14, 1967 in the form of a program guide from Commissioner Harold Howe II to the chief state school officers. This memo called for "parent participation" but was not specific on the nature of participation. The second set of basic criteria in March, 1968, on Title I went a step further. It called for involvement of parents "in the early stages of program planning and in discussions concerning the needs of children in the various eligible attendance areas." Four months later, in July of 1968, USOE issued a separate memo stating "local advisory committee *will need to be established* for the planning, operation, and appraisal of comprehensive compensatory education programs."

This last memo brought the education lobbies into action against formal parent committees. Seventeen days later USOE retreated through another memo that in effect told the states to do as they pleased.

Subsequently, USOE's Division of Compensatory Education convinced the Nixon Administration to recommend that local advisory committees for Title I be included in the law. The administration amendment was eliminated on the House floor, and the April 1970 Act extending ESEA further confused the matter with unclear language on USOE's authority.

During the following six months representatives of the public school lobby met with USOE and flatly asserted that requiring councils was an unacceptable provision. Unlike the past, however, USOE was also under pressure from the other side, particularly groups coordinated by the Washington Research Project and the NAACP. Finally in October, 1970, a compromise emerged from USOE requiring "system wide" parent councils. Whether the requirement will survive congressional scrutiny, or be effectively enforced by chief state school officers who opposed even milder versions of the October, 1970, guidelines, remains to be seen.

Student impact on policy has grown in numerous directions, but has rarely focused on federal categorical programs. The focus of student attention has been student's rights, minority studies, due process, etc. It is quite possible that students will get around to federal programs. A 1970 survey of cities by students actively supported the minority group causes in some instances. An underlying theme in a large amount of the protest was an insistence that school personnel be more responsive to curriculum needs felt by students. Students also demanded smaller class sizes, more counselors, bilingual instruction, etc.[11]

It seems feasible that these growing student demands could be linked to the reallocation of federal categorical funds. Students need information on the potential of federal programs for meeting their curricular and programatic desires. Parent participation and student participation have not worked in concert under Title I ESEA. Such an alliance could be a partial counterweight to professional education dominance in policy making for federal aid.

Teacher Organizations and Federal Aid

At the Washington level, teacher organizations present a two-front lobby effort—the NEA and the AFT (represented in large part by its parent AFL-CIO). Teacher organizations have traditionally favored general aid (particularly for salaries), elimination of special programs for private schools, and resistance to supporting alternatives to public schools. NEA proposed that the federal government should assume one-third of all public school costs (over $13 billion in FY 1972). NEA has supported categorical programs, but only as an interim political necessity until general aid can be passed.

In a recent statement before the House Education Committee NEA's John Lumley contended:

We are tired of American education being studied, analyzed, probed, researched, surveyed, and polled . . . the solutions are not national. What is needed in Chicago is different from what is needed in Lame Deer, Montana. . .

In its policy positions, the NEA has consistently resisted legislation which would undermine the autonomy of state and local governments in the formulation and administration of school systems.[12]

In short, NEA reflects a strong local control bias that runs counter to explicit federal regulations in categorical programs.

AFT is primarily interested in national support to help achieve certain staffing ratios—e.g., twelve pupils per teacher, and no more than twenty pupils per class or twenty class periods per week. AFT believes the deployment and the use of paraprofessionals or teachers (or other educational personnel) should be determined according to local circumstances. AFT also sponsored a study calling for equalizing per child expenditures among the states. Again, we see no particular support by this lobby for federal categorical aid. The point here is that the growing power of national teachers' organizations is not oriented toward a strong federal-state stance on implementing the letter and spirit of categorical programs.[13]

For a number of reasons, including those cited above, teachers have exercised very slight influence on the planning and initial design of local proposals for federal categorical aid. A national survey by the National Advisory Council on Education of Disadvantaged Children concluded that federal projects were devised in central offices with little or no teacher input.[14] After the money was obtained, teachers were informed of the project and their role in its implementation. In short, teachers are only slightly more influential than parents.

This lack of teacher influence has also led to a low priority for the crucial component of teacher in-service training.[15]

Federal Categories and Comprehensive Planning

While the array of categorical grants reflect national problems, they do not embody any explicit overall national policy. Since no one was sure what types of federal programs would be effective, the prevalent view of the mid-sixties was that almost any good idea was worth a try. For instance, we now have over one hundred and seventy grants-in-aid that relate to urban education. Moreover, "hardening of the categories" set in quite early whereby each federal program was administered independently from related categorical programs. For example, it is rare to see a city that links EPDA teacher training to a Title I program that is reinforced by Title III of ESEA and NDEA. Various categorical programs usually operate in relative isolation spread around the city, and rarely concentrate in one school and/or its feeder system.

The response of the Office of Education to this confusing and independently operated array of categorical programs was originally to turn to the states for comprehensive statewide planning. In 1968 the Office of Education urged state departments to become the leading force in the consolidation and coordination of federal categorical programs through developing comprehensive plans, application forms, and evaluation reports based on statewide priorities. The states were to develop a strategy and plan for integrating, coordinating, and focusing diverse categorical programs on a limited number of high priority activities and populations. Implicit in OE's rationale for comprehensive statewide planning was that the needs of the cities and their disadvantaged students would be placed at or near the top of a state plan priority list. Consequently, cities could begin to get a larger share of grants allocated to the states and then allocated to localities through statewide plans. Moreover, the various categorical programs like EPDA, Title III, and Title I could be linked together in comprehensive action programs concentrating on the inner city.

In effect, the Office of Education answer to the most pressing problems of federalism in education is further strengthening of the state departments. More federal money was given to upgrade and add more state administrative personnel to carry out comprehensive statewide planning.[16]

The need and potential for a statewide plan with an urban priority is demonstrated by the following data. Excepting Title I and PL874, all major federal education programs operate through state plans that allow the state considerable latitude in distribution of the federal grant within the state. The state plan establishes priorities for types of school districts within the state. In a

1965 self-survey by state departments of education, only ten states claimed to have even a partially developed study and planning capacity. Since 1965, out of their total state and federal funds, the state departments have been using only 4 percent for "study, planning, developing, and evaluating state education programs." According to the 1968 Federal Advisory Council on State Departments, "there is no evidence that it provides for comprehensive planning to any significant degree."[17]

Systems of comprehensive state planning for federal aid should include the following elements:

1. An assessment of state needs—this could be based on achievement tests, measures of social economic status, attitude surveys, etc.
2. Establishment of statewide priorities based on the needs assessment. Given the limitation on total federal funds, priorities must be few and not all inclusive.
3. The coordination of various categorical federal programs to develop critical mass. Federal aid should be treated as a single fund and critical mass developed by linking ESEA and NDEA program expenditures with EPDA, Vocational Education, etc.
4. The targeting of unified federal funds to the state priority areas—e.g., central cities, migrants, etc.
5. Focus and reinforcement of federal aid by linking it to changes in state aid based on the state priorities. State aid will buttress the federal aid flow and also be targeted.
6. Institution of a process of control and monitoring. Comprehensive planning is more than making projections and setting targets.

Comprehensive state planning necessitates such federal aid administrative changes as: a consolidated application form that integrates several federal categories; a consolidated and improved management information system; and consolidated monitoring of LEA programs. Such broad-scale changes in the states can only succeed if the federal government is agreeable, indeed enthusiastic, about packaging the various categories. However, since each federal category is some congressman's footnote in history and some OE bureaucrat's base of expertise, fragmentation is extremely difficult to overcome. Not unexpectedly, we found little evidence of comprehensive planning in the states we studied with the exception of Michigan and to some extent New York.

As the term "comprehensive" is used here it does not require the planner "to choose among alternatives after careful and complete study of all possible courses of action and all their possible consequences and after an evaluation of those consequences in the lights of one's values."[18] Education planners and budgeters have limited and inadequate information and lack a clear ordering of values and objectives. Essentially the planning effort we describe would necessitate a modest and pragmatic effort to stretch the use of analysis at the margins.

As of now federal aid is rarely allocated with any recognition of operational objectives. The process described in 1-6 above would effect a substantial change in the processes and quality of public choice in federal aid allocation. As Charles Schultze observes, comprehensive planning cannot be substituted for political bargaining, but:

While it is often strategically and tactically important for participants in the bargaining process to conceal their objectives from their adversaries, it hardly behooves them to conceal them from themselves.[19]

We did not find coordination of state priorities to focus federal programs on urban areas with their high proportions of disadvantaged children. Title I did, of course, lock in on cities, at least outside the South. But other federal programs tended to work in opposite directions. The fact that the programs which tended to be non-urban were also state plan programs—as opposed to Title I which requires no state plan because of the statutory prescription of the distributional formula—was far from coincidental. It is noteworthy that the recent cutback in federal funds earmarked for state planning and evaluation is occurring at the same time that special revenue sharing proposes to give the states much more flexibility by removing many categorical strings.[20] The Nixon Administration's proposed Allied Services Act would also encourage state comprehensive planning as the concept is used here.

The Administrators and Their Agencies

Behind the processes and dynamics of the chain of intergovernmental relationships are the organizations and individuals who draft the regulations and conduct the negotiations. Without an understanding of these bureaucrats and bureaucracies, our view of federal aid administration would be only two dimensional—flat and lacking in reality.

Federal civil servants are a conscientious group who, for the most part, will attempt to adjust as top federal policy makers change, elections approach, or congressional amendments respond to pleas from established recipients who are no longer favored. But with the emphasis on the poor and the non-whites that emerged in the 1960s, a particular problem became apparent: civil servants knew very little about the life style and problems of disadvantaged minorities. A lack of minorities in top federal grants administrative positions demonstrates one aspect of this problem. The "other America" was neglected in professional training as well as in public policy. Prior to the late sixties, professional training in schools of education and public administration contained meager content on administering programs directed at the disadvantaged.

When priorities change, a federal civil servant will be in better position for promotion if he is not identified solely with an outmoded cause (particularly if it is an emphasis of the prior administration). Promotions within grade are automatic and job security is assured. In sum, the economic incentives for civil servants to implement rapidly and completely new administration policies are at best unclear. This is especially true when favoritism for the disadvantaged in grants will lead to conflict between federal officials and their professional and state-local colleagues thus jeopardizing "good working relationships" for the future. With these professional state-local colleagues the federal administrator must work under different future priorities and on other positions.

The White House staff concentrates on new legislation and overall budget decisions with few resources for oversight and supervision of the implementation of individual grants through the federal system. It is in part the aggregate of these individual grant decisions that determine the gap between promise and performance of federal categorical aid. Revised legislative provisions can rarely sweep away such inadequacies in the implementation process.

Thus the oversight of categorical grant administration is left to the Office of Management and Budget. OMB has no field staff; yet it is out in the field where the programs reach the intended beneficiaries and where political compromises are made that dilute funds for the poor. Finally, it is out in the field where the overlap and confusion of federal programs lead to funding delays and fragmentation of effort.

Despite their unease about agency implementation capability, budget examiners must spend most of their time in Washington dealing with agency officials on financial issues. While OMB has expanded its economic analysis staff, the economic analysts were in a separate organization area from the budget examiners who had direct leverage on agency implementation policies.

The reorganization announced by President Nixon in 1969 should improve management oversight capability. Indeed it was an acknowledgement of weaknesses in this area. It is too soon, however, to evaluate whether the formation of a management branch will make a big difference, especially in view of the continued absence of any field staff.

The General Accounting Office is an arm of the Congress with general responsibility for reviewing the administration of programs. GAO's concept of "comprehensive audit" includes analysis of administrative procedures and program effectiveness as well as the traditional focus on verifying vouchers. In short, GAO has a hunting license to comment on any aspect of program performance in addition to checking the bookkeeping. Because GAO has a limited staff trained to perform comprehensive audits, many years can elapse before the GAO auditors examine a new categorical program; and even then GAO resorts to spot checks. For instance, 19,000 LEAs receive federal grants, and GAO can cover only a small fraction of those each year. Auditors tend to go where there are demonstrated problems or particular congressional interest. Under these circumstances, the program may be so discredited or riddled with administrative problems that a salvage operation is unlikely.

The federal domestic agencies have greatly expanded their planning and evaluation staffs. These staffs, however, focus on *post facto* evaluation of program outcomes, e.g., have children learned, job trainees been placed, or new jobs created. Not only does this after the fact orientation result in a time lag before the assessment of categorical programs; more important, it frequently overlooks a detailed examination of political and administrative process and delivery services. While such evaluations can sometimes reveal whether a program has not met its goals, they can rarely explain why. Consequently, the evaluations are of limited use in preparing a report such as this or in recommending new approaches for administrative policy.

State Administration: Structure and Personnel

Federal categorical programs for the disadvantaged are filtered through a specific state and local administrative context. Political scientists employ the term "political culture" when they analyze comparative state politics.[21] The political culture of the states we studied are quite different with regard to such things as:

1. urban/rural conflict and bias in state administration
2. tradition of "localism"—e.g., how much do state officials defer to local judgments or assert substantive state leadership
3. impact of pressure groups on administrative decisions
4. professionalism, performance, and competence of state agency employees
5. role of the governor in administrative oversight.

The performance of state officials varies greatly and sweeping generalizations are impossible. It is demonstrable that *some* state and local agencies are hostile or indifferent to many federal categorical thrusts aimed at the disadvantaged.

But federal officials cannot bypass the bad ones and work through the good ones. In many states and localities, the political and administrative reward structure offers little for the bold administrator who favors the disadvantaged. All the problems of the merit system and professional working relationships apply here as well as at the federal level. State administrators understand federal priorities are likely to change, and if federal policies conflict with the state orientation to the disadvantaged, it is the long-term state policies that determine an administrator's job success.

For many years, state administrative pay scales have lagged behind federal and private salaries. It is not unusual for a federal administrator of a categorical program to be making $20,000 and his state counterpart $14,000, or less. In Texas, for instance, state education administrators are returning to high school teaching jobs because of their higher pay scales. The Texas teachers' lobby has been successful in raising the state minimum teachers salary schedule, but the state administrative employees have less political clout throughout the state. State employee salary maximums are constrained by low ceilings for top state administrators (who often make less than \$25,000) and grade promotions are rarely as rapid as are those in federal service. All of these salary factors tend to militate against a first-rate administrative staff, although many very able people remain in state government at a considerable financial sacrifice.

A 1967 report summarized the background of SEA personnel in this manner:

The most obvious generalization which can be made in summarizing our analysis is that the professional personnel in each of the states we studied comprise extremely homogeneous groups. These State Departments of Education are largely composed of men who have lived their lives in the rural areas of the states they serve; who have gone to State teachers' college and perhaps the State university; who had begun careers as professional educators, generally in rural schools, before entering the department; and who had been invited to join the department by another member of the State Department of Education.[22]

State government has a tradition of limited gubernatorial supervision of state administration. We have already commented on the limits of the White House staff for oversight of implementation. In state government, the problem is even worse. Governors have rarely taken an interest in the management side of government. The political rewards rarely lie in that direction, and central budget and management resources are meager and inadequate. This small staff is a reflection of the general understaffed condition of state government. In many states, individual departments are in important ways autonomous from central executive control.

For example, state education agencies in twelve states are responsible to an elected lay state board of education. State boards are sometimes elected by the legislature (New York) or in other states selected with staggered terms by the governor (California). In twenty-one states the chief state school officer is elected directly and thereby maintains a political base distinct from the governor's. Usually state boards of education meet once a month, have no staff, and put most of their energies into demanding outside jobs. While most governors have budgetary control over state funds, state agencies are relatively free to proceed without gubernatorial or legislative oversight on federal funds. State administrators are in an intermediate position—responsible neither to federal executives nor governors.

The policy consequences for categorical aid of this administrative independence are difficult to assess. In some cases independence from the governor may assist state agencies in reaching disadvantaged populations who are a minority of the electorate. In other instances, a governor may be unable to bring his agencies into line even though he is enthusiastic about reinforcing the national objective of categorical aid. Where federal programs involve a substantial state role, we do know there is no way to assure uniform program administration by working through sympathetic governors. This insulation from central executive control also makes state agencies more vulnerable to cooptation by established special interest groups. State agencies have rarely had enough support from governors and legislators to adequately staff their needs. Consequently, federal money under Title V ESEA (about $27 million) and a 1 percent administrative overhead charge on other federal titles have provided the bulk of growth in state education agencies since 1965. For example, in Texas 70 percent of the SEA is financed from federal money. Despite this impressive growth, state administrators claim that they are chained to their desks with paperwork, and thus rarely able to monitor categorical programs at the LEA level. Funds are even more scarce for evaluation or they are diverted from evaluation to other SEA operations.

In 1970 the Urban Institute made an in-depth study of several states and their conclusions are illustrative:

There are not enough people working in evaluation at the State level and possibly not enough of the right kind of people. State evaluation efforts are badly understaffed either because the SEA has not allocated sufficient positions for evaluation or because the positions which are allocated go unfilled. Salaries paid State evaluation personnel (and other State personnel as well) are often not competitive with those paid by large urban or suburban school districts or with the salaries a qualified evaluation specialist could command in the market place. . .

But in every case, the Federal funds have been spread across a variety of State agency activities, only some of which are directly related to evaluation.[23]

An overarching problem of state administration in general, but particularly in education, is the norm of "localism." The respect and deference to local control, strongest in New England, maintains a firm foothold in all states. In education, "the religion of localism" is a shorthand expression of a sociological norm which says that the local communities should be the dominant partners in the American governmental mix of federal, state, and local entities. This means that the LEA should have the major voice in determining policies, directions and operations of schools. Localism helps to restrict the prerogatives, scope, and style of SEA operations. As the Urban Institute study concluded:

SEAs have played a traditionally passive role in the direction of education. SEA personnel typically cajole, suggest, urge and perhaps even exhort—but almost never *require*—LEAs to make appropriate changes in educational practice.[24]

In spite of all the problems detailed above, several states have been more aggressive than the federal government in advancing the interests of the disadvantaged. We shall return to these success stories in another section of this chapter. We shall also examine the problems of direct USOE administration.

Local Educational Agencies and Federal Categorical Aid

Local educational agencies provide the cutting edge of categorical aid—the contact between teacher and child. To a substantial extent both the problems and attributes of overall LEA performance apply to federal aid. But federal aid also contains some particular attributes and drawbacks in this local context.

Federal categorical aid is designed to be a catalyst or stimulus for LEA attention to particular national objectives. Federal aid has had a significant impact as a 1965 study of innovation in six large cities concluded:

It is clear that the emerging role of the Federal government through the Office of Education is an external force promoting the greatest changes in the large city districts that has been witnessed in the course of their history . . . Compensatory education was virtually non-existent prior to federal aid. The proliferation of experimental programs can be traced directly to the influence of federal aid policies. Pre-school education is now widely accepted under "Headstart" auspices.[25]

In a large number of cases, federal aid has elevated a new breed of teachers and administrators with special concern and expertise with disadvantaged youth. However, we do not know how often federal categorical programs have been a stimulus to broad scale change in the entire LEA. There are numerous instances where federal projects have been strictly confined to specific showcase demonstration attendance areas. Business as usual even in these showcase areas is resumed after federal funds are phased out, or federal funds have been in place so long that district-wide routine takes over. There are special problems (as discussed in a subsequent section) in insuring that federal funds even reach the target group specified in the categorical legislation much less change the basic instructional approach.

As in state government, local goals may have a very different emphasis than the federal category. A federal goal of innovative programs for the disadvantaged may conflict with a local goal to provide a teacher salary increase and thereby stabilize property tax rates. In such cases, the administrative "muscle" of federal and state governments may not be sufficient to overcome local resistance or modification to better meet the local priority. In school desegregation, for example, southern LEA reactions were along a range of compliance:

1. *Voluntary non-compliance*—i.e., close the schools entirely.
2. *Involuntary minimal compliance*—appeal all adverse decisions and otherwise delay change by every means. Grant claim only to specific class of black litigants.
3. *Involuntary token compliance*—desegregate after adverse decision, yet use alternative which desegregates the least.
4. *Involuntary moderate compliance*—same as 3, but make wider plans for desegregation without effectuating it on a compulsory basis.
5. *Voluntary minimal compliance*—i.e., move before threat of litigation, with compliance only minimal.
6. *Voluntary compliance*—providing full compliance without threat of litigation.[26]

Distribution of federal categorical aid titles, such as ESEA I, falls on a similar spectrum. Some districts would channel all the funds to the disadvantaged, while others would only move after court suits or after they saw funds withheld by USOE in a nearby state. Indeed, California and Mississippi probably stand at the opposite poles of this Title I continuum. In short, federal agencies are ineffective on their own in imposing a uniform high quality implementation policy for specific categorical legislation across a pluralistic national school system. In desegregation it required a statute backed by willing courts and Congress, energetic enforcers, and a supportive public even to dent resistance in the deep South. National concern has never been so forceful or focused on the proper implementation of particular categorical programs for minorities.

Even if an LEA school board and superintendent are enthusiastic supporters of a federal categorical priority, it is still a long implementation chain to the teacher in the classroom. Most large LEAs have a federal projects officer whose job is "to get our fair share of the federal money." Federal projects are viewed as ephemeral funds that come late in the year and can disappear at the whim of Congress or a new USOE bureaucrat. Consequently, federal categorical aid is often administered like "soft money" so that its withdrawal will not upset the "regular program." The result is a lack of lasting impact from federal funds on the mainline instructional effort.

Nor does a superintendent or school board who are enthusiastic with regard to a federal program guarantee an enthusiastic local bureaucratic response. Most key administrators have risen through the chairs during lengthy bureaucratic careers. Few of them are likely to revolutionize traditional ways of allocating money or educating children simply on the strength of federal funds which average only 7 percent of their total revenues. Superintendents frequently find they cannot implement their own, no less federal, priorities through an encrusted bureaucracy. Teachers may be willing, but federal funds are rarely accompanied by the lead time, planning, and in-service training to change teaching behavior. The normal procedure is little or no planning and a one or two week superficial teacher orientation.

At the bottom of the implementation chain is the teacher who has a pocket veto on instructional goals of federal categorical programs. We have almost no information on the educational process for special federal programs once the classroom door closes. We do know that federal aid has rarely considered the magnitude of teacher training needed or the special organizational goals of the increasingly powerful teacher organizations.

Title-by-Title Analysis of Some Significant Aid Programs

Having traced the intergovernmental chain of administration from the federal through the local levels, and having identified some of the characteristics of the respective bureaucracies involved at each level, we turn now to the subject of their labors, the federal aid programs which are their responsibility to administer. Focusing on specific titles of specific aid programs, we highlight what we consider to be some of the more significant characteristics of the federal aid legislation and some of the events that have shaped their operation.

ESEA Title I and Multiple Objectives

Title I is the largest federal aid program ($1.5 billion) and is targeted to disadvantaged youth. The political disputes over concentration and comparability demonstrate the general problem of categorical aid.

The inclusion of numerous different and sometimes conflicting policy objectives in Title I assisted speedy congressional passage. It also has led to unfulfilled expectation and erosion of public support for such categorical aid. The array of interests and decentralized power centers in the American polity are reflected in the diverse objectives embodied in Title I: (a) establishing a precedent for large-scale federal aid, partly as a necessary prelude for a shift to general aid, (2) encouraging educational reform through priority to the disadvantaged, (3) speeding the pace of school desegregation, (4) strengthening the staff capacity of SEAs and LEAs, (5) meeting health and welfare needs of poor children, and (6) increasing in educational attainment and reduction of dropouts. The interested parties in the evaluation stage after Title I was implemented could not be expected to agree on the ordering of priorities in their evaluative conclusions. Moreover, new and additional priorities were bound to emerge as the funds had an impact at the local level. In effect, while much of the criticism of Title I has included "evaluations" of Title I's performance, evaluators' perspectives and criteria were influenced by their particular ranking of the different policy objectives enumerated above.

It is true that the pupil achievement results on Title I are at best unknown and at worst very discouraging. But to evaluate whether a program that reaches nine million children "works" on the single dimension of achievement test scores is to ignore the multitude of other political objectives embedded in Title I. Title I's defenders point to such positive outcomes as the fiscal equalization impact of Title I funds and the concern it has generated among educators all over the nation for the previously neglected disadvantaged child. Others have contended Title I funds were intended to be "a sugar solvent" to help ease acceptance by the South of black children rather than forsake the federal financial windfall. In effect, Title I held out so many different aspirations to so many different constituencies that inevitably several of these aspirations were never met. Perhaps multiple objectives in large-scale federal programs is a formula for insuring that no single objective will be substantially accomplished. The recent agitation by the National Welfare Rights Organization for a Title I clothing allowance reflects their view that the child welfare objectives of Title I have been slighted by education administrators. In short, Title I funds are spread over too many objectives. Not enough funds are available to satisfy each of the objectives, which leads to pressures for reallocation, and the lack of satisfactory fulfillment of any objective.

ESEA-Title II

This small program reached only slightly more than $100 million, but it is an interesting test case of the flexible state plan method of categorical aid. A primary political motive for Title II was its potential for channeling funds to private schools. Indeed, Title II ESEA was never viewed by its 1965 legislative framers as a target program for the disadvantaged. Nevertheless, a "need" orientation was inserted in the Act through a provision requiring the state plan to "Take into consideration the relative need of the children and teachers of the State for such library resources, textbooks, or other instructional materials." USOE did not define "relative need" and the "take into consideration" language left the ultimate decision in states' hands. During the first two years of the 1965 Act USOE paid little attention to how the states were defining relative need. California, for example, allocated Title II money on the basis of average daily attendance and assessed valuation. This formula is not an accurate indicator of need. In 1968, USOE requested California to tighten up "relative need" and the formula now includes three factors:

$$\frac{State\ Average\ Assessed\ Valuation\ per\ ADA}{District\ Assessed\ Valuation\ Per\ ADA}$$

$$\frac{District\ Tax\ Rate}{State\ Median\ Tax\ Rate}$$

$$\frac{State\ Book\ Average\ per\ ADA}{District\ Book\ Average\ per\ ADA}$$

While these factors seem reasonable need factors given the multiple objectives of Title II, wealthy white suburban districts in the Bay Area display more need under this California formula than heavily black Oakland.[27]

New York State defines Title II "need" through four criteria that may conflict with each other:

1. large urban centers with critical education needs related to economic and educational deprivation
2. school districts with critical educational needs created by severe financial need
3. school districts with critical shortages of school library resources
4. school districts with student enrollments large enough to insure a full scope of educational programs.

The legislative history of Title II reveals several conflicting definitions of relative need. The legislative intent indicates rapidly growing white suburban districts may have the greatest need because their libraries are not yet stocked with a large number of books. Such a perspective overlooks inner city libraries which may have numerous books, but their contents may be outdated and irrelevant for a newly arrived black population. Such decisions on need call for subjective judgments by literature experts which cannot be incorporated into a statewide financial distribution formula. An objective of Title II was to reorient local priorities so that they favored more library books and instructional materials regardless of whether the LEA was wealthy or poor. Moreover, the private schools were a prime target for funds and they usually do not enroll as large a number of disadvantaged pupils as public schools.

Again, we see multiple objectives in a federal program deflecting concentration of limited resources from the disadvantaged.

Vocational Education and Federal Aid

Federal involvement in vocational education began in 1917. The legislative history indicates the goals of the program were directed to training in seven occupational categories with a minimum of federal direction or involvement. The first basic reconsideration since 1917 came with the 1963 Act. A panel of consultants reported prior to the 1963 Act that low enrollments in urban centers were especially disturbing. As Garth Mangum stressed "Little was being done to serve youths whose socio-economic or academic handicaps made it difficult for them to profit from regular programs. Vocational education was neither retraining potential dropouts nor preparing them for employment."[28]

Although the VEA Act of 1963 was supposedly passed to correct the above problem, the federal-state reporting system on whether any objectives were being met was grossly inadequate. No significant changes were made in the reporting forms in 1964. Though the 1963 Act's philosophy was to refocus efforts on people rather than occupational groups, there are no demographic characteristics reported beyond the sex of the students. In an era of concern with racial discrimination and poverty, data on age, race, education, and family income were not collected. Though groups with special needs were supposed to receive special treatment, there are no data to identify them nor to describe the content of courses allegedly designed for them. Consequently, assessments of the 1963 Act and of the 1968 Act at this point depend upon limited fragmentary official data, partial studies by various researchers, and personal observation and judgment.

One of these researchers, Garth Mangum, concluded with respect to the 1963 Act:

Expenditures have increased, but the expansion has been largely in the old occupational categories except for the addition of a new category of office occupations. Vocational education is not yet adequately responsive to the needs of the labor market, little recognition has been given to new occupations, few innovative programs are underway, and there is little coordination between general and vocational education.[29]

As an obstacle to change Mangum highlights the lack of national leadership by USOE:

The agency has a long history of providing matching funds without prescribing objectives, establishing substantial guidelines, or evaluating state and local accomplishment.[30]

While VEA Act of 1963 directed that emphasis be changed from occupational categories to groups of people, most states continued to organize administration around the traditional categories. The state plan was a misnomer. It remains today merely a legal agreement by the states to comply with federal laws in the use of the federal funds. Mangum concluded that no state plan with its accompanying projected activities has been disapproved, and there was little evidence that they are seriously studied by USOE. Lacking public or administrative pressure or support, the disadvantaged continued to be left out by the traditional delivery system.

Another state arbitrarily reported ten percent of its secondary students as being in the special needs category without creating any special needs courses. A technical school in another state reacted that it had spent years building an image with employers and was not going to risk that image by enrolling less than the best. In another case, the State Director of Vocational Education arbitrarily announced that he would allocate no funds to post-secondary training.[31]

The U.S. Senate Committee on Labor and Public Welfare concluded that only 1 percent of the federal funds were spent on special needs students (handicapped and disadvantaged) from 1963-1968.

The 1968 Act attempted to make legislative changes in administrative behavior, with at best minimal results. Several of our studies vividly illustrate how state administration of the provisions requiring earmarking of 15% of the funds for the disadvantaged and the provision encouraging better manpower surveys were effectively defeated through inadequate implementation. Funds not earmarked for "special needs" categories are allotted in many states under traditional formulas that discriminate against the central city poor. Texas merges its federal VE money with its basic state aid formula that is now the subject of several court suits because of its discriminatory effect on minorities, the poor, and low wealth school districts. California now uses an allocation formula instead of the individual project application required from 1963-1968. But the formula is designed to insure that the same LEAs get about the same amounts they were receiving before the 1968 Act.[32]

Emergency School Assistance Program (ESAP) and ESEA Title I:
Similar Problems,

In 1970, Congress enacted the Emergency School Assistance Program. Funded for two years at $75 million per year, ESAP was designed, in part, to assist school districts in meeting problems associated with desegation. In 1972, Congress extended the program and increased its funding to $2 billion. Despite this expansion, research from the first year of ESAP demonstrates that the errors of omission and commission in Title I are being repeated again.[33] Very little has changed in the political underpinnings of the present distribution system. We will not discuss the desegregation aspects of ESAP but will focus on program design and implementation. However, the absence of strong initiative and administrative effectiveness clearly results, in part, from the political controversy that envelops the desegregation issue.

As in the first year of Title I, ESAP grants had to be disbursed without adequate planning or lead time. Local grants were approved without sufficient USOE review or documentation. GAO stressed that the weaknesses in HEW procedures were due "to a large degree, to HEW's policy of emphasizing the emergency nature of ESAP and to its desire for expeditious funding at the expense of . . . the adequacy of described program activities in satisfying ESAP requirements." ESAP grants were made by USOE regional offices which, we stressed earlier, were inadequately staffed initially and have never been strengthened. The lack of lead time in federal education programs has always been the main complaint of SEA and LEA administrators. Whatever the reasons, ESAP makes one dubious that a crucial difference in federal education administration would result from USOE assumption of state prerogatives. Indeed USOE did not do any better in administering ESAP than the least effective SEAs did in implementing Title I.

In both Title I and ESAP, USOE did not require high standards on the educational design components (teacher training, textbooks, curriculum, and comprehensiveness). The National Advisory Council on Education of Disadvantaged Children concluded in 1966:

For the most part, however, Title I projects are piecemeal fragmented efforts at remediation or vaguely directed "enrichment." It is extremely rare to find strategically planned, comprehensive programs for change based on four essential needs: adapting academic content to the special problems of disadvantaged children, improved in-service training of teachers, attention to nutrition and other health needs, and involvement of parents and community agencies in planning and assistance to school programs.

In 1970, the NAACP and other groups concluded about ESAP:

The Title IV [of the 1964 Civil Rights Act] Office (USOE) has abandoned the mandate of the Regulations, under which the decision whether, and to what extent, a district funded was to have been based on the promise the district's proposal showed of dealing comprehensively and effectively with special problems of desegregation . . . First, some proposals which did include a comprehensive treatment of desegregation were severely cut, apparently because the districts were not large enough to warrant grants of the size needed. On the other hand, a large number of very small grants were made—grants too small to deal comprehensively with the problems of the district.

The Title I Advisory Council found in 1967 that teacher aides were being used for the most menial of tasks, and teachers were not trained to use the aides. While the NAACP survey found more money spent for teacher aides and teacher training than for any other single purpose, it asserted that frequently no effort was made to tie the need for aides to desegregation. For instance, ESAP aides were hired to keep libraries open. In short, both Title I and ESAP funds are frequently not directed to the "special education needs of the children," and both acts funded numerous fragmented efforts. As the discussion of multi-pocketed budgeting revealed, LEAs are able to divert federal funds to match their own priorities which are usually not congruent with the federal legislation. Federal funds become a small piece of the total funds in an ongoing local education political system. The use of the federal funds is as likely to reflect the dominant viewpoint in that local political system as it is to mirror the intent of the federal statute.

Education Professions Development Act
and Teacher Training in Title I

In a recent report, the National Advisory Council on Education Professions Development criticizes the quality of policy formulation as it relates to the federal government's efforts in training and development of educational personnel.[34] Specifically, (1) on some important issues the policy positions of the agency are not indicated; and (2) existing policy statements tend to be neither informative nor based on any systematic analysis of the issues.

Part I of the Council's report stresses the need for "policies of effective means" (policies which indicate actions to be taken to achieve the broad goals outlined in other higher level policy statements). These policy statements are especially necessary so that those public officials in non-federal levels can engage in sound planning to meet goals articulated by the federal government. The council recommended there be program personnel sufficient to engage in policy formulation rather than just program administration (which is usually a more pressing activity). Policy is defined as "simply a declaration which will clearly communicate the ends and means intended in a given effort, and the rationale by which the ends and means were determined."

The Advisory Council's conclusions are an accurate assessment of one of the key problems of EPDA. There has been no operational strategy or ranking of objectives to ascertain if the program was making progress toward some goals. Congress viewed EPDA largely as a manpower program to fill shortages and upgrade skills. USOE administrators stress the reform elements in EPDA in terms of local school operations and university training efforts. It has never been clear who the primary clients or target groups of EPDA are: teachers, disadvantaged kids, unskilled poor people, institutions of higher education, or administrators. In its brief history since 1967, EPDA has tried to affect each of these groups without any consistent or sustained focus. In the first year, 89 percent of the EPDA funds went to universities and 11 percent to LEAs. Subsequently, funding for universities has sharply decreased, and the LEAs now receive the larger share. The NSF institutes for science and math teachers operated at a level of $550 million for several years and reached a very large number of the total teaching force. In contrast, EPDA has changed from emphasis yearly and thus had little impact on the total target group.

EPDA has never attempted to be the teacher training arm for other federal aid programs such as Title I or vocational education. Unfortunately, the efforts at teacher involvement and in-service experiences under Title I have not been adequate either. The attitudes and skills of teachers are crucial in improving the education of disadvantaged children. If no force were required other than an expanded number of workshops, and in-service seminars, the road to change would be relatively easy. Teachers reflect the attitudes of society. Society applies value judgments of "good" and "bad" to such common aspects of child behavior as use of language, cleanliness, orderliness, management of time, diligence in lessons, and homework.

The structure of our educational system often inhibits internal efforts toward teacher improvement. The teacher usually practices in the hallowed privacy of a classroom. Rarely does one teacher see another work. Exceptionally talented teachers exist in almost every school, but they are separated from the teacher in the next room by an impenetrable wall of professional isolationism.

In 1967 the National Advisory Council on the Education of the Disadvantaged Children conducted nationwide observation of Title I programs. Three out of four of the Title I programs examined had an in-service training component. However, the council concluded:

But most training programs were regarded by the consultant-observers as being too short and too limited in content to be highly effective. Most were held during the regular school year, and took place during a couple of hours after school each day, lasting for less than 10 days. The most frequent emphasis in training was on techniques for teaching remedial classes. A few programs, however, included sensitivity training, involving group dynamics and attempts to make teachers more aware of their own feelings as way of heightening their sensitivity to the feelings of children. These few programs, when they included practical work with children, seemed to have produced striking results.[35]

In short, we have no evidence as yet that federal aid has caused much change in teacher class-room behavior nor has it been designed well to accomplish this essential objective.

Summing Up

In summarizing the important findings of our study, we have taken an even-handed approach by attempting to point out both the central tendencies as well as the range of disparities which were encountered both in the analysis of fiscal flows and in the results of the state studies. To stress the differences would provide few common threads for policy makers to use in their efforts to improve federal policy toward education. A treatment that emphasizes only generalizations applicable to all states and school districts, however, would obscure the need for policies broad enough to encompass crucial variations in state financial and behavioral patterns.

It may be useful, in this final summary, to return to the beginning and remind ourselves of the substantial elements of commonality we found in the financial aspects. In most of the large central cities of the nation, particularly those in the northeast and midwest, an extremely discouraging financial pattern prevails. When the finances of the central city were contrasted with those of their suburban rings, the result of a demographic and economic "sorting-out" process was readily apparent. In comparison with the suburbs, the central cities had populations which were proportionately more impoverished and more heavily composed of ethnic and racial minorities. The pupil population of the central cities includes disproportionate numbers of the foreign born, handicapped, racial minorities, and the poor—people whose education requires far more intensive resource use than is true for the more socially advantaged pupils in most suburbs; yet central city per pupil expenditures were frequently less than or only marginally higher than the surrounding suburbs. Because of generally higher price and salary levels in the large city education systems, equal amounts of money tends to provide less education in cities than it does in suburban school districts.

During the last decade, the central city has lost its pre-eminence in the proportion of metropolitan activity, as measured by such indicators as retail sales; the bulk of retail sales activity is now located in the suburbs rather than in the core cities. Property bases—of direct interest to education since the local share of school revenues is drawn from the property tax—grew only a fraction as quickly over the last decade in central cities in most sections of the nation as they did in the outside central city areas of the SMSAs.

As a result of both the relative decline in their fiscal situation and the greater demands for public services in heavily urbanized areas—demands for police, public health, transportation, and, in some cities, welfare—tax effort (as a proportion of per capita income) and expenditures for public services were considerably higher in most core cities than in suburban areas of the nation's largest SMSAs.

In addition to these generalizations, our data revealed numerous exceptions as well. Some districts in the suburban ring were heavily urban in composition and suffered from many of the problems ascribed to central cities. Some cities, particularly the newer cities of the west, tend to be less densely populated and less afflicted with the urban fiscal phenomenon than are the older cities of the midwest and northeast. Nonetheless, the general trend is evident. Therefore, we have taken the complex and widespread pathology that affects the largest cities of the nation as the backdrop of our examination of the fiscal impact of federal aid to education.

Our examination of the impact of total federal aid of education led us to this conclusion: while central cities received somewhat more federal aid than suburbs in four states, the amount was far too small to overcome the advantage that the suburbs held in local revenues and state aid in those states. School districts in nonmetropolitan areas, largely rural, tended to receive more federal aid than those in metropolitan areas. In three of the four states for which we have comparable data, rural areas received more federal aid per pupil than did even the central cities. In general, however, federal aid in the aggregate was more responsive to urban fiscal problems than was state aid; yet when total federal aid was disaggregated into its component programs, the degree of responsiveness varied markedly.

For example, ESEA I appeared to be the primary source of the sensitivity to urban and to rural school finance problems. Its poverty-related formula funnelled money into cities in ways that state aid formulas, usually geared to property value per pupil (a measure that ignores the real financial problems in large cities) did not. Districts with large proportions of nonwhite pupils and districts with low median family income levels received the highest proportions of Title I funds. But many other federal programs appeared neutral to such factors, and a number of programs, such as NDEA and ESEA III, frequently worked to make the rich districts richer. In a number of instances, in ESEA II and III, Vocational Education, and NDEA III, major cities have received even less aid than should have been allotted to them in view of just their proportion of their state's pupil population. When comparative cost levels and the more costly educational needs of central city students are taken into account, the pattern becomes more discriminatory still.

Why do these patterns appear? What causes the somewhat greater urban and poverty orientation of federal aid than of state and local funds? Let us begin by noting the immense areas for state discretion that exist in the allocation of most federal programs. The discretion is partly a result of statutory language that permits state development of distributional formulas and procedures, and partly the result of a lack of enthusiasm that USOE administrators have for enforcing or policing aid programs. Yet ESEA I—the categorical program with the least leeway for state discretion in its distribution—was the most instrumental in providing funds for central cities, the poor, and areas with high proportions of minority pupils despite the problems of program implementation we have noted. The programs most amenable to state determination of need factors in the allocation to school districts were the programs that were most likely to aid suburban areas more than core cities. Urban school lobbies in most of the states in our study, it will be remembered, have not yet mobilized to turn the flows of federal funds to their advantage.

But the conclusion should not be drawn that all rigid federal distribution formulas will help the urban areas, the poor, and the members of the minority groups. Impacted Areas Aid (P.L. 874), another program whose distribution formula leaves little room for state action, was relatively neutral regarding the factors noted above, showing a relatively random distribution in regard to those variables. Nor is it justified to conclude that all state discretion will work against urban districts. In Michigan, for example, we noted a fairly consistent priority for the central cities and the poor that filtered through the administrative apparatus of the education department.

In analyzing the fiscal impact of federal aid in relation to state and local revenue patterns, we examined whether federal aid offset the wealth-based disparities that tend to characterize the state and local patterns. In terms of property valuation, we did not find that total federal aid was strongly equalizing. The reason for this lies in the fact that urban areas, which attract substantially higher shares of federal aid than do their suburbs, tend to have relatively high property tax rolls. A better index of fiscal capacity would be the district income level, and in that regard federal aid does tend to equalize because of the effects of ESEA I.

A stronger relationship exists between some rough indexes of educational need and federal aid both in the aggregate and in particular regard to Title I. Strong positive correlations between the proportion of non-white pupils and federal assistance were found in our work, and other investigators have found a similar phenomenon regarding the flow of federal aid and the incidence of low achievement scores. In short, Title I in particular, and total amounts of federal aid to a lesser extent, provide more aid to areas with greater proportions of high-need students. Unfortunately, the magnitudes of aid involved are seldom equal to the immense cost of effective education of the poor and culturally deprived.

While we drew upon a single year, usually 1967, to illustrate a number of these points in the first chapter of this volume, the data contained similar information for a four-year period. This longitudinal dimension revealed some rather strange characteristics of federal aid as it finally reaches individual school districts. From year to year, independent of total appropriations levels passed by the Congress, amounts of federal aid vary at the district level. Part of the problem is, of course, the timing of congressional action, which usually occurs well into the school year in which the funds are meant to be spent. Another component is the letter of credit procedures through which the USOE and the state education agencies authorize school systems to spend at a percentage of the previous year's grant pending final action on appropriations. Other factors have to do with the LEA's ability in aidsmanship. Yet for whatever reasons, such overall trends as the following appeared in our data: in 1967-68, at a time when total appropriations for elementary and secondary education were increasing by several hundred million dollars, nearly half the school districts in the metropolitan areas of the five states received less federal aid than they did the previous years. Of the remaining metropolitan districts, 30 percent received more aid and only 25 percent remained stable.

The impact of such irregularity or undependability in revenues combined with the small relative amounts that federal aid constitutes of school budgets has contributed to the low profile nature of the politics of federal aid allocations. Schoolmen often feel that the race is hardly worth the prize. Nor are they willing to risk key employees or essential programs to the vagaries and uncertainties of federal revenues. As the fiscal pinch tightens, however, federal aid, with all its shortcomings, is becoming more central to the politics of education.

Here, too, the variations on the theme must not be overlooked. While for the nation as a whole the proportion of total elementary and secondary revenues contributed by the federal government hovers around 7 percent, federal aid averages between 3 and 22 percent among the fifty states. For particular school districts and types of districts, the variance is far greater. Thus, in 1968, federal aid surely played a far different role in the impoverished Edgewood, Texas, school district, where it accounted for $108 of the $356 per pupil the district had in per pupil revenues, than it did in neighboring Alamo Heights, where federal funds constituted only $36 of $594 in per pupil revenues.

Recommendations

The purpose for which this study of federal aid to education was undertaken was to assist in making future educational policy more enlightened and more effective than that of the present. We hope that the description and analysis which has gone before will contribute to that goal. For that reason we have presented the results of our work in some detail so that readers could share as fully as possible the information that we have had before us and thus draw their own conclusions about needed changes. But besides presenting the evidence, we think it important also to present the major recommendations that we have arrived at in the course of our research. We make no claims, however, that our views are free of value orientations. What we have done, however, is to make as explicit as we could the reasoning and the biases which underly our suggestions so that the reader may discount our proposals on the grounds of disagreement with our logic, our biases, or our reading of the facts.

1. *Federal education policies should emphasize differential administration.*

Our studies disclosed a vast range of administrative and fiscal behavior among the states of our study. What makes this data even more striking is the fact that the states we studied, while differing in regional distribution and in a variety of characteristics, were all relatively urbanized and highly populous states. We concluded, therefore, that federal administrative practices which use one set of regulations to cover a variety of state practices are doomed, and that more flexible approaches are needed. Flexibility would permit administration by state education departments capable of supervising and guiding their LEAs, or if the state department were incapable, such flexibility would enable a program to be administered through direct federal-to-local relations. Anarchy is inconsistent with responsible government, yet anarchy is what characterizes the administration of many federal programs. Certainly, the U.S. Office of Education is not equipped to administer federal aid programs for the entire nation, but it could develop a capability to conduct them better than they are now being done in many states. And that, we contend, is little more than USOE's basic responsibility.

2. *The political processes related to the allocation of federal educational resources should be opened up to a wider range of interest representatives and general government officials.*

The implementation strategy of federal aid since 1958 has been essentially top-down. Federal and state standards were supposedly designed to insure that LEAs responded to federal categorical priorities. The program negotiations were conducted among professional administrators at the three levels with little involvement of parents, teacher organizations, students, and community agencies. This study, however, demonstrates that the top-down strategy of regulations and guidelines contains neither the sanctions or incentives sufficient to accomplish the legislative framer's categorical purposes in 50 states and 17,000 LEAs. Moreover, the top-down strategy does not have sufficient leverage to reorient classroom practice or to insure that money always reaches the intended targets.

A potentially more effective system would be to reverse substantially the flow of sanctions and incentives so that students, parents, and teachers have the desire and means to accomplish federal purposes. We need an intensive analysis of the experiences of parent councils in Title I ESEA and other federal domestic programs. Parent councils that were particularly effective could serve as models.

If changes in federal guidelines would promote more effective councils, such changes should be mandated. Moreover, there is some basis for hope that we can design federal aid so that the growing influence of teacher organizations is directed toward some of the same goals as federal categorical legislation. In essence, the best we can hope for in a number of federal programs is that they will give teachers an environment in which to change.

If federal aid is to be coordinated with other programs of government, particularly with state priorities for education, general government officials and broader based coalitions of individuals with an interest in education must be involved in the allocation processes. At present state legislators and governors are frequently unaware of the vast discretion that could be exercised in allocating federal funds. Similarly, we found that urban interests, whose stake in federal aid is an important one, are often unorganized, uninterested, and, therefore, ineffective in influencing the administration of discretionary federal programs in their state. Until those patterns are changed, states are unlikely to allocate resources in proportion to pressing educational needs.

3. *Title I of the Elementary and Secondary Education Act should be vastly increased in funding.*

While our studies have uncovered a host of problems related to Title I of ESEA, we are strong in our recommendation that its funding should be brought up to the levels envisioned in the legislation. Only when it is funded in the manner originally intended can it fairly be judged. While the evaluation of the educational benefits of Title I are mixed, as a fiscal device its record is clearly the best of any program in American educational finance. Its funds are concentrated on overburdened central cities and impoverished rural areas. It places resources where needs are greatest. Much still must be learned about how best to teach the children of the poor, but that is no excuse for failing to make available to teachers with the most difficult tasks the greater resources that Title I was meant to commit.

Comparability requirements must be enforced; resources should be focused more carefully; program priorities should be implemented by state education departments; evaluations of the effectiveness of programs should be made more useful; and many other improvements should be initiated. Despite its faults Title I has not failed. It has succeeded admirably in serving one of the legislative purposes set forth in the Act, namely to assist school districts in meeting the costs brought on by heavy concentrations of educationally disadvantaged people. In regard to its purpose of improving the education of the poor, the Congress and the educational community have failed Title I. We propose that it be given a fair trial.

4. *In addition to the continuation of categorical aid programs aimed at specific national purposes, new federal aid programs should be designed to serve as a lever to change the course of state policy.*

While recommendations for untied block grants in education are popular in Washington as this is written, the principal authors of this volume oppose such aid. We believe that the record of the states as discussed in our research does not warrant confidence that the allocation of federal funds will be any more rational or equitable than it has been in the past. Instead, we would propose that aid be given for general educational purposes so long as the state meets certain requirements.

For example, the federal government might require that states engage in some form of comprehensive planning or priority setting as they sought to meet the educational needs of their citizens. While, again, no particular method need be provided for the nation as a whole, an encouragement could be given to different processes in a number of states that would prove of real benefit. Similarly, a federal requirement that states move toward systems of assessment of the outputs of their educational programs would be another of these broad, but, we believe, highly needed changes. Clearly, the states would require technical assistance and additional funds to improve achievement testing and longitudinal evaluation, but once again encouraging a more sensible method of resource allocation would be of long range national benefit. Lastly, a provision for public disclosure of statewide achievement testing data might open a portion of the closed system of educational policy making.[36] At present, citizens have little means of judging school performance. The ability to make some sorts of comparisons among schools and school systems would introduce a measure of responsibility into a system that at present has none. It would serve, we believe, to bring the schools closer to the communities they serve, and would permit parents to play a more realistic part than they now do in school affairs.

5. *Federal aid should be addressed to eliminating the wealth-and need-based disparities that characterize state patterns of raising and distributing revenues for education.*

American school finance, on both the revenue and expenditure sides, is riddled with inequity and irrationality. As one looks at the data on the distribution of revenues, one finds a strong correspondence in state after state between the property wealth and the income of the district on the one hand and their level of spending on education on the other. If one believes, as we do, that greater resources should be spent on the education of children who are demonstrably the least likely to succeed—the physically or mentally handicapped, the poor, the members of racial minorities—then the present pattern of resource allocation is simply wrong. For it is the communities that are the richest, the whitest, and the most socially advantaged that usually lead their areas in the quality and quantity of school services. Large cities and heavily urbanized areas seldom receive school revenues in proportion to the more difficult educational tasks they must perform; the higher urban cost levels that prevail, or the heavier demands that are placed upon their tax bases for a wide and costly variety of municipal services. Poor rural areas, too, almost invariably lag far behind the rest of the state in the quality of schooling they provide. In short, the current distribution of educational resources does not correspond to the distribution of what we believe are the highest priority educational needs of the nation.

Tax rates for education are generally lower in those districts with highest property valuation yet the yield of those lower rates is frequently far higher than the yield of the higher rates of poorer districts. In the urbanized areas, while tax rates for education are frequently relatively low, the total tax rates for all services tend to be far higher in proportion to the income of their residents than is true in other areas of the state. Thus in regard to taxes, education tends to extort a heavier burden from those who are less able to bear it. To the authors of these recommendations, a revenue policy of that kind violates the most elementary concepts of fairness in taxation.

Since the fall of 1972, courts in five states have issued ringing opinions declaring that the Fourteenth Amendment of the federal Constitution prohibits finance systems that exhibit these characteristics. In particular, they have laid the responsibility for eliminating wealth based disparities upon the states. While at this writing, the outcome in the Supreme Court is still to be determined and while none of the courts have yet formulated standards as to precisely what will satisfy the new legal doctrine, a number of estimates of the costs of eliminating the legal wrongs are available. If the cases come to mean that wealth-based disparities must be eliminated, and if expenditure levels of the more favored communities are not to be noticeably reduced, the bill for the nation as a whole may run to $9 billion. If additional sums are to be focused on the disadvantaged or on low achieving pupils, the cost could well be $13 to $14 billion. We believe that costs of these magnitudes are simply unlikely to come from the regressive and relatively inelastic tax structures of state governments.

We would propose, then, that a federal responsibility for assisting the states to meet the decisions of the courts and the dictates of equity and rationality should become a national policy. Such a policy would be consistent with the direction of major federal education programs to date, which as our data have shown, are far more equitable and rational in their distribution than are state aid funds or the distribution of local revenues. While the magnitudes of federal aid would be far in excess of those that the federal government has customarily provided, we maintain that they are not at all inconsistent with the national interest in the education of all citizens. In a country whose economy is national in scope, where mobility within and among regions is high, and where the democratic process rests upon an educated citizenry, the provision of 25 to 35 percent of educational expenditures from federal sources would be entirely consistent with the federal benefit from American public education.

Notes

1. This ignores School Assistance and Federally Affected Areas (Impacted) which the writers regard as essentially general aid.

2. For the particular problems of cities in federal aid see James Guthrie, "City Schools in a Federal Vise," *Education and Urban Society* (Feb., 1970).

3. For an analysis of these nonstatutory controls see Michael W. Kirst, *Government Without Passing Laws* (Chapel Hill: U.N.C. Press, 1969).

4. For instance, see letter of January 20, 1971 from Commissioner Marland to William J. Dodd, Superintendent of Public Education in Louisiana.

5. David O. Porter et. al., "The Mobilization of Federal Aid by Local Schools: A Political and Economic Analysis," Report submitted to the Syracuse University Research Corporation.

6. Jerome Murphy, "Title I of ESEA," *Harvard Educational Review*, Vol. 41, No. 1, Feb., 1971.

7. Murphy, op. cit., page 45.

8. We believe this is a crucial reason that federal influence is more limited in education than Martha Derthick found in her study of welfare administration in Massachusetts. Education is a state function under our constitution which has resulted in less bargaining resources for USOE than federal welfare administrators, see Martha Derthick *The Influence of Federal Grants* (Cambridge: Harvard, 1970).

9. M.W. Kirst and Decker Walker, "An Analysis of Curriculum Policy Making," *Review of Educational Research*, Dec., 1971.

10. Murphy, op. cit., passim.

11. Raphael O. Nystrand, "High School Students as Policy Advocates," *Theory into Practice*, Vol. VIII, October 1969.

12. U.S. House of Representatives, *Needs of Elementary and Secondary Education for the Seventies*, 91st Congress: First Session, pp. 406-409.

13. Ibid., p. 29.

14. Co-author Kirst was Associate Director of the Council and analyzed reports on this teacher involvement component from observers who visited 86 school districts in 43 states. Almost 30 percent of Title I expenditure occurred in counties observed by Council staff.

15. For specific comments on this see the reports of the National Advisory Council on Disadvantaged Children for January 31, 1967 and December 5, 1966.

16. This money is part of Title V ESEA (Sections 503 and 505).

17. U.S. Office of Education (1968) *Focus on the Future: Education in the States* (OE 23 050-68) Washington.

18. Charles Lindblom and David Braybrooke, *A Strategy of Decision* (The Free Press, 1963), p. 40.

19. Charles Schultze, *The Politics and Economics of Public Spending* (Washington, D.C.: Brookings, 1970), p. 66.

20. OMB eliminated the state planning funds for FY 1972 under Section 503 of Title V ESEA.

21. See Frank Munger (editor), *American State Politics* (New York: Crowell, 1966).

22. David J. Kirby and Thomas A. Tollman, "Background and Career Patterns of State Department Personnel", in Roald F. Campbell, Gerald E.

Sroufe, and Donald H. Layton (eds.), *Strengthening State Departments of Education* (Chicago, Illinois Midwest Administration Center, June 1967), p. 39.

23. Bayla F. White et. al., *Monitoring and Evaluation: A State Survey* (unpublished paper for the USOE Title I Task Force by the Urban Institute, Washington, D.C., 1970).

24. Ibid.

25. Marilyn Gittell, *Six Urban School Districts* (New York: Praeger, 1968).

26. The writers are indebted to Professor Frederick Wirt for this classification.

27. For instance, Walnut Creek, California, a middle class Oakland suburb, has a total need factor of 2.90 compared to Oakland's 2.56.

28. Garth L. Mangum, *Reorienting Vocational Education*. (Institute of Labor and Industrial Relations: University of Michigan, 1968).

29. Mangum, op. cit., p. 21.

30. Ibid.

31. Ibid.

32. See Chapter 6, "The Politics of Federal Aid to Education in Texas," and Chapter 3, "The Politics of Federal Aid to Education in California."

33. ESAP comments drawn from Senate Select Committee on Equal Educational Opportunity Committee Print, *Emergency School Assistance Program: Background and Evaluation*, 92nd Congress, 1st Session.

34. National Advisory Council on Education Professions, *Windows to the Bureaucracy* (March, 1971).

35. National Advisory Council on the Education of Disadvantaged Children, *Annual Report* (January 31, 1968), p. 21.

36. Such systems would be designed to prevent disclosure of the records of individual pupils to insure against violations of privacy.

Index

Educational Conference Board (ECB), 327, 334–340, 352
Educational Improvement Act, 95
Educational Innovation Advisory Commission, 122–123
Educational Laboratories, 98
Educational Reform, Commission on, 143
Educational Research Commission, 123
Educational Research and Statistics, Bureau of, 67, 303, 319
Educational Services, Bureau of, 22, 152, 177
Eisenhower, Dwight D., administration of, 138–139, 243
El Centro College, 266
Elazar, Daniel J., cited, 250, 289–290
Elections, effect on education, 138, 199
Elementary schools, public, 2, 6–7, 24, 54, 63, 72, 107, 143, 174, 198, 226, 228, 268, 317, 326, 329, 348, 363, 366, 369
Elementary and Secondary education, 115, 194, 261, 265, 294, 314, 401–402
Elementary and Secondary Education, Bureau of, 210, 213, 221, 223, 230, 252
Elementary and Secondary Education Act of 1965 (ESEA), aid and effectiveness of, 3, 6, 21–23, 26–27, 32, 44, 52, 64, 67, 71, 382–384, 389–393, 400–403; amendments of 1968, 319; in California, 79, 92–95, 98–101, 121–122; and "creative tension," 377–378; in Massachusetts, 194, 196, 198–199, 229; in Michigan, 132–134, 156, 165, 169, 177, 182, 188; in New York, 326–328, 331–359, 365–371; in Texas, 236–237, 240, 248, 255–256, 269, 272; in Virginia, 287–289, 293, 301, 303–305, 316, 318, 320
Elementary and Secondary General Information Survey (ELSEGIS), 47–49, 54
Eliot, Thomas, cited, 136
Elite and Specialized Interviewing, 62
Emergency School Assistance Program (ESAP), 300, 396–397
Empire State Federation of Teachers, 339
Employment, opportunities for, 9, 47, 102, 166, 168
Employment Service and Security, Bureau of, 172, 220
Emotionally disturbed children, 15, 182–184
English, study of, 102, 159, 174, 315
Enrollment: non-white, 39, 295; on per capita basis, 132; pre-kindergarten, 143; public schools, 13, 15, 17, 49–50, 156, 259, 312, 317, 393
Entitlement system, 111–112, 114

Environment, influence of, 64, 155
Episcopal Church, 292
Equal protection clause, 1
Equality of educational opportunities, 21–22, 148, 155, 188
Equalization, concept and forms of, 37, 42, 79, 132–133, 143
Equipment and materials, educational, 3, 32, 45, 157, 173, 176, 268, 307, 314–316
Ethnic compositions, 47–48, 107, 199
Executive branch of state government, 131
Expenditures, pupil, 11, 182–183, 220, 272, 284, 286; Headstart program, 7, 47; non-conforming, 281, 307
Experimental Elementary Programs (EEP), 357
Experimental school programs, 123, 174, 308, 358
Extremism, racial, 295

Factionalism, educational, 68
Family incomes, composition of, 6–9, 17, 20, 30, 33, 36–37, 50–51, 55, 107–108, 135, 141, 156, 158, 173–174, 186, 210, 212, 327, 352, 394, 400
Favoritism, rural, and New York State, 236, 243
Federal Advisory Council, 97, 384
Federal aid, impact and implementation of, 1–5, 20–25, 47, 39, 61–64, 68, 77, 84, 93, 101, 125, 131, 175, 198, 251, 331
Feedback, sources of, 125
Field trips, importance of, 211
Film library, educational, 365
Finances of Large City School Systems, 32
Fiscal problems, 45, 99, 367
Five Primary Schools (5P), 356, 358
Fleischmann Commission, 340, 342
Food services, 53, 158–159
Foundation program formula, 262–263
Fourteenth Amendment, 1
Fringe benefits, teacher, 342
Fuller, Edgar, cited, 243
Funds and funding: federal, 78, 86, 122, 193, 229, 249; local and city, 228, 259; programs for, 174, 225, 358, 367; restrictions on, 116, 172; state, 303, 307

Gardner, John, cited, 296
Garms, Professor, cited, 11
General Accounting Office (GAO), 386
General Education Services, 153
General Laws of 1965, 206
Geography, influence of, 74, 114, 120, 124, 133, 162, 166, 174, 182, 199, 310, 318–319, 335
Georgia school system, 34
Ghetto districts, 220, 257

420

About the Authors

Joel S. Berke directs the Educational Finance and Governance Program of the Syracuse University Research Corporation and teaches political science at Syracuse University. He is the coauthor of *Financing Equal Educational Opportunity: Alternatives for State Finance* and of numerous articles in law reviews, scholarly journals, and public affairs periodicals. He has directed research projects for the New York State (Fleishmann) Commission on Education, the President's Commission on School Finance, and he currently heads a long-term finance study for the United Stated Office of Education.

Michael W. Kirst is Professor of Education and Business Administration at Stanford. He has held a number of federal posts related to educational policy analysis and formulation with the Bureau of the Budget, the USOE Bureau of Elementary and Secondary Education, the Commissioner's Ad Hoc Education Financing Group, and the Senate Committee on Labor and Public Welfare. His books include *Government Without Passing Laws, The Political Web of American Schools*, and *State, School and Politics: Research Directions*. He is currently conducting a study of the finances of public education in Florida.

Stephen K. Bailey is Chairman of the Policy Institute of the Syracuse University Research Corporation. Among his writings are *Schoolmen and Politics* and *ESEA: The Office of Education Administers a Law*.

Alan K. Campbel is Dean of the Maxwell Graduate School of Citizenship and Public Affairs, Syracuse University, and coauthor with Seymour Sacks of *Metropolitan America: Fiscal Patterns and Governmental Systems*.

Laurence Iannaccone, Professor of Education at the University of California at Riverside, is the author of *Politics in Education*.

Edith K. Mosher is Associate Professor of Educational Administration at the School of Education and Research Associate of the Bureau of Educational Research, University of Virginia. She coauthored *ESEA: The Office of Education Administers a Law*.

Seymour Sacks, author of *City Schools/Suburban Schools: A History of Fiscal Conflict*, is Professor of Economics at the Maxwell Graduate School of Syracuse University.

Jay D. Scribner is Associated Professor of Educational Administration at UCLA and editor of *Education and Urban Society*.

Frederick M. Wirt, author of *The Political Web of American Schools* and *Northern School Desegregation*, is currently Director of the Policy Sciences Graduate Program at the University of Maryland Baltimore County.